MONTESSORI FOR EVERY FAMILY

MONTESSORI FOR EVERY FAMILY

A practical parenting guide
to living, loving, and learning

TIM SELDIN and LORNA McGRATH
THE MONTESSORI FOUNDATION

CONTENTS

Chapter 3
FAMILY LIFE THROUGH A MONTESSORI LENS

FOREWORD

Many people worldwide have heard of Montessori schools and, whether through reputation or personal experience, are impressed with the beauty, calm, and order of Montessori classes as well as the independence, maturity, and kindness of children educated in the Montessori way.

An often-asked question is, what is the secret that allows one or two adults to manage large groups of children in an atmosphere of peace? The answer is, to a large degree, that Montessori teachers consciously learn to establish cooperative classroom communities. This book is intended to show parents how they can apply the same principles to their family's daily life.

As authors, we can barely remember a time when we weren't involved in the world of Montessori education – for us, it is a way of life. This book draws on our personal experiences as children, as parents, as Montessori guides, and as parenting coaches to many families who have sought a better way to raise their families in a spirit of kindness, respect, and partnership. Much of what we have learned came from observing and working with parents and children, and from raising our own families.

Being a parent is a full-time job. In the past, mums tended to stay at home to look after children while dads went out to work. Today, families of all shapes and sizes – whether mums and dads, same-sex couples, single-parent households, grandparents raising grandchildren, or blended families – juggle the responsibilities of work and parenting. Young children are often cared for by others, while older children spend much of the day at school and after-school activities.

❝ ❞

Children's brains are programmed to learn; stimulating them in developmentally appropriate ways is key in the early years.

At the same time, there is a growing awareness of how important the right environment and experiences are for infants, toddlers, and young children. We understand children's brains are programmed to learn, which is why stimulating them in developmentally appropriate ways is especially essential in the early years. And it never stops. As children grow, they continue to need time, attention, engagement, and support, all the way into young adulthood.

Most of us long to give our children the best home environment that we possibly can, within the limits of our time and resources. The mission that we undertake as parents is not simply to feed, cuddle, and protect our children. We also want to teach them to become independent, self-confident, successful adults, who are happy and fulfilled. While that journey takes many years, it helps to have an idea of where we are heading and why we do what we do. If you are eager for a fresh perspective and some practical suggestions,

then this book is for you. We hope that it will encourage you to enjoy your time with your children more than ever. It is filled not only with practical guidance and ideas for activities to do together, but also with the message that life is meant to be celebrated. The small, everyday things that we can do to mark occasions and to reaffirm our love for one another can make all the difference, both for our children, and for us, as mums, dads, grandparents, or guardians.

Tim Seldin

Donna W Bruth

Teaching our children the small ways in which they can celebrate life daily is part of creating a stimulating and harmonious home.

WHAT IS MONTESSORI?

MONTESSORI PHILOSOPHY

The term "Montessori" refers to more than 22,000 schools in more than 110 countries who follow the approach pioneered by Dr Maria Montessori. Its philosophy involves a way of organizing classrooms and of helping children to learn, as well as a way of thinking about relationships that can be applied at home, in the workplace, and beyond.

Montessori as a way of life

Most people think of Montessori as a pre-school curriculum and educational approach used with very young children. While it is true that the first Montessori schools were developed with children under the age of seven, today they serve children of all ages, from the youngest up through the secondary school years. Moreover, beyond the school environment, core Montessori principles are now commonly extended into family life and businesses and used as a template for social institutions.

The Montessori way of thinking encompasses many things, but fundamentally it is a way of creating a culture that helps people of all ages to work together in peaceful, mutually supportive ways. Its approach is counter-intuitive to the more familiar one of top-down authority and control, with rewards and punishments and external judgments about whether work is up to scratch. Montessori does encourage habits of excellence and the pursuit of carrying out tasks extremely well, however, it relies on helping children to internalize values, work habits, social skills, thinking, and problem solving to achieve goals. It allows children to find, or rediscover, their own voice, learn to work together in ways that minimize conflict, be in touch with their true feelings, and become appropriately assertive in ways that are mutually respectful. This way of life tends to lead Montessori children to experience great satisfaction and connection with others at home, school, and, later on, at work.

The foundation years

One of the original discoveries of Dr Maria Montessori was that the most important time in a child's education is not the years from twelve to eighteen, but rather the first six years of life. When many people assumed that children were just playing – indeed, we still use the term "pre-school" for centres that care for young children – she realized that, in reality, these are the years when a child's brain and nervous system develop most fully.

This development goes far beyond our normal academic concepts of maths and reading skills. Children are developing foundational skills and understanding

66 99

Montessori is a way of creating a culture that helps people of all ages to work together in peaceful, mutually supportive ways.

Giving children access to books
and quality reference materials is a cornerstone of Montessori, helping them to develop a habit of learning for life.

that will shape them for the rest of their lives. For example, they are learning about balance and coordination; executive function skills, such as organizing and planning; the first levels of independence; and vocabulary and language skills. They are also developing an inner sense of order; a sense of social norms and values; and positive attitudes about their gender, racial, ethnic, and spiritual identity. This is the time of life when children are learning how to learn.

Ideally, having an understanding of the Montessori approach before a first child is born would allow families to create, from the start, a home that supports a collaborative and cooperative culture. However, any family can begin to benefit from the insights of Montessori philosophy whenever they discover it, and families with children of all ages can learn how Montessori educators cultivate environments that are calm, peaceful, and cooperative.

" "

Montessori teaches us the art of hearing what our children are saying to us, monitoring our own thoughts, and being consistent in our responses.

Montessori encourages hands-on learning that allows children to develop practical skills and gain a deeper understanding of certain concepts.

A Montessori-inspired home

Incorporating the Montessori philosophy into the home in practical ways helps children to embrace learning.

- Montessori-inspired homes recognize the value of hands-on learning. Parents understand that many of the skills and concepts children are asked to learn are abstract, and that text books rarely bring them to life. Rather than focusing on rote drill and memory, parents offer experiences that help their children to understand and use concepts.

- Families recognize the importance of books and connect children with libraries, both physical and online, to introduce them to esteemed literature and reference materials.

- Montessori-inspired homes value the importance of being outdoors as a family: gardening, discovering and caring for the natural world, hiking, and exploring.

A concept of leadership

Montessori teachers usually undergo a year or more of training to learn how to teach in the Montessori way. As part of their study, they take a course in Montessori classroom leadership, which shows them how to follow a systematic approach to establish a Montessori culture and routines to allow children choice with clear limits. These essential skills help teachers build a cooperative classroom community. This concept of leadership can be extended into the family home, with the practice of "Montessori family leadership", where strategies for developing healthy family relationships help build a special sense of community in the home.

Montessori family leadership is not about discipline in the sense of establishing ground rules and using a system of rewards and punishments to try to control behaviour. Instead, it is an approach to cultivating a culture of kindness, warmth, mutual respect, and a common adherence to ways of conducting day-to-day life. It is about helping our children to understand their emotions and express these in ways that are respectful and appropriate; figure out how to find their own voice without harming others; and learn that all conflict should be resolved non-violently and to the mutual satisfaction of all parties wherever possible.

The Montessori philosophy also recognizes that each child and each family is different. What Montessori teaches is the art of hearing what our children are saying, paying attention to what is happening, monitoring our own thoughts, and following principles that tend to minimize stress, increase consistency in our responses, and that enable families to build happy and harmonious homes.

Spending time together as a family, exploring and being outdoors, engenders a mutually supportive family culture.

KEY MONTESSORI PRINCIPLES

The Montessori principles set out here can be applied in the home, providing a valuable starting point for parents to help them create a family life inspired by the ethos of Montessori.

1

Be consistent

Teach children clear guidelines and reliably reinforce these by your example and leadership. When your child tests limits, be consistent and kind but firm to keep them on track.

2

Practise mutual respect

Our words and deeds should never shame. Speaking to your child with kindness and respect – picturing the adult they will become – is most likely to elicit the best in them.

3

Recognize uniqueness

Each child has their own voice and may see or respond to situations in their own way. Resist comparing children to each other or yourself. Cherish what makes a child unique.

4

Foster a sense of order

To help children think logically and follow a sequence of steps, we need our own sense of calm and order. An organized home with routines set up helps us work towards this goal.

5

Encourage rather than praise

Constantly praising children to show our approval can lead to them craving praise. By encouraging, we invite them to carry on and convey that their effort and choices are recognized.

6
Instil intrinsic motivation

When you teach correct behaviour, model it consistently, and recognize and appreciate it, it tends to become second nature. Aim to instil the habit that this is the way we do things.

7
Give freedom within limits

Creating conditions where children have appropriate levels of freedom of movement and choice of activity within clear, safe limits helps develop independence and self-discipline.

8
Support life-long learning

Ask children the right questions rather than give answers. Learning *how* to learn, understanding concepts, and thinking deeply and creatively help us navigate life.

10
Promote grace and courtesy

We help children develop grace – control of the body – and manners, its social equivalent, so they show respect and avoid hurting others, or embarrassing themselves or others.

9
Build autonomy

Part of our job is to help children master physical, intellectual, and social skills. Our goal is to raise a child who stands next to us as a young member of the community of adults.

11
Instil personal responsibility

When we take responsibility for our actions and provide an emotionally safe space where mistakes are seen as learning opportunities, we help children to "own" their behaviour.

MONTESSORI
FAMILY LIFE

MONTESSORI FOR ALL FAMILIES

Montessori offers a perspective on the world and promotes interpersonal relationships based on partnership. Parents who are drawn to the Montessori way come from all walks of life. Though families may have different backgrounds, those who follow the Montessori philosophy and principles, whether by sending their children to a Montessori school or by embracing Montessori in the home, tend to have much in common.

A courageous choice

It can take courage to be a Montessori parent. This is because Montessori encourages children to think for themselves and articulate their own opinions. For example, there may be moments when it would be much easier for parents of a six-year-old if their child obediently accepted their simple explanation for why it is not practical to create a full recycling centre in the middle of the kitchen. By encouraging independent thought and reasoning, Montessori challenges parents to help children explore projects and find practical solutions so that children learn how things work and what challenges a project might present.

A common outlook

The Montessori approach senses that children are capable of amazing things from a very young age. It believes that this is the case regardless of gender, race, or ethnicity. It recognizes that children from all families, regardless of social class, income, and family structure can develop their full human potential when they are given the right stimulation and emotional support from the outset. Following Montessori principles does not mean overhauling the home or buying special learning tools. Instead, parents nurture kindness and empathy in their children and encourage the development of their innate intelligence, curiosity, creativity, and sense of wonder.

Being a Montessori family is about seeing children as unique human beings, with their own personalities, interests, and emotions, no matter how young. It recognizes the importance of helping them learn to do things for themselves so they develop independence and realize their own abilities and the value of their voice in the world.

A collective aim

Montessori families believe they can help to build a better world by teaching peace within the home: how to resolve conflicts without violence, hear and cherish one another, and live in a spirit of collaboration and partnership rather than short-sightedness and self-interest. Even if, initially, Montessori is discovered in search of good childcare, families who embrace Montessori come to recognize

that the way to work for a better future for all is by teaching our children a way of living. When the fundamental principles resonate, Montessori is already, or will probably become, a wonderful fit for your family.

" "

With the right stimulation and emotional support from the outset, children can develop their full potential.

Montessori challenges parents to listen to children and foster a sense of curiosity in them through exploration and discovery.

FAMILY VALUES

We pass down our world-view to our children. When we raise a child, whether as their biological parents, adoptive parents, as a single parent, in a foster family, or in an extended family that includes grandparents, each of us has values we pass on.

A clear message

In Montessori-inspired homes, parents promote a set of core family values and fundamental goals. Being clear about what our values are and what we hold dear is important. However, we cannot simply impose our values on our children without displaying these values, too.

Striving to be on the same page as a co-parent, and being consistent in the way we act and react on a day-to-day basis, increases the likelihood that the messages that your child receives from you will be absorbed and understood and that your child will learn from the example that you set.

Identifying your values

To ensure that children are clear about family values, it is helpful first to clarify the values of each adult in your family unit. Look for the values that you hold in common and identify areas where you disagree, then explore these together to see if you can reach some agreement. For example, do you share the same views regarding your child's religious education? If not, can you find a solution that works for you both? Also, how do you perceive the role of each parent? If one prefers to avoid conflict, does this leave the other parent enforcing rules?

As well as absorbing our values, children can also unconsciously absorb our biases towards or

Listening and conversing with each family member, from youngest to oldest, helps to reinforce important Montessori values such as mutual respect.

against certain areas, so it is important, too, to examine any preconceptions you have. Ideally, parents-to-be would consciously address their values in preparation for parenthood, then on an ongoing basis in their lives together, to make sure that everyday words and actions continue to convey the lessons they intend to teach.

While a family's values can be determined by many factors, including ethnicity, faith, political perspective, and social attitudes, in Montessori, certain common values are aspired to, which

form a solid foundation on which to build family life:

- **Families nurture curiosity**, creativity, and imagination in each other.
- **They strive to exhibit** a habit of doing things well, a passion for excellence.
- **Universal values**, such as non-violence, honesty, kindness, empathy, and respect, are taught and shared.
- **Children are helped** to develop a global perspective and embrace differences that are the hallmark of human beings.
- **A family tradition** of service to others is encouraged.
- **Gender-based roles** are discouraged.
- **Families listen** and speak to each other with respect and thoughtfulness.
- **Conversations are** invited to discuss how each person feels if a situation arises.
- **Each person tries** to express intentions clearly and ensure actions reflect words.
- **Conflicts or concerns** are resolved directly and peacefully with the person involved, rather than harbouring resentment or complaining to others.
- **Responsibilities are shared** and each person's contribution is valued.
- **Mistakes are seen** as chances to learn.
- **Each person is treated** equitably and families strive to address implicit bias.

FAMILY CULTURE

A family's culture is informed by its values. Families following the Montessori way develop a culture that nurtures respect, kindness, and collaboration. This may be expressed in the home environment, in meeting children's emotional needs, by maintaining traditions, being respectful, listening intently, and communicating thoughtfully.

An engaged child

In a Montessori-inspired family culture, children are encouraged to help with decision making, express feelings, and to try new ideas. While to some this may sound like a recipe for chaos, rebellion, and disorder, in the context of the parents being the leaders in the family, setting the tone based on their values, this is not the case. Montessori parenting aims to set limits without limiting potential, finding a balance between guiding a child and allowing for individuality and autonomy.

Challenging our perceptions

Giving children a voice can mean we may need to let go of preconceived ideas about how we think things should be and understand that we cannot mould our children like clay into the image that we have in mind. Instead, we allow them to reveal their unique personality and interests, giving them freedom within limits.

Avoiding gender-stereotyped roles can be one way to allow children to explore their own interests. For example, each person can help with the dishes, cook, or do household chores. And as children grow, helping to plan the family budget and become involved with money matters can allow them to help with decisions.

Montessori family meetings

A key element for creating a Montessori-based family culture is a weekly family meeting where the whole family, across the generations, sits together to solve

The family meeting format

There are four parts to family meetings, as set out below. Pages 66–67 show you how to put these into practice.

- Appreciations and acknowledgments. Each person offers and receives appreciation or acknowledgment for things they have done in the week.
- Getting started. The family member facilitating the meeting guides the family through the agenda.
- What's coming up? Family members share what is coming up for them during the week so that everyone can be mutually supportive.
- Family fun! The facilitator chooses an easy, fun activity, such as a bike ride or playing a game, lasting no longer than 10 minutes, to close the meeting, .

How meetings take shape is governed by the age of the children. For younger families, settings remain informal and at the child's level.

problems, make agreements, learn leadership skills, think creatively, listen, share thoughts and ideas, and enjoy each other's company. By brainstorming issues, the family can explore possible solutions together. When this is done well, it fosters creative thinking, collaboration, and respect.

Family members take turns to facilitate meetings, with younger members observing and learning from older ones (see p.64). Meetings provide a forum for family members to participate in honest, open communication with each other.

They are an important way for your child to express feelings, work out problems, and keep connections strong, providing a chance for them to converse on a deeper level than is the case with digital communication and even face-to-face catch-ups at meals.

Holding regular meetings, with no interruptions or distractions, gives the sense that family time together is valuable and that each person is an important part of the family. Follow the guidelines on pages 64–67 for how to hold your weekly family meetings.

A PARENTING PARTNERSHIP

Whether your parenting partner is your spouse or civil partner, your ex, a good friend, your parents, or whoever shares parenting responsibilities with you on a regular basis, it is important to have an ongoing conversation about parenting.

Starting the conversation

Being sure that you and your parenting partner are on the same page when it comes to your child's behaviour and

values is important in providing both consistency for your child and harmony in your adult relationship. Ideally, couples who wish to start a family would discuss child-raising practices before having a child, but most of us do not manage to do this. Instead, we have a child and then, not until we are in the middle of a situation, do we start to think about how we can best parent together or what parenting values we have in common.

To begin a conversation about parenting practices, you and your partner may want to each think about

Discussing your views together and finding common ground can help you to parent consistently and thoughtfully.

" "

Talking together about your hopes and thoughts for your child as they grow leads to a strong and loving parenting partnership.

how you envision your child when they are 18 and how you can help them to prepare successfully for adulthood. You might hope your child will value honesty and have empathy and courage. Or that they will be able to receive an education that provides them with a valuable skill set, instils confidence, and allows choice in future work. Or is their ability to be happy most important to you? You may wish that your child will grow to become a responsible adult who shows respect for others and the planet. And you may hope that they will have the confidence to express themselves.

Each try writing your thoughts down, giving yourselves enough time to really gather them together before sharing them with each other. A day or so later, share your thoughts together. See where you have similar hopes, and talk about where your views differ. Give some thought to what you can do as

parents to foster those goals as your children grow, from toddlerhood through to young adults.

Looking back

As you talk through these hopes, begin a discussion about what you each think about parenting; for example, what are your views on discipline? Look back and discuss how your parents handled tricky situations, such as a public meltdown, or what they did when you and your siblings argued. Are there aspects of parenting you would handle differently? Keep discussing how you both experienced family life as you grew up and return to this discussion as your child grows, asking each other how you want to resolve situations and to parent.

Even if you and your partner were brought up in similar homes with similar values and goals, you are still likely to have differences in your parenting approaches. Find out what you agree on and what you do not. Can you work out a compromise? If you have children from a previous relationship, talk to your new partner about your parenting practices. Work together to give your children as much consistency, routine, and love as possible. Brainstorming together can help you find common ground and solutions that will work for you both and other family members who care for your child.

LOOKING AFTER YOUR RELATIONSHIP

Cherishing your relationship with your partner as you experience the joys and challenges of parenting takes patience, understanding, communication, and commitment. While it is easy to see shortcomings in our partners, modelling an approach with our own behaviour can be a more constructive way to build a supportive partnership and, in turn, a harmonious family home.

Listen, understand, and agree

Paying attention and listening carefully to each other is a crucial aspect of finding agreement and keeping your relationship intact. When you have a conversation, it is extremely important that you both feel that the other person is truly present and engaged.

Sometimes our partner may just need to talk and to be heard. They are not asking us to help them solve a problem or make their feelings go away. Instead, they are seeking a safe space to express their frustration, anxiety, or other feelings.

If your parenting partner is upset or wants to discuss an issue they consider to be important, make a conscious effort to stop what you are doing and focus your attention fully. Listen carefully and be sure that your partner senses that you

Spending dedicated time with your partner helps to nurture your relationship and provides children with a model for a loving bond.

are truly attempting to understand. As well as listening, check whether your understanding of what they are trying to say is correct. You could say, "I think what I'm hearing you say is…", then let your partner explain if this is wrong. Listening in this way can open the door to brainstorm ideas, draw up priorities, and agree on solutions that can be applied to parenting, the whole family, and to your relationship.

Acknowledge challenges

It is important to acknowledge to each other that child-rearing will be a busy, often challenging, time in the cycle of your relationship. Despite this busyness, avoid putting your relationship on hold while your children grow up, thinking that you will be able to pick it up where you left off. Focusing solely on children while they grow up, without paying attention to your adult relationship, can leave you trying to remember what you have in common with each other once your children leave home.

Taking time for yourselves as adults not only keeps your relationship intact but also provides a model for your children in how to care for each other. Trying new things together,

Visualizing your needs

To be sure that you both have the necessary energy and calmness for parenting, take time to renew and refresh your bodies, minds, and spirits. A simple visualization can help you both to think about your own needs so that you can be the best version of yourselves for your family.

Imagine a glass full of your best energy, patience, empathy, and sense of calm. Now imagine two or three empty cups and that each family member is thirsty. You fill their cups daily so by the end of the day your glass is empty. You are tired and need to refresh yourself to refill your parenting glass. Think of what you can do daily to achieve this, whether you read a book, go for a run, dance, sing, sit quietly to collect your thoughts, or take a bath. Find what works and make it part of your daily routine.

whether a pottery class, yoga, hiking, or woodwork, can be an excellent way to avoid getting into a rut.

Take care of yourselves

As parents, you are in a position of nurturing and supporting each of your family members. Sometimes, though, while busy taking care of others, we fail to care for ourselves. The visualization exercise above can help you to take stock and assess your own needs.

CHALLENGING YOUR PERCEPTIONS

As parents, we often question whether we are doing a good enough job. Self-doubt can be common, especially for first-time parents. Thinking about your own behaviour and mindset is an excellent way to encourage your child's growth and learning.

Opening our minds

The real preparation for parenting is the study of ourselves. To be highly effective parents, we need to do far more than learn parenting strategies, even where these have been shown to work and have been used successfully for many years. Beyond these strategies, we need to explore our own ways of thinking about – and interacting with – our children and our parenting partner, or other caregivers.

An important part of the parenting process is to ask yourself if you are ready to challenge the messages you received from your own parents. You may decide that you wish to raise your child differently from how you were raised by your parents, not necessarily as a criticism of your parents, but rather because you feel that you will improve on some of their methods. However, even with these intentions, you may sometimes catch yourself sounding like your parents and realize that you have been programmed to repeat the mindset and parenting practices that you experienced as a child.

Adapting your thinking

It is good to know that, if you do find yourself responding to your child's behaviour in a way that does not feel right, you can change your thinking.

First, try to explore the ways in which you think about your child and your responses to their behaviour. Some of your thought patterns may be extremely positive and effective, shaped by childhood memories of the times when

Identifying thought patterns

Here are just a few examples of conscious and unconscious thought patterns that we inherit from our own childhood. Exploring these on your own, and/or with your parenting partner, can help you to question these perceptions.

- Children should play quietly and not interrupt adults.
- I want to be my child's best friend.
- Boys are better at maths and science than girls.
- When I tell my child something, I should have to say it only once.
- I should always correct my child's mistakes.
- I should never let my child feel that they have failed.

Our own childhoods and relationships with our parents shape and influence our parenting in the here and now.

your parents did an incredible job with love, kindness, and consistency. Other habits of thinking may be shaped by less positive childhood experiences and may lead you to behave negatively, interfering with your goal of creating a calm and peaceful home.

Whether habits of thinking are conscious or unconscious, they shape how you feel and how you interact. You can adapt thought patterns you are conscious of most easily. To adapt unconscious thinking, you also need to identify which thoughts shape the way you react emotionally and instinctively to your child. Once you are aware of these unconscious ways of thinking about and responding to your child

and others, you can begin to re-examine and rethink your parenting practices.

For example, you may have an ingrained thought process that girls are easier to manage than boys, or vice versa. If this is your unconscious thought process, common parenting issues that arise may confirm this bias, and raising your child may feel like a challenge. Your perception about the differences between girls and boys will influence the way that you interact with your child and colour your relationship as your child will sense your frustration and perception that they are difficult and harder to manage. Checking your bias can help you adjust your internal mindset, bringing greater harmony to your relationship.

SEEING THE WORLD THROUGH YOUR CHILD'S EYES

One of the keys to creating a calm and peaceful home is to learn how to see the world from your child's perspective. Dr Maria Montessori challenged us to "follow the child". To do this, first we must have a sense of how children think, feel, and react.

Your child's perspective

When a young child looks up at an adult they love, from their perspective of two or three feet tall, the adult seems like a giant. To a child, the size and strength of the adult makes them seem all powerful. When children are small, this impression can make them feel overwhelmed, powerless, and without a voice.

Carrying out a simple exercise can help you appreciate the world literally from your young child's perspective. When your child is asleep, get down on the floor and observe your surroundings, or take a video of how your house looks from your child's height. The dramatically different perspective is likely to be striking.

As a parent, you are not only taller and stronger than your young child, you are also the one who meets their needs, who says "yes" or "no", pays attention, or ignores them. If we do not always understand what our children are trying to tell us, our children need to find ways to get our attention and communicate their desires by trial and error. By trying to see the world from your child's perspective, you can better understand how your child might be thinking and feeling. This can help you to respond more effectively.

Your growing child

As your child grows, their thoughts and communication skills develop. Of course, each child is unique. No matter what age they are, some seem to accept their parent's guidance easily, while others may test everything their parents say or do. Your job as a parent is to listen to and try to understand your child, help them gain confidence, and find their own identity.

> **" "**
>
> Appreciating how your child sees the adults and world around them will help you to understand what they are trying to communicate and to respond to their needs.

Thinking about how it feels to be small can help you to appreciate your child's perspective.

- **Before your child can talk**, they cry, smile, or coo to get attention. They do not even truly recognize that they are separate beings from their primary caregivers.

- **From toddlerhood**, children gain words and are also likely to communicate their needs through tears, heart-melting smiles, tantrums, and pouting. Your young child is learning slowly to recognize the needs of others as well as their own, to communicate with words, and gain skills that foster independence. They begin to realize that they have their own unique voice and that they can communicate respectfully and do things for themselves.

- **In the primary school years**, children become better at communicating. They are increasingly interested in their peers and their relationships and preoccupied by rules and fairness, wanting to make up their own rules and try them out. They are beginning to sense their own independence and autonomy. As parents, we start to feel more comfortable and confident in their ability to make decisions and handle certain situations on their own or with a little help from adults.

- **Adolescence** sits between childhood and adulthood. One moment, teenagers act or feel like children, the next like adults. Bodies grow and change overnight. Teens want to know what their place is in the world and how they can make a difference. They become interested in sexuality, their own and others, and want to try out different ideas to discover their values and beliefs, which may or may not be the same as their parents.

AN EMOTIONALLY SAFE ENVIRONMENT

Just as we prepare the physical environment for our families, when we create a Montessori-inspired home, consciously preparing the emotional environment is equally crucial, ensuring that we nurture a sense of emotional safety for each member of the family.

Respecting your child

It is important that we see our children as independent human beings deserving of warmth and respect. Our children are far more sensitive to our influences than we may realize, so being careful about what we do or say in front of them is key. If you speak to the very best within your child, include them in family life, show concern for their feelings, and respect their interests, they are more likely to live up to your expectations. The following strategies will help you to create a safe emotional environment for everyone in your home.

- **Create consistency and routine**. Make daily and weekly schedules that are predictable, but not rigid. Children feel comfortable and secure when they have a sense of family routine. Being consistent in

Talking calmly and avoiding a cross encounter if your child arrives home later than agreed is more likely to make them reflect on their behaviour and to avoid being late in the future.

your responses, too, and reacting respectfully to everyday situations creates a sense of safety, making it clear that your love is not conditional based on behaviour – even if you disagree with your child's behaviour, you accept and love them.

- **Set clear expectations** and boundaries positively. When children know what is expected, they are more likely to behave as we desire, within our boundaries. Convey expectations in terms of the behaviour you wish to see, rather than the behaviour you do not. For example, if your child shouts in the home, you might say, "Please use your inside voice", rather than, "Stop shouting in the house." Describing expectations in negative terms can be heard as a command, which can trigger resentment and lead to the opposite behaviour as your child tries to prove autonomy.

- **Be comfortable with mistakes**. Dr Montessori's advice was to help children to learn how to do things for themselves. Children make mistakes and can learn from them. They may forget to water the plants or to walk the dog, and older children may miss homework dates, stay up too late, or not manage to get home at an agreed time. When dealing with their mistakes, we hope children will learn valuable lessons rather than feel scolded. The word "discipline" means to teach and to learn (see p.40). Presenting everyday living skills allows children to practise and become more aware of how their words and actions affect others. If we protect children from mistakes that seem obvious to us, we can inhibit their independent learning process and they can be easily overwhelmed when we jump in with a quick solution.

- **Provide a "quiet" space** for thoughtful reflection (see pp.156–159). In Montessori-inspired homes, families create comfortable places where each family member can go when they are upset or disturbing the harmony of the home. This is the opposite of a "time out" space, used when parents are at a loss. Time out is usually felt as a punishment, sending a message that children are bad and need to leave. This works only as long as children dislike the experience enough to modify their behaviour. A quiet space for each family member helps individuals to calm themselves and consider their actions and words so that they can take responsibility, rejoin the family, and do things differently in the future.

TALKING TO YOUR CHILD

As children grow, they will hear and see things they do not understand and may want to learn more about them. While you may feel comfortable answering certain questions, there may be other topics that you find harder to discuss.

Looking at issues

Topics you may need to tackle could include:

- Questions related to current affairs.
- Anti-racism and social justice.
- Religion and moral dilemmas.
- Sexuality and gender.
- Separation and divorce.
- Illness and death.

Use these guidelines to help you navigate tricky conversations.

- **Give children** only as much information as they can absorb. The length and depth of explanations depends on a child's age and level of maturity. For example, if your three-year-old asks where babies come from, your answer should be brief and factual. Most young children do not need to know the details from conception to birth. Your pre-adolescent, however, not only wants to know, but needs to know. The same applies to all "sticky" questions.

- **Be honest** with your child about your feelings. If you feel uncomfortable about a topic, express this, keeping their age and maturity level in mind. Children of all ages pick up on feelings and body language, not just words, and sense when you are not being honest about how you feel.

- **Separation and divorce** can be hard to discuss. Children can sometimes feel they are to blame. They need to know that they are not responsible and that both parents love them, no matter what. The most difficult part of this conversation is explaining why you have separated while keeping the best interests of your child in mind, for example, by not blaming your co-parent.

- **Different families** have different beliefs. Talk to your child about how families can hold very different views on issues such as politics, faith, ethical and moral questions, and family culture. Do clarify your family's core values, but recognize and respect other families' rights to hold their own opinions. Montessori-inspired families are likely to share many values and beliefs, but there will always be unique perspectives and traditions.

- **Be guided** by your family's core values and beliefs when answering your child's questions. If you discussed these with your parenting partner at the start of your relationship and agreed on them, this will be helpful when it comes to answering questions. When you feel secure about your values and beliefs and aligned with your parenting partner, your child is also likely to feel secure.

- **Children may be reluctant** to talk about certain topics. There may be a topic or situation you think you ought to discuss but sense they will find it embarrassing, uncomfortable, or upsetting and they, or you, might prefer to avoid a conversation. First, let them know that you need to talk. Ask if they are willing to talk now. If they seem distressed, it may be wise to give them time to calm down as pursuing it when they are upset can make it hard for them to express themselves or hear what you need to say. Be clear, though, that you cannot avoid difficult conversations. You could say something like, "We do need to talk, but I can see that you are upset. Let's talk a little later when you are ready."

Finding a comfortable and relaxed place to talk about difficult-to-discuss topics can help your child to listen and engage more easily.

A HOME FOR ALL AGES

In a Montessori-inspired home, parents give thought and attention to preparing an environment where all family members feel included and at ease. There are simple things you can do to help make your home a comfortable and welcoming place for you and your family.

drawers in bedrooms and books in bookcases or on shelves, have a space for arts and crafts' materials; shelves for children's toys and activities; areas for reading and study; and places to prepare food and to sit down and eat.

An inviting home

How we set up our home can promote cooperation, calmness, and a sense of routine, ensuring that where we live is a place in which each family member feels comfortable. This can be achieved whether your home is large or small and without the need to spend lots of money. With Montessori, beauty, order, and comfort all play a role.

- **Create beauty**. Ideally, your home should communicate to everyone in the family that this is a place we care about and feel comfortable in. When you walk in the door, seeing a space that is clean and neat, that has beauty and is inviting, will help each person in the family feel they want to take care of their home and that it is a place for every one of them.

- **Think about creating order** in your home – a place for everything and everything in its place. As well as keeping clothing in wardrobes and

Creating an orderly home, with accessible spaces for clothes and everyday objects, helps to promote harmony and a sense of calm.

Clutter inhibits our ability to focus. Many families collect a lot of "stuff" for children. However, having everything out at one time can make it hard for children to focus on any one thing. Rather than a toy box or series of containers, display toys, games, and art supplies on shelves, then rotate activities and toys as your child's interests change.

- **Think about comfort**. Aim to create a home that is comfortable for everyone. When you have a baby, think about the furniture you choose and about whether you wish to have valuable or breakable objects or furniture that is not child-friendly in the house as they grow. Consider how you can create a home that is both beautiful to you as adults and which you can welcome others into, but where you do not feel anxious about things being spilled or broken by young children. Having a home that is practical as well as comfortable avoids creating arguments over dirt, spills, or marks on furniture. While you want to teach your child family ground rules, you also want to be realistic and focus on raising your child and helping them to learn, rather than on keeping a perfectly furnished home.

How spaces can evolve

As your children grow, your home will gradually change as they become more independent, taller, and develop different interests and needs.

For example, you may have modified your child's bedroom when they were younger to ensure that items such as clothing were accessible for their height. As your child grows, as well as raising items to match their taller stature, your child may also want to have a say in the decor of their room, and will also need dedicated areas to read, write, and to work on a computer.

Planning for the whole family

An important aspect of preparing your home with everyone in mind is to consciously design spaces where your child can either help you with a task or be comfortably present while you do something else. For example, having a small table and chair in a family room or kitchen creates a space where your young child can work on a puzzle, write, or draw while you get on with tasks. This lets your child know that their presence is welcome. Whether they participate in the same activity as other family members or do their own activity in their dedicated space when others are busy, they feel fully included in family life.

MISBEHAVIOUR IS COMMUNICATION

We all have emotional needs. When these needs are met, we can be our best selves and are able to show compassion and empathy, to collaborate with others, to lead others benevolently, and to accomplish tasks and activities that we set out to do.

Our core emotional needs

Adults and children have the same set of core emotional needs that, when met, help us to live harmoniously and productively. We need to feel loved and lovable; to have some control over our lives; to feel a sense of belonging; and to feel that we are valuable and capable.

When we feel that one or more of these needs is not being met, we might take things personally, become cranky or defensive, seek attention, engage in power struggles, say and do hurtful things, or withdraw and hide.

When children behave in these ways, we call it misbehaviour. Often, children do not understand exactly what they are feeling or how to ask for their needs to be met, so acting out can be their only way to let us know something is wrong. They are not misbehaving, but are unconsciously trying to communicate their need for reassurance that they are loved, that they are able to have some control, and that they are an important and useful member of their family.

The more we understand what our children are trying to tell us and meet their needs before they act out, the more likely they will be to cooperate rather than challenge; use kind words and actions rather than be mean or hurtful; to help out and be independent rather than hide away in their rooms for much of the time; and to allow you to have time with others or alone rather than constantly demand attention.

Relationship "accounts"

Thinking about your relationship with your child as a savings account that you can invest in to meet their emotional needs can help avoid perceived misbehaviours

❝ ❞

Children act out if they feel their emotional needs are not being met – to communicate that they need reassurance they are loved, valued, have some control, and belong.

Encouraging your child and noticing when they are doing something well, helps them to feel capable and builds up your relationship "account".

and cultivate and sustain harmonious family life. The things you do or say can "build up" or "draw down" this account. Responding to your child's behaviour by punishing, yelling, shaming, comparing them with siblings, ignoring them, name-calling, threatening, or disempowering them by doing too much for them, can all draw down your relationship with your child.

The types of behaviour that help build your relationship as well as meet your child's emotional needs include:

- **Being emotionally present**, listening intently, and giving your full attention.

- **Encouraging your child**.

- **Noticing** what they do right.

- **Being consistent**.

- **Making agreements** and talking about problem solving together.

Be consciously aware of how many times during the day you are "drawing down" rather than "building up" your relationship with your child. If it helps, keep a record to see if you are managing to invest more in "building up" rather than "drawing down". When you build up your relationship, observe how this affects your child's behaviour.

This idea of relationship accounts applies to each relationship within the family and can likewise be used to pay particular attention to nurturing your relationship with your parenting partner.

RETHINKING DISCIPLINE

When we think of discipline, we often think of using punishment and reward to control a child's behaviour. In fact, the original meaning of the word "discipline" is "to learn" or "to teach". When we see discipline as a teaching tool, we set our children up for success.

In Montessori thinking, rather than employ a system of rewards and punishments to encourage children to behave in the way we would like them to, instead we help children to develop independence, inner discipline, and intrinsic motivation.

Why some methods can fail

So why does Montessori avoid the often favoured use of punishment and reward? Rewards work to motivate people to behave in a certain way. Likewise, the threat of punishment tends to motivate people to avoid certain behaviours. However, both work only when someone is watching, when children believe they will be seen or caught, and depend on whether they care enough about the promised reward or the threatened punishment to modify their behaviour.

In Montessori, the goal is for children to internalize their family's values and norms of behaviour, whether or not other family members are present.

Fostering intrinsic motivation

Intrinsic motivation – an inner voice about who we are and how we behave – is an internal and enduring means of learning and sustaining behaviours that lead to calm and positive relationships.

When children follow and respect house rules, they develop intrinsic motivation, as they understand the importance of caring for their home and the living things within it.

All children misbehave at times. It is inevitable that they will be disagreeable or test limits when they are unsure of our expectations. However, we do not have to fight constant battles, never have a minute to ourselves, or often deal with children who are being aggressive or hurtful with their words or actions.

As parents, we can proactively teach children values and good behaviour by modelling these ourselves. Meeting your child's emotional needs (see p.38) can also help minimize misbehaviour. When your child's emotional needs are understood and met, they are more likely to be cooperative and able to go about their daily routines independently. See some useful strategies on pages 168–171.

Moreover, when we respond to children by being kind and firm, with the intention of helping them gain skills and understand what we expect from their behaviour, family harmony is enhanced, even in challenging situations.

Setting "house rules"

Children need consistent guidelines on how and what to do at home to navigate everyday family life successfully. When clear expectations are set out by house rules (see above), which are consistently reinforced, children develop a sense of safety, security, and order.

Setting house rules

The older your child, the more detailed house rules can become. A broad, all-inclusive set of house rules might look like this:

1. In our home, we take care of all living things – plants, animals, and people.

2. We take care of the objects in our home.

Discuss together what taking care of living things and objects involves. For example, your child may question why they cannot sit on the table. You could explain that this is because it could be unsafe, could cause damage, and upsets the sense of order, and is therefore non-negotiable and should be followed consistently.

House rules are the common rules of everyday life that each family member is expected to follow. Anything that involves safety, damage, or destruction should be non-negotiable. Beyond this, rules can be open for discussion. There may be certain things that adults can do and children cannot, which sit outside house rules, but avoid double standards, which children may legitimately perceive as unfair and can lead to resentment.

House rules provide the framework for determining what is negotiable and what is not, in turn helping to avoid frequent power struggles.

RESPONDING INSTEAD OF REACTING

It is inevitable that unpleasant, challenging, or embarrassing situations will occur between you and your child in the parenting years. When a situation arises, how you interact – whether you react or respond – will be important in shaping your relationship.

A critical moment

How you react to difficult situations with your child can make all the difference to how you build your relationship with each other and how you are able to nurture your child's independence, sense of responsibility, and growth. There are several key Montessori principles that you support when you respond to a situation in a considered way instead of react immediately. When you respond thoughtfully, you are helping your child to develop autonomy, promoting good manners – grace and courtesy – in your family, practising mutual respect, and instilling a sense of personal responsibility. Victor Frankl, a survivor of the Holocaust, psychologist, and author has been attributed with the quote:

Constructively working together with your child to correct a mishap can provide a valuable learning opportunity.

❝ ❞

Thinking about your responses to challenging situations with your child can help you to find more positive outcomes in moments of stress.

"Between the stimulus and the response, there is a space. In that space is our power to choose our response. In our response lies our growth and our freedom."

This concept of "a space" can help us to think about how we respond as parents, allowing us to envisage a space between the time that something occurs between you and your child and the time when you react or respond to the situation. The space represents an important moment where you can ensure that you are responding thoughtfully instead of reacting impulsively on autopilot. Often, when we react we make a situation worse and undermine the values that we were hoping to reinforce.

Pause for thought

Upsetting situations can develop quickly between a parent and child, often leaving little time to think through a response. You may recall instances when you have said something to your child or done something and almost instantly realized it was out of line with Montessori principles – if you already practise these – and your family values. Even if you expressed regret inwardly, or out loud, for reacting in this way, your child may have walked away from the situation with a sense of shame, guilt, or hurt.

By thinking about how we can reinforce family values before challenging situations arise, we become better at finding positive outcomes for our children in moments of stress.

As long as a situation is not an emergency, practising pausing for a few seconds to centre yourself can allow you to be more thoughtful in your responses. When you feel challenged, taking a few deep breaths, counting in your mind to three, or turning away for a few seconds, can help you to create the space where you can grow and be free to choose what your response is going to be.

A positive outcome

Thinking about how a scenario could play out, or reviewing a situation in the past, can help you consider how your response or reaction can make a difference.

For example, if a young child accidentally spills their drink at a family gathering, a parent may think they were not paying attention and react crossly, saying, "You are being clumsy, please be more careful! You stand aside and I'll clear up." The child in turn feels shamed and embarrassed.

Alternatively, the parent could pause, then respond calmly, saying, "I'm sorry this happened. We will get it cleaned up. If you get a towel, we can clean it up together." This response helps the child to become more responsible, learn a new skill, and to see grace and courtesy in action.

MINIMIZING CONFLICT

Some squabbles and disagreements are inevitable in life. They may arise when a child does not want to share or take turns; when they are unhappy about doing a chore; or are trying to get attention. While it is not possible to avoid conflict completely (see pages 108–111 for strategies to disarm squabbles) there are steps you can take to minimize disagreements.

Identifying areas of conflict

There are many ways to prevent disagreements from arising at home. One of the best ways to avoid conflict is to have weekly family meetings (see pp.22–23 and pp.64–67) where you can discuss situations that often lead to squabbles. Here, issues that family members might disagree about, such as family chores, can be resolved peacefully.

❝ ❞

Talking through potential areas of dispute at weekly family meetings can be one of the best ways to avoid disagreements arising.

With areas such as chores, for children from two to three years up (see pp.106–107), you could agree to make a list of tasks in chart form, so that names can be added as the family decides who will be responsible for each job. Add your chores to the list, too, so your child sees that you also have work to do around the house. Allowing your child to have a choice of one or more chores, rather than assigning chores to them, gives them a sense of ownership and choice, helping to minimize conflict. You could also rotate chores weekly or monthly to avoid your child tiring of a task, keeping complaints down and interest up.

Another way to avoid or prevent conflict in the family is to ensure that everyone understands and agrees to follow the house rules (see p.41). Your agreed house rules help individual family members to keep on track with expectations for behaviour.

Setting an example

Your goal is to help your child learn how to manage their feelings, how to listen to others as well as talk, and how to come to some kind of agreement about what will happen next. When your child observes you working out everyday challenges with others peacefully and treating others with kindness, respect, and understanding, they will learn from your example. When a disagreement does arise, your child needs to learn how to respond, how to work out differences, and how to compromise, creating a solution that works for both parties involved in the conflict.

Containing conflict

Often, parents do not know how to help children who are starting a dispute to settle down and resolve conflict peacefully. They either become part of the battle, worsening the conflict, or they impose their authority, demanding that children quieten down and stop fighting, which is unhelpful for the children. If conflict starts, following the rules of engagement set out below can be helpful.

- **Your role** is to facilitate learning, rather than participate in the struggle.

- **Let go of preconceived ideas** about who started it, who should know better, or what the outcome should be. Both children are responsible. Avoid judgment and strive to stay neutral.

- **Guide the children** to find their own resolution, rather than solving an issue for them.

Agreeing on a family chores rota shows children that each person has a part to play and defines roles.

BEING FULLY PRESENT

Occasionally, we all need someone we love, respect, or admire – whether a partner, friend, relative, or colleague – to pay attention briefly just to us. If we do not get this attention, we may feel discouraged, disappointed, ignored, sad, determined, or unimportant.

How receiving attention helps

When we feel we have not received attention, we may try harder and even do something inappropriate to get it. Or we may give up and no longer expect to receive attention, or we may seek it from others. Children, like adults, need to be acknowledged, valued, and loved. If your child continually seeks attention, they are demonstrating that there is a greater emotional need that is not yet being met. Giving your child 100 per cent of your attention for just a few moments can give them that boost, allowing them to carry on with what they were doing, or need to start doing, independently. Children and adults can be more autonomous when their emotional needs are met (see p.38).

There are some key elements to bear in mind when you wish to give your child your 100 per cent focused attention.

- **Make sure there are no distractions**. You cannot be effective if multitasking, for example, driving the car, making dinner, texting, or looking at a screen.

- **A moment can be enough**. Just a brief moment only of your fully focused attention lets your child know that they are important and that you care.

- **Be fully present** when your child needs you to be. Children so often seem to need our attention at inconvenient moments. For example, your child may want your attention when everyone is rushing to get ready for work or school. Rather than see their behaviour as annoying, consider it is an opportunity to meet their needs so that they can carry on without you. If you put other tasks on hold for a moment and attend to your child's need for attention, everyone will be happier and more productive.

When your child needs your attention

Notice signs that your child might benefit from a moment of your undivided attention:

- Is your child ignoring a request and being disruptive rather than cooperative?
- Has your child asked you a simple question?
- Is your child being particularly clingy?

" "

Giving your full attention for just a moment meets your child's emotional needs and promotes independence.

Making eye contact, ensuring your body language is open, and listening fully all signal that you are giving your child your complete attention.

- **A verbal response** is not always needed. We tend to talk too much, instead of being quiet and present. Children often just want you to be there with them. They might simply need to sit on your lap for a minute, for you to look at something special with them, such as a butterfly, or to tell you something that they are planning to do. If you feel that a verbal response is needed, make sure that it is heartfelt, such as, "That is beautiful", or, "It is so special to sit with you". Often, we jump into adult problem solving or information-gathering mode with responses such

as, "Let's look up what kind of butterfly that is", or, "I know how you can get that done. You should…". When children need our focused attention, this is a moment for emotionally bonding with them. They are not looking for information or solutions, but for connection with you.

When you are fully present with your child for a brief moment of time, you invest in your relationship and the dividends are invaluable. Your child feels loved and important and has less need to misbehave.

47

ENCOURAGEMENT VERSUS PRAISE

We often confuse praise with encouragement. However, these are quite different and have very different results. Encouragement helps develop and support intrinsic motivation, while praise does the opposite.

How praise affects us

Praise tends to promote dependence on the approval of others. It is a type of external reward, as opposed to the intrinsic motivation that comes from encouragement. When children engage in everyday activities such as painting a picture, tidying their room, raking leaves, or achieving a good grade on a test, parents can either encourage or praise them. When we immediately tell our children how much we love what they have done, how proud it makes us feel, and how much we want them to do it again, we may do so innocently. Our intention is not to turn the focus onto ourselves; however, this quick praise tends to make children dependent on our approval. If we say "Good work!" or "I love that!" time and again, our words

" "

Children experience a sense of self-satisfaction and pride when encouraged, which helps them to grow in confidence.

Though your child may not carry out a job to your standards, they are learning to take pride in performing a task.

tend to become meaningless and children can become "praise junkies". Breaking the cycle of meaningless praise is incredibly beneficial for children.

Praise involves judgment, approval from others, focus on outcome, and competition. It does not give a child any usable feedback for future activities. If at your annual work review, your employer gave you a list of five areas of your job and for each made comments such as "fine job", "excellent work", "good reviews", you might feel pleased, but would not have any useful information to help you grow professionally.

The power of encouragement

An encouraging review might include an employer also suggesting you think about how to develop organizational or leadership skills, strategies, and ways to meet goals in a timely manner or to be a self-starter. Likewise, if you ask questions that help your child to reflect on what they have done and how they feel, they are able to experience self-satisfaction and a sense of accomplishment. Their confidence will grow and they will be more likely to try new things and learn for the sake of learning, encouraged by their own sense of pride. Encouragement is based on acceptance, process, learning, gaining skills, and pleasure.

The art of encouragement

Children gain so many benefits when we encourage rather than praise. They can see themselves as contributing members of their families, schools, and communities.

- Point out how much work they put into a project, their focus on detail, and their concentration and perseverance.
- Ask what your child liked best about a process, what media worked best for them, how they felt when they completed it, and how it helped others.

Focusing on the process

An important observation is that from birth to about six years of age, children are in a developmental stage where the process is more important than the outcome. They do things out of interest and enjoyment in an activity and, usually, are not concerned with the final result. For example, a young child helping to sort clean laundry focuses on getting it out of the machine or off the dryer, helping to carry the laundry basket to the place where it will be folded, then sorting and folding items. Whether or not socks are matched or towels folded as you would wish is not important to them. For a young child, the sense of achievement comes from the process of getting the laundry from dryer to drawer.

49

HELPING YOUR CHILD TO BE INDEPENDENT

One of our goals as parents is to help our children develop a sense of independence and autonomy while also understanding that we are all, at the same time, interdependent. We teach this to our children step by step, as they grow from early childhood to adulthood.

Being your child's mentor

The ways in which we respond to our children when they feel as if they need assistance can lead them either to feel self-confident and capable or that they are dependent on others. We should be their mentors and trusted guides rather than their "fixers". Our responses are meant to help them become emotionally strong and resilient.

66 99

Maria Montessori said that if young children had the right words, they would ask us, 'Help me learn how to do this for myself'.

Your child starts to learn from the day they are born. Everything is a first-time experience. Most of us are aware of this when our children are infants. However, once children take their first steps, it can be easy for parents to forget that they are constantly teaching their children what to do and how to be. As your child grows, they will continue to learn everyday skills from you, from how to wash their hands and face as a toddler, to managing an allowance when older. Sometimes you will teach your child lessons intentionally, while at other times your child learns simply by watching you. Each time you teach a skill, or help them gain understanding, they become more capable and confident.

Guiding your child

You are your child's first and most influential teacher. The best teachers ask questions that help children think about a situation and plan their next step, rather than give all the answers or solutions, or do things for them. The aim is to empower children to be independent.

There may be times when your child says, "Nobody will play with me at school"; "I can't do this science project"; "I fell and scraped my knee; it hurts"; or "I wanted to wear this outfit today and it's in the laundry". Take a

Working side by side lets your child observe how you carry out a task.

moment to centre yourself before responding so that you can give support and guidance, if needed. First, acknowledge their feelings. Then respond with caring questions that will help them develop relationships, complete homework, take care of themselves, accomplish tasks, and solve problems. When your child reaches out to you and your response is to guide them lovingly, they learn that they are capable and that it is okay to ask for help when needed.

Follow a few basic principles when you want to teach your child to do something correctly, whether tying a shoelace or helping to wash the dishes:

- **Be very thoughtful** about the steps they need to follow to accomplish the task correctly.

- **Show them how** to do the task slowly and carefully, step by step, inviting them to try it for themselves.

- **Try to be silent** while showing them how to do something, saving words until the end of the task. Demonstrate a skill slowly and carefully so your child can watch what you do, then try it too. Expect mistakes at first. Each mistake provides an opportunity to learn, whether that is how to do a task correctly, or, for example, how to clean up an accidental mess.

FAMILY LIFE THROUGH A MONTESSORI LENS

A STIMULATING HOME ENVIRONMENT

Just as Montessori classrooms are designed with the children who learn there in mind, you can create a Montessori-inspired home environment for each family member.

Montessori classrooms deliberately create an environment that promotes a sense of order, independence, comfort, intellectual stimulation and engagement, and love of learning for all members of the classroom community, no matter what age, interests, or skill level. This is referred to as a "Montessori-prepared environment". Likewise, you can build a Montessori-prepared home environment with some simple steps, taking into account the ages, interests, and skills of each member of your family.

" "

An organized, aesthetically appealing environment that reflects your family's interests is key to creating a stimulating family home for all.

THE KEY PRINCIPLES

Following three basic principles will help you to plan, prepare, and enjoy a family home that embraces Montessori's approach.

Whether your home is small or spacious, ensuring that it is well organized; making it aesthetically appealing; and reflecting your interests in your home environment will all create a home that reflects Montessori values and principles.

Have a place for everything

Organizing your home so that items are stored methodically and can be easily found, systems are maintained, and your environment is free of clutter creates a sense of order with everything in its set place. When your child can access items from a young age, this facilitates their ability to be increasingly independent by learning practical skills that allow them to participate in all aspects of family life.

Create aesthetic appeal

Try to create a home that feels warm, inviting, clean, and comfortable for each family member and for guests. Of course, what appeals to your child may not appeal to you. This can be reflected in their own space; for example, by painting their room a colour they love, or by referencing a part of contemporary culture or history they are fascinated by in the decor.

Reflect your interests

Fill your home with stimulating items such as books, art, music, and things to do and learn, that reflect and support each family member's interests. Include skills and interests of your own that you would like to introduce to your child. Elements might be as varied as celebrations and symbols of your faith or traditions; a nature corner; a workout area; a library collection; pets; a telescope; a creative projects area; or a place to listen to music. Create a home where exploring and developing ideas and interests together is a family goal.

Ensuring that items in your home are organized instils the idea that everything has a dedicated place.

THE BEDROOM

Your child's bedroom is their personal space. Even if sharing with a sibling, children have a special attachment to their room. Help your child to create and maintain a room that conveys warmth, comfort, safety, and order, and reflects their personality and changing interests.

An emerging identity

When your child is an infant or toddler, you decide on furnishings, toys, and clothing. By the age of three, your child may have their own ideas and can begin to have a say in how their room is arranged. At first, involve them just a little. For example, you may choose an elephant picture and have two places in mind for it. Offer them a choice, "Do you want the elephant near your wardrobe or your bed?". The older the child, the more collaborative the process; and eventually your child will do most of the planning.

Allowing your child to help plan and design their room fosters independence, creative thinking, problem solving, and a sense of order. Creating a room for and with them will result in one that they are excited about, comfortable in, and love.

What to consider

Use these guidelines for a Montessori-inspired bedroom for all ages.

- **Decide on house rules**. Follow your family values to decide on some basic rules for what your child can bring into their room. For example, can food be eaten there? Can computers, phones, screens, and video games, or pets be allowed at any time?

- **Hang items at your child's eye level**. Get down to their height to see where to put photos, pinboards, and art.

- **Help your child create order**. Display toys and belongings in a visually appealing way. Using containers or toy boxes to store items may feel like an easy way to keep your child's room tidy; however, children can be overwhelmed when faced with too many things thrown together in a disorderly way. When each item has a set place, you help your child experience a sense of order. With practice and consistency, your child will develop a habit of putting items back in their designated place. Instead of using large containers or overcrowding shelves, display just eight to 12 items on accessible shelves when your child is young to instil this habit. If they tire of an activity, put it away for a while and bring out something else to ignite new interest.

- **Make clothing accessible** for young children. Lower wardrobe rails and use the bottom drawer of dressers for their clothes. This appeals to their sense of order, and when they can start to dress themselves, at around 18 months, helps them to do this independently.

- **Choose furniture** for your child's size and needs. Whether a first bed, a mattress on the floor, or a bunk bed, try to ensure that your child has a place to sleep that is comfortable, safe, and allows them independence. If there is space, a child-sized table and chair are a welcome addition to a child's room.

- **Make room for books**. With Montessori, books are revered and considered precious. They are usually found in every room of the house. Have a dedicated space for books in your child's room to help them learn to treat books with care and respect.

- **Think about lighting**. Nothing is better than natural daylight, but consider the artificial lighting in your child's room, too. It is important for their room to be well lit, with various sources of light that will allow them to read, write, draw, and do other activities without straining their eyes.

Arrange your child's room to suit their perspective – making sure that activities are within reach and wall hangings placed at their eye level.

Ages and stages

18 months–6 years
Do not overwhelm your child with too many toys. Choose fewer toys that are durable, beautiful, and made from natural materials, rather than lots of plastic and battery-run toys.

6–12 years
During this stage, a desk, reading lamp, and chair give your child a space to study. Limit the use of digital devices in bedrooms.

12–18 years
Allow your adolescent child to do most of the planning and arranging in their bedroom, with your consent and advice.

THE KITCHEN

The kitchen is often the hub of family life, a place where family members gather to prepare food, to talk, and to be close to one another. Young children, in particular, enjoy helping out in the kitchen and spending time with parents while they work there.

An accessible space

Organize the kitchen to assist and encourage your child to develop the everyday skills that allow them to be helpful and become independent. When everything has a place and is accessible, you create a sense of order that helps your child to navigate the kitchen calmly and confidently. Working together to prepare meals and clean up not only helps your child develop useful life skills, but also creates a family community. For young children, simple adjustments make it easy for them to help out.

- **Set aside a low refrigerator shelf** to store prepared drinks or a small jug of water, fruit, and ingredients for sandwiches and snacks. Allowing your child to help themselves to a snack or drink teaches them self-regulation.

Easily accessible plates, cups, bowls, and eating utensils encourage independence in your young child.

Ages and stages

18 months–6 years
Place items in reach, so even very young children can help to prep, independently get food for themselves, and clean up. As impulse control and coordination grow, use child-sized ceramic plates, glasses, and metal cutlery (use a butter knife until about the age of four).

6–12 years
Your child can help with simple cooking tasks. Teach them about basic nutrition, cleaning surfaces and utensils, and safe food storage.

12–18 years
Teens can help with meal planning, grocery shopping, cooking, and cleaning up.

OUR STORY

Throughout the stages of Otis' life so far, we have made a point to set up the spaces in the house so that they are functional and accessible for a three-foot person, allowing him to be engaged and safe.

He has his own cupboard in the kitchen with his plates and utensils so that he can access them when he is getting lunch or a snack. He also has a step stool in the kitchen so that he can reach the worktop and help prepare some of his food. He especially likes to help us with cookies, cakes, and bread – bread-making is his favourite! He has some experience with this culinary art as he has baked bread at school. He is so proud when he shows us how to knead the dough. By giving him ownership and providing a right-sized kitchen environment, he has freedom to organize things how he likes them, while at the same time keeping items safe and tidy.

Brendan and Ann Marie, parents of Otis, aged four

- **Use non-breakable containers** for peanut butter, jams, and spreads so your child can successfully get out and put away ingredients while they are working on holding and carrying skills.

- **If space allows**, a child-sized table and chair allows young children to set up and eat their food independently.

- **Put plates, cups**, and napkins in a low cupboard or on a low shelf. Store cutlery in a low drawer or basket. Ideally, use child-sized metal cutlery (see box, opposite), either custom-made or smaller items from your set. Using unbreakable plates and cups until three to four years of age helps children to gain skills confidently and safely.

Prepping and clearing up

A sturdy stool or a set of small, stable steps allows a young child to help wash up or prep food at a worktop. Show your child how to wipe the counter after use to instil this habit for life. A child-sized broom, dustpan and brush, and mop will mean that, from a young age, your child can help to clean the kitchen floor.

EATING AREAS

Whether you have a separate dining room, or meals are shared around the kitchen table, aim to make your mealtimes a pleasant experience for everyone (see pp.78–81). Encourage children to help in both setting the table and cleaning up after a meal.

Setting the table

Getting your child involved regularly in setting the table for the family or guests provides an invaluable lesson in everyday living skills. Making the table look inviting and orderly emphasizes that mealtimes are valued moments for all.

House rules for family meals

Meals are a time to be together, enjoy your food, and talk about your day (see pp.78–81). House rules, such as the ones below, can make mealtimes enjoyable and harmonious.

- Set a rule that digital devices, television, or loud music are not allowed at meals so you avoid these distractions.

- Consider how long children should stay at the table. For example, if parents and/or older children are engaged in conversations that a younger child finds uninteresting, may they ask to be excused, or should they wait until everyone has finished eating or they are excused by an adult?

- Agree that everyone helps to clean up: clearing plates; putting waste in a compost container or a bin; and washing up, or scraping or rinsing dishes then loading the dishwasher.

If you use a tablecloth, encourage your child to help with this. They can carry it to the table, unfold it and arrange it, and put soiled cloths in the laundry. Your younger child will most likely need help placing a tablecloth, even on a small table. Placemats, used with or without a cloth, can be easier for a young child to arrange, and these also help to create a feeling of order.

Montessori encourages using cloth napkins to model the principle of reusing items rather than disposing of paper napkins. Your child can also learn the skill of folding or rolling them, how to use them, and how to launder them.

As soon as your child develops sufficient coordination and shows interest, they can help to carry plates to the table, setting one on each placemat or on the cloth in front of each chair. They can also collect and bring cutlery to the table. Show them how to carry knives, forks, and spoons safely and place them correctly.

" "

Involving your child in preparing the table for a meal and clearing up afterwards helps them to feel that they have an important role to play.

Think about the eating experience from your child's perspective. For example, are dishes and jugs light enough for them to lift and manage?

Ages and stages

18 months–6 years
Your toddler can carry cutlery and napkins in a basket to the table for you or an older sibling to set out. From around the age of three, as strength and coordination develop, they can help set up and clean the table.

6–12 years
Your child can start to handle more delicate dishes and place glasses at each setting now, and help to wash up or load the dishwasher.

12–18 years
Teens can engage in the entire mealtime process. They can also model grace and courtesy for younger siblings.

Your child may need help carrying heavy jugs of water or drinks to the table. Think of ways to make this task possible, even for younger children. For example, you could carry a large jug of water to the table and your child could carry a smaller, child-sized jug.

Learning table manners
The dinner table provides a perfect opportunity to model and teach grace and courtesy on a daily basis. Family members practise and use manners when interacting, and they move carefully and thoughtfully when setting the table, passing food, pouring drinks, and cleaning up when the meal is done.

Like any lesson you teach your child, teaching table manners involves first modelling the behaviour you are looking for in them. Give short, simple lessons on the right way to do things, such as eating soup with a spoon, cutting food, or asking politely and responding with "thank you".

If your child drops or spills something, treat it as a chance to teach them how to clean up. If they forget to ask politely or say "thank you", respectfully remind them how to ask so that they are not embarrassed or pushed into a power struggle.

FAMILY ROOMS AND PLAYROOMS

A family or play area – whether your home's living room, a separate room, or a designated space in a room – provides an informal area where families can gather together to play with toys, watch television, play video or board games, or enjoy other similar activities. This shared space promotes and enhances your family community.

Keep things in order

As with other rooms in your home, try to create and maintain order in this informal area. All too quickly, toys can end up scattered from one end of the room to the other, becoming an obstacle underfoot and a challenge to put away. Consider the following when organizing the family room.

- **Think about how** family members typically like to use this space. For example, does your family love to watch television together or enjoy playing multi-person video games? Or do you use the family room as a place to read quietly, or as a space where toys are played with and stored? Consider the space you have available, what your family's focus will be for most of the time, and what sort of furniture will work best in this family space.

- **Find ways to arrange toys**, games, craft materials, or other items you wish to keep here neatly in the available space. Shelves or wall hooks can store items in an orderly way, while a sturdy basket or bin can hold bulkier items such as building blocks and construction materials. Do what makes sense in the space that you have. Organizing in this way helps each family member follow the principle that everything has its own place where it is kept when not in use.

Ages and stages

18 months–6 years
Be sure your child can reach books and play items safely. Place anything that can be easily broken or pulled down out of reach.

6–12 years
Continue to teach your child to be mindful of others in the common space, putting away items after use, asking others if the television will disturb them, and sharing with siblings.

12–18 years
Work out house rules around impromptu visits from friends to assess when they use the shared family space or their bedroom.

With a little planning, family rooms and playrooms can be organized so that family members can enjoy activities side by side, in a harmonious manner.

- **Establish a rule** that family members can take out just one or two things at any one time so others in the family can move around safely. A rolled mat or rug in the room that your child can take out and spread on the floor to define their play area can be helpful, giving them a dedicated space, for example, to construct items with building or interlocking blocks or to work on a floor puzzle. Depending on your child's and family's interests and the space, you may also want to have a table and chairs where children and others can sit to work on puzzles or non-messy craft projects.

- **Are any activities not allowed here**? For example, do you want to avoid energetic games, such as tag or play wrestling, and are snacks allowed?

- **Bear in mind** that some house rules, such as taking good care of things, not playing music too loudly, and not leaving leftover food in a room, apply to all areas of the house because they involve being considerate of others and keeping each other safe.

EVERYDAY STRATEGIES
FAMILY MEETINGS

The concept of the family meeting, introduced on pages 22–23, is one of the most important Montessori strategies for creating an atmosphere of inclusion in your family. In family meetings, each person is included and has a voice at the table.

The lessons learned at weekly family meetings are invaluable during your child's years at home with you. They will continue to use the skills they learned at these meetings when they start their own family, and in their work life and community life.

Meetings are facilitated by family members on a rotating basis, with each person having an opportunity to lead. The role of facilitator may come more naturally to some who have had plenty of experience in meetings, while others are learning this valuable life skill. By starting with the oldest, children can observe and prepare for this role – children as young as four, with help from an older family member, can begin to facilitate. By rotating leadership, each person has the chance to be empowered as a leader and supported in learning this new skill.

Meetings normally run for 20–30 minutes, including a closing fun activity. If an issue is not resolved in this time-frame, it can be carried over to the following week. They should follow a set format for consistency, as outlined on pages 66–67.

" "

Family meetings, where each person is given a turn to express their feelings and ideas, promote open communication.

" " OUR STORY

When our oldest child, Cooper, was about five years old and our daughter, Madeline, was two years old, we took a parenting class because we were starting to question whether we were on the right track for Montessori kids. One of the most valuable practices that we learned was the importance of a weekly family meeting.

We began to have our meetings right away. We hadn't realized how much a toddler takes in from family conversations, even when we thought she was just playing with her toys. Each child in their own time became a good facilitator, leader, and creative problem solver. They were also empathetic and appreciative of each other and us.

We also noticed that as time went by and our children got close to the end of their primary school years, our meetings changed a bit. They became less regular and more casual than when the children were younger. Everyone had busy schedules, but when one of us had something to discuss as a family we would all make time to chat and figure things out together.

One of my most cherished parts of a meeting is the time for acknowledgments and appreciations. The children always remind us if we forget to include that time, even when we are all very busy.

Jon and Sophie, parents of Cooper, aged 18 and Madeline, aged 15

FAMILY MEETINGS IN PRACTICE

1
Starting the family meeting

Weekly family meetings, ideally at a set time, begin with appreciations or acknowledgments. This gives children and parents a moment to express positivity about being together and is a chance to look at each person's growth and contributions. The facilitator starts, choosing a family member and thanking them for one thing they did or helped with during the week, then other family members follow.

2
Discussing issues

In the week, family members add items for discussion to a blank agenda. At the meeting, the facilitator runs through these. When an item is raised, everyone brainstorms, so children practise being part of a team that problem solves without blame or shame. The meeting leader gains valuable skills in helping others to be creative, thoughtful, and to stay on task. They may also decide to postpone an item until the next week.

3
What is coming up?

Each person shares their activities or obligations for the coming week; for example, a child may have a dance performance one evening, and a parent a work presentation one day. Sharing what will be happening in the coming week gives everyone a sense of what to expect and means they can support and help each other. Children learn to be sensitive to others' needs, concerns, challenges, and activities.

4
Finishing off

After spending 15–20 minutes in discussion, the last 10 minutes or so of the meeting are spent enjoying a family activity, chosen by the facilitator. Ideally, activities involve all family members and are interactive, such as a game or a short walk, rather than passive or screen-based. Ending in this way gives everyone a boost and ensures that each family member leaves on a positive note.

" "

Taking part in family meetings
shows children how to problem
solve with others.

All members of
the family – including
visiting grandparents
and relatives – take part
in family meetings.

MESSY SPACES

Hobbies, interests, and activities can be messy, and items for projects may need to be left in place so that they can be returned to on another day. Allocating a "messy space" in your home allows family members to pursue interests without creating chaos.

Ordered "messy" spaces

Finding a space where your child can pursue messy activities fosters creativity. Younger children are also likely to want to be around you as much as possible, so when planning a messy space, think about the activities that each family member enjoys and consider whether these can be done in the same space.

Ages and stages

18 months–6 years
Lay down a heavy plastic covering on the floor in part of a room, or put a washable cover on a child-sized table. Place paints, brushes, clay, or other supplies on a small shelf, or designated area of a shelf. You might wish to purchase a child-sized easel. Be present when your child is working in this area to guide them and ensure safety.

6–12 years
Provide advanced art and craft materials and tools in line with interests and skills. As your child gets older, they can work without constant supervision.

12–18 years
Evolve this space to reflect more focused interests as your child gets older.

Providing your child with an area to enjoy messy activities allows them to engage freely in creative pursuits.

66 99 OUR STORY

I started noticing that my son's backpack was full of what I considered rubbish – broken rubber bands, the inner ring from a roll of tape, and bits of string. I asked him what they were for and he just said that he needed them. I cleared out any insect-attracting items such as broken crackers and left the rest for whatever it was he had in mind. Then I noticed items moving from the recycling bin to his bedroom: egg boxes, milk cartons, cardboard boxes of various sizes.

He said that he needed them all. So, we agreed that he would keep them in a designated "messy" area in his room, then I took a deep breath and went

with it. One day, he emerged with a "smoothie shop" made out of the cardboard and rubbish, each part thoughtfully glued together. With grace and courtesy, he took our orders and we played along. He was so proud, and I silently thanked his Montessori teachers for showing us how to let him follow his interests.

Tara, mother of John, aged seven

As with other areas, keep order in mind when planning a messy space so that utensils for activities are easily located and items are unlikely to be knocked over. Clutter and disorder compromise safety and make it harder to concentrate on the project at hand.

Being creative with space

If you do not have a spare room to turn into a messy space, think about how to provide a creative area for your child in a bedroom, kitchen, or living room (see Ages and Stages, opposite). Your child's needs will vary depending on their age and interests, but the basic concept remains the same: your child feels they have the freedom to explore hobbies and interests while you maintain order and avoid mess. By providing a controlled environment for your child to create, construct, and explore at home, you encourage creative thinking and self-expression.

OUTDOOR SPACES

Montessori teaches children that they are part of the natural world and that all living things are interdependent. Think about how to use outdoor environments to teach your child about nature, support their development, and enjoy family time.

Spending time outdoors

Most children love to be outdoors, to wander around and explore, to climb trees, to look at flowers and berries, and perhaps play with a family pet. Many children also enjoy working in a garden or outside space and, when given the opportunity, feeding small animals such as rabbits, ducks, and chickens.

Ages and stages

18 months–6 years
Draw your child's attention to plants, trees, seeds, berries, and small animals, helping them to recognize and name them.

6–12 years
Work as a family to keep your environment tidy: rake leaves, pick up twigs, and trim bushes. By 12, your child might help to mow a lawn.

12–18 years
Let your teen develop gardening interests, for example, by growing herbs from seed.

Whether you live in a flat without a garden, have a small outside space, or an area big enough for some play equipment, finding ways to give your child the opportunity to play and learn outdoors is invaluable.

A stimulating space

Depending on your child's age, family interests, and space, as well as your local climate, consider the following when planning how to enjoy outdoor environments with your child:

- **Whether in your garden or a park**, find areas for your child to run and play. As well as providing the exhilarating opportunity to run, this helps them to gain dexterity, agility, and muscle tone. Where possible, using equipment such as a child-sized basketball hoop or a sports net can also be stimulating.

- **Think about outdoor activities** that feed your child's imagination. This

" "

Giving your child the chance to play and learn outdoors is an invaluable way to support their development and teach them about the natural world.

Spending time outdoors with your child gives you an opportunity to introduce them to the cycles of nature and to teach them to respect their environment.

could be a simple sandpit or swing; or, if space allows, climbing equipment, a playhouse, or even a basic treehouse.

- **If there is space**, an outdoor table allows you to eat meals together in the open or to enjoy activities such as reading and drawing outside.

- **Plan a shady area** to offer protection from the sun.

- **Think about creating** a family garden to plant and grow flowers and vegetables (see p.112). This could be in a small garden plot, in a container, or in a window box.

- **Find out about** local parks, hiking trails, or community gardens that you can enjoy as a family.

- **For a more ambitious project**, if you have space, you might consider building a home for a few small farm animals to care for. Alternatively, enjoy a trip to a small petting farm.

Stewards of the earth

Sharing the world of nature with your child – whether when on a nature hunt in your garden, hiking on a countryside trail, or growing herbs on a windowsill – teaches them that we are all connected to nature and dependent on it. From the start of their life, spending time with your child outdoors helps them to appreciate the relationship between living things and the environment.

- Being outside helps them to learn that each plant and animal is affected by the climate, soil, and geographical features of its environment, as well as by the other plants and animals that live there, each one striving to feed, grow, and reproduce. Your child will develop an attitude of stewardship towards the earth: caring for wild areas as well as pockets of nature in the city or suburb.

- Teach your child to treat living things with care. Explain that you should gather flowers for a set purpose only, and not over-pick a plant. Fresh wildflowers can be dried, pressed, or put in a vase to preserve them for as long as possible. Encourage them to study flowers, comparing species, and counting petals and stamens. As the weather changes, they can look for nuts, fruits, and berries, noticing how these are distributed and which animals forage them.

DAILY ROUTINES

One of the defining concepts of a Montessori-inspired home is to prepare an environment where children can learn to be independent, self-disciplined, and organized each day.

This is a very different philosophy from permissive parenting, where children have no limits on their behaviour or the choices they make. It also differs from families where the parents make the rules and the children are expected to follow routines and decisions made for them. The Montessori approach is authoritative – firm at the edges, warm and empathetic at heart. The goal is to teach children to recognize that their voice matters. They can do things for themselves, learning how to be increasingly masterful and independent, while at the same time, understanding that with freedom comes responsibility. In this section, we explore the daily structures and routines that will help your child to develop and thrive.

" "

Building in routines to certain parts of your day can help children to feel supported by a structure and teaches them to be independent.

A FLEXIBLE FRAMEWORK

Children tend to respond best when there is just the right amount of structure and routine in their daily lives – not too much and not too little, a sort of "Goldilocks" approach.

The main areas where routines help families are when getting up and ready in the morning and during mealtimes and bedtime. How you structure your family's free time and manage screen time are also key.

Routines involve thinking about a daily sequence of steps that can be helpful when followed in a particular situation. While the sequence does not need to be rigid, your child should feel supported by a structure, which in turn reduces stress and squabbles.

Times of transition

There are times when children need to transition from one activity, or part of the day, to another. For example, moving from breakfast to play time, or transitioning from school to extracurricular activities. As you guide your child, you can work out if they need help to transition or manage this easily. Be aware of their personality and needs. Is a gentle reminder enough, or do they need concrete support to transition? If so, certain tactics can be helpful.

- **Consider setting a kitchen timer**, say, for ten minutes, to focus your child on tasks such as getting dressed and ready for breakfast.

- **A calming strategy** can help your child transition from playing outside to coming in for dinner. For example, invite them to sit on the doorstep to have a drink of water and catch their breath before coming in. Remind them what you need to do together to get the table ready or prep food.

- **Some children respond well** to a checklist. This could be written, or made up of simple illustrations that represent actions, such as getting out of bed or brushing their teeth.

A visual checklist of what needs to be done at certain times of the day can be a useful tool for some children.

GETTING READY FOR THE DAY: YOUNG CHILDREN

From 18 months to six years, children need direction and structure in their day. At the same time, Montessori encourages us to "follow the child". Aim to balance your child's need for structure and routine with the recognition that each child is unique.

Setting the tone

Montessori said that adults need to prepare themselves so that they can set the tone for the day with their calm, quiet presence. Following a routine whereby you wake early to enjoy a jog, listen to quiet music while thinking about the day ahead, or read a chapter of an enjoyable book ensures a more relaxed start to the day, in turn helping your young child to feel calm and reassured.

A smooth start

Consistency and routine are essential for young children to develop trust and feel assured that their needs will be met. However, plans should not be rigid and must be designed with the individual child in mind. Here are some ideas to consider for the start of the day.

- **Prepare clothing choices** and lunches with your child the night before. You can also set up the table for breakfast

Setting out clothes the night before is a simple task that saves valuable time during busy mornings.

and encourage three- to five-year-olds to begin to serve themselves in the morning. If your child takes a packed lunch to school, they may enjoy helping to make this so that they can have a say on what goes in their lunchbox. Offer healthy choices. By being part of this process, they are learning to select food from different food groups and to balance their diet. They are also more likely to eat food when they have been involved in the decision making. Invite your toddler to help make snacks at weekends to prepare them for this task.

- **Develop a list of tasks** – whether a mental list or a written one – that need to be done at the start of the day. Include every task – whether big or small – from feeding and dressing your baby to supervising older children while they have breakfast to eating your own breakfast. Then work out at a family meeting who is responsible for each task. A regular set of morning tasks helps young children develop habits and a rhythm.

Some children fall easily into a pattern, while others may need a chart, which could be in the form of illustrations, to keep them on track.

- **Give yourself and your child** plenty of time to get ready in the morning to allow for plans going awry, such as a cup of juice being spilt, a dog walking slowly, or a toddler who does not get to their potty in time.

66 99 OUR STORY

After he had got dressed, I saw my son shuffling, as children do when they need their potty. I asked if he needed to use his potty and he replied, "No". As we got ready to leave the house, his feet started to shuffle faster. "Are you sure?". Again he said "No".

His shuffling became more urgent. I said, "I think you need to go" and lifted him to carry him to the potty. I felt a warm trickle against my hip and knew that I had invited myself to experience the consequences of waiting too long.

With my toddler, I had to remove soiled clothes, put them in the laundry, and find new clothes. The lesson I was trying to instil in him I had to practise, too. In my rush I was trying to avoid the unavoidable. He might have made it to the potty if I had stopped and said at the start, "Let's go ahead and try."

Alicia (@montessibaby @teachlearnmontessori), mother of Charlie, aged two

GETTING READY FOR THE DAY: OLDER CHILDREN

From the age of six, up through the adolescent years, your child becomes increasingly able to take on more responsibilities, organize their time, and put the family values that they learned from you in their early years into practice.

Tools for life

Your child practises using the skills, knowledge, and beliefs they have acquired as they navigate each day. As they use these tools, inevitably making some mistakes along the way,

they are preparing themselves to be on their own and independent one day. Creating routines from the start, when your child is very young, can minimize stress and helps your child feel capable.

Bear in mind that six- to seven-year-olds and 10- to 12-year-olds are beginning new stages of development. As children enter a new stage, they sometimes seem to have lost or forgotten much of what they learned earlier. They may seem easily distracted, clumsy, and very disorganized. As their bodies and minds change, this can be confusing and disrupt their usual sense of order and routine. Doing as much preparation as you can the night before makes morning routines easier to follow and gives you time to deal with any hiccups patiently.

A start-the-day plan

Just as when your child was younger, think about what needs to be done to prepare for the day, and make plans so everyone can get off to a good start.

- **In the evenings**, encourage your child to put homework and books into their backpacks as they complete a piece of work or when family study time is over, so these are packed for the morning. If your child takes a

A moment of complete focus

Busy mornings can make it hard to give your complete attention to your child. If your child asks you to look at something that interests them while you are getting ready in the morning, you may be tempted to put them off. As a result, they may feel brushed aside and be less cooperative.

A different outcome
Now, imagine stopping for a few minutes and focusing totally on the thing that caught their attention, sharing their wonder or interest. Your child's needs will have been met and what might have escalated into a time-consuming, energy-sapping situation, instead becomes a special moment. Everyone is able to get back on task and feel good about themselves and each other.

packed lunch to school, they can prepare this the night before, either with your assistance or on their own. Your child can also set out the clothing they will need for school and any after-school activities.

- **Your child can use an alarm clock** now. They can also dress, groom, and feed themselves. Bear in mind, adolescents struggle to wake early. Studies show that their biorhythms change so they are programmed to stay up later and sleep in longer. If your child's school does not take this into account by starting lessons later, suggest your child sets their alarm earlier to allow more time to wake up.

- **Encourage siblings of different ages** to work together. For example, an older sibling could get breakfast ready while the younger sibling feeds a pet. An older child could also help by brushing and tying back a younger one's hair.

- **Assign each person a task** – whether locking doors, turning off lights, or clearing food and dirty dishes – that needs to be taken care of before you can all leave the house.

- **Be prepared for journeys**. If you drive your child to school, who is driving? Who will buckle up young children? If your child takes public transport, is their travel card ready?

Working together as a family to get ready in the mornings can be time-efficient and creates an atmosphere of mutual support.

MEALTIMES: YOUNG CHILDREN

From 18 months to six years of age, mealtimes evolve. In their first three years, you may choose to feed your child before you eat; however, the sooner you can eat some or all of your meals together, the greater the benefits for your child.

Early skills

Your young child will naturally eat smaller amounts of food and eat more often than you. As their feeding pattern starts to align with your own, and once they can feed themselves, provide a chair that they can safely sit in to join you at the family table. By their first birthday, or before, they will probably be able to eat at the table with you, sharing family meals together.

By around 18 months old, your child becomes more skilled with their hands and fingers, alternating between eating with fingers and utensils, when food has been cut up. Teach them step by step how to use cutlery. Ideally, avoid plastic and use child-sized metal cutlery (see p.58). Start with a butter knife so they can learn to hold it correctly, apply soft spreads, and slice soft foods. By about four years of age, show them how to use a knife with a pointed edge to cut through food that requires more control. Introducing utensils that are similar to the ones that you use makes your child feel empowered and helps them master real cutlery with safety and control.

Eating together

Encourage your young child to try new foods and eat a balanced diet. If they have strong preferences for unhealthy foods or resist a new food, recognize their preferences, limit how often you offer them, and continue to offer a range of healthy foods. Getting them involved in prepping meals can be helpful.

If your child refuses a meal you have made, acknowledge their opinion, then gently but consistently encourage them to try it. If they still refuse, they can join you at the table for mealtime conversation. Do not force them to eat, put a plate in front of them, prepare different food, or bribe them with dessert. Instead, let them know there is food if they change their mind, and trust they will eat when hungry. If they become disruptive, invite them to visit their quiet place (see pp.156–159).

By three to six years of age, children are able to practise manners (see p.61) and put the Montessori principles of grace and courtesy into practice: eating carefully, engaging in mealtime conversations, and helping with cleaning up.

" "

As your child grows, they can learn that mealtimes provide a perfect opportunity to talk and engage together as a family.

Using child-sized metal cutlery encourages your child to practise the skills needed during mealtimes.

Cleaning faces and hands

Helping your young child to clean themselves at the end of a meal can be a wonderful learning opportunity for them and a chance for you to provide gentle care. However, adults often tend to race through this part of the meal. They may quickly grab a face cloth, rush up behind their little one, hold onto their face from behind, and briskly wipe their child's face and hands. Imagine how unpleasant it would feel if someone bigger and stronger than you did the same thing to you. In addition, by doing this, your child does not learn anything about how to take care of themselves.

Instead, have on hand two warm, moist cloths, one for yourself and one for your child. Get down to their level, face to face. Show your child how you gently wipe your own face. Then let them try to wipe their face. If their face is not quite clean, finish off, wiping it gently and carefully for them, but only after they have had a go. Do the same to teach them how to clean their hands and fingers. You could have a bowl of clean, warm water on the table – out of your child's reach – to rinse the cloths between wiping your faces and hands. In this way, cleaning up after a meal will become a routine that your child looks forward to rather than dreads.

MEALTIMES: OLDER CHILDREN

As children grow, sitting down as a family and sharing food without screens or interruptions from phones is increasingly rare. Make a commitment to each other that mealtimes will be a period when you spend dedicated time together: work is set aside and calls or text messages dealt with afterwards.

A rewarding time

Eating with older children can be richly rewarding. These ideas and guidelines can help make mealtimes a treasured part of the day.

- **Dress up the table**. Favour sitting at a table instead of a breakfast bar. A touch of formality at times lends a festive spirit to meals.

- **Create a family circle**. If you wish, join hands and share a moment of silence, reflecting on the day. Say thank you for simple blessings, and thank the cook – not for how tasty the meal is, but to appreciate the effort that went into preparing it.

- **Check in with each other**. At the start of the meal, you might want to take turns, informally, to tell the rest of the family about your day. Family members can share anything they feel comfortable saying to the whole family. It might be something that

went well, or was a challenge, or was upsetting or stressful. There might be an area where someone feels they need to learn something new to be able to handle their work or social life more effectively. This can be a time to keep each other in the loop and, occasionally, to make a commitment to yourself or others in the family.

- **Have real conversations**. Current events, life, and work can be intriguing. Some families enjoy lively discussions at mealtimes. The key for parents is to listen and enquire, as much as to tell stories or teach lessons. If there is an awkward moment when no one has a topic of interest, allow this. After a short silence, your child may recall something they want to share.

- **Stick to topics everyone likes**. Notice what your family enjoys exploring. Your child may feel left out of conversations about adult matters that do not interest them, so make time to talk to your partner away from the table.

- **Help your child** to continue to develop grace, courtesy, and manners (see p.61). Teach these from a positive perspective rather than scolding or shaming. Help them to learn how to eat politely, sit up, pass items, and listen without interrupting. Teach awareness of others, for example, by not taking more than their share;

and model how to ask to be excused gracefully if conversations go on for longer than they prefer.

- **If your child is in a play**, or learning a poem, they might like to recite some lines. While Montessori avoids challenges that overwhelm a child's ability and makes them feel ashamed, it does recognize that memorizing lines is a useful skill. Many of us have snippets of poetry learned as children

that we treasure. Make the experience fun, not a burden. Gauge if your child loves it, or would really rather avoid this.

- **In warmer months**, try to spend time outside after dinner to promote your child's appreciation of the natural world and extend this positive family time. Ideally, leave phones inside so you have everyone's attention. Notice the sun setting; collect leaves; play tag; feel an evening breeze; or just quietly talk.

Older children take an active role at meals, helping themselves to food and making sure others have what they need.

EVERYDAY STRATEGIES

NATURAL CONSEQUENCES

As parents, we are often reluctant to allow our children to experience the inevitable outcome of a wrong step or action. However, shielding children in this way means that they often fail to learn valuable life lessons.

A traditional approach to parenting has been to try to teach children lessons by lecturing and punishing them for perceived misbehaviour, and sometimes giving them no option but to behave in a certain way. However, the most common outcome of this approach is that children end up feeling as though they are disappointing their parents. When they are made to feel worse by punitive tactics, children do not tend to respond by reflecting on their behaviour and improving it for the better.

Natural consequences are the best way to teach children because consequences speak for themselves in many everyday situations. When parents do not interfere with natural consequences and allow children to experience the results of their actions, children tend to remember lessons better. In Montessori-inspired homes, parents use natural consequences often, instead of assigning punishments or rescuing children from real-life lessons. Pages 84–85 outline helpful guidelines for using natural consequences.

❝ ❞

Children are more likely to learn lessons when they are allowed to experience the consequences of their actions.

" " OUR STORY

Jasmine, my three-and-a-half-year-old, loves to make her own decisions. One chilly morning we were getting dressed. We had nothing special planned – just spending time in the garden and around the house. When I asked her to put on extra layers so she didn't get cold outside, she danced off in the opposite direction singing, 'No, no, no, I don't like to wear those clothes! Oh no, no, no.'

I knew she would be cold. However, rather than tell her that she would not be allowed outside without extra layers, I decided that using natural consequences on this occasion would be a far more helpful lesson. She pulled on her wellies and headed outside, without her coat. Within moments of playing in her mud 'kitchen', she turned and asked, 'Mum, where's the thing that's hot from the kettle?' I looked at her and held back a smile. 'Are you asking about the hot-water bottle?' I said. 'Yes,' she said, 'I think I need it. My hands are cold and I'm shivering. I want to put my coat on.'

My smile grew – I was so proud. The natural consequences technique had worked so well and the best part was, it had avoided causing conflict or hurting her feelings by insisting she wear her coat when she had made a choice not to. 'Okay,' I said to her, 'let's go in; I'll get the hot-water bottle and you get your coat on.' She looked up at me with her cold little hands outstretched, smiled, and said, 'Thanks, Mum.'

Chaneen (@chaneensaliee), mother of Jasmine, aged three, and Ocean, aged one

NATURAL CONSEQUENCES IN PRACTICE

Let the consequence speak

Take care to allow the consequence to teach the lesson instead of you – resist the temptation to point it out in advance. Telling your child ahead of time what the outcome of an action may be – for example, "If you forget your lunchbox, you'll be hungry" – ruins the effect of the experience.

Do not shame your child

After your child has experienced a natural consequence, do not rub this in or shame them, for example, by saying, "I told you that you would be hungry. If you had remembered your lunchbox, that would not have been the case." Your child is probably well aware of the result.

" "

A natural consequence speaks for itself. There is no need to chastise or lecture.

> **Giving your** child responsibility for certain tasks and actions can mean they learn by natural consequences.

Do not rescue your child

Avoid solving your child's problem, for example, by dropping off their lunch at school. Allowing the natural consequence often leads children to problem solve and remember things instead of depending on you. A child whose parents always remember is likely to often forget.

Avoid punishments

Do not punish your child after a natural consequence. The consequence is enough to teach the lesson. For instance, if they do not get ready for bed in time, naturally this means there is not time for a story before lights out. Adding on a punishment – "There will be no more bedtime stories for a month!"– is most likely to make your child feel resentful and to act out.

When to avoid this strategy

The following are clear occasions when natural consequences should not be used.

If your child could be harmed. For example, you would not let a young child near a hot stove to feel the heat in order to teach them not to touch it.

The consequence is too removed from the action. For instance, if your child is in charge of watering a house plant and forgets to do so, do not expect them to connect it dying two weeks later with this action.

If an action harms property or others. For example, your child learns not to kick a ball inside if it damages walls or hurts someone, but this lesson comes at a cost to your home and others.

If your child does not care about the result. For example, you may decide to let them feel a little hungry for a while if they do not come to dinner when asked, but this will not work if they had a big snack before dinner.

LEAVING FOR THE DAY

Setting off for the day, whether to a childminder, nursery, or school, is a time of transition in your child's daily routine. Being organized, punctual, and positive helps your child to start their day confidently.

The importance of punctuality

Getting ready each day (see pp.74–77), leaving the house on time when travelling to daycare or school, and undertaking a journey, all teach your child valuable life lessons. They are learning to separate from you, to keep themselves safe, grow in independence, and develop a sense of responsibility.

Being punctual is a key life lesson. Your child learns this by arriving at school on time – having navigated their morning routine with your help – and by learning that they can count on you to pick them up punctually each day. Being on time for arrival and pick-up and ensuring that your child knows who is meeting them helps them to feel emotionally secure and confident.

The journey

Taking your young child to daycare or school can provide wonderful moments – you may engage in a conversation; your child may spend time reading if you are driving; or you might observe the sunrise or enjoy seeing plants and animals in the natural world on your walk.

You may also need to manage stressful moments. Giving children allocated roles can help to avoid flash points. For example, if your child resists wearing a seat belt, putting them in charge of ensuring that everyone is buckled up, including themselves, gives them a sense of responsibility and helps them understand the importance of this task.

If siblings squabble on the way, simply stop, if possible, then make it clear to them that you will resume the journey when they are ready to converse quietly and respectfully.

Ages and stages

18 months–6 years
Help very young children with tasks such as putting on shoes, dressing, and gathering their lunch and belongings. Your goal is for them to become increasingly independent during these years and to care for themselves.

6–12 years
Now your child can manage practical skills, put more emphasis on them taking responsibility for organizing themselves.

12–18 years
As teens focus on friends, activities, and social lives, their minds can become somewhat chaotic and disorganized and there may be a lack of attention to detail. Offer renewed support, if needed, to help keep them on track.

A positive start to the day

Some young children may experience a degree of separation anxiety when they are dropped off at daycare or school. This is a normal part of early development. As they get older, they may become anxious again when starting a new school or activity, if they are concerned about exams, or if there is conflict with a peer. Some supportive strategies can help:

- **Visit your child's** new childminder, nursery, or school with them before they start, so they can see their new environment and meet staff or carers and other children. If possible, arrange a play date with another family, so your child knows someone from the outset.

- **Be honest with a young child** to build trust. When you leave, be positive about their day, let them know where you are going and when you will be back, then say a quick goodbye.

- **As they grow**, agree where and when to say "goodbye", whether at the school gate, on the way, or at home. Send them off on a positive note, encouraging their skills and talents.

- **Your child may be apprehensive** when starting secondary school. Encourage them to share any concerns. Listen without offering solutions or sympathy. Talking things through can help them to find their own solution. If they ask for advice, offer suggestions in question form; for example, "I wonder what would happen if you told your new friend how you feel?". Your child needs a listening ear, advice if requested, and guidance on safety and ethics. Beyond this, making their own mistakes helps them to learn.

Getting packed and ready the night before promotes good timekeeping skills.

FREE TIME AND WEEKENDS: YOUNG CHILDREN

At 18 months, the structure of each day should be similar for your child to provide consistency and routine. Keep mealtimes, naps, and bedtimes at weekends as close to their weekday schedule as possible. As they grow, children become able to cope with more flexible routines at weekends.

Family time

When your child is young, family life at weekends and holiday times is likely to be simple and not overly structured. However, leisure time does allow you to spend time together on family activities both at and away from home and to introduce new experiences and people into your child's life. In these

Tackling tasks together helps to build strong family connections.

formative years, your child will get to know extended family members and friends, forming lasting bonds, for example with grandparents.

Natural activities for children

In the early years, the leisure time activities you plan with your child can support their physical, social, and emotional development and help them learn important life skills. Choose activities that promote hand–eye coordination and brain development and ones that involve working in collaboration to develop social skills and build strong family connections.

- **Your young child** is building strength and coordination. Engage them in activities that develop large muscle control, balance, coordination, and muscle tone, and that teach them to enjoy moving. Try moving quickly or slowly to music together, singing, or doing yoga. They could walk heel-to-toe while carrying an object – often practised in Montessori schools. Play games where you mirror their actions as they move their legs or hands, or vice versa. Or set up an indoors or outdoors obstacle course.

- **Set aside time** for your child to join you on projects. Hobbies such as woodwork

Quiet time

Young children are naturally active. It is important to balance their time with quiet activities during free time, just as you would on weekdays, such as listening to music together or sharing a story.

Build in time, too, for your child to occupy themselves. They can play quietly near you while you are busy with tasks. As well as giving you time to get jobs done or follow your own interests, this also helps your child to learn to make choices for themselves.

develop hand–eye coordination. Around the age of four, children can start to use child-sized tools, such as a small hammer or child-safe saw, wearing safety goggles and supervised by you.

- **Use extra time at weekends** to spend time in the kitchen with your child. Cooking or baking projects, such as making soup from scratch, or baking bread, pizza, or cookies, are ideal for parents and young children. Take your time to teach them basic prepping and cooking skills.

- **Plan family activities**, whether clearing up leaves, enjoying a walk, or working on an art project together.

FREE TIME AND WEEKENDS: OLDER CHILDREN

As your child grows beyond the early childhood years, your family's free time, weekends, and holidays might change as your child's interests, needs, and level of independence evolve. Ensuring you continue to spend time with them while also allowing them to expand their interests is a question of balance.

Out-of-school activities are a great outlet and help children to learn about sensible scheduling.

The need for balance

As your child grows, after-school and weekend activities and, increasingly, a desire to spend more time with friends, often away from home, compete for their time. Avoid over-scheduling free time now because this can create overload for all. Build in time with your child by watching or taking part in some of their activities and enjoying outings together. Bear in mind that each family member needs time to relax, do chores, and follow their own interests.

A family discussion

To promote balance and understanding, use family meetings to discuss whether new activities can comfortably fit in with existing plans. Discuss how they impact each person. Make decisions that take into account what is important to you all: what do we have time for, how much will it cost, and is it within our budget? This helps your child to think about others; decide what they really value; and to understand how much goes into making decisions about their activities.

• **Involve your child fully** in choosing their extracurricular activities. Discuss the cost, travel time, whether a new activity will interfere with family commitments, and the overall time

" " OUR STORY

Having four children and being part of a community within the school, church, and neighbourhood, all involving extracurricular activities, we saw that our lives were going to get busier than we knew would be healthy for us.

My wife and I made the choice to carve out family time each week. Saturday become a family fun day, dedicated to time just for us to spend the day together, primarily at home, with bike rides, walks, reading books, enjoying games, cooking, baking, and eating. Occasionally we will have outings to a zoo, restaurant, or another place that we view as a treat. Sunday, after church, we treat as a rest day and also do necessary household chores, with exceptions made for out-of-town visitors or special celebrations and gatherings.

David, father of Eden, aged 10, Eli, aged eight, Ewan, aged six, and Ethan, aged four

commitment that would be required from each family member.

- **Even activities or classes** that you feel are non-negotiable, such as those related to education, faith, or culture, are best discussed openly so your child understands why they are important.

- **Consider limits**. These may focus on whether you feel an activity is safe. You can also set limits to help children learn about commitments, rather than flit arbitrarily between activities. For example, if they want music lessons, agree on a time commitment so you do not sign up for a series of lessons only for them to want to drop out several weeks later.

In adolescence especially, these discussions are key. Adolescents want to separate from parents, feeling they are individuals with their own voice. Talking and debating ideas keeps communication open and promotes understanding. Adolescents need to be able to make choices, but parents need to help them see the ramifications. If they insist, at times you may have to allow them to experience the consequences of choosing unwisely.

MANAGING SCREEN TIME: YOUNG CHILDREN

From the very start of your child's life, talk to your parenting partner about how much screen time your child will be allowed. Review your own screen time habits now, too, bearing in mind that your habits and behaviour set an example for your child. Work out some screen house rules for the whole family (see p.96).

Your child's influences

Children's values and knowledge about the world have traditionally been shaped by five cultural influences: home, school, youth groups and activities, faith-based organizations, and peers. Television has also competed for children's attention, joined today by games and apps on digital devices and consoles, social media, and online videos, which represent a sixth, incredibly powerful culture over which many parents have limited knowledge and exercise little control. Face-to-face communication is increasingly sacrificed as even young children are silent and absorbed in their digital devices.

Types of learning

Slick marketing often sets out to convince parents that babies and young children learn faster when exposed to technology. However, studies suggest that they learn best by interacting with hands-on, three-dimensional materials;

Keeping your young child company while they are engaged in screen time creates a positive experience for you both.

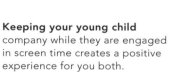

from real-world experiences; and from other people. When writing about children under six years old, Montessori said, "Never give something to the mind before you give it to the hand." Today, brain research confirms this fundamental principle. For young children, the physical act of counting out forks and knives, pouring juice, or building a puzzle, provides a more solid learning base than interacting with a two-dimensional screen with a finger or a mouse.

A balanced approach

If you think some digital media, apps, and television programmes could have some value for your child, aim to keep the time they spend in front of a screen to a minimum and use this time as an opportunity to interact with them. You might snuggle up and read an e-book or watch a child's programme together.

Avoid relying on digital devices to keep your child calm and quiet or as a way to occupy them while you are busy. This could lead to them becoming dependent on technology, rather than human beings, for comfort and care.

Be aware, too, that screen time can have long-term consequences for your young child's ability to attend to tasks. Studies show that children who engage with digital devices and televisions daily

Screen time recommendations

The following guidelines can help you to regulate your young child's screen time:

- From birth to two years, keep screen time to a minimum. If possible, no screen time is best. For three- to six-year-olds, limit screen time to one to two hours a day. Other screens nearby should be counted in your child's screen time as younger children constantly absorb the stimuli around them.

- Be very selective before introducing technology into your child's life. Watch and listen to programmes and games and gauge their appropriateness.

- Spend screen-free time with your child.

- Treat technology as a tool, not a toy, especially below the age of six.

- Make agreements with others close to your child about the use of technology around and with your child.

from one to three years old are more likely to find it hard to focus once at school. Children and adults can experience symptoms of addiction from excessive screen time, and screen time and digital devices can also interfere with sleep. Moderation and balance when using screens is key to supporting happy, healthy relationships, learning, and positive behaviour.

MANAGING SCREEN TIME: OLDER CHILDREN

From the primary school years, up through adolescence, technology and digital media can be useful when your child is researching a subject, and games and videos can be a valued source of entertainment. However, problems can arise if there is unlimited access to screens without attention to the quality of the material.

A healthy balance

As your child grows, they may need to use a computer or tablet to help with work. However, you may want to agree to a time limit on the amount of free time they spend on screens. Use family meetings to discuss a balance between sedentary activities and physical and interactive ones. Drawing up house rules (see p.96) can be helpful.

The hazards of screen time

It is easy for children and adults to lose a sense of time and reality when looking at a screen, whether passively consuming content, which requires little effort; or engaged in social media or games, which can become addictive. Be aware that you are modelling behaviour and try to avoid being absorbed in your own devices when together as a family.

You will need to make decisions constantly about what to allow into your home, so think carefully about the level of violence your child is exposed to, from enacted murders, to fights, crashes, and explosions. The values and problem-solving approaches in media aimed at children are often very different from those of a Montessori-inspired home.

Quality screen time

Some basic guidelines can help you to select programming that enhances your child's understanding of the world, ignites awareness, curiosity, and imagination in a positive manner, and hopefully reinforces your positive values.

- **Documentaries** – whether about nature, science, history, space, or technology – can be educational, informative, and at times age specific. Avoid "educational" children's programmes that promote learning by memorization, rather than fostering understanding of concepts or ideas.

- **Choose films and shows** that present compelling stories and characters, whether fictional, biographical, or portraying a time or event in history. Montessori aims to limit exposure to non-realistic, fantastical stories, even though some can be positive and entertaining. Expose your child to stories that showcase respect and kindness, and have a positive, but realistic, message.

- **Avoid content** that is misleading; filled with sarcasm and ridicule; humour based on a character being embarrassed or hurt; or that undermines family values that aim to teach children to be advocates for justice, kindness, compassion, and peaceful conflict resolution.

- **Think about content**. Research games, films, and shows on trusted online guides for families to make sure

they are age-appropriate. Look for quality content, too, just as you would with reading material. Choose videos that are enjoyable, clear, that appear to be accurate, do not glorify cruelty or violence, and do not contain sexual situations that would make you or your child feel awkward.

- **Use family meetings** to help your child understand why your family's values on digital content may be in conflict with their friend's family values.

Exposing your child to programmes that adhere to your core family values is a great way to promote positive messages.

HOUSE RULES FOR SCREEN TIME

Prioritize reaching a general consensus about the use of digital devices and media for different age levels as soon as possible. Aim to strike a balance between access to digital media and enjoying a family life that supports your values.

The role of house rules

It is important to create house rules around digital devices and the media that you are comfortable allowing your child to engage with. When they are young, it is easy to draw up rules. As children grow, they will question and debate why rules are needed, so establishing house rules that make sense and that you are willing to follow is key. While the rules will no doubt need adapting as your child grows, they should be based on your family values, be fair, and be followed consistently. They should recognize that time spent on screens can be positive, but should not interfere with family connections or tasks. Be sure that others who spend time with your child, such as grandparents, friends, or babysitters, know the rules.

Family time without digital distractions shows children how to balance activities.

Be a good role model and follow your family's house rules for digital devices and media. Consider the following:

- **Put your smartphone** away when dropping off and picking up your child and avoid non-essential phone calls when travelling with them.

- **As with any life situation** that could harm your child, prepare them to keep themselves safe by discussing internet safety rules.

- **Avoid screens in bedrooms**. They can interfere with sleep, expose children to unwanted content, and pull them away from interacting with others.

- **Learn how to use** parental control software to limit your child's screen time and access to concerning content.

- **Set up media-free** family time when you focus on reading, games, or real-life experiences such as mealtimes, bedtime, and outings.

- **Ensure children spend** as much time each day reading, exercising, and playing as they do on a screen.

- **If a rule is broken**, discuss consequences that are reasonable, respectful, responsible, and related.

- **Know what your child** is watching and listening to and chat about it with them.

Using social media safely

Be guided by your family values when talking to your child about using social media safely and thoughtfully, and think about how you use it, too.

- Discuss being thoughtful before posting online photos or videos. Could they embarrass them one day or compromise the family's privacy? Apply this principle to yourself before posting images of your child.

- Exercise caution when texting. Texting takes away two important aspects of communication: you cannot see the recipient or hear their tone of voice. This makes it hard to interpret messages that involve emotions, leading to misunderstandings. Suggest your child sticks to messages that give information and saves those that involve emotions for face-to-face conversations.

- Discuss hazards such as the addictive nature of social media; making or receiving mean-spirited comments, which can step over into online bullying; presenting a more exciting life than is the reality; and the risk of connecting with a stranger who may present a danger.

- Avoid "over-parenting". While helpful, technology can mean parents communicate with and monitor their children too much. This can inhibit children from practising life skills such as problem solving and remembering, which increase confidence in their ability to care for themselves when away from you and help them to develop a strong sense of autonomy.

BEDTIME: YOUNG CHILDREN

Sleeping arrangements for babies and toddlers are a topic of debate and are influenced by a family's beliefs, culture, and values. In a Montessori-inspired home, parents strive to help children become independent, including when going to sleep. There are no strict rules, but the aim is for them to settle themselves and sleep on their own. By the age of six, their bedtime routine will be well established.

Independent sleeping

Your child's sleep environment helps them to learn to sleep independently.

- Once your toddler begins to try to climb out of their cot, lower the sides so that they can get in and out safely. When you feel they are ready, move them to a child's bed or a regular-size single bed.

- From about 18 months until three years old, a gate in the bedroom door helps your child to stay in their room at night. Ensure that the room is completely safe in case they wake up and are alone. This safe environment encourages independence.

- Some young children might want a prop to help them sleep independently. A nightlight and/or a soft toy can be reassuring and comforting.

- Most children settle down more easily in a calm, uncluttered bedroom (see pp.56–57), following a nightly routine.

Winding down

Moving from active play to a quiet and calm state, ready for sleep, can be a difficult transition for your child.

Young children can be overstimulated by a lot of activity around them, time spent looking at or being near screens, or by loud noise in the house at bedtime.

After your child's evening meal, choose soothing activities. A warm bath, a story, or just snuggling in a comfy chair, can all help your child feel ready for sleep. Be cautious about props or actions for soothing infants and toddlers; for example, using a motorized swing or rocking an infant or toddler in your arms until they are asleep. While these can be calming, you should put your child in their bed before they fall asleep so that they become used to being put down awake and falling asleep alone.

By about three years of age, your child can be more actively involved in their bedtime routine. To help them transition from play time to bedtime, you could encourage a habit of getting ready for bed earlier. This can become a looked-forward-to time where they engage in quiet activities such as looking at books – with you or on their own – before getting into bed, or cuddling a favourite soft toy. By five or six years of age, children can usually read quietly by themselves in bed with the lights on.

" "

Bedtime is a time of transition for your young child that requires a change of pace to help them settle down.

Developing habits such as quietly reading at bedtime gives children helpful tools for settling to sleep.

Settling to sleep

How you say goodnight to your child and handle nighttime waking plays an important part in encouraging them to settle down and sleep independently.

- **A comforting routine** can be tucking them in, saying goodnight, then returning for "whispers" and lights off as they settle. Whispering messages of love creates an intimacy that sends them to sleep feeling cherished.

- **At 18 months to two years**, if your child wakes, go to their room quietly, but do not pick them up or move them to your room. Wait a minute or two to see if they settle. If you feel they need help, spend a few minutes talking to them gently. Say it is still night and sleep time. From about three years, if they wake from a bad dream, reassure them calmly that you understand it was scary but you are there and their room is safe.

BEDTIME: OLDER CHILDREN

In the primary and secondary school years, bedtime routines evolve. Help children to associate the bedroom with a place to relax and sleep. Ensure that their environment promotes good habits and ideally avoids screen time interfering with their sleep, health, and development.

Adapting bedtime

During the primary school years, children may push for a later bedtime. As they approach adolescence, they often stay up increasingly late in defiance of wishes. Research suggests that there is a neurological basis for a teenager's tendency to stay up later. Teenagers may also enjoy staying up late because this is something they were not allowed to do when younger.

Your goal is to ensure that throughout primary school and adolescence, children continue to get adequate rest. Discuss a nighttime routine that helps your child to prepare for sleep at a reasonable time, adapting this as they get older. Adolescents in particular are keen not to miss out on online activities and social media chat with peers. Talk to them about how to navigate this, explaining that friends will still be happy to chat the following day, and help them find ways to sign off at night with friends. Helping them to let go and make good choices is a valuable lesson.

A healthy bedtime routine

It is important that children maintain good nighttime routines. Adopting a firm policy that digital devices are kept out of bedrooms when winding down is advised. It is wise to set a rule when your child is very young to not allow devices in the bedroom because once they are allowed, it is hard to establish in your child's mind that at bedtime the bedroom is a place to sleep and dress. It can also

How technology affects sleep

Consider the following when thinking about the effect of technology on your child's sleep.

- Be mindful of how flashing lights and noise affect our brains as we drift off to sleep. Falling asleep to bright images from a digital device or the sound of a television can affect our ability to reach the calm, deep sleep we need to restore ourselves.

- Social media and online games can be addictive and watching films and surfing the net can lead a child to stay awake late into the night.

- Gaming devices let children play in real time with players on different time zones, who are also complete strangers.

be difficult to monitor what they watch or do online when this takes place behind a closed door. Digital devices are also very stimulating and tend to keep our brains active, making it difficult to fall asleep.

If you find consistently enforcing this policy proves difficult, at least strive to have a clear lights-out policy that you check up on. You could say that all digital technology should be turned off and left outside of the bedroom after a certain time, adjusting this time as children get older.

Recommendations from sleep experts on how to prepare for sleep include:

- **Dim the bedroom lights**.
- **Advise your child** to use their bed only for calming activities that help with falling asleep.
- **For older children**, recommend that they turn music off or down before bedtime.
- **If older children** consume caffeine, they should avoid this after 2pm.
- **If adolescents wake in the night**, advise them to get out of bed without waking others, and, quietly, do something relaxing.

" "

Bedtime routines will naturally evolve as children grow, but should still be designed to promote adequate and restful sleep.

Keeping phones in a designated place at night, away from bedrooms, can be a family rule.

HELPING AT HOME

Family life is where children learn the basic skills of living with others and taking care of a home environment. Those habits and skills form a foundation for the rest of their lives.

Montessori teaching believes that children learn what they live – that is, they learn from their daily experiences. The everyday tasks involved with family living help children to learn how to understand, appreciate, and work together with other members of the family – to be an active member of the family community. We all have our own distinct personalities and ways of approaching everyday life. By finding ways to work together, your child learns how to be part of a team, a skill that will help them throughout life – in study, work, and when establishing a family of their own.

66 99

Caring for the home environment
is part of what defines being in a family
community, with each family member
taking responsibility for tasks.

SKILLS FOR LIFE

We want children to understand that, while we love them, we expect them to help out. This teaches them about structure, shared responsibility, how we depend on one another, the value of teamwork, and the importance of doing a job well.

Working together

Your young child's concept of how to do a task will not, necessarily, match yours. Initially, you are teaching them how to do a job step by step. If they make a mistake, repeat a lesson without shame or blame, but with firm, gentle encouragement. As they grow, keep the following in mind:

- **Your child's sense of time** is not the same as yours. Children under the age of six often become distracted, showing the natural tendency of young children to live in the moment.

- **Young children** may be more focused on the process rather than completing a job. Recognize their contribution and progress, appreciating that it takes time for them to develop lifelong habits.

- **Your child needs** to be independent and feel valued, both great motivators. Instead of thinking of chores as onerous tasks, see them as an opportunity for your child to contribute meaningfully.

With your help and guidance, very young children often embrace the chance to help around the home, working close to you.

- **Young children**, especially, enjoy being with us. They participate not just to make you happy, but to be at your side. Harness this desire to get them into a pattern of routine tasks, working in harmony as you teach them skills.

- **As your child grows**, they may have more school work and activities. It is completely reasonable to expect them to continue contributing to chores and to build these into their schedule.

103

COOKING

A large part of the enjoyment of any meal is involvement in the preparation of the food. Montessori emphasizes how important it is to allow children to have a meaningful part in family life as soon as they are able to.

Scaffolding skills

When guided by patient adults and given the right tools, even very young children can help to prepare food. For instance, your toddler can learn to peel a tangerine or use a butter knife to slice a banana or spread peanut butter. As your child becomes increasingly dexterous with their hands and fingers, they can master more complex cooking skills and also combine skills. So your five-year-old can use newly acquired reading skills to follow simple recipes, and as your child grows, they can use their increased understanding and abilities to follow multi-step recipes, to double or triple ingredients, and to become more independent in the kitchen.

Working alongside each other independently – ready to guide if needed – builds your child's confidence in their skills and ability.

❝ ❞
Cooking with children can be messy. Take it slowly and think of spills as part of the process, teaching them to mop, wipe, and sweep.

Planning ahead

Preparation and thought enhance the joy of cooking with your child, allowing you both to concentrate on the process and working together, rather than being frustrated if ingredients are not available or you need to hunt for a tool mid-step. Your child can also learn self-preparation – how to wash their hands, put on an apron, and cover their hair or tie it back.

- **Provide proper tools** – blunt knives can be more dangerous than sharp ones – and show how equipment is used to slice, grate, or peel safely.

- **Let your child know** that they must have your permission or supervision when using the oven or hob.

- **Prep ingredients.** Help your child understand the importance of following recipes and measuring, especially for baking. But flag up chances for creativity, too, such as when making a fruit salad.

A complete task

Montessori teaches that tasks have a beginning, middle, and end, so cleaning is an important part of cooking. Cleaning up together as you go along teaches your child to do this methodically. This then ceases to be overwhelming, instilling the skill in a manageable way and ensuring that your child cleans up automatically each time.

Using a butter knife helps your child safely learn skills such as chopping at a young age.

Ages and stages

18 months–6 years
Hands are the first tools. Start with foods that your child can prep by hand, such as peeling an orange. As they grow, they can use a butter knife to slice soft foods such as bananas, celery, or cucumber and to apply spreads. From as early as three years, they can peel with a peeler or cut with an apple cutter, progressing to a sharp knife. They can also make a fruit salad, prepare biscuits, flatbreads, or muffins following a simple recipe, and add skills by baking with yeast.

6–12 years
Your child may be quite skilled now and creative. They can prepare a variety of foods, using more complex tools such as a food processor, electric mixer, and, with supervision, the oven. They can also read and follow recipes with multiple steps, and double, triple, or halve a recipe using maths skills.

12–18 years
Give scope for your child to fill a leadership role – budgeting for a meal, expanding a recipe, and inviting guests. Encourage them to make a range of food, from omelettes to fish, roasted veg, soups, and desserts.

CLEANING AND FAMILY CHORES

As with daily routines and other family structures, children can begin to help out with everyday chores at a much earlier age than most parents ever imagine. Encouraging your child to get involved with household jobs facilitates their independence.

How your child can help

Children can begin to help out with chores as young as two or three years old. If tasks are introduced correctly, your child not only learns useful skills, but also understands that everyone pitches in. A child-sized broom or mop are useful tools for your young child. However, there are many ways they can help out without needing special equipment. For example, they can make their bed, put dirty clothes in the laundry, fold clean clothes, wipe and dust, water indoor plants, and help in the kitchen. As they grow, they can also learn to use equipment such as the vacuum cleaner or the kitchen mop to keep the house clean.

Getting your child involved

Think about your child and their abilities and consider what they are ready to help with and what they show interest in. Rather than tell a very young child that it is their job to do something, instead, deliberately organize your home so they

Everyday tasks, such as washing and drying dishes, provide an opportunity for children to work together and learn basic skills.

Feeling in charge of a task can be a good motivator for a child and builds their confidence.

can safely and easily work with you. For example, if they enjoy taking things out and putting them back, work together to unload clothes from the washing machine into the laundry basket.

As your child grows, they may express a desire to be involved. At around four or five years old, you may notice that they are developing routines around small jobs. As well as engineering your home so they know where tools for helping out are and can access them, talk to them about how much you value their contribution. Agree on some initial jobs to do routinely together, or that they might do on their own. Once they master a task, give simple reminders. For example, if they learn to water a house plant, encourage them to check it daily to see if it is dry, explaining that overwatering drowns the roots.

Ages and stages

18 months–6 years
Most young children want to do what you do and can enjoy tasks that we see as chores. If wiping the table, they are likely to be more interested in wetting a cloth, wiping, rinsing the cloth, then drying the table, than ensuring the table is clean. Let them enjoy the process.

6–12 years
Teach your child more advanced skills now, such as removing stains, vacuuming, scrubbing pans, and cleaning the car to help them feel a sense of ownership and pride in their home.

12–18 years
Teens may prefer to be with friends, study, or focus on other activities. Use family meetings to keep them focused on the need to share in household chores as they prepare for adulthood.

Suggest this could become one of their jobs. Agree to a list of regular tasks for each family member at a family meeting.

If your older child is a reluctant helper, this may be a sign they struggle with a task or are avoiding it. Try giving them ownership of a task. For example, if they fail to put dirty clothes in the laundry, put them in charge of making sure that everyone does this. This gives them a feeling of leadership and responsibility.

EVERYDAY STRATEGIES

DISARMING SQUABBLES

Disagreements are part of life and dealing with conflict is a learning process. As parents, our role is to guide children through conflict, with a sibling, cousin, or friend, to help them to reach a peaceful resolution.

Peaceful conflict resolution skills are valuable throughout life. The sooner children learn these skills, the more independent they can be in working out disagreements by themselves. They also become better at listening to others' needs and expressing their own. Your role is to help your child learn to solve problems peacefully and independently, rather than to judge and come up with solutions. At times, you may be able to prevent conflict escalating by simply doing something comical or unexpected to break the tension. Or, children may be able to solve a situation

without your help. Resist the urge to jump in. Instead, give them a minute to see if a disagreement calms down or escalates. If it escalates, try the strategies on pages 110–111; these deal with conflict both in the moment and, when emotions are too high to problem solve on the spot, show you how to take a break and follow through later to ensure that ongoing conflict is resolved.

Holding hands is one of the simplest ways to help children listen to each other and resolve disagreements.

❝ ❞ OUR STORY

When my children were six and 10 years old, they had a brain teaser puzzle and were both fascinated by it. Quickly, this puzzle game became the centre of attention and they fought over it frequently.

To find a fair solution about how to share this favourite toy, I waited for a moment when they were both calm, then sat them down and we brainstormed some solutions for how they might take turns with the puzzle.

It was decided that the toy would stay downstairs on a shelf so that it was available for both of them to play with. They agreed that once one of them was having a turn playing with it, they could continue playing with it for as long as they wanted to during that play session. When they had finished, they had to return it to its place on the shelf so that it was available for their sibling.

My daughter wrote down the rule on a piece of paper, which they both signed. They shook hands to show their agreement, and the 'contract' was hung on the shelf next to the toy. I was impressed by how well they responded to the conflict resolution strategy.

Carine (@montessorifamilyuk), mother of Lily, aged 13 and Louis, aged nine

DISARMING SQUABBLES IN PRACTICE

1
Be a calming presence

Move close to the two squabbling parties, doing this slowly and calmly. Once you are close, get down to the children's eye level and look at them both calmly and kindly so they understand that you are not going to become part of the conflict.

2
Be gently authoritative

Put a hand gently on each of them to help calm them, then just wait for them to stop squabbling. If they are arguing over an object, when they begin to calm down, hold out your hand to signal that you want the item in question. Do not speak until they give it to you.

3
Express your thanks

Thank them for ending the squabble. If children were arguing over an object or a toy that they have handed to you, put this to one side. This signals that you have not confiscated it, but they should return to it only when they can do so peacefully.

4
Show belief

Assure both parties that you are confident they can work out whatever it was they were squabbling about and find a solution together that they are both happy with. Allow them the time and space they need for this problem-solving process.

"

Gently guiding children on conflict resolution gives them the skills to resolve disputes independently in future.

5

Take a break if needed

If either child is simply too upset to engage in solving the dispute on the spot, ask both parties to take a break, then follow through later to find a solution. When ready, ask them to hold hands – this action has a calming effect on the whole body.

6

Help them to listen and talk

While they are holding hands, guide each child to take turns listening and talking to each other, reassuring them that they will each have a chance to talk. Take care not to judge the situation yourself or to offer ready-made solutions.

7

Get them to say how they feel

Help children through the process step by step, so they learn to speak for themselves and express their feelings and ideas. For example, ask the first child to tell you why they are upset and how they feel. Acknowledge their feelings. Then ask them to tell the other child how they felt and what they would like them to do, such as return a pen.

8

Help them find resolution

Ask the second child to give their side; perhaps they needed the pen and it was not being used. Ask them to think how they could resolve the dispute. For example, could they ask for the pen politely? Invite them to try this. If this does not work, continue to guide the children, suggesting they take a break if needed and return to the dispute later. Follow this through.

GARDENING

Nurturing a garden, or finding an opportunity for your child to enjoy gardening in a community, can be an invaluable experience for them. As well as showing them how to save money by growing high-quality fresh produce, they will also be surrounded by beauty and will learn about the seasons, ecosystems, and nature.

Ages and stages

18 months–6 years
Your child learns basic tasks in a very experiential way now. With child-sized tools and gloves, they can use a trowel and help you to dig and hoe. They can plant seeds, rake, weed, and gather ripe produce.

6–12 years
The garden is a living laboratory for the natural world now. From water systems for maintaining growth, to seasonal changes, to the systems and cycles of living things, the science of nature stimulates your child's mind and raises their awareness of the impact of humans on nature.

12–18 years
Adolescents should continue to help out in the garden. They may become interested in different types of gardening, such as organic versus the use of pesticides and fertilizers. Encourage them to explore their values and beliefs.

Creative spaces

Gardening can be enjoyed in a variety of spaces. If you have a garden, you can set aside a small plot for your child to grow produce. Alternatively, grow edible and decorative plants indoors in containers, on a balcony, by windows or in window boxes, and even under grow lights. Or find out about sharing a space in a community garden or signing up for an allotment.

Nurturing your space

Gardens are a natural classroom. Whatever space you have available, encouraging your child to help out in the garden provides them with numerous learning opportunities. Getting involved in gardening also helps children to form a deep sense of connection to – and appreciation for – the natural world.

- **Children can learn practical skills**, such as how to start seeds off indoors and then transplant the seedlings outside to grow at the correct time of the year.

- **Teach your child** how to take care of the garden and plants. At a family meeting, discuss how to share the responsibility of caring for all the living things in the garden. Depending on your child's age, they can help out with tasks such as watering, weeding, and harvesting, with help or independently.

Working together with older siblings or parents helps children learn how to nurture and care for plants.

- **Planning a garden**, or garden plot, helps your child to learn maths skills and graphing. Work with them to measure the area available for growing plants. Draw a map and calculate the space needed for each plant when mature and the number of plants that will fit in the space.

- **As your child observes nature**, they can expand and enrich their vocabulary, by learning the names of the parts of flowers and plants, and by identifying flowers, plants, seeds, vegetables, herbs, and insects. You can also teach them the names of local wildflowers and trees.

- **Your child can explore processes**, life cycles, and insect communities. Indoors or outside, you can set up a small composting bin, or a worm or ant farm. If you find a cocoon or chrysalis on a small branch, your child can observe it from day to day in place or take it indoors and set it in a suitable container to wait for the moth or butterfly to emerge.

- **The garden is a science lab**. Your child can witness and appreciate the web of life, the seasons, the weather, and, of course, botany. They can learn the difference between the plants you deliberately grow and weeds.

PETS

Our pets offer us companionship, love, and loyalty, and give our children the chance to learn how to care for them. If you have a family pet, or are thinking of getting one, you will need to model how to care for it, guiding your child on how to treat a pet, the responsibilities involved in caring for it, and how to cope with the experience of illness and possibly death.

Choosing a pet

It is important to be very thoughtful when considering getting a family pet. First, bear in mind the age of your child. If you have a pet when your child is born, they will grow up learning how to interact with and care for it. If you do not already have a pet, it is advisable to wait until your child is at least four years old. By this age, most children have enough maturity and self-control to be able to welcome a new animal safely. Discuss choosing a pet at a family meeting, or over several family meetings. Think together about the space,

> " "
> Choosing a pet should be a carefully considered decision, discussed and agreed by each family member.

Learning how to handle and care for a family pet teaches your child important lessons about responsibility and kindness.

time, and attention you can give a pet and research different animals. Help your child learn about the nature and care of dogs, cats, and smaller caged pets. Talking to them about a pet's needs and what is realistic for your family in terms of the space you can offer a pet, helps them to understand the care involved, the role they will be expected to play, and why it is important to think about the pet's needs first and whether you can meet them. Before you make a decision, consider your child's instincts and personality. Some animals are better around children than others, and vice versa.

Caring for pets

Your child will naturally learn how to care for your pet by watching you do this. Involve your child in a pet's care by allowing them to feed or water them, clean their cage, or brush them.

Spending time with a pet, whether playing with them, walking them, teaching them tricks, caring for them, or helping to socialize a new pet into your home, provides invaluable lessons for your child. When caring for an animal, your child learns about kindness and empathy, and about being careful in their movements so a pet is not hurt, dropped, or played with roughly. They also learn about compassion and the responsibility of caring for a dependent creature, and about respect for all creatures.

Ages and stages

18 months–6 years
Young children can begin to help parents and older siblings to care for family pets, for example, setting out a bowl of water or accompanying another family member when walking the dog. They can learn to play with a pet with care and consideration.

6–12 years
As children grow, they gradually learn more about the responsibility of caring for pets. They can help with grooming and training. You can encourage your child's interest in the biology and care of your pet's species.

12–18 years
Be clear you expect your teen to carry on helping to care for family pets. Some teens may want to learn more about animals and animal care and may express interest, for example, in volunteering at an animal shelter or getting involved in training and competitions. Encourage their interests.

Losing a pet

If a pet dies, your family will join together in the grieving process. This may be your child's first experience of such a difficult life situation. It is important to talk to them about how they are feeling. You can discuss your family's beliefs and guide them on moving forward while still remembering and honouring the pet they have lost.

LEARNING AT HOME

Your child is learning from birth, if not before, and will continue to learn throughout their life. We learn through our experiences – the things your child encounters daily will shape their learning.

You are and always will be your child's most important teacher. Some families choose to home-school their children. Whether or not you do this, your child will still learn informally from you during the time you spend together. How you act and speak – both consciously and unconsciously – will inevitably influence your child. They will hear what you say, observe what you do, and participate in experiences, planned or unplanned, that have the potential to teach them how the world works and how to do things for themselves.

" "

Your child learns every day through real-life experiences, by watching you and others, helping with tasks, exploring ideas, and discovering new things.

LESSONS AWAY FROM THE CLASSROOM

It is important for parents to be aware that learning does not happen in the classroom only and that many key life lessons do not involve textbooks.

Your child learns from everyday life – through trial and error experiences; by exploring ideas; through independent discovery; by participating in tasks with others; or by observing others. You are constantly involved in helping your child to learn – not only concepts and skills, but also to develop a lifelong love of learning. Memorizing the right answers helps them to pass a test, but learning how to learn will get them through life.

Curious to learn

In a Montessori-inspired home, learning is viewed as a journey, not as a burden or a race. Some children do love competitive learning, but learning does not need to take place in a formal setting, with children competing for grades. Ideally, children learn because they are curious, rather than as a response to external motivation or to prove that they can do something. As a parent, your goal is to consciously help your child to not only develop basic skills that are taught in school, but also to develop a love of

learning and master practical everyday living skills not taught in school. You can also promote cultural literacy on universal topics – in science, technology, invention, and medicine; in arts and literature; in health and wellness; and in current affairs.

Lessons at home happen naturally – at meals, family meetings, and when talking, reading, and playing games. Often, the best way to help your child learn is to ask questions and listen rather than give answers. Learning should be a fundamental aspect of family life for all.

Embarking on projects with your child provides them with hands-on learning opportunities.

MAKING LEARNING FUN

We often struggle with the idea that learning can be fun – some of us may have negative recollections of learning experiences at school. However, we learn best when we have fun and enjoy ourselves. Children find learning fun when they are engaged. Thinking about a learning experience in your childhood that was enjoyable can help you to find ways to ensure that learning is not difficult or boring for your child.

Ages and stages

18 months–6 years
Your child loves to do things with you. Helping you sweep, wash up, or prep food is joyful for them. Avoid flash cards, online learning, or textbooks – keep activities hands-on.

6–12 years
Help your child retain a sense of curiosity and enthusiasm. Follow their interests and keep absorbing books that reflect school topics. Watch short educational programmes together, visit museums, and attend live performances. Keep learning experiential.

12–18 years
Help adolescents feel that learning makes sense, is exciting and satisfying, and can reveal interests and passions. Studying with friends, gently supervised, can satisfy their desire for social interaction while getting work done.

Individual learning pathways

Learning becomes natural and enjoyable when it is an experience that is free from embarrassment and intimidation. Sometimes children feel that they are not able to compete, whether with other children in the family or even with their parents. It is important to be aware that everyone learns things in their own way and at their own pace. It is also crucial to be mindful that on the path from being a beginner to mastering a task, mistakes can happen, whether playing a tune on the piano or baking a cake. Children learn both from the things that turn out just right, and, if they feel safe, from their mistakes. Natural consequences (see pp.82–85), assuming everyone is safe, allow your child to discover by doing.

Hands-on learning

Giving your child extra school work to do at home to "reinforce" learning can backfire. Some parents find it comforting to have additional textbooks at home that their child spends time working on, either on their own or with a parent. While some children may enjoy this, many do not. Instead, they learn to either tolerate the extra work as inevitable or they resist, often by letting their minds drift off, which leads parents to pester them. With a Montessori approach, parents are generally urged not to use textbooks or test papers at all,

" "

The home is a place where your child can explore and discover in a relaxed environment.

Activities such as making a favourite cake, engage your child willingly in enjoyable learning tasks.

in particular with young children, unless they actually request them. Instead, parents are encouraged to think about their home as a place where children can explore and learn, having fun as they do so. Some children are happy to explore and discover on their own, while others like to watch someone doing something to see how it works before trying it for themselves. The following suggestions help to make learning at home fun:

- **Making learning into a game** can be helpful for younger children. Games such as "I spy" help your child to think about sounds and letters. Other observation games, such as seeing how often you can spot a certain word on street signs, build basic skills such as word recognition and counting.

- **As your child grows**, allow them to participate freely in everyday tasks so they learn by doing things with you. You can find opportunities for learning at home in a range of activities, from baking a cake to sorting socks or washing the car, to more ambitious projects such as building a birdhouse or renovating a piece of furniture.

STIMULATING YOUR CHILD'S MIND: YOUNG CHILDREN

The human brain is hardwired to respond to and learn from stimulation and interactions with the environment and other people. When your young child's developing mind is engaged appropriately, they not only grasp specific concepts and master skills, they also form neural pathways in the brain that facilitate their future learning.

Ideal learning moments

Young children pass through stages where they are particularly sensitive to certain kinds of learning. Some stages occur naturally, without help from you, such as when your child learns to take their first steps, from which they go on to walk, run, then jump. Sensitive periods can also offer wonderful opportunities to stimulate your child's brain. During the first six years of life, your child learns through exposure and

Introducing experiences to your child, such as dancing, can ignite an interest.

66 99 OUR STORY

My son is two years old and fascinated by lorries. One day, he scribbled on his favourite toy lorry with a brown marker. I walked into the room just as he was finishing. Looking pleased, he stood up and announced, 'I will clean it now!'. I immediately thought, 'Oh no. This is going to be a disaster!', but I took a breath and decided not to interrupt.

He rushed to the bathroom for the foaming soap dispenser. He lathered his hands and rubbed the lorry in a circular motion, then left to fetch a cup. I offered to help him move the lorry to our front steps, to avoid the inevitable mess, and he agreed. I then sat there as he poured water and marvelled as it ran off the lorry. He ran inside for a towel and dried every drop. I just gave him a few coaching words to help with the clean up. He was beaming with pride as he negotiated whether to put away the soap or towel first and experienced the unparalleled feeling of independence at being the person to decide this, as well as at the feeling of satisfaction from the 'big work' he had carried out.

Alicia (@montessibaby @teachlearnmontessori) mother of Charlie, aged two

their senses. For example, you can introduce a foreign language or music from birth by speaking the language or playing music in their presence. The connection between lived experience and your child's brain development means it is important to introduce stimulating activities and experiences consciously into family life.

- **Maria Montessori** used the metaphor of sowing seeds of interest and culture like wildflower seeds. You do not know which seeds of learning will germinate and thrive, but your child is likely to develop a sense of curiosity, creativity, wonder, and imagination.

- **Another lesson** from Montessori is to "follow the child". Pay attention to what they are drawn to and think of practical ways to help them develop an interest. Be mindful, too, not to pressure them to do things that they do not enjoy as this may lead them to become resistant. Avoid overstimulating them, too. If they become irritable or distracted, let them pursue other activities of their choice.

STIMULATING YOUR CHILD'S MIND: OLDER CHILDREN

Children are naturally curious and, as they grow, continue to ask "what" and "why" questions, especially in the primary school years. A fundamental way to stimulate their minds is to talk with one another constantly, as well as play games and share experiences.

Working out the answers

Your child knows that you have far more experience and knowledge than they do, so it is only natural that they will ask you for answers to their questions.

Conversing with grandparents and older relatives can give children a new perspective.

To keep their mind engaged and encourage their inquisitiveness, your goal is to help them to learn that they can figure things out for themselves, and to teach them that we continue to learn throughout our lives.

- **Think about how conversations** can help your child to explore topics. For example, if your young child asks you why the sun looks so big at the end of the day, you may or may not know the answer, but you can use an online search engine together or show them how to look up information about the atmosphere in an encyclopedia. The search results will no doubt lead to videos and articles that will help both you and your child to gain a better understanding of what is going on in the atmosphere. Your child sees that you are learning, too.

- **Talk about shared experiences**. Whether you are watching a television documentary, film, or drama with your child, reading the same book, or have enjoyed an outing together, talk to them about it. For example, discuss what they found most interesting about a film or book. Was there a character they particularly enjoyed watching and how would they describe them to someone else?

Or, if you have been on an outing, what did they find the most interesting or enjoyable part of their trip?

- **Arranging conversations** between your child, yourself, and their grandparents or other older relatives can be an enjoyable and interesting way to stimulate your child's mind. You might consider recording the conversation for posterity. Children love to hear the stories that older family members have to tell. They can be fascinated by stories from grandparents about what it was like when they were growing up and how they came to live where they do. These stories not only carry on your family history, but they can also be intellectually stimulating. Do, however, watch out for signs that your child is no longer interested in a conversation.

- **Ask your child** to tell a story (if they enjoy this). Mastering the art of creating a tale or writing and acting out a short play can be extremely stimulating for children.

- **Introduce "heroes"** into your child's life. Is there a heroic character, either living or from the past, with whom they can identify and will find thought-provoking? This is especially important for families who are raising

❝ ❞

Talk to your child about your shared experiences – what did they like best about a film, book, or an outing you enjoyed together?

children who come from an ethnic or religious background that is a minority in their local community, because children need to feel connected to history.

- **As your child grows**, continue to provide games and suggest activities that engage their mind. Make sure that games evolve in line with their age. Think, too, about different types of activities, from ones they can enjoy on their own, such as building and construction blocks and jigsaw puzzles, to action games played with others, to advanced strategy games such as chess or role-play. Older children can also enjoy teaching younger children skills, and grandparents and parents how to keep up with technology.

INVESTIGATION AND DISCOVERY

Very young children ask questions to start a conversation rather than wanting to get a detailed explanation – they are simply exploring ideas. As your child grows, their exploration of topics of interest becomes more detailed and in depth, and the breadth of their interests is likely to widen.

Young explorers

Four- and five-year-old children tend to learn through their senses while exploring anything that captures their interest. In a Montessori classroom, special learning materials help them to do this while developing foundational skills in reading, writing, mathematics, measuring, organizing, and observing. Even though you may not have these learning materials at home, you can consciously help your child to discover how to learn in a Montessori way.

For example, your young child may be interested in a butterfly in the garden. With your help and guidance, they can look through a book of butterflies from the library or in your home or search online to find out its name. Depending on their level of interest, they may be delighted with the information on how the caterpillar evolves into the butterfly,

Ages and stages

18 months–6 years
Allow your child to explore activities without your interference when they are engaged and focused. Observe them. If they become frustrated, watch for another minute or two to see if they can work something out. This helps them build perseverance and determination. Offer help if they are stuck.

6–12 years
Encourage your child to ask questions, read, and learn about whatever catches their interest. If you can, suggest they talk to someone you know who has professional insight into a field they enjoy.

12–18 years
Let your adolescent explore, investigate, and discover answers through research, travel, joining a debating team, or getting involved with a youth organization for a political party.

how long it takes for that to happen, and what the caterpillar eats. After that, they may move on quickly to another interest. Or, they might be interested in seeing what a chrysalis looks like. If you find a chrysalis attached to a branch, you could even bring this inside and put it in a terrarium or suitable container to allow the butterfly to emerge, which can be an unforgettable experience for a child.

Learning to combine skills

In the primary school years, children are interested in the "how" and "why" and have vivid imaginations. They want to delve into subjects that catch their attention and are usually able to carry out simple research on their own to investigate and discover information, through a process of asking a question and developing a theory, experimenting in some way to test the theory, or researching to discover the answer.

At home, investigation and discovery can be initiated by you or your child when questions are asked. Even though your child engages in more abstract thinking now, they still enjoy practical learning and discoveries can involve combining reading, writing, and calculating with hands-on learning (see box, right).

Changing interests

In adolescence, children can start to focus more on relationships with peers, gender identity, sexuality, social justice, global situations, family values, and how they fit in and can make a difference. They may question why you support a political party and may want to gain a better understanding of the differences between organized religions. They may also be interested in ancestors: where they came from, what was going on in the world

Close-up observation can be an engaging way for young children to investigate and learn.

when they were alive, and the impact world events had on them. Engaging in deep discussions, even if these lead to disagreements at times, helps your child to explore and discover now.

Hands-on learning

Thinking about how you might approach a project such as building a birdhouse, illustrates how you can help your child to combine skills as they move through the primary years.

The questions your child might need to ask could include, what type of bird is in your garden and what kind of bird would they like to attract? Does this kind of bird live in the area? How big are they, and what predators do they have? Work together with your child to find the answers. Then start to design the house together. Choose the wood, work out the dimensions, saw and glue the pieces, and hang the birdhouse in a suitable spot. Finally, your child can wait for the birds to appear and record their observations.

GAMES AND ACTIVITIES TO STIMULATE THE MIND

Your child's brain develops through interacting with the environment. They learn by watching, hearing, thinking, and doing. As a parent, you can tailor activities to help your child develop their inner sense of order, concentration, problem-solving skills, language, and independence.

Learning through play

Many activities that entertain your child also help to strengthen their problem-solving skills, develop their memory, and increase their knowledge. Watch your child to see how they engage with activities and try not to interrupt them when they are concentrating on something.

- **Children enjoy creating patterns**. Activities that involve sorting, nesting, and stacking as well as recognizing the pattern in which blocks and objects can be arranged, engage sensory awareness and coordination.

Provide opportunities to recognize, repeat, or create patterns, for example with beads, coloured blocks in geometric shapes, or mosaics. You can also have fun creating patterns through movement, which builds memory and pattern recognition and develops coordination. Try performing a movement, dance step, or clapping in a specific pattern or beat, and ask your child to repeat your actions.

- **Touch recognition games** also develop sensory awareness. Place objects in a bag. Invite your child to put their hand in and determine what the object is simply by touching it.

- **Games involving puzzles** develop your child's problem-solving and maths skills as well as their

From building blocks to threading beads, children of different ages enjoy creating patterns with colours and shapes.

focus. These can range from first jigsaw puzzles, with just a few pieces and knobs to hold, to complex jigsaw puzzles for older children. Introduce abstract puzzle challenges, too, from simple "dot to dots" to crossword puzzles and word and number games.

- **Strategy games and activities**, such as noughts and crosses, puzzle cubes, or board and card games, contribute to brain development by encouraging planning and logic skills and also teach your child to play by the rules. Games with dice help with number recognition and simple maths.

- **Introduce activities** that build memory and observation skills. At around three years of age, show your child three or four objects. Ask them to close their eyes, remove one, then ask them which is missing. As they get older, use picture pair cards to test memory and focus. Or play a film clip, then see if your child can recall details.

- **Story games** develop language skills, memory, and imagination. In the early years, play oral games where you take turns to add a sound, word, or sentence to create a story, challenging your child to remember and incorporate what the previous person said. As they grow, many children develop

Ages and stages

18 months–6 years
In the early years, activities that involve manipulating parts, such as building blocks, puzzles, or putting matching objects together, are key to stimulating your child's mind. Montessori said you cannot give anything to the mind without first giving it to the hand.

6–12 years
Many children continue to enjoy building with blocks or other materials, making models, or playing strategy games.

12–18 years
Teens enjoy playing games with friends. See if they are open to having friends over to join in a family activity. They may enjoy competing as well as challenging board and video games.

vivid imaginations and enjoy creating and telling stories. Take turns to make up a story then tell them in a way that makes them come alive. This stimulates the brain in ways that are different from listening to a story or reading. It also develops memory as your child keeps track of the story, its characters, the sequence of events, and what will happen next. Children who create and tell stories tend to have a stronger vocabulary and use of language.

ACTION GAMES AND ACTIVITIES

Games and activities at home that involve movement not only help to ensure that your child gets valuable exercise and enjoys family time, but also develop coordination, strength, and agility, both physical and mental.

- **Many activities develop** your child's hand–eye coordination, important for everyday tasks and skills such as

Ages and stages

18 months–6 years
Young children learn as they move. At this developmental stage, they are working on coordination, strength, and agility. Simple games that involve movements such as running, jumping, hopping, and moving under and over things all contribute to the development of their confidence and grace.

6–12 years
Children often enjoy active outdoor games now, such as catching and other ball games and tag. They may also enjoy gentler activities such as yoga and dance.

12–18 years
Teenagers are most likely to enjoy team sports. Many also enjoy running, cycling, or power walking with friends.

writing and drawing and helpful for participating in sports. Young children can start by gently tossing a bean bag into a basket from a few steps back. As their skill grows, you could create a slanted board with holes as targets so your child can play at a more advanced level. Other games that involve aiming for a target, such as croquet, or simple catch games with a ball, also improve your child's hand–eye coordination.

- **Home obstacle courses** are enjoyed by children of many ages. These help children to develop their balance and coordination, movement, visual perception, and problem-solving skills. Whether you set up an obstacle course indoors in your living room using chairs, pillows, boxes, and other suitable items, or outside in your garden, aim to create a structure that involves your child climbing, crawling under objects, jumping, hopping, and walking.

- **Scavenger hunts** are great fun for children and allow them to be actively involved in reading a list, searching for items, and working as a team. The idea is that this is collaborative rather than competitive. Choose from a variety of themes, such as a hunt for

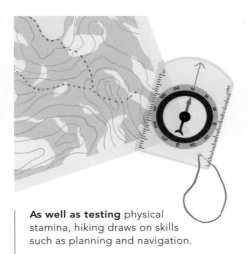

As well as testing physical stamina, hiking draws on skills such as planning and navigation.

children the opportunity to not only enjoy nature and get some exercise, but to also learn how to follow a map and/or pay attention to the landmarks you pass along the way. With older children, hikes can last for hours, or maybe even overnight. Hikes can be especially valuable if you involve your child in thinking about what you need to bring, from snacks and water to a first-aid kit, extra socks, rain gear, or a compass. They can help to gather the items and pack a backpack.

- **Some families enjoy** practising yoga together, whether with an instructor, from a video, or by preparing yoga "posture" cards for their children to try. Yoga not only leads to good balance, flexibility, strength, and inner calm, it also contributes to children's brain development, coordination, and "body mapping" – the self-awareness of our bodies in relation to our surroundings.

- **A dance off** can be fun for the entire family. This develops your child's coordination and helps them to enjoy movement. Try dancing to energetic music in an informal competition, either together or individually, where you dance until one of you is declared the winner by mutual consent.

items around the home, or for nature items in the garden or local park, then make a list of items for the hunt. Smaller children can team up with an older sibling or parent; older children might work individually or in a team. Give your child or team a certain amount of time to find the items listed. At the end of the hunt, gather around and share the items you have found.

- **Hiking** is a valuable experience for children of any age. Children need to spend time outdoors, and benefit greatly from the companionship of family walks. Longer hikes offer

SHARING BOOKS

Reading together is one of the best ways for families to stimulate their minds and feel closer to each other. If you enjoy reading and integrate it into family life, your child is likely to enjoy the benefits of sharing books and reading throughout their life.

Introducing books

No child is too young to enjoy snuggling with a parent or older sibling as they are read a story. When choosing books for your toddler, bear in mind that they are developing their visual sense so large illustrations with minimal text is ideal. As your toddler learns vocabulary, point to pictures and name them, then to the word describing the picture, drawing your finger across it as you say the word. As their vocabulary grows, progress to picture books with sentences.

Montessori teaches children the sounds of letters before their names so they learn to read phonetically. Say the sounds when pointing to a letter. For example, for the letter "s", say "sssssss" instead of "esss".

Young readers

Many children start to read on their own, or with help, around the age of five. Offer books with exciting vocabulary and captivating content. Keep the following in mind when selecting books for children aged 18 months to six years:

- **Very young children** cannot easily distinguish between fantasy and reality. Their understanding of the world is based on what they can touch, smell, see, hear, and taste. Look for books with fairly realistic illustrations instead of books that show animal characters acting and dressing like people, which give children a false impression

Sharing books with a looked-up-to older sibling can be a magical experience for a young child.

of how real animals behave. While some classic books do this, try to stick in the main to books with realistic stories and illustrations.

- **Rhyming stories** are fun and natural for children. Rhyme and repetition also help them to remember stories. Young children may repeat learned words and sentences while looking at a book, before they know how to read.

- **When your child** is around four years old, read short chapter books to them, a chapter at a time, as well as picture books. Chat about the characters, the story, and how they felt about a chapter.

Broadening horizons

In the primary years, children move into a period of imagination and creativity, making up their own stories. Read books to them now that are several levels above their own. They also want to know the how and why. Encourage them to use libraries – at home, in school, or public ones – as well as online sources to gather information from encyclopedias, dictionaries, and other non-fiction sources.

For reluctant readers, comics, magazines, and audio books can help develop an interest in reading.

In adolescence, your child becomes more interested in relationships with others and enjoys books and stories that explore moral or social situations.

Ages and stages

18 months–6 years
For toddlers, choose board books with real-life photos or drawings, without words near the picture, or with an explanatory word on a separate page. Young children love books that rhyme. Encourage your child to join in with rhyming words or repeated phrases. Form a habit of reading regularly with your child, not just at bedtime.

6–12 years
Try starting a family book club, where you ask open-ended questions to help your child formulate and express ideas.

12–18 years
Adolescents may start to read a diverse range of material. As well as fiction, they may increasingly read non-fiction, such as biographies, autobiographies, and topical books, for pleasure. Help them access more diverse reading material.

Looking after books

When you begin reading with your child, as well as teaching them about words and stories, you are also showing them how to handle books carefully, turning the pages gently.

Show your child that care must be taken not to step on books; that they should not be thrown; and that, like other objects, they need to be put away when finished.

ENJOYING ART

As well as being part of our history and a way of understanding other people's experiences, art is also a form of personal expression, like poetry, song, dance, and telling stories. It is a form of human connection that can evoke feelings, thoughts, and hopefully appreciation and understanding. Montessori encourages families to expose children to as many forms of art as possible.

Ages and stages

18 months–6 years
From painting with water on smooth stone to using paints, clay, or crayons, children can explore colour and different media now, developing hand–eye coordination and expression. Visit a gallery if they enjoy this.

6–12 years
Some children may continue to enjoy creating art and appreciating others' art. Encourage them to frame and display their favourite work. Continue to invite them to visit galleries with you.

12–18 years
An interest in art may be rediscovered now, providing adolescents with a vehicle for self-expression and creativity that helps them to clarify their identity. Students may explore digital art and photography.

Introducing your child to art

Exposing children to art and crafts – together with music, dance, film, and theatre – and surrounding them with art in our homes, helps them to have a sense of the vibrant texture of the world and our common history. When your child is young, display art from your family's culture and from other cultures and familiarize them with well-known artists from around the world.

A creative environment

Artistic creativity is one of the many ways that children can express their personalities and intelligence. As well as being an expression of personal experience, it also plays a key role in developing learning, problem-solving abilities, and planning skills. Encouraging the artistic side of your child's personality can pay dividends for life.

- **Set up a prepared environment** that encourages creativity. This space could include media such as paints, collage materials, pastels or charcoal, or sculpting clay, depending on changing interests. For a young child, start with a small table and chair, if possible, with paper and some type of storage facility or drawers where they can put crayons, markers, small pompoms, feathers, and other things that could be used for craft projects.

" "

Encouraging your child's interest in art and giving them room to be creative provides them with experiences that will endure.

Letting your child explore art from an early age fosters creativity and aids motor development.

- **Young children** start off by using their hands to create finger paintings or drawings in a tray of sand. They need plenty of practice to develop the muscles in their hands and fingers and coordinate their movements before using tools such as pencils, crayons, or paintbrushes. They usually love the process of creating, and are less concerned with how the art looks. However, they feel pride when their art is displayed at home. Plan how to display and share their favourite work.

- **School-aged children** may develop an interest in a particular art form or media. This might signal a shift in their attention, from simply exploring and working with media to being more focused on a finished product.

They may enjoy finding objects to use in nature or from a charity shop as their imagination and creativity blossom. Peer interaction is also important now. They might wish to join an art class with their peers or integrate an art activity into their birthday celebration.

- **If your child joins an art class**, help them explore themes. Discuss the lesson with them and, if they are interested, visit a museum or watch a film about a particular artist together. Encourage them to source library books or online material that illustrates a style they are interested in, such as still life, or discusses an artist whose work centres around the style. They could also set up a still-life arrangement to practise at home.

LEARNING ABOUT MONEY MANAGEMENT

A long-term goal in Montessori-inspired homes is to teach children about money and the part it plays in our lives. Learning to manage money involves developing a wide range of everyday skills and helping your child to grow up with a balanced set of values on money, possessions, savings, investments, charitable giving, and debt.

Ages and stages

18 months–6 years
Giving a small allowance, starting around the age of four, can help you guide your child into thoughtful habits around using money.

6–12 years
Adjust your child's allowance to reflect the items they will need to buy. Learning to live within an allowance is a key skill. If they spend it too quickly, let the natural consequence of not having enough teach them to be more conscious of spending in future.

12–18 years
By adolescence, your child has hopefully learned to be careful with money. You may need to increase their allowance so they can save for bigger purchases, helping them learn more about planning ahead and avoiding impulse buys.

Setting an example

Helping your child to understand and use money wisely is one of the steps to them becoming independent, resilient, responsible, and innovative planners, decision makers, and problem solvers. Children absorb life lessons about money from observing how their parents spend it, share it, and save it. These lessons begin as your child watches you use money, for example, as you pay for things at a shop.

How you talk about money influences your child's ideas about abundance or scarcity and models money decision-making behaviour. For example, hearing thoughtful discussions about expenses, budgeting, and investments teaches your child the importance of talking about finances. Even if you do not directly involve them, your child sees, hears, and senses these patterns in your life.

You can also help school-aged children to become financially literate by explaining the difference between an asset, which appreciates in value and, ideally, brings some income, and a liability, which depreciates in value and costs money to own. Your child can learn that things that we need, such as a home or perhaps a car, cost us money to maintain, and that understanding the costs involved is important to a family's decision-making process.

The benefits of an allowance

Giving your child an allowance from four to five years old helps them start to think about money management. Talk to them about having their own money and how they can spend it wisely, use it for a worthy cause, or save it. Show an older child how to create a written budget, using their allowance as their income to determine expenses and plan savings. From an early age, help them to think about making good spending choices. They should consider the need versus the desire (see below); the value versus the cost; and the total amount that they have available to spend. These valuable steps help them to manage and track money independently and responsibly.

Wanting and needing

Be thoughtful before buying something just because your child wants it. Help them to distinguish between things they need, such as equipment for a class they have enrolled in, and things they want, such as a new toy. Save the latter for special occasions or, even better, help them learn to save and maybe earn extra money so that, in time, they can buy it themselves.

Find practical ways to teach your child to avoid impulse buys. You could plan a meal together. Compile a grocery list and shop for the food together, buying only the items on the list. Ask them to add up prices as you go along. This teaches them how to choose between brands, stick to a list, and keep track of expenditure.

Sticking to a planned list while shopping with your child teaches them a valuable life lesson.

Teaching your child the fundamentals of savings and investments helps to prepare them for the future.

Building on an allowance

As your child grows, they may want to buy more expensive items and their allowance, even with savings put aside, may not be enough. This can be a chance for you to help them explore ways to earn additional income. They might do jobs around the house above and beyond their usual tasks, as well as for other people. Also, with or without your help, they might look at ideas for starting a small business of some sort, whether running a cake stall, helping out in a family business, or starting a small business of their own. This sort of venture helps your child to become innovative, independent, and responsible while earning extra money.

Keeping balances in check

Once your child has learned the basic principles of budgeting, help them to develop this practical life skill, showing them how to ensure bills get paid, look at cash flow projection, and reconcile expenditure and balances.

- **Whether you have** paper bank statements or bank online, talk to your child about the different ways to make payments and how to check these against your statement at the end of the month, to be sure that the figures tally. If you have home accounting software, show your child how this works for setting up accounts, entering incoming bills, and planning what needs to be paid and when.

- **Older children can learn** how to keep track of their expenses, read a bank statement, or use spreadsheet software to develop a monthly budget and compare actual expenses against their budget. They can project how well they are working towards long-term saving or investment goals.

Credit and savings

Using credit wisely is another important lesson for your child. Ideally, large items are paid for fully upfront. If you need to finance something over time, teach your child how to look for the best terms and to factor ongoing costs into their budget.

It is a good idea to make savings a deliberate part of your child's money

66 99 OUR STORY

My seven-year-old grandson wanted a mountain trail bike so that he could join his older brother, who had a trail bike of his own, on rides through the nearby park.

His mum and I talked about the possibility of getting him one as a birthday present, but we felt that he was now old enough to contribute to its cost. Together, we proposed that she and I would each cover a third of the cost, and he could earn his share by walking the family dog and giving it its weekly bath for two months. He earned his share, week by week, and took special pride when it was time to go to a bike shop and pick out his own bike.

David, grandfather of Asher, aged seven

planning. Some families simply regard savings as a family expense, while others view them as an opportunity to teach children to save for large purchases, unexpected trips or activities, or emergencies. How much your child saves now is not significant, but the lessons they learn from this are valuable.

66 99

As your child gets older, they will become more involved in managing their own money and can start to plan for their future.

Planning ahead

Your child will become increasingly involved in managing their money and future plans. Show them how to plan by working together on a "family strategic plan". This includes what the family wants, what you need to do to get it, who will be involved, and how long it will take to achieve. It could include future plans for your teenager, such as the costs of further education, starting a business, or travel. Help them look at ways to create money through investments, whether they partner in a business venture, develop a source of passive earnings, or learn about the stock market. Choosing companies to invest in gives them the chance to explore if there are some whose mission and practices better reflect their personal values.

HOMEWORK

Too often, homework is a battleground between parents and child. Regular homework is not part of Montessori schooling, but for families where schools do set homework, there are ways for parents to make it a positive learning experience rather than a struggle.

The Montessori approach

In Montessori, traditional homework is not the norm. Instead, "school work" done at home is usually an outgrowth of what children are interested in, whether that is reading, making a presentation, planning and budgeting family meals, or writing invitations, letters, emails, or an article. There may be a test to study for or a project or research to do, but most academic work is done in school hours, with at-home projects used to put

children's knowledge or skills to practical use. Home time is for absorbing, reflecting on, and internalizing information learned at school.

"Family learning time"

Whatever your child's homework regime, the Montessori ethos can help families to set up a basic routine to make work that is done in home time more pleasant for everyone. Before a school year starts, discuss "family learning time" at a family meeting. Think about when and where this will happen, what type of activities each of you will do, and how it will help. Agree on and stick to a time and place for the whole family to engage in a learning activity – whether reading, doing online research, or working on the measurements and design for a model. By preparing for this time and letting everyone express their thoughts, you reinforce the idea that each member of the family is a lifelong learner, that learning is enjoyable, and that it is important to be present so that each of you can work individually or ask for help.

- **At weekly family meetings,** let each person share what they have coming up that week. One parent might be preparing a work presentation, a child might have a test to study for, another may have chapters of a book to read and report on, and the other parent

Being mindful of your message

Keep in mind that your own approach to work sets an example for your child. If you talk about your work negatively and approach it as a chore, you signal to your child that work is not enjoyable and is something that simply has to be endured, in contrast to relaxing leisure time. Conversely, expressing the satisfaction you take from your work shows your child that work can be a fulfilling endeavour that forms an integral part of life.

may be doing genealogy research. This conversation means each family member knows what's coming up and makes it easier for everyone to understand and support each other.

- **At the start of daily** family learning time, check in with your child. What do they need to achieve? Share what you hope to accomplish. This will help your child to structure their learning time and set them up for success.

Ages and stages

18 months–6 years
Read, read, read; count everything; match and sort. Create and act out a sketch and sing and dance together!

6–12 years
Help your child to be organized. Help them manage large projects but don't do them. Ask about work, but don't say how to do it.

12–18 years
Ensure your child has the support for more advanced assignments. This gives them the sense that if they need extra guidance or time you are there, but that they are able.

Quietly sharing a space while each family member enjoys learning time creates a focused and mutually supportive homework environment.

Show an interest in your child's work, but encourage them to find their own solutions.

" "

With the right approach and encouragement, children will explore and learn about whatever captures their attention.

the ability to apply skills and knowledge in new situations. Moreover, when parents and teachers use rewards and pressure to try to get children to work, children can end up resistant and resentful of lessons, teachers, homework, and tests. Test anxiety is a major concern. Many parents want to help children not only succeed, but also excel and feel they need to give them an external push.

Why children learn

The purpose of education is not only to pass exams, but also to become a well informed and thoughtful member of the adult community and someone who can adapt to an ever-changing world.

Children are usually born intelligent, curious, and creative. When given the chance, they will explore whatever captures their attention without needing encouragement or external structure.

There is growing concern that often school work is orientated to memorization more than understanding in context or

Your role as a parent

As well as providing the structure and support discussed on pages 138–139, consider the following when thinking about how to help your child manage and enjoy homework.

- **Pay attention** to how much work they have. Does it seem interesting or mundane; how much time do they need to spend on it; and do they seem to be coping or seem stressed, resentful, or exhausted? If they are working until late at night or seem anxious – respectfully talk to their teacher, who can identify if your child is being given too much work and/or needs additional support.

- **Avoid the temptation** to add out-of-school academic enrichment or support, unless you have a good reason to believe your child needs it, or they ask for it and find it enjoyable.

- **Learning should be interesting** and enjoyable, not something dreaded and resented. Many parents feel they need to spend time doing extra work with their child. This is great if you both enjoy it, but is a very bad idea if either of you gets frustrated and discouraged.

- **Treat your child's homework** as their task. If they ask for help, ask them to explain what they have in mind and how they aim to achieve it. This helps them to understand what needs to be done and how to get organized. Do not take over, partially or completely. Projects are given so that students learn by doing something and demonstrate understanding through completing them (see also p.142). If you do the thinking, your child will not learn.

66 99   OUR STORY

When my son, Joseph, reached secondary school, he often struggled to complete homework on time. He was unprepared, uncooperative, and full of excuses. Reasoning didn't work, so we decided to talk about it at our weekly family meeting rather than try to deal with it in the heat of the moment. The calm nature of weekly meetings made it possible to express our concern and commitment to helping him succeed.

I asked Joseph whether there was anything that we could do to help him get his work done, other than doing it for him. He described feeling overwhelmed at all the things he had to do, and saw his tendency to get bogged down. We agreed to try to help him list and prioritize work, and to think what he would need to do to accomplish each piece. He had always been an active child, so we suggested that he complete a task, put it in his bag, then do some press-ups or other physical activity as a 'brain break'. For him, this worked. He would periodically ask for help, and I would check in with him to see how he was doing, offer words of encouragement about his effort and progress, and congratulate him when the day's tasks were done.

Daniel, father of Joseph, now aged 15

HELPING WITH PROJECTS

Your school-aged child will periodically have more substantial homework projects – such as learning lines, making a model, or setting up an experiment – which require preparation over days, weeks, or longer. Your role is to support them in developing the planning and organizational skills required.

Ages and stages

18 months–6 years
At around aged four or five, your child may announce that it is their turn to "show and tell", or that they need to learn the lines of a song. Encourage them, give choices, and help them take the lead confidently.

6–12 years
For long projects, avoid last-minute scrambles, taking the lead, or doing too much for them. As well as helping them to think through the project and note each step as it is completed, commend them along the way for their effort and progress.

12–18 years
Children can face more and increasingly complex projects. Ask questions to help them focus their efforts on what is due, when, what steps are involved, and how they can manage it with minimal stress. Encourage rather than rescue them.

How you can assist
The aim is to help your child learn how to think through and carry out a larger project by coaching and inspiring them, but never doing the work for them. Instead, ask questions and help them to organize their thoughts if needed.

An organized approach
Weekly family meetings are an ideal time to keep abreast of more involved school commitments. As each family member shares what is coming up over the weeks ahead, you can note major projects or events in your diary. If your child mentions a school project, set up a time to discuss its details and to offer your support. This helps to avoid the frustration and stress of learning about important plans at the last minute.

You can guide your child and support and encourage the completion of their project by helping them to develop skills steadily; to learn how to organize their thoughts; to prepare a timeline and plan the steps; and to think through what materials and resources they will need.

Practical help
The range of projects can vary widely depending on the age of your child, the approach of their school, and the subject matter. Do not expect perfection. Instead, help your child to feel comfortable doing the project

" "

Asking your child questions and helping them to organize their thoughts supports your child and encourages them to think for themselves.

themselves and to try to improve with each new assignment. There are a number of ways to support them.

- **If your child is preparing** an oral or written report on a book, or a class presentation, for example, about a historical figure or event, help them find ways to add interest. They could prepare a PowerPoint presentation, use props, or dress up as a character.

- **Brainstorm ideas** for science projects together. Coach your child in the planning: how they will conduct the experiment; how they will display the research and results; and how they will explain it to others.

- **If your child is memorizing lines** for a play or class reading, offer to listen as they practise. Gently coach them on how to dramatize the message and prompt them to think about how well they are doing. For example, after listening, ask how they felt about it.

What did they think went well and what might they do differently? This approach avoids them feeling they are not good enough. You could also offer to record them. Encourage them to watch and critique themselves. If you have a knack for drama, and your child does not feel uncomfortable, you could show them how you might do it. Be mindful that they only have so much emotional energy to work on a project like this at any one time.

- **Encourage them** to help prepare any costume or props. This will help them feel that they have been involved in every aspect of an endeavour.

Suggesting creative ways to engage in a project, such as dressing up, can help your child find new ways to explore topics.

SPENDING TIME TOGETHER

It is easy to be part of the same family, living in the same home, and yet to spend relatively little quality time with one another.

Spending time together is important for every member of the family. If you have a partner, spend time with each other in meaningful communication and nurture your relationship. However your family unit is made up, the goal in a Montessori home is to nurture a family that is close, cooperative, and mutually supportive. It is also important to be mindful that, while your family has an identity of its own, it is made up of unique individuals, each with their own interests and distinct personalities. Forging a family is about creating a small community of individuals — of parents, children, and sometimes extended family, all living together.

❝ ❞

The time that you spend together in mutually enjoyable activities helps to strengthen family bonds and individual relationships.

NURTURING YOUR FAMILY

Spending quality time together is important for strengthening family relationships. There are many ways to build this together time into family life, from the routine of everyday life to enjoying outings and planned trips together.

Being together

Each day we have opportunities to connect with each other, at mealtimes, on the way to school, or relaxing in the evening. Beyond these everyday routines, building in time together – playing, learning, travelling, reading, and sharing stories – helps to build the family unit. Creating and sharing memories and traditions is also important. These become part of the ongoing story that your child will pass on to their own family when asked about their childhood. You also nurture your family when you enjoy projects and activities together, such as embarking on a small building project.

It is important, too, to set aside your digital devices so you focus on each other. Disconnecting from the digital world and our separate activities is vital to enable us to reconnect with each other and put our relationships foremost.

Setting aside time to enjoy activities as a family helps to build and nurture each relationship.

SHARING FAMILY STORIES

Family stories are usually shared spontaneously and informally in everyday family life. Children can benefit in big and small ways from knowing more about the lives of the people in their families, both those who are alive now and from stories about their ancestors.

Opportunities for family stories

Being open to the many chances that arise in family life to share and pass down family stories can help your child to feel a sense of belonging. These family stories can bring up emotions for the people involved, of humour, sadness, appreciation, or love. Sharing stories with your child and displaying emotions helps your child to explore their own emotions.

You may find stories are sparked by your child asking about your childhood, or when asking their grandparents about what it was like when they were growing up. Stories may also come up at family gatherings when someone is reminiscing, or when visiting a place where you lived or visited frequently as a child.

• **Family stories can provide** an opportunity for humour. They are often comical and funny and your child will love enjoying the merriment

and laughter they create. Do be careful to ensure that the humour you enjoy does not include sarcasm or making fun of other family members, but rather that it teaches your child that an optimistic view of situations helps families to build resilience and healthy attitudes, no matter what comes along in life. Demonstrating this gentle family humour teaches your child how shared stories can generate laughter and a feeling of warmth that everyone can enjoy.

Ages and stages

18 months–6 years
Your young child loves to hear you tell stories about your family and will often ask you to tell stories again and again. Other family members may chime in as stories are retold and become part of the fabric of family life.

6–12 years
Your child may be keenly interested in delving deeper now, talking with grandparents and other relatives about their childhood experiences, going through photo albums, and even doing online family research.

12–18 years
Teenagers may lose interest in family history for a time, or interest may grow. They may want to create their own family history, collecting photos and recording interviews with family members to make an oral history.

> "
Telling family stories
when opportunities present
themselves gives your child
a strong sense of belonging.

Weave in stories about family
and ancestors when looking at
photographs to help your child
feel a sense of shared history.

- **Family stories** can hold valuable lessons for children about topics such as bravery, getting through hard times, standing up for family beliefs, or about practical matters such as starting a business.

Bringing ancestors to life

When stories have been told over several generations, find ways to help to make them more real for your child. If you have old photographs of the people in the story, show these to your child. Visiting a grave to put down some flowers can also bring up memories and stories.

During the primary and adolescent years, your child may become more interested in who their ancestors were, especially if they can link them to a topic they are studying in history. For example, they may be intrigued by the women's fight for the right to vote, where a great, great grandmother may have been part of the movement, or how their great-grandparents' life was affected by war. Sharing stories about them can help to make that part of history come alive. If ancestors migrated, children can learn about the part of the world they were born in and what life was like there.

EVERYDAY STRATEGIES

MAKING AGREEMENTS

Disagreements are part of everyday life. Resolving conflict and making agreements with your child after a dispute is important for them to learn about their relationships with siblings, parents, friends, or other relatives, and live peacefully together.

When children disagree with each other, parents act as facilitators to help them think through what happened and how they can resolve conflict (see pp.108–111).

Similarly, when you and your child disagree, the Montessori approach is for you, as the parent, to engage with them so that you can resolve the conflict and reach an agreement. Whether your child badgers you to buy something, fails to do a chore, or, as a teenager, spends money unwisely, your role is to model peaceful conflict resolution skills.

If emotions are running high after a disagreement with your child, it can be best to disengage and take a break before trying to resolve things. Wait for a neutral moment, when you are both calm, before discussing it. It is vital, as a parent, to stay calm and somewhat detached to avoid being defensive. It is also important to separate the "deed" from the "doer", so your child knows that, no matter what they say or do, you love them. The strategy on pages 150–151 showcases how to reach an agreement peacefully.

" "

Waiting for a quiet, calm moment to discuss disputes can help you and your child to reach agreements amicably.

" " **OUR STORY**

Our youngest child is still at home while our two older children are at college. After some time, she began to feel lonely without her older brother and sister around. So she did something she does not often do, she asked for something – she began asking us for a dog.

My wife and I were concerned that she would quickly tire of the responsibilities of having a pet. So we began to prep her for ownership of a dog by carefully explaining all of the work and obligation that would follow. Her desire for a dog was not thwarted. We then made an agreement that she would be completely responsible for its care.

The day we brought home the puppy she took to him immediately, naming him Ollie. From day one, she exceeded our expectations for how she would care and attend to the puppy in every single area. As with most 14-year-old children, the reality for Mattison was the hard work of being responsible for caring for another life. We do help from time to time, but we do not take over. We let her go through it, without bailing her out, without being a crutch, without allowing her to abdicate the responsibility that she asked for, and she has grown a great deal in light of it. No matter the situation, she does what she has to do to make Ollie's existence a good one.

Michael, father of Isaiah, aged 23, Morgan, aged 22, and Mattison, aged 14

MAKING AGREEMENTS IN PRACTICE

Wait for a calm moment

If, for example, you are drawn into an argument with your child when you are out shopping together because you have said you will not buy something that they want, try to stick to your guns but resist getting drawn into a big dispute in the shop. Instead, wait until you get home and are both feeling calmer, then revisit what happened at the shop. You might say to your child, "We need to talk about what happened when we were at the shop today."

Acknowledge their feelings

Begin by letting your child know that both of you played a part in the problem. You might say something like, "I know that we both argued about what to buy when we were at the shop. I don't like to argue and make a fuss in a shop, and I'm pretty sure you don't like that either. Am I right?". This not only lets your child know that both of you have some responsibility in continuing to argue in the shop, but it also lets them know that you care about their feelings.

Talking together calmly after a dispute can help you and your child to avoid a similar situation in the future.

Reach an agreement

Once you have acknowledged what happened and have made it clear that you both had a part to play, invite your child to help you think of some ways to resolve the situation and avoid it happening again. For example, you might decide to not shop together if it is not necessary, to leave a shop if an argument starts, or to use an agreed signal to stop if an argument begins. Once you have talked through your ideas, choose one that you both agree on and try it out.

❝ ❞

Agreeing that you both played a part in a disagreement helps your child to understand that you are seeing both sides.

Choose future consequences

If your child does not follow through with an agreement, talk again. You might make a new agreement with consequences that you work out together. If a situation affects the whole family, you could discuss it at a family meeting. The point of a consequence is not to punish your child but to teach them. You are helping them to stop behaving inappropriately; to understand your concern; and to behave responsibly. When choosing a consequence, ask yourself the following:

Have you ensured that the chosen consequence relates to the situation?

Is this consequence a reasonable expectation for your child?

Does the consequence show respect to your child and the family?

Will the consequence help your child to take responsibility?

PLAYING TOGETHER

Competition is often used in schools, in children's sports, and by adults to externally motivate children into an artificial spirit of competition. In contrast, Montessori encourages a spirit of friendly, cooperative work and play that can appear very different from the typical competitive mindset that many cultures take for granted.

A different approach

Many think that a Montessori philosophy does not recognize competition. Montessori does appreciate that many situations involve competition – at school, work, and in the home – and sees this as a natural part of life, where sometimes we win and other times we do not. However, Montessori nurtures a spirit of cooperation and collaboration, rather than promoting the sense that life is a competition for attention or a prize.

Often, visitors to a Montessori classroom are surprised to see children of different ages getting along so well. The wonderful spirit of collaboration and sharing that is promoted allows children to work and play together or beside each other, enjoying both the experience of shared time and the celebration of each other's unique achievements and milestones. Children help each other to be successful. There is an absence of one-upmanship and children appreciate each other's accomplishments.

A spirit of cooperation

In Montessori-inspired homes, parents celebrate each family member as unique, with their own gifts, challenges, and rates of progress. They recognize and appreciate each person and what they have accomplished on a task, and encourage other family members to acknowledge and appreciate other's accomplishments and achievements at family meetings and in everyday life.

Ages and stages

18 months–6 years
Model sharing and cooperating for your two-to-three-year-old and help them to use words to express needs. From three to five years, they are ready to learn about sharing.

6–12 years
Learning a new sport or skill during these years can be frustrating for your child. Helping them to be comfortable with the journey of learning and the idea that this may include losing from time to time teaches them an important life lesson.

12–18 years
These years can be challenging as teens may pull away or be frustrated with younger siblings. Find ways to keep them connected to the family and also welcome their friends.

Learning to share

In the first six years of life, children are learning how to be in relationships. In their first two to three years, dependent on their parents for their care, they tend to think the world revolves around them.

Between two and three years of age, they begin to realize that they are separate from their caregivers – they can do things on their own and can express their needs verbally. As they become increasingly capable, act as a guide and mentor, helping them to cooperate and become aware of others' needs.

At this age, children find it hard to share toys and their parents' attention. Some parents try to persuade children to share. Do not force sharing now. Your child prefers to play on their own, with others close by, and is just learning what sharing means. They do not understand the difference between sharing a toy for a time and giving it away for ever. Help older siblings to understand this. You could suggest older children play with something else for a little while. With children over three years old, facilitate a conflict resolution scenario if a squabble over sharing arises (see pp.108–111).

At three to five years of age, children start to master turn-taking. Show them how to share respectfully, guiding them through situations and modelling appropriate behaviour.

Enjoying competitive play

Through the primary school years and adolescence, children often enjoy competing and are more focused on outcomes. Help them to recognize that learning a new concept or skill is a process that involves mistakes. Also, that playing together, whether a ball game, a board game, or charades, is something that we choose to do voluntarily because we enjoy it. This helps children compete in a way that is healthy for their relationships.

Mutually enjoyable activities help children have fun participating and competing without feeling pressured to succeed.

FAMILY PROJECTS

Getting involved in a family project gives you and your child an opportunity to plan and work together and brings a sense of accomplishment. Ideally, such projects bring you closer and leave your child feeling that it was an enjoyable experience and that they also gained practical life skills.

Working together

Whether your family project is a large job that needs to be done in or around the house, or something you are making for your child to enjoy, the idea of working together is the real goal. Obviously, the practicality of the entire family working together depends on your own skills and the age of your children.

- Projects that could involve the whole family range from assembling a new bed or item of furniture for your child's bedroom to building a deck where the family can enjoy meals and spend time together outside.

- Creating a play area for your child, such as a sandpit, setting up outdoor play equipment, painting a small play table indoors, or even the construction of a treehouse can be something that the family undertakes together.

- A family project outside of the home could involve some sort of community service project. You might volunteer for a worthy cause, such as delivering meals or preparing food packages for needy families or helping out at a food bank, or work together, for example, to help clean up a public park or river bank.

Willing helpers

When you embark on a family project with your child, it is important to consider how they feel. Do you think they feel coerced into helping and possibly resentful, or do you think they are feeling that spending family time working together on something beyond their routine household chores is a positive experience?

As a parent, your aim is to help your child understand that each family member does need to help out in some way and that at times we do not always

Ages and stages

18 months–6 years
Your toddler may be aware that a project is underway. By three to four years, a child can have some supervised involvement. By five to six, they can handle child-sized tools and work independently on some parts of a project.

6–12 years
Your child may suggest a project or make a meaningful contribution to the planning process. They can learn a lot by helping. Find jobs they can do safely according to their age, strength, and maturity.

12–18 years
Adolescents should be able to plan, organize, and complete many projects on their own, or with some support. They can play a full role, planning and using tools correctly.

Collaborative projects teach your child about teamwork and completing tasks.

have a choice. To work in harmony on family projects, it is important to minimize stress and to disarm any squabbles that arise among family members as calmly as possible. This helps your child to come away from early experiences feeling positive about the time they spent working together or helping with a chore.

Realistic expectations

Be careful not to set unrealistic expectations for how long or how hard your child will work on a project and be practical about how much help they can give you at a certain age. Appreciate that their ability to maintain focus and

interest on a particular task and their level of commitment to completing a project are likely to differ from yours. The goal of embarking on family projects together is not simply to get the job done, it is to lead your child to understand that there are times when everyone needs to pitch in, and that this is a normal and positive part of family life. Ideally, your child will come away from a completed project with a sense that this was something you achieved by working together. Over time, they may develop a sense of shared responsibility and pride and accomplishment when a project is carried out successfully.

EVERYDAY STRATEGIES
A QUIET SPACE

We all experience emotions such as frustration, anger, disappointment, or loneliness. How we express these at times can be hurtful or damaging. In Montessori, all emotions are seen as part of life. We want to help children to recognize emotions, self-calm, and learn to express how they feel.

When your child is young, often their first instinct when upset is to cry, hit, or throw something. You can begin to help them recognize and identify feelings, giving them new vocabulary to start to express themselves with words rather than behaviour. Simply telling them to calm down is unlikely to work and can trigger fresh upset because they have not been taught how to do this. Instead you could say, "I can tell that you are upset/angry. Breathing deeply and slowly can help. Let's try it together."

Once you have introduced the idea of emotions to your child, at a family meeting, discuss creating a "quiet space" for each family member (see pp.158–159). This is a comfortable place where they can go when upset to calm down, coming back to the family when they feel better and are ready to interact appropriately.

The goal is not to punish but to teach – the true meaning of discipline (see p.40). Your child begins to learn about emotions, how these affect behaviour, and to behave more appropriately in future.

" "

A quiet space helps your child to think about their emotions and begin to see how these can affect their behaviour.

" " OUR STORY

When our children were about four and seven years old, we started to discuss the idea of creating a quiet place for each family member. When they were younger, we tried to help them put words to their emotions so that they could calmly express how they were feeling. Still, sometimes there were outbursts for one reason or another, so we thought quiet places might give each of us a place to go to calm down and feel centred.

Both Clark, the eldest, and Natalie were very enthusiastic about the idea of a quiet place. Clark wondered if his quiet place could be outside, dribbling and shooting his basketball into the hoop in our driveway. Natalie wanted to have an area in her bedroom for art work and a cosy space where she could snuggle up with her stuffed toy animals. I chose my small computer room where my music could be played, and my wife chose her rocking chair in our bedroom.

Although we weren't certain at first whether this strategy would work, we found that each person's idea worked for them. Our quiet spaces definitely helped when one of us needed some time alone to regroup. We still use those spaces today.

Robert and Ruth, parents of Clark, aged 14 and Natalie, aged 11

A QUIET SPACE IN PRACTICE

Talk about privacy

At the family meeting, discuss how each person's quiet space is a private place where they can be alone and calm down. It is the opposite of "time out", used by parents as a last resort and which can make children resentful and unlikely to reflect on behaviour.

Make it a joint decision

Work with your child to decide where their quiet space will be. Involving them in the decision helps them to feel that this is their chosen space and is most likely to lead to their cooperation and willingness to embrace the concept of a quiet, self-calming space.

A tool for all

Agree on a guideline that anyone in the family can suggest to another family member that it might be helpful for them to take a quiet break. Discuss this at the family meeting, when everyone is calm and there is a feeling of being part of a team.

Agree to accept suggestions

Make an agreement that each family member will listen to and cooperate with a parent's or sibling's suggestion to take a quiet break. If someone agrees to this at the meeting but does not carry through when a situation arises, try the strategies, opposite.

Create your quiet spaces

Discuss each person's space. Some find activity calming. The "what and where" could be a cosy corner; a rocking chair; playing a ball game; or being in the garden or a workshop. There might be books, cushions, music and headphones; a fish tank; paints or clay; or even a miniature Zen garden.

Avoid time limits

Do not set a time limit on the person taking a break. In contrast to "time out", a self-quieting space is designed to help your child self-regulate: to know when they are upset and need a break, to take time to think about a problem, and know when they are calm enough to rejoin the family.

When your child says "no"

If your child says "no" in words or actions when you ask them to visit their quiet space, try the following:

Bear in mind they may think it is a punishment, especially if an older child has experienced "time out" before. You may need to stay with them the first few times to let them know that this is a comforting place. Once they settle in leave them so they can experience self-calming on their own.

Be the model for your child. Go to your quiet place. Use strategies such as deep breathing or reading. Say, "I feel better now" on your return.

As a last resort, ask if they need your help going to their quiet space. If so, lovingly guide or carry them there.

"

A quiet space provides a place where family members can think about a situation and regain a sense of calmness.

A comfortable self-quieting space encourages self-reflection and helps to promote self-regulation.

ENJOYING NATURE TOGETHER

Montessori values include caring for and preserving our natural resources and the planet, and placing an emphasis on families spending time in nature. Being in nature together enhances relationships and helps your child to develop a strong sense of connection to the natural world. This might even lead to them becoming involved in the protection of the natural environment.

Observing nature

Studies show that children who connect with nature seem to be calmer and more grounded than those who spend more time indoors, often on digital devices. As a family, spending time in nature – whether gardening, walking in the park, hiking in woods, or consciously observing nature up close in any or all of these settings – is enjoyable, affordable, and good for the physical and mental health of all.

Spending time together in natural environments engenders a connection to, and respect for, nature.

- **Equip your child** with tools, such as a magnifying glass, a bug box or jar, and a small guidebook to help them collect and identify items you find on nature excursions. If you have space at home, you and your child could create a nature area to display your finds.

- **Help your young child** notice plants and animals at different stages of development. They can use their magnifying glass to observe objects such as eggs, perhaps taking photos of them before they hatch. Teach them the important lesson of not disturbing natural processes and letting creatures exist in their natural setting.

- **Help your child** become a detailed nature observer. Suggest they choose a place to sit, in your garden or other natural environment, and spend five minutes really looking closely at this spot. After five minutes, they can talk about, write, or draw what they noticed. Ask them questions about what they observed, such as, "What colours did you see in the grass? Did you see any insects? What sounds did you hear?".

- **Your older child** might like to keep a nature journal. This could be a written or photographic record, or you could encourage them to draw plants from nature, which might lead them to

---

Ages and stages

18 months–6 years
This is a crucial time in your child's development for connecting with nature. Spend as much time as possible outdoors: playing, exploring, eating, and relaxing, to help your child develop a deep sense of being part of the natural world.

6–12 years
Longer, more involved activities, such as staying up late to star gaze, hiking, and fishing, stimulate the mind now, as well as exercise the body and help families bond.

12–18 years
Teenagers may enjoy joining the family in activities such as jogging, cycling, camping, and canoeing. They may like to draw from nature and practise nature photography.

---

develop an interest in botanical illustration. Drawing from nature will help them to notice small details that they might otherwise miss. You could create a digital journal together, with video clips of the passage of time, perhaps recording something you both planted while it grows.

- **Encourage your child** to write poems and stories that capture the sense of wonder in nature.

OUT AND ABOUT: YOUNG CHILDREN

Whether going to the shops, the park, or on a longer outing, going out with children aged 18 months to six years involves ensuring you have everything you need to care for them away from home. With some thoughtful planning, this challenge becomes manageable.

Your child's needs

In Montessori-inspired homes, parents consciously show respect, empathy, understanding, and consideration for their children from birth onwards. This means planning ahead before leaving the house to make outings as comfortable and pleasant as possible for everyone. Whether your child adapts easily to changes in their routine, or struggles to cope with disruption, show them respect and consideration before leaving the house. Ask yourself why you are going out and whose needs will the trip meet: yours, your child's, or both of yours? Once you have decided on a trip, taking into account all your child's needs – for clothing and food throughout your trip – will help you plan. When you are out, being aware of the signs that your child is tired and irritable will also ensure that you are thinking of their needs.

A little independence

When toddlers and young children are engaged in play dates with friends at the park or spend time at a playground, they begin to move away from their parents slightly as they play. Naturally, you will stay close by to keep an eye on them, and they will return to you every so often to make sure that you are still there, but this activity means they are starting to experience a degree of independence. These are times when you can teach your child to stay within sight, to hold hands when crossing streets, and to take turns.

Thinking about stamina

When planning a family outing with your young child, bear in mind that, as well as being costly, large amusement parks or events with long queues and crowds of

When children are bored

Parents often worry about children being bored, for example, if an outing is not stimulating enough.

Encouraging your child from as young as two years of age to be creative and think for themselves means they will rarely be bored because they will learn how to find things to do, to build, or to discover for themselves. Conversely, when constantly entertained and engaged, they can feel at a loss if left to their own devices.

" " OUR STORY

Whether I'm heading out with my toddler for a few hours or for an entire day, I always try to prepare to ensure as smooth an outing as possible. For us, this looks like packing up some engaging activities for the inevitably long car ride – such as various books, mess-free art options, and anything that involves magnets – and a healthy snack or a picnic lunch.

I also make sure that I have all of the necessary clothing items, including extras, depending on the weather and our destination of choice. Knowing I have an extra outfit in the car allows me the mental ease of letting go of any worries I may have of them getting dirty, and I am able to let her explore her surroundings freely, which almost always includes getting wet and muddy!

Most importantly, I plan for plenty of time at the destination of choice. Allowing for ample time once we arrive takes away any unnecessary pressure of time constraints and gives her the respect and freedom to explore to her heart's content.

Lauren (@modernmontimama), mother of A, aged two and K, newborn

Being prepared before heading out with your young child demonstrates your consideration of their needs.

people can often end up as a stressful experience for younger children. This type of trip is better suited for older children who have more stamina and independence. When planning outings with your young child, opt for simpler, smaller activities without too many distractions. These activities can often provide fun learning experiences and, ideally, there will be plenty of space to move around in and relax.

OUT AND ABOUT: OLDER CHILDREN

When deciding on outings with primary school-aged children and adolescents, planning ahead is key to ensure that everyone is happy and to avoid power struggles or exhausted children having a meltdown. Your goal is to enjoy positive experiences that form lasting and loving memories.

Routine outings

Routine shopping trips or similar outings may be unavoidable with your child. However, many children do not enjoy shopping, unless it is to buy something that they want, and it is common for parents and children to feel frustrated.

If your child feels involved in a shopping trip they are likely to be more engaged, which will set both you and your child up for a more enjoyable experience. You could talk to them about what needs to be accomplished and they could help to prepare a shopping list. On a supermarket trip, ask a primary school-aged child to lead the way to different parts of the shop. Although you want them to stay close to you, you can help them to feel as though they are playing an important part by guiding the trolley carefully around other shoppers.

With an older child, consider a strategy for dividing up the shopping, perhaps putting them in charge of finding certain items on the list while you shop in another section.

Identifying shared interests

Family meetings (see pp.22–23 and 64–67) are the best place for families to explore what they wish to do in the week.

Use your weekly family meeting to list all the activities that members of your family currently enjoy doing together. The concept of doing things together that you all wish to do – rather than doing something that an individual is interested in – is crucial to ensure that everyone has a positive experience.

Bear in mind, too, that some family members like to set plans far in advance, while others might prefer to be more spontaneous. Being aware of these different preferences can help you balance each others' needs.

66 99

When your child feels involved in an outing, whether a routine shopping trip or a planned activity, they are more likely to be actively engaged.

Planned trips

Recreational activities are a chance to enjoy time together in new environments. You can expose your child to activities that involve being with others as well as experiences that require you to stay together and take care of each other.

- **Bear in mind that long journeys** can be challenging, so think carefully before routinely taking children on a long road trip. If you do need to travel far, try to turn the journey into a family bonding experience by singing together, conversing, playing games, telling stories, or listening to an audio book that everyone enjoys. Ideally, avoid downloading films and programmes onto devices that your child watches on their own. While this may stop them from becoming irritable, it means that family members are in their own worlds rather than bonding with each other.

- **Help your child to learn** how to enjoy experiences and notice what is going on. Find activities that the whole family will enjoy. This might be going on a hike at the weekend or enjoying hobbies together such as cycling, canoeing or kayaking, or fishing, where you can enjoy nature

and get some exercise. You might take binoculars to look for birds and wildlife together. Outings that involve visiting local fairs, farmers' markets, or a festival can open up new worlds to your child while also helping them to learn life skills such as moving calmly through a crowd.

The time spent getting to a destination provides a perfect opportunity to chat together without distractions.

SPECIAL OUTINGS

Enjoy outings with your child that are outside of your everyday norm, such as visiting a restaurant, museum, or a public event. These outings expose them to experiences that you feel are an important part of growing up, where they can learn about the community and culture in which they live, and may develop an interest in new activities, places, or ideas. You can also teach them how to behave politely, appropriately, and safely in a particular situation.

Ages and stages

18 months–6 years
Choose outings carefully now to minimize disruption to routines and avoid your child becoming overstimulated. Pack activities such as colouring books. Be ready to leave if they show signs of being tired.

6–12 years
Guide your child on how to behave in an audience or at a restaurant, how to stay safe at a public event, and how to manage on long journeys. Include them in planning snacks and activities.

12–18 years
Your teen should be quite independent when choosing clothing and packing for outings. Check on their plan without micromanaging.

What to consider
When choosing a special outing for the family, take into account the age of your child and their readiness. From an early age, you can begin to teach your child how to be well behaved and considerate of others in a new situation. However, do consider whether it is reasonable to ask your child to participate in a particular event or outing where you can predict they are likely to lose interest quickly or where you think they will lack stamina. For example, is your very young child likely to become restless and behave inappropriately in a restaurant?

Introducing new experiences
Special outings can help your child to develop new skills and an appreciation and understanding of a variety of experiences. You can help them learn to stretch their interests and begin to be aware of and appreciate new activities when you introduce them in the right way.

- **Before going out**, let your child know what the outing will involve, how you expect them to behave, and the appropriate dress for the outing.

- **When you introduce** your child to a new situation, it is wise to expose them only briefly at first. If, for example, they have to sit through a long play or an entire sporting event, this can leave them feeling tired

Introducing your child to new experiences, such as visiting a gallery, broadens their horizons.

and grumpy and also feeling reluctant to repeat the experience. Your aim is for them to think of the outing as a positive experience.

Choosing outings

Think about experiences that you believe will be exciting, affordable, and practical for your family, whether in your local community, a day trip close by, or as a holiday. Ideally, a family outing or holiday will help your child to become aware of the things your community and beyond have to offer. This could be a new type of cuisine, an exhibit at a local gallery, a play the whole family might enjoy, or enjoying new landscapes.

It is important to include older children, in particular, in planning during family meetings, as they will have their own ideas. You could give them an open-ended choice, discussing timings, costs, and points of interest. Or suggest two or three possibilities that you have considered in advance. This ensures that they are aware that you are considering a particular trip, helps them to get some idea of what the experience might be like, and, hopefully, makes them feel that they were part of the decision-making process.

EVERYDAY STRATEGIES
REFOCUSING MISBEHAVIOUR

No matter how many preventative strategies you put into place and how much you read up on parenting, your child will at times misbehave. They are in the process of trying to manage emotions, express their needs appropriately, and understand their boundaries and limits.

Your response to your child's behaviour can have a positive or negative effect on how they learn communication skills, resolve problems, and take responsibility for actions. Parental responses that uphold Montessori values include remaining calm when interacting with your child; recognizing that they are learning; avoiding taking their behaviour personally; and helping them to work through concerns. There are many reasons why a child's behaviour may be challenging, disruptive, or aggressive. Irritability and being out of sorts can be due to hunger, tiredness, feeling unwell, or sensitivity to changes. Being aware of your child's physical needs and thinking ahead help. Behavioural issues also arise when your child is trying to convey their emotional needs – to feel loved, to have control, to belong, and to feel valued (see p.38) The strategies on pages 170–171 will help you to deal with challenging behaviour that arises from these needs.

" "

Your child is learning to express their needs appropriately and to understand their boundaries and limits.

" " OUR STORY

We noticed that our eight-year-old daughter seemed to whine and fuss or simply disappear when it was time to do the least little thing, from getting her own breakfast to making her bed to choosing her clothes for an outing. We knew that she was perfectly capable of doing these everyday tasks on her own, but... it just wasn't happening.

So, I decided to break down the tasks into smaller steps that she could succeed at and build up her self-confidence. However, that didn't work and things seemed to get even worse. She became sadder and disappeared to her room more frequently. Finally, after looking for patterns and deciding that it wasn't a simple matter of, for example, her being tired, or trying to test limits, it dawned on me to check my own feelings when situations came up. When I began to pay attention to how I felt instead of just noticing my daughter's actions, I realized I was feeling annoyed. I was then able to look beyond my annoyance and see that what she really wanted was my attention.

She and I talked about how she was feeling and how she could talk to me about her thoughts, then we came up with some ideas to help her feel that she was loved and important. She asked if I could join her in cleaning her room sometimes. She also asked if we could have some snuggle and reading-together time before we turned the lights out at bedtime. It was amazing how easy it was to meet her needs when I realized what the whining and fussing were all about.

Jane, mother of Cheryl, aged eight

REFOCUSING MISBEHAVIOUR IN PRACTICE

A need to feel loved

If a child constantly seeks attention, even when you are busy, they need reassurance that you love them. Notice when they approach. Without talking, reach out with a loving gesture to signal to them to come closer. Do not halt your task. This simple action can help to avoid their behaviour escalating.

A need to feel some control

If your child challenges your authority, for example, refusing to do a task, they need to feel that they can make decisions. If a dispute is important, at a calm time, invite them to talk. Say you know that they feel nagged but a solution needs to be found. Work on one together, and stick gently to this.

A need to belong

If your child is unkind to you or others, they need assurance that you accept them, if not the behaviour, and that they are integral to the family. For example, a child may feel left out when a new baby arrives and say they hate them. Try saying, "I understand how you feel; the baby takes up my time, I'm sorry. Let's find ways to spend time together."

A positive gesture can reassure a child that they are loved, while you also signal that you have an important task to do.

A need to feel valued

If your child seems discouraged, they may need reassurance that they are capable. Break tasks down into steps. Encourage them to do the first step. Acknowledge this when it is done. You might finish the task, then next time encourage them to add a step so they build on small successes.

Dealing with power struggles

As well as talking to find a solution when your child challenges you (see opposite), there are some additional ways to deal with power struggles:

Give choices. These can be narrow choices, for example, deciding between two types of clothing.

Let go of your position. Sometimes we find it hard to listen to our child's ideas. Children can be very creative and may find a different solution that achieves the same goal. Be prepared to listen to their solutions.

Put them in charge. For example, if you are having a battle about a task, putting them in charge gives them a sense of leadership.

Use one word on tasks that you have already agreed they will do. For example, about loading the dishwasher, simply say "Dishes".

Agree a signal. If power struggles are frequent, find a signal that you can both use if you feel one starting, to remind you both to stop and start again.

THE BIRTH OF A CHILD

When a child is born, whether a first child or a sibling, it changes the family dynamic. Preparing for your baby's arrival involves practical considerations, such as reviewing the space in your home and the supplies that you will need, as well as preparing older siblings to welcome the new baby and working with your partner.

Being prepared

Think about the space available for sleeping, playing, changing, clothing, and feeding. If your new baby will need to share a bedroom with a sibling, talk to your older child about this to prepare them for their new roommate.

This is also the time for first-time parents to discuss parenting practices, discipline, and family values (see pp.20–21).

New family dynamics

With your new baby's arrival, much of the family focus will be on interacting with and caring for them. Nurture relationships during these years, spending time with your partner and sharing caregiving. A new baby can have a dramatic effect on older siblings, who can wonder where they fit into the family and feel that the new baby receives everyone's attention. Your goal is to help them feel a sense

" "

A baby's arrival can shift focus in a family, and siblings may need guidance to feel a sense of connection.

Showing your child how to handle and care for the baby, with your supervision, helps them to embrace their new sibling.

❝ ❞ OUR STORY

As any new parent, the birth of our first child brought feelings I had never felt or experienced before. With the waves of emotion, I felt a fuller person. I was proud, happy, and in love with my daughter and had dreams for her future. I also became more fearful and anxious for her and the world she was brought into.

When my wife was expecting our second child, our daughter fell in love with my wife's growing tummy. She listened, watched, and touched. We told her how her brother was growing. The day of the arrival came and I took her to her favourite shop to pick out a special present for her brother. We did this for our third child and in both cases the siblings were welcomed with complete joy. For the announcement of our fourth child, my wife came home with balloons and a cake. Two of our children celebrated. The other one broke down in tears and with great sadness cried out, "Another one!". Fast forward four years and our four children are with each other seven days a week, and live in love and peace... mostly.

David, father of Eden, aged 10, Eli, aged eight, Ewan, aged six, and Ethan, aged four

of family connection – that there is enough love for everyone and that they can play a key role as the older sibling. Before the birth, discuss what will happen, answer questions about how things will change, and reassure them that each family member is important. A child may hear these words and not take them seriously and may feel left out or resentful. Look for signs that they feel this way, listen if they voice concerns, and answer questions honestly to minimize worries or fears.

- **Invite siblings** to join in with welcoming the baby. They can help to prepare their room or pick out books for them.

- **After the birth**, depending on their age and interest, siblings can help bathe, feed, or read to the baby.

WHEN FAMILIES CHANGE

When families evolve and grow through adoption, fostering, or when two people with children from previous relationships become partners and form a blended family, often a number of new relationships between adults and children need to be forged and well-established routines adjusted.

Family structures

Each family is unique and families have many different faces. The strategies and guidelines discussed throughout this book apply to all family structures. In a home inspired by the Montessori ethos, the aim is to create an environment where children and other family members can grow and develop deep

❝ ❞

Whatever the make-up of your family, the aim of parents is to create a home where family members can develop deep bonds with each other.

bonds with each other. Hopefully, these bonds are profoundly positive, kind, mutually supportive, and filled with love and respect.

When households change, new relationships may need to be formed, for example, between older children and adults previously unknown to each other. Additional time and care may need to be taken to ensure that each person feels loved, heard, and that they belong, and also to help new family members learn to live together in harmony.

Challenges for families

When a new adult or adults come into a child's life, there are often many fresh challenges for the child to face.

With blended families, a child may have already been through the trauma of separation, divorce, or a parent dying. They face additional challenges when a new adult partners with their parent and becomes part of the child's life. It can be awkward or difficult for a child to accept, and hopefully come to love, a new parent figure. Children may also need to adjust to new siblings, whether these are the children of a parent's new partner, or children are joined together in families through adoption or fostering.

Some children can find this an incredibly joyful experience. Other children may feel sad, afraid, resentful, or confused. The process of helping

Creating a welcoming environment for a child helps to ease the transition into their new home.

children adjust to each situation requires a lot of patience, love, and everyday parenting skills.

- **If you are in a couple**, work closely to form a united parenting team. Try to understand what each child is going through, and present a warm, loving, and consistent set of guidelines as the new family dynamic evolves. With blended families, respect for all the members of all the families involved is sometimes the most challenging and the most important lesson for both children and adults to learn.

- **If older children**, originally from different households, are becoming part of the same household, allow the children time to get to know each other so they can settle in gradually to their new, expanded family. Give each family member in the household time to bond before taking a holiday or introducing a new family member to people in your extended family.

- **If you choose to foster or adopt**, involve any children of your own in the process. Talk to your children at a family meeting about what this means and how it could affect your family life.

- **Be patient**, kind, and consistent in helping new children to understand and become accustomed to a family culture and house rules (see pages 22 and 41) that may be different from the ones they are used to.

GUIDING SIBLINGS

The family is a safe place for siblings to learn to communicate, collaborate, share, and disagree, secure in their love for each other. As parents, our goal is to guide siblings through their interactions with each other and help them to develop the skills needed to create rich and loving relationships inside and outside of the family.

Respecting relationships

Each child is a unique human being and their relationship with a sibling may not be as you imagined it, or how you experienced sibling relationships as a child. Different personalities and interests as well as age differences between siblings can sometimes cause children either to be very close and share many interests, or to prefer to engage in their own activities.

Patterns of behaviour

Falling-outs between siblings are common in families, and, ultimately, you may have to get involved to help sort out disagreements. Whether one child is trying to get their sibling into trouble or is trying to get your attention, patterns of behaviour can develop. Watch for these patterns at different stages as your children grow. Try to stay calm and observe what is going on objectively and use strategies to short-circuit behaviour before it gets started or goes too far. Try the strategies on pages 108–111 to disarm squabbles; pages 156–159 for quiet, self-calming spaces; and pages 168–171 for refocusing common misbehaviours.

A secure sense of belonging

Your goal is to try to ensure that each child feels that they belong, that they are seen for who they are, that they are loved and respected, and that their voice matters.

- Teach your child that, while their voice is heard, they need to respect others and to not be mean or hurtful.
- Help your children to learn how to see, listen, and appreciate one another and how to support each member of the family.

Dealing with disagreements

Sibling rivalry is common in many families and can be challenging for all. This may take the form of a child vying for your attention by doing something that they believe will make you proud or elicit praise, but that actually creates disharmony within the family, or that tests your family's house rules (see p.41). Help your children to understand that there are consistent, fair, loving, and firm limits for behaviour within the family.

Using the weekly family meeting to discuss disagreements and come up with solutions; spending some private time with an individual child having a quiet conversation about squabbles with siblings; or engaging in a pleasant activity with the whole family, helps siblings to learn how to get along and resolve their disagreements.

- **Help siblings** to enjoy family activities harmoniously by giving each child the opportunity to lead and helping older children to recognize that younger siblings are learning about turn-taking.

- **Be aware of how you respond** to your children. Try to put judgments aside; focus on facts rather than emotions; and stay calm, firm, and consistent.

" "

Siblings sometimes have squabbles, but the family is a safe place for them to learn to communicate with each other.

Ensuring that children feel listened to and can see that family rules are applied fairly, helps siblings co-exist peacefully.

FAMILY TRADITIONS AND CELEBRATIONS

The traditions and celebrations that families enjoy create comforting patterns during the childhood years and help parents to underscore the message that their children are loved and cherished.

Celebrating the traditions passed down to us from our parents, perhaps creating a few new ones, and discovering the traditions of our own and other cultures and faiths, opens us to the wonder and delight of life. Certain celebrations, whether or not we formally belong to an organized faith, can also help us to teach our children in simple ways the moral and spiritual lessons of love, kindness, joy, and confidence in the fundamental goodness of life. Creating everyday routines that celebrate family life also fosters a sense of safety and security.

" "

Enjoying celebrations together and following and creating family traditions nurture your child's sense of joy and appreciation of life.

A SENSE OF WONDER

One of the most precious gifts that we can give our children, through celebrations and family traditions, is an education of the heart, nurturing their sense of joy and appreciation of life, providing a sense of the poetic, and connecting them to humanity.

Passing on traditions

Family life is often hectic and stressful and, all too soon, children shift their focus from family to friends.

- **Activities and events** such as birthdays, or a trip or holiday that you enjoy on an annual or regular basis, perhaps involving the whole family, are a chance to spend time together and to reconnect with our sense of curiosity and joy.

- **Family traditions** and celebrations can also help us to reconnect with nature. Children can help us get back in touch with the beauty of the world as we gather shells, shout into the wind, fly a kite, or leave a trail of footprints in the sand. Being alive to the beauty of our world and the seasons nurtures a spirit of inner peace and reverence for life. Without a sense of wonder, the world becomes commonplace, but, when we open ourselves to a sense of wonder, our souls can stir.

Customs such as annual holidays that strengthen bonds and create precious memories are deeply reassuring.

EVERYDAY TRADITIONS IN FAMILY LIFE

Family traditions can be both large and small. As well as annual festivities, acts of kindness and celebration can be woven into everyday family life. These small, thoughtful acts and activities enrich your child's world. Children will often remember, cherish, and pass on some of the day-to-day family rituals that you create and share.

Expressing gratitude

Creating traditions that help family members to express their thanks to each other regularly is an important part of family life. As well as starting family meetings with a moment to appreciate and acknowledge what family members may have done (see p.22 and p.66), you can also create simple, everyday ways for family members to record acknowledgments and express thanks to each other. By helping children to recognize the importance of expressing gratitude, we teach them social skills and help them to build strong relationships.

- **A "thank you" board** in the kitchen, or simply a piece of paper displayed on the fridge, can be a place for family members to say thank you to each other.

- **A "kindness" wreath** can be a fun way to express thanks. Each time someone notices a kindness, they add a ribbon to a wire frame, creating a colourful wreath.

- **In your child's early years**, slipping a note into their lunchbox can mean a great deal to them. You could leave a humorous, caring message, or perhaps just a few words of love and encouragement.

Simple, loving gestures can create a tradition that your child carries forward through their life.

Creating memories

Everyday traditions can also be created around mealtimes and at other moments when the family is all together. At meals, maybe at weekends, adorning the table with candles, flowers, and special dishes can add a touch of festivity, and thanks and gratitude can also be expressed now (see p.80).

After dinner, you could set aside time every now and then for a family literature activity. The idea of this tradition is to create a positive experience and fond memories and teach your child about enjoying non-screen based activities that include interaction with others and foster a love of literature. This might be just half an hour where you read aloud to one another, perhaps a poem or extract from a book, and share cherished tales before getting on with other activities such as hobbies, homework, or watching television.

This can encourage your child to think about and discuss a story or book that touches on emotions or sparks the imagination. When your child is old enough to read, if they wish, they can take a turn to read aloud. The experience should be fun and not a burden, so gauge if this is something they are happy to do.

Ages and stages

18 months–6 years
Establish a tradition of calling the family to dinner. You could sing a song, ring a bell, or quietly go about and invite each person to the table. At the table, you might have a tradition of saying a prayer of thanks or reading a poem before you start to eat.

6–12 years
At bedtime, ask your child what was the worst and best thing about their day; what made them laugh; and what did they learn?

12–18 years
As you would with a younger child, check in with your teenager in the evening. Reflect with them on their day and share something about your day.

" "

Small, everyday acts of kindness and celebration can become a part of your family life, creating traditions that your child may continue.

CELEBRATING THE SEASONS

Seasons mark the passing of time in our natural world. In many families, there may be traditions that are shared throughout the wider culture, and, of course, your family can create seasonal traditions of their own.

Observing the seasons

Whether seasonal changes are distinct or there is little difference from one season to the next, no matter where you live there are seasonal changes. Days grow longer or shorter, animals migrate to or from a region, plants flower and fruits ripen, wildlife offspring are born, or the weather may be drier or more rainy. Observing seasons teaches your child about the natural changes that occur over the year. Draw their attention to small details that they might overlook.

Marking the seasons

There are many ways that people celebrate the solstices, when we pass from one season to the next. Your family might choose to celebrate the beginning of a new season by placing something that is symbolic or representative of the season, either indoors or outside. These actions help young children to sense the passage of time and the continuity of the seasons. Your child can enjoy learning about why the items that you have chosen to bring into your home or to decorate your home with are connected to the seasons.

While the seasons may look different in each part of the world, and the traditions that are celebrated where you live may be different from elsewhere, there will almost certainly be common ways in which the passage of time is marked and the seasons celebrated. These rituals will normally involve decorations, foods, activities, and traditional events.

Ages and stages

18 months–6 years
Draw your child's attention to visible signs of a change of season, such as the first spring buds, and talk about the seasonal equinox. At around four to five years, enrol your child to help with seasonal decorations.

6–12 years
Your child takes great pleasure in helping with seasonal decor or projects. Help them understand the symbolism behind traditions.

12–18 years
Help your child recognize that they will be able to carry on seasonal traditions. Gently encourage them to participate or take the lead in traditions.

A **seasonal** nature table develops your child's awareness of the patterns of nature where you live.

- **Think of ways** to signal the seasons. In northern hemispheres, a pumpkin, or a wreath with colourful vines, leaves, nuts, and berries can signify autumn; while holly and evergreen branches announce winter. In subtropical areas, palm fronds may be gathered. A display of seasonal flowers or a basket filled with seasonal produce also celebrate the seasons.

- **Young children enjoy** thinking about and remembering things that are typically associated with the seasons. For example, winter coats, raking leaves, sledging, and cooking traditional dishes and hearty soups are associated with colder months.

- **Children love to gather** items that represent the seasons and special holidays. Keep some of them from year to year. Pack them away and joyfully take them out as part of your annual traditions. Other annual family traditions might include forcing bulbs to flower inside in spring, filling vases with branches from flowering trees or bushes, or growing tiny meadows of grass in baskets filled with potting soil.

CELEBRATORY FAMILY GATHERINGS

Many family gatherings centre around the life cycle of the family, with families gathering to celebrate or commemorate significant life events, depending on a family's beliefs, customs, and cultural traditions.

Celebrating anniversaries

Wedding anniversaries, birthdays, the anniversary of a death, cultural or national holidays, or annual reunions, are all times when families gather to celebrate their connection and reminisce.

Ages and stages

18 months–6 years
Try not to go overboard with birthdays. Create a tradition of celebrating your child's growth, keeping it simple, focusing on them, and letting family members share their love and appreciation for a child's unique qualities.

6–12 years
Help your child to appreciate what an occasion is about rather than think of it solely as a time to collect gifts.

12–18 years
Major rites of passage mark the transition to adulthood now. Help your child to focus on the symbolism of an occasion and on the dignity and importance of the milestone.

Wedding anniversaries are a chance to share photos and videos with your child. You can recount your special day and establish the idea of a family history.

Birthdays are particularly special for your child because they honour the start of their life and their awareness of time and history through their personal story. As well as a cake, gifts, and a birthday song, there are plenty of ways you can choose to mark this day.

- **Try introducing the idea** of the cycle and length of time that it takes the earth to rotate around the sun. Invite guests to sit in a circle. Place a candle in the middle to represent the sun and give your child a globe to represent the Earth. Say that it takes one year for the Earth to revolve around the sun, and that, since the day your child was born, it has travelled around the sun a set amount of times – the age of your child. While your child carries the globe slowly around the circle for each year of their life, recount a brief story and share photos from each year.

- **Light a special candle**. Gather around it and ask your child to share the most significant events of the last year and their dreams for the coming one. Express your hopes for them for the year ahead.

- **Every year**, add items to a time capsule for your child. Seal it and put it away, to be opened on their twenty-first birthday. Include photos, artefacts, and a letter from you, reminiscing about milestones and events. Your child can look forward to opening this storehouse of treasured memories.

Rites of passage

Formal rites of passage occasions, such as baptisms, graduations, weddings, or funerals, may involve your child sitting through a ceremony or attending an animated party that may overwhelm them.

Be respectful of your child and give thought to how they might participate, if at all. Avoid asking them to carry out a role that they will struggle with. Think about whether a young child will be able to behave appropriately in an audience, congregation, or celebration, and how you can help them to have a positive experience that does not disturb others.

Balance finding ways for them to participate and form memories and bonds with being sensitive to what they can cope with. For example, you might arrange for them to attend just for a short time, to form a special memory.

Gathering to celebrate an anniversary gives families a sense of belonging, togetherness, and shared love.

INDEX

REFERENCES

Page 100, Bedtime: Older Children
"Adolescent changes in homeostatic and circadian regulation of sleep", *Developmental Neuroscience*, 2017, DOI: 10.1159/000216538

FURTHER READING

The Discovery of the Child, Maria Montessori, The Clio Series, Vol. 2, 1997

The Child in the Family, Maria Montessori, Montessori-Pierson Publishing Company, 2007

Montessori from the Start, Paula Polk Lillard and Lynn Lillard Jessen, Schocken Books (a division of Random House Books, Inc), 2003

Montessori for a Better World, Aline D. Wolf, Parent Child Press (a division of Montessori Services), 2017

How to Raise an Amazing Child: The Montessori Way (2nd edition), Tim Seldin, DK Publishing, 2017

ACKNOWLEDGMENTS

The authors would like to thank their families for their patience and support now and over the years. They are definitely the "wind beneath our wings". We also appreciate our many friends and colleagues who offer advice and counsel, which have been invaluable during our careers.

Dorling Kindersley would like to thank the following for their contributions:

Alicia Diaz-David @montessibaby @teachlearnmontessori

Chaneen Saliee @chaneensaliee

Carine Robin @montessorifamilyuk

Lauren Weber @modernmontimama

Claire Wedderburn-Maxwell for proofreading and Vanessa Bird for indexing.

ABOUT THE AUTHORS

Tim Seldin is the President of the Montessori Foundation and Chair of the International Montessori Council. During his more than 40 years of experience in Montessori education, Tim served as a Montessori guide, Headmaster of the Barrie School in Silver Spring, Maryland (which was his own alma mater from age two through to high school graduation), and as Executive Director of the NewGate School in Sarasota, Florida.

Tim was the co-founder and Director of the Institute for Advanced Montessori Studies, and the Center for Guided Montessori Studies. He earned a BA in History and Philosophy from Georgetown University, an M.Ed in Educational Administration and Supervision from The American University, and his Montessori certification from the American Montessori Society. Tim is the author of several books on Montessori education, including *How to Raise An Amazing Child*; *Building a World-class Montessori School*; *The Montessori Way* with Dr Paul Epstein; *Finding the Perfect Match – Recruit and Retain Your Ideal Enrollment*; *Master Teachers – Model Programs*; *Starting a New Montessori School*; *Celebrations of Life*; and *The World in the Palm of Her Hand*.

Tim is the father and step-father of five former Montessori students and grandfather of a new generation of Montessori students. He lives on a small vineyard north of Sarasota, Florida, with his wife, Joyce St Giermaine, and their horses, dogs, and cats.

Lorna McGrath is the Director of the Montessori Family Alliance, a division of the Montessori Foundation and host of the Montessori Family Life Webinar Series.

During her career in education, she has taught in Montessori classrooms for three–six-year-olds as well as in the public sector for middle and high school students. She spent many years as the Associate Head of NewGate School in Sarasota, Florida, and is a member of its Board of Trustees. She is an adult educator in several Montessori Teacher Education Centers in the US and China. She received her BS in Home Economics Education, an M.Ed with a concentration in Family Counselling, and holds an American Montessori Society teacher's credential. She is a trained parenting instructor and is the creator of *The Parenting Puzzle: The Basics*, a course that helps align home practices with Montessori values and principles.

Lorna and her husband, Larry, enjoy interacting with their adult children who grew up in Montessori schools. They are especially thrilled that their grandson attends a Montessori school now. In her spare time, Lorna loves gardening, making quilts and other sewing projects, and travelling with Larry.

Project Editor Claire Cross
Project Designer Vanessa Hamilton
Senior Designer Barbara Zuniga
Managing Editor Dawn Henderson
Managing Art Editor Marianne Markham
Senior Production Editor Tony Phipps
Senior Jacket Designer Nicola Powling
Jacket Coordinator Lucy Philpott
Art Director Maxine Pedliham
Publishing Director Katie Cowan

Illustrator Yeji Kim

First published in Great Britain in 2021
by Dorling Kindersley Limited
DK, One Embassy Gardens, 8 Viaduct
Gardens, London, SW11 7BW

The authorised representative in the EEA is
Dorling Kindersley Verlag GmbH. Arnulfstr. 124,
80636 Munich, Germany

Copyright © 2021 Dorling Kindersley Limited
A Penguin Random House Company
10 9 8 7 6 5 4 3 2 1
001–322814–August/2021

A CIP catalogue record for this book is
available from the British Library.
ISBN: 978-0-2414-8156-1

Printed and bound in China

For the curious
www.dk.com

This book was made with Forest Stewardship Council™
certified paper – one small step in DK's commitment to
a sustainable future. For more information go to
www.dk.com/our-green-pledge

MERCEDES
IN MOTORSPORT

MERCEDES
IN MOTORSPORT

PIONEERS TO PERFECTION
By **Alan Henry** Foreword by **Norbert Haug**

Front endpaper: Rudolf Caracciola's Mercedes W125 heads Bernd Rosemeyer's Auto Union through Casino Square in front of the Hotel de Paris during the controversial 1937 Monaco Grand Prix when his team-mate Manfred von Brauchitsch won the race against team orders. (Ludvigsen Library)

Rear endpaper: Fangio (no.18) and Kling on their way to a decisive 1–2 finish, Reims 1954. (DaimlerChrysler Classic Archive)

First published in February 2001

A catalogue record for this book is available from the British Library

ISBN 1 85960 658 X

Library of Congress catalog card no. 00-135964

Haynes North America Inc.,
861 Lawrence Drive, Newbury Park,
California 91320, USA.

Published by Haynes Publishing, Sparkford,
Nr Yeovil, Somerset BA22 7JJ, UK.

Tel: 01963 442030 Fax: 01963 440001
Int.tel: +44 1963 442030 Fax: +44 1963 440001
E-mail: sales@haynes-manuals.co.uk
Web site: www.haynes.co.uk

Designed by G&M,
Raunds, Northamptonshire
Printed and bound in England by
J. H. Haynes & Co. Ltd, Sparkford

CONTENTS

FOREWORD

*by Norbert Haug, Mercedes-Benz Motorsport Director
and Vice President of DaimlerChrysler*

*Norbert Haug …
committed to excellence.*
(DaimlerChrysler
Classic Archive)

MERCEDES-BENZ HAS THE LONGEST established tradition in motorsport of just about any automobile manufacturer in history. From the early years of last century, through to the achievements of the legendary Silver Arrows in the 1930s to Fangio's two World Championships, and on to the present day and our close connection with McLaren, the Mercedes name has always been associated with a commitment to excellence and a determination to succeed on the race tracks of the world.

Yet I would like to think it is more than that. Everybody who works at Mercedes is proud of the historic silver thread of motorsporting tradition which we cherish and encourage.

We have also always been keen to encourage enthusiastic and talented young drivers. In the 1930s that tradition was established when Mercedes team manager Alfred Neubauer used to conduct tests for promising young hopefuls at the Nürburgring, and I am very satisfied that we have maintained such forward-thinking traditions in the present era.

ACKNOWLEDGEMENTS

THERE ARE MANY PEOPLE who have helped field my detailed queries during the course of the research for this volume. Foremost amongst them I would like to thank Norbert Haug, the Mercedes-Benz Motorsport Director, and now a Vice President of DaimlerChrysler, not only for his patient assistance but also for contributing the Foreword. My friend Wolfgang Schattling, who is responsible for Mercedes motor racing press and public relations, also went out of his way to assist with valuable information and by steering me in the right direction.

His colleagues Xander Heijnen and Frank Reichert were consistently willing and helpful, while both Max-Gerrit von Pein, Director DaimlerChrysler Classic, together with Thomas Weimper and his colleagues of the DaimlerChrysler archives team, offered valuable assistance with photographs and other crucial information.

I would like to thank Wolfgang Wilhelm for his excellent work as MB's official photographer at the races over recent years. Much of his work is also featured in the later section of this book. Also thanks and appreciation to Paul Parker at Ludvigsen Associates in London for filling some crucial gaps in the photographic coverage.

For reflecting on happy days past, my sincere thanks go to Sir Stirling Moss, Hans Herrmann, Jochen Mass, Manfred von Brauchitsch, Eugen Böhringer, Desmond Titterington, Rauno Aaltonen, Chris Nixon, Günther Molter and Stuart Turner; to Graham Robson for valuable help in putting the early 1960s rally scene into a clearer perspective; to Nigel Roebuck for interview material with Karl Kling and other crucial information; to Doug Nye for his help in marshalling personal recollections of our mutual friend, the late Denis Jenkinson; to Tim Wright at LAT Photographic; to John Evans, formerly of Mercedes-Benz UK; and to David Tremayne for checking material about Mercedes' record-breaking efforts before the war. I was also delighted to have the opportunity to speak with John Dugdale, shortly before he died, about his time as a staff writer for *Autocar* in the 1930s when he was a good friend of Dick Seaman.

On contemporary Mercedes racing issues I would like to thank a friend of 30 years standing, Ron Dennis CBE, now Chief Executive Officer and Chairman of the TAG McLaren Group. He, together with Adrian Newey, Professor Jurgen Hubbert, Jo Ramirez, Martin Whitmarsh, Mika Hakkinen, David Coulthard, Mark Blundell, Mauricio Gugelmin and Mario Illien have helped me steadily to glean much information over several seasons.

Finally, my appreciation is due to my long-time colleague Maurice Hamilton for fascinating material from an interview with Al Unser Jr about the Mercedes pushrod engine development programme which led to the American driver's memorable Indy 500 victory for the works Penske team in 1994.

Alan Henry
Tillingham, Essex
January 2001

INTRODUCTION

THIS VOLUME IS INTENDED to offer an essentially anecdotal over-view of the racing achievements of Mercedes-Benz. It involves examining a remarkable motor racing heritage, from 1894, when the primitive Daimler V2 engine won the world's first motor race, to the moment when Mika Hakkinen clinched his second World Championship title driving for the McLaren-Mercedes team in the very last Grand Prix of the millennium, and on through the maiden season of the new century.

The Mercedes-Benz brand has always pursued motor racing for two distinct purposes. First, for its advertising and promotional value. Second – and perhaps even more crucially – because its mechanics, designers, engineers and directors believe that motorsport is a crucible for technical development which can produce spin-offs that benefit production cars.

Bearing in mind the depth of Mercedes's involvement over the decades and the diversity of its achievement, one could have expected the company to take a rather self-satisfied view of its history. That is far from the case. Whereas during the 1950s Enzo Ferrari was quite happy to push his obsolete Grand Prix cars out of the racing depart-

Count Zborowski at the wheel of a Mercedes, no. 26, at the last time control point before reaching the end of the long-distance Paris-Vienna race in 1902. (David Hodges Collection)

ment to rot in lean-to sheds in the open, Mercedes has always been extremely committed to maintaining links with its motor racing heritage.

Many Mercedes competition cars from generations past are not only displayed in the extensive museum at the company's Stuttgart-Unterturkheim headquarters, but are also regularly and meticulously prepared by a dedicated department for display and demonstration throughout the world.

As long ago as 1958 Peter Collins and Tony Brooks thrilled spectators at Oulton Park with demonstrations of pre-war Mercedes Grand Prix cars – and the Stirling Moss/Denis Jenkinson 1955 Mille Miglia-winning 300SLR has probably covered almost as many miles in demonstrations over the past 45 years as it did during its active competition career.

Moreover, the Mercedes racing history is regularly harnessed as a dynamic promotional tool. For example the launch of the current E-class models in Britain was celebrated by an advertisement in which a silver saloon lined up alongside the legendary 1955 Mille Miglia 300SLR still carrying its winning number 722. Even more recently, there was a light-hearted portrayal of a black A190 being apparently serviced by the McLaren-Mercedes pit crew at a

Three generations of race-bred Mercedes: the 1999 McLaren-Mercedes MP4/14 which carried Mika Hakkinen to his second World Championship; the prototype of the sensational Mercedes McLaren SLR coupé which will be built at McLaren's new technology centre, Paragon, near Woking, from 2003; and the one-off, race-derived 300SLR 'gullwing' coupé used by racing engineer Rudolf Uhlenhaut as his high performance road car in the mid-1950s. (DaimlerChrysler)

Class act. For the 1994 DTM season the baton was assumed by the new C-class Mercedes saloon which had taken over from the 190 range as the 'Baby Benz'. (DaimlerChrysler)

London kerbside, while a traffic warden looks on. This is powerful, almost subliminal, imagery. But it works well.

Yet it is the anecdotes, memories and gossip from generations of motor races past which have really drawn me into writing this volume. Many of the leading players, particularly from the pre-war era, are now long gone, so I have been left no choice but to use an interpretive approach.

With that in mind, I hope the Mercedes enthusiast will approach this book in an indulgent frame of mind. If you feel, for example, that I have been too hard on Dick Seaman for what appears to be an overtly selfish personal life, too indulgent towards Hermann Lang, who seems to have been the most charming and self-effacing of the pre-war Mercedes drivers, and a touch ambivalent towards the legendary team manager Alfred Neubauer, who many I spoke to regarded as a little too much of a showman, then I will quite understand.

The fascination of carrying out what amounts to journalistic archaeology in assessing some of the key players in the Mercedes-Benz racing story has certainly been an absorbing task. Right or wrong, I hope it will hold the readers' attention.

FOUNDATIONS, 1894–1914

THE FIRST RECORDED MOTORISED competition was the Paris-to-Rouen trial in 1894, organised by the Parisian newspaper *Le Petit Journal* to publicise the fledgeling motor car. With a first prize of 5,000 francs, this was a well-supported event. Those were pioneering days when anything seemed possible. Of the 102 machines offered for entry there were no fewer than 20 differing means of propulsion. Some 30 had petrol engines. There were also 28 steam cars, vehicles propelled by compressed air, gravity, levers or springs – and even one which claimed

to derive its power from the weight of its passengers alone. Only 21 of these aspiring competitors were accepted, 13 of which were powered by a Daimler V2 engine manufactured in France under licence.

The judges were looking for vehicles that demonstrated safety, economy and ease of handling over the 80-mile race distance, rather than sheer speed. In the end, a 20hp De Dion Bouton steam car finished first, in front of a couple of Daimler-engined Peugeots and a Panhard Levassor. But first prize was shared between the Panhard and the Peugeot,

Baron Henri de Rothschild at the wheel of his 35hp Mercedes at the 1901 Nice race meeting which was so heavily promoted by Emil Jellinek, whose young daughter's christian name would become famous around the world. (DaimlerChrysler Classic Archive)

while second place went to the De Dion Bouton 'which, although first from the point of view of time, did not fulfil the conditions of the contest'.

That V2 engine was the brainchild of Gottlieb Daimler (1834–1900), whose name would be partnered with that of Carl Benz (1844–1929) to become one of the most famous car makers of all time. In an industry with a notoriously high attrition rate, it was not until more than 100 years later, when the global alliance was forged between Daimler-Benz and the Chrysler Corporation in 1998, that the famous Daimler-Benz name was consigned to the history books.

Gottlieb Daimler was a far-sighted man. In some notes penned in 1894 he observed: 'Success is always the surest indication of fulfilment of purpose and it represents the true value of a new invention, particularly if the latter becomes firmly and permanently established.' Gottlieb

Daimler had built his first car in 1886, powered by a derivation of the single-cylinder engine he had originally designed three years earlier. By then Carl Benz had been in business for three years, establishing Benz & Co. Rheinisch Gasmotoren, based in Mannheim, which would become the parent company of the Benz firm.

Ten years on, cars were becoming ever more sophisticated, with Daimler machines moving from two- to four-cylinder engines. Sadly, during August 1899 Gottlieb Daimler's health began to deteriorate and he died on 6 March 1900. Thereafter, his lifelong friend Wilhelm Maybach assumed all responsibility for the technical work previously borne by Daimler.

Benz had turned out a total of 2,000 cars by the end of 1899 and his company's annual production was now just short of 600 machines. This made Benz the world's leading car maker in terms of output and its sales were handled by

In the 1903 Gordon Bennett race Camille Jenatzy won by almost 12 minutes, making an average speed of 49.2mph for the entire 327.5-mile distance. (David Hodges Collection)

agencies as far afield as Berlin, Dresden, Krefeld, Paris, London, Brussels, St Petersburg, Moscow, Vienna, Milan, Basle, Buenos Aires, Singapore, Mexico City and Cape Town. Interestingly, despite the obvious interest that motor racing had aroused in many countries, Carl Benz seemed ambivalent about participating. On the one hand he could accept that it added to the development of the touring car, which was the rationale of racing, but it had been very much against his wishes that Emile Roger, his representative in Paris, took part in that first trial from Paris to Rouen. However, as reports of the 1894 event repeatedly referred to the car as a 'Roger' rather than a 'Benz' he decided that two of his own cars should contest the first Paris-Bordeaux-Paris road race the following year.

In November 1895, a Benz car also took part in the first motor race in the USA, while the first competition in which Benz cars competed in Germany took place in 1898 over a 33.5-mile road circuit linking Berlin-Potsdam-Berlin. It was during the Nice competition week in 1899 that the name Mercedes appeared. Using this pseudonym – the first name of his ten-year-old daughter – Emil Jellinek entered in the 23hp Daimler Phoenix which had just been completed. In his great enthusiasm for motoring, Jellinek had over the previous two years ordered a number of Daimler cars and, thanks to his social prominence among what would today be described as the 'jet set' on the French Riviera, this Austrian businessman and entrepreneur played a significant role in establishing the company's reputation.

Unfortunately, in March 1900, Daimler driver Wilhelm Bauer – factory foreman at the Cannstatt plant and an excellent driver – was killed competing in the La Turbie hill climb, near Nice. As a result of this disaster the Daimler factory decided to withdraw from motoring contests. But Jellinek robustly opposed this policy and lobbied the company to reverse its stance, maintaining that what was needed was a car with a lower centre of gravity and a longer wheelbase. Supported by Maybach, Jellinek eventually won the argument, not least because he said that he was prepared to buy a series of cars from the Daimler factory. However, he made the order on the condition that he was to have the sole rights to sell these cars in Austria, Hungary, France and America where they would be named 'Mercedes'. In all other countries, they were to be known as the 'New Daimler'.

Thus the first Mercedes car proper was despatched to Pau, in south-west France, for its maiden race on 17 February 1901. Unfortunately, the new machine had been very hurriedly prepared and jammed in gear shortly after the start and had to be retired. Jellinek was not impressed. The Cannstatt factory was soon under pressure to ensure that the car was in perfect order for the forthcoming 'Nice week' which lasted from 25–29 March and was particularly important to the patron of the project.

As things transpired, all was well. On the La Turbie hill climb, for example, Wilhelm Werner averaged 31.9mph in the new Mercedes compared with the 19.5mph achieved the previous year by the Daimler Phoenix. Werner also won the 244-mile road race from Nice to Aix-en-Provence and back. It was reportedly something of an eye-opener for many spectators when the same car which had won the long-distance race, the hill climb and the one-mile sprint during this festival of speed could be seen driving through Nice barely a quarter of an hour after the end of the last event, an elegant four-seater tourer. Paul Meyan, the General Secretary of the Automobile Club de France, remarked with great perspicacity: 'We have entered the Mercedes era'.

The name Mercedes became rapidly established. Moreover, its fame would not simply be confined to those countries mentioned in the contract with Jellinek. In due course Mercedes became the name for the products of the Daimler-Motoren-Gesellschaft (DMG) and in 1902 was registered as an official patent and trademark.

The next two years saw considerable development at the Daimler factory and by 1903 the company had produced a 90hp machine which averaged 74.3mph at the Nice races. After this it was decided to enter one of these cars in the

Gordon Bennett road race in Ireland. Disastrously, just a few weeks before the event the factory at Cannstatt, together with the 90hp racing cars, were totally destroyed in a devastating fire. This resulted in the German team having to use the smaller 60hp cars loaned back to the factory by several obliging private owners. After the fire, a new plant was erected on the site of what has become the present DaimlerChrysler HQ at Untertürkheim.

The 1903 Gordon Bennett race, held on a closed circuit of roads near Dublin, saw a trio of 60hp Mercedes ranged against three 40hp Napiers, two 100hp Panhards, one 80hp Mors, two 80hp Winstons and an 80hp Peerless. At the wheel of one of the Mercedes, Camille Jenatzy won the race by almost 12 minutes, making an average speed of 49.2mph for the entire 327.5-mile distance. It was regarded as the most important victory in the short history of the marque. One contemporary magazine report noted: 'With these vehicles, which before the race had had a rather gruelling journey from Cannstatt to Ireland, the Mercedes team beat everyone, and this victory must be regarded as the triumph of all that is best in motor engineering'.

Otto Salzer at the wheel of the chain-driven, four-cylinder 130hp Mercedes at the 1908 French Grand Prix. (DaimlerChrysler Classic Archive)

CAMILLE JENATZY
Obsessed with engineering

This red-bearded Belgian was born in Brussels on 4 November 1868. As a young man scarcely out of his teens he was obsessed with engineering, the intricacies of bicycles and the fledgeling internal combustion engine. His father had founded Belgium's first rubber processing plant, but Camille was extremely keen to develop an electric car and pursued this technology with considerable zest.

Eventually, however, he convinced himself that while such power units were fine for short sprint events, a proper piston-engined machine was necessary if he was to go racing seriously. Consequently he purchased a 16hp Mors which he raced with intermittent success, eventually building his own car which he crashed heavily in the 1902 Circuit des Ardennes. He was about to give up racing for good and concentrate his efforts on the family tyre business when the Mercedes team offered him the ride which saw him win the 1903 Gordon Bennett victory. The following year he would return to the same event and finish second.

Thereafter, it was downhill for Jenatzy's career. In 1905 he failed to finish the Gordon Bennett event, the Vanderbilt Cup and the Circuit des Ardennes. In the inaugural French Grand Prix in 1906 he was running almost last when he dropped out. At the end of 1907, when he was 39, Mercedes dispensed with his services. He briefly raced a Mors the following year but then retired for good.

On 7 October 1913, Camille Jenatzy was seriously wounded in a shooting accident during a wild boar hunt. He died in his own Mercedes as his friends rushed him to hospital.

Camille Jenatzy takes the start of the 1903 Gordon-Bennett race in Ireland at the wheel of the 60hp Mercedes, in this case a car borrowed from a customer as a hastily-arranged stand-in for the 90hp machine which had been destroyed in a disastrous fire at the Cannstatt factory. He won that race … (DaimlerChrysler Classic Archive)

… and finished second the following year. (David Hodges Collection)

The epic town-to-town races had by now become unacceptably dangerous. The 1903 Paris-Madrid road race had wrought carnage among competitors and spectators through a succession of accidents with primitive machines plunging into the crowds who lined the very edge of the route. Henceforth international racing increasingly developed on closed circuits, which were more organised and tightly controlled, but still laid out on public highways.

The first official 'Grand Prize' took place in 1906 at Le Mans. Grandstands, pit areas, and safety fencing were erected at a circuit to the east of the city. A specially laid wooden road linked two sections of the Routes Nationales, along which much of the circuit was organised. The Grand Prix de l'ACF – in effect the first official French GP – was

won by Hungarian driver Ferenc Szisz whose Renault took over 11 hours to complete the course. He achieved an average speed of 63mph which was quite astonishing considering how his car's solid tyres and cart-sprung suspension must have reacted to the bumpy, rutted roads on which the event took place.

To prevent Mercedes from swamping the field, the cunning French organisers had limited each team's entry to no more than three cars. The Mercedes cars were driven by Jenatzy, Vincenzo Florio – who would later co-found the legendary Targa Florio road race in Sicily – and the little-known Mariaux.

The 769-mile race was a gruelling affair, split over two days. Competitors had to cover six laps on each day. After

Victor Hémery's Benz, which finished second at the 1908 French Grand Prix, leaves Pierrons's Motobloc after an incident at Eu. (David Hodges Collection)

the first day the cars were placed overnight in a *parc fermé*, and then resumed next day at time intervals corresponding to their previous finishing positions, a staggered system which made the race extremely difficult for spectators to follow.

On the second day Jenatzy was suffering with eye problems which prevented him from taking part, so his place was taken by J.T. Burton-Alexander, a newcomer who had never driven on the circuit before. But a combination of inexperienced drivers, tyre problems, and poor track conditions conspired to ensure that the Mercedes runners finished the event as distant also-rans.

By 1907, although technical development might have been painfully slow and unco-ordinated, the idea of a 'Grand Prix formula' was now becoming established. Initially this was based on fuel consumption, with around

30-litres per 100km permitted. Szisz's success at Le Mans ensured that this would become one of the most highly-regarded events on the fast-expanding international racing calendar.

In 1907 the race was won by Felice Nazzaro in a Fiat, and again Mercedes was decisively outclassed. Paul Daimler – Gottlieb's oldest son, who became Technical Director of the company in 1902 – had extensively revised the Mercedes GP challenger, with a short wheelbase, wider track and lower centre of gravity, although not as low as many of its key rivals. That season the French Grand Prix was switched to a 47.74-mile circuit close to Dieppe. After the experience of the protracted race the previous year, the organisers decided to shorten the event to ten laps, again split over two days. The three Mercedes entries were driven by Jenatzy, Otto

Théodore Pilette brings his Mercedes to the pre-race examination before the 1913 French Grand Prix at Le Mans. Pilette, Mercedes' Belgian agent, had been refused entry for the Grand Prix at Amiens which was for manufacturers only. However he brought a team of four white Mercedes cars to Le Mans – and took a third and fourth, the last chain-driven cars to race at Grand Prix level. (David Hodges Collection)

CHRISTIAN LAUTENSCHLAGER
Long and loyal service

Christian Lautenschlager's life embraced the first half century of cars and motorsport and, in particular, some of the most spectacularly successful years for the Mercedes marque to whose legend he made his own fair contribution.

Born in Magstadt, near Stuttgart, on 14 April 1877, he began working for the Daimler company aged 22 and quickly attracted the attention of both Gottlieb Daimler and Wilhelm Maybach. Although quite a modest personality, Lautenschlager developed a shrewd taste for financial reward. In 1908 he would collect the lion's share of 80,000 gold marks which were put up as the prize fund for the French GP at Dieppe which he won commandingly. After that, Lautenschlager retired to work in the factory and would not reappear until the 1913 French Grand Prix where he finished sixth.

On 4 July 1914 – the day after the assassination of Archduke Franz Ferdinand in Sarajevo, which would trigger the First World War – Lautenschlager produced what was perhaps his greatest victory, leading Louis Wagner and Otto Salzer home for a Mercedes 1–2–3 finish in the French Grand Prix at Lyon.

After the war, Lautenschlager remained the Mercedes factory's principal driver, although he only drove in occasional events and never matched his pre-war pace. The 1924 Targa Florio was his final race outing after which he worked in the Mercedes factory for the rest of his life.

In the spring of 1954, Christian Lautenschlager died in his sleep in the cottage which had been provided for him in his retirement by Daimler-Benz in recognition of his long and devoted service to the company. A fittingly untragic end, perhaps, for one of the survivors from the pioneering days of motorsport.

Christian Lautenschlager's Mercedes developed 140hp at 1,600rpm at the 1908 French Grand Prix, and won, despite nine changes of tyres. (David Hodges Collection)

Salzer and Victor Hémery. Salzer ran fourth on the opening lap, but eventually fell back and retired. At the chequered flag the sole surviving Mercedes, driven by Hémery, finished tenth.

Things would be dramatically different in 1908, however, despite predictions that the French would retain the upper hand. Halfway through the race six out of the nine German cars were lying in the top ten places, in stark contrast to just four of the 24 French entries. Christian Lautenschlager's Mercedes developed 140hp at 1,600rpm – not bad from a 12.7-litre engine! – and while the car was extremely modern in most respects, its chain-drive to the rear axle was a transmission system antique in the extreme. Even at this early stage in the development of the automobile, of the 48 competitors who started in Dieppe, 19 had propeller shaft transmissions. It is also worth mentioning that Paul Daimler and his colleagues were certainly receptive to the issue of driver safety, if only by the primitive standards of the age. For the first time in a racing Mercedes, the rear bodywork was designed to come up to the driver's hips, thereby offering a degree of basic protection in the event of an accident.

Despite being forced to change his tyres no fewer than nine times, Lautenschlager eventually came home a convincing winner. 'The Mercedes pilot drove very consistently,' wrote Gerald Rose, a contemporary observer. 'In the corners he took no unnecessary risks, preferring to use the power of his car on the straight, prolonging the life of his tyres into the bargain.' On the face of it, the outsider had come home! Bookmakers around the circuit had quoted Lautenschlager at 8/1 against, but a small group of punters had still taken the chance and now found themselves rewarded.

Meanwhile, there had been changes in the key personnel within the DMG organisation. Most notable was the departure of the highly-regarded Wilhelm Maybach who had picked up the engineering torch which had maintained the company's reputation in the years following the death of Gottlieb Daimler. This great engineer never worked again in a similar role through to his death in 1929.

In 1909, faced with a Europe-wide recession, Benz and 15 other companies, including Daimler, signed an agreement not to take part in major motor racing events until further notice. It was widely felt that the current over-engined GP cars had become too expensive a luxury. This deal – signed by all the car makers, with a $20,000 penalty in the event of a breach – remained in force until 1912. It did not, however, prevent them from supplying cars for privateers wanting to compete.

The French Grand Prix was duly revived in 1912 and a

Mercedes was developed for the 1914 race to a new formula that limited engine capacity to 4.5 litres. This machine had a four-cylinder engine developing 115bhp at a then remarkable 3,200rpm and duly provided the means for Lautenschlager to score his memorable second victory (see sidebar).

In that race, Max Sailer – who later became plant manager at Untertürkheim, head of the racing department in the 1930s and eventually chief engineer of Daimler-Benz AG – ran ahead of the pack as 'hare', trying to force the opposition into racing at an unnecessarily gruelling pace. Although Lautenschlager won thanks largely to his strategy of frequent tyre changes, his veteran team-mate Louis Wagner shrugged such considerations aside. In his view, tyre changes represented an unnecessary interruption to the progress of the race.

After the race the three cars returned to Untertürkheim where the drivers were duly fêted by the factory workforce. Then the winning car was transported to Berlin for a week's display before being shipped to London where it was to be exhibited in the UK importer's showroom in Shaftesbury Avenue. Alas, by the time the Mercedes arrived in London the First World War was four days old and the car, as Karl

Changing tyres during the 1914 French Grand Prix, Louis Wagner uses a copper hammer to loosen the securing nut of one of the spoked wire wheels. (DaimlerChrysler Classic Archive)

Safety, of the drivers or onlookers, was not high on anyone's list of priorities at the 1914 French Grand Prix as Lautenschlager sped towards his second win. (David Hodges Collection)

Ludvigsen so accurately observed in *Mercedes-Benz: Quicksilver Century*, 'was now a prisoner of war'. It would remain in London, crated and stored, until after the end of hostilities.

By now, Mercedes racers had made their début in the USA, which would become a major export target for the German car maker. In 1911, before the first 500-mile race at Indianapolis, the 'Blitzen Benz' driven by 'Wild Bob' Burman set an unofficial average speed record of 141.732mph at Daytona Beach, although its 21.5-litre engine size meant that it was not eligible to enter the race itself. However a 9.5-litre Mercedes was driven into fourth place by Spencer Wishart. In 1912 Ralph de Palma used

one of the 1908 Grand Prix Mercedes to qualify second and build up a four-lap lead only for a con-rod to break with just four miles to run to the chequered flag. Heartbroken, de Palma and his mechanic Rupert Jeffkins pushed the ailing car over the finishing line to be classified eleventh.

Three years after suffering this acute disappointment, luck was on de Palma's side. This time he was driving a modified version of the 1914 lightweight GP racer in the 1915 event, battling for most of the way with Dario Resta's Peugeot. With three laps to go the car's engine yet again threw a con-rod, but now de Palma was able to nurse his stricken machine home to win at an average speed of 89.84mph, a record which would stand for another seven years.

BLITZEN BENZ
Fastest car on the planet

The Blitzen Benz was the brainchild of Victor Hémery who, early in 1909, had obtained permission from the Benz management to produce a car with the potential of breaking the 200kph mark. Hémery decided that the new Brooklands banked circuit in Surrey would be the ideal venue for his attempt. He came close, but the banking proved to be punishing in the extreme, and he simply could not manage to achieve the 200kph average required over the measured mile.

Eventually the car was taken to Daytona where it was sold to American Ernie Moross who, in turn, nominated Barney Oldfield, a former racing cyclist with an unquenchable lust for speed, to drive it. On 16 March 1910 Oldfield easily topped the 200kph record, marking out the 200bhp, 21.5-litre machine as the fastest car in the world.

Barney Oldfield in the Blitzen Benz in which he would also unofficially break the world speed record at Daytona Beach. (David Hodges Collection)

GROWING TO MATURITY, 1919–1934

THE EFFECTS OF THE FIRST WORLD WAR on the social fabric of Europe were considerable. Most crucially for the evolution of the commercial future of the Daimler AG, Germany would be subjected to economic problems resulting in the collapse of her monetary system and the emergence of the National Socialist era.

From a technological viewpoint, the company's aviation engine department began as early as 1915 to experiment with supercharging, with both piston and vane compressors being evaluated in the development process. By 1918 Roots blowers had been adopted for the majority of the Mercedes supercharged aero engines, which enabled the planes into which they were fitted to climb quicker and fly higher than the equivalent without this boost.

Mercedes were not slow to recognise the potential of adapting this technology for cars. The first two road-going models were displayed at the 1921 Berlin Motor Show, with the two-bladed Roots blower fitted vertically on the front of the engine, driven by a small multiple disc clutch and bevel gearing. The supercharger did not operate all the time, but could be activated – by pressing the accelerator right down to the floor – when additional power was required.

On the motorsport front, it was not until after the First World War that Grand Prix racing developed an identifiable pattern which would form the foundations from which the sport would evolve. In 1921 Grand Prix racing was revived under a 3-litre limit which was then reduced to 2 litres

Max Sailer, aged 41, at the wheel of the 1923 Mercedes Indianapolis challenger. From left behind the car: von Gontard, son of the DMG board chairman, Christian Werner, Karl Sailer (nephew of Max), co-driver Hans Rieger, mechanics Gustav Auer and Jakob Krauss, engineer Louis Schwitzer, Christian Lautenschlager and engine test mechanic Otto Weber. (Ludvigsen Library)

from 1922 to 25 inclusive. The 1922 season also saw the construction of the world's first permanent Grand Prix circuit, in the former royal park at Monza, on the northern fringes of Milan. Seven years later Monaco would host its first race, and names such as Delage, Bugatti, Mercedes-Benz and Alfa Romeo became increasingly familiar thanks to their on-track achievements.

Initial post-war prospects were not particularly encouraging for Mercedes. A cartel of British and French trade groups had agreed not to stage any major races in 1919 and 1920 and, although the French Grand Prix resumed in 1921, it was out of bounds to German and Austrian entries until as late as 1924. However, there were other possibilities to be explored. Max Sailer ventured to Sicily to compete in the 1921 Targa Florio with a heavily modified touring 28/95 Mercedes roadster and returned duly encouraged having finished second. The following year it was decided to compete in the smaller 'Voiturette' class for 1.5-litre cars and, to that end, to supercharge one of the 1.5-litre Mercedes to supplement the modified 1914 Grand Prix cars which would be driven by Lautenschlager, Sailer and eventual winner Count Giulio Masetti.

In 1923 Mercedes also sent a team of works cars across the Atlantic to take part in the Indianapolis 500, competing with the first supercharged cars to be seen at the Brickyard. Lautenschlager, by then approaching the sunset of his active career, Sailer and Christian Werner were the nominated drivers on this occasion. The Mercedes proved capable of a respectable turn of speed against the Bugatti, Duesenberg, Miller and Packard opposition. But the sudden power delivery when the supercharger chimed in made the narrow-tyre cars extremely precarious to control on the brick surface track made treacherously slippery by a mixture of rain and oil.

Overall, the Mercedes performance on this banked oval was not an unqualified success and they started 15th (Werner), 17th (Lautenschlager) and 20th (Sailer) on the grid. Lautenschlager and his mechanic Jakob Krauss were out after only nine laps when they skidded into the retaining wall, and the other two cars were slowed by too many pit stops. In the end Max Sailer – relieved after 73 laps by his cousin Karl – finished eighth with Werner 11th, acutely disappointed as that meant he ended up one place away from the prize money.

In 1924 Ferdinand Porsche joined the Daimler company in Stuttgart, the great Austrian engineer having transferred from the Vienna-based Austro-Daimler company; aspiring racer Alfred Neubauer accompanied him. At Austro-Daimler, Porsche had been responsible for the design of the 'Sascha' models which distinguished themselves in the

1922 Targa Florio and, under his direction, Mercedes fitted its four-cylinder 2-litre engine with a supercharger. The resultant package enabled Christian Werner to win the 1924 Targa Florio.

Porsche also settled down to develop a new supercharged eight-cylinder car for that year's Italian Grand Prix. The race was originally scheduled to take place at the start of September. However, when Fiat withdrew its entries and Mercedes indicated that it was having problems with a new engine, the Italian organisers obligingly postponed the event until the following month.

Having been one of the first seriously to embrace supercharger technology, Porsche was determined to run the new eight-cylinder engine to high levels of boost. To this end Porsche had opted to make its eight individual cylinder heads from bronze, as a means of enhancing heat dissipation. Unfortunately the bronze castings had suffered from unwelcome porosity, so the engines were re-worked with steel cylinders incorporating welded steel water jackets. The engines developed a claimed 170bhp at 7,000rpm, running 14psi supercharger boost pressure, which meant they went into the rescheduled Monza race with a 15bhp edge over their most powerful rivals, the elegant Alfa Romeo P2s.

No fewer than four of the eight-cylinder M218s were fielded at Monza. They were shared between Christian Werner, Count Giulio Masetti, Count Louis Zborowski, Alfred Neubauer, and rising star Rudolf Caracciola.

Christian Werner in the 2-litre supercharged Mercedes which held third place in the 1923 Indianapolis 500 before valve problems dropped it to 11th at the finish. (Ludvigsen Library)

Rudolf Caracciola and his riding mechanic Eugen Salzer were the somewhat surprised winners of the 1926 German Grand Prix at Avus in the eight-cylinder Mercedes designed by Professor Porsche. Caracciola invested all his winnings in setting up a Mercedes dealership in Berlin's fashionable Kurfürstendam. (DaimlerChrysler Classic Archive)

Caracciola, a 23-year-old innkeeper's son from Remagen on the River Rhine, had carved out quite a reputation at the wheel of a privately-owned SSK Mercedes sports car.

In practice Neubauer reported that his car was extremely unstable at the Lesmo turn. In the race, at the same point in the circuit, tragedy struck when Zborowski – whose father had been killed in 1903 driving a Mercedes in a hill climb – crashed fatally when he ran off the road and hit a tree. Mercedes director Max Sailer withdrew his remaining works drivers from the race out of respect for their popular colleague. These incidents gave the supercharged eight-cylinder Mercedes something of a reputation for precarious handling, yet it would be tamed by Caracciola to good effect, as we shall see shortly.

Of course, in those distant days motor racing was a more relaxed, less intense affair than it is today, with events more evenly spaced throughout the year. Drivers in the 1920s and 1930s were physically tough in a rough and ready way, requiring endurance and great strength to manhandle their machinery around the makeshift circuits. Yet the sport was also extremely social, and anybody reading contemporary

reflections could be excused for thinking that off-track activities amounted to a succession of riotous parties.

Caracciola in particular recalled an episode when the Mercedes squad was preparing for the 1924 Klausen hill climb in Switzerland. The drivers and team management convened in a small hotel in the Lin Valley where, once the efforts of the day were past, everybody let their hair down in quite dramatic fashion. He recalled: 'Otto Merz was usually the chief figure among the noisy, laughing drivers. He was as strong as a bear and he loved to show off his strength. While I was sitting at the table, minding my own business, his big hand reached through my legs to the back rung of the chair and lifted me bodily, holding me up in the air with me kicking and laughing.'

Merz then took bets with his colleagues that he could slam a nail through the table top with his bare hands. 'For each millimetre the nail emerges beneath, I get a bottle of champagne,' he said. One of the other drivers took him up on his bet and Merz duly won four bottles of bubbly. 'We decided to drink [them] the following day, either to celebrate victory or to console ourselves in defeat. It turned

The front row of the starting grid for the inaugural race at the Nürburgring in 1927. Rudolf Caracciola (1) and Adolf Rosenberger (2) are competing with the new Model S Mercedes… (DaimlerChrysler Classic Archive)

… and they're off! Caracciola won the first race, ahead of Rosenberger. The German Grand Prix, held there the following month, was another home victory, won by Otto Merz from Christian Werner and Willy Walb. (David Hodges Collection)

out that the bottles were drunk to victory, because Merz was first in the racing car class and I was the winner in the sports car class.'

In 1924, the Daimler-Motoren-Gessellschaft and Benz & Cie entered into a partnership which resulted in the complete amalgamation between the two companies on 28/29 June 1926. At that time there were 86 motor manufacturers in Germany producing some 144 models. The economic slump of the mid-1920s meant that there was considerable over-capacity in the industry and the newly formed Daimler-Benz AG would undergo a stern programme of product rationalisation over the next few years in order to guarantee its economic survival.

Only a fortnight after the merger, the first so-called German Grand Prix officially took place on a makeshift 12.15-mile circuit at Avus, this being a section of the Berlin to Potsdam autobahn with connecting loops at either end. The Automobilklub von Deutschland, which had recently been admitted to membership of the AIACR (Association Internationale des Automobile Clubs Reconnus), had hoped to supplement the field by including cars of up to 3-litres rather than simply those for the then-current 1.5-litre Grand Prix formula.

The rules were also framed to admit sports cars into the field. Mercedes duly fielded two eight-cylinder supercharged 'eights', for Adolf Rosenberger and the youthful Caracciola who – though entered – had never managed to get the chance of taking the wheel in the previous Italian Grand Prix at Monza. Rosenberger forced his car into an early lead but crashed at the North Turn on the wet track surface, smashing into a timekeepers' roadside hut and killing the three occupants. In chaotic wet/dry conditions Caracciola confessed that he'd really no idea precisely where he was running in the field, fighting off his tiredness in an effort to respond to encouraging pit signals from Max Sailer.

In the end he managed to win at an average speed of 83.719mph. Not only was it the moment when Rudi

Otto Merz, 1927 German Grand Prix winner. (David Hodges Collection)

Caracciola with the SSK, 1928. (David Hodges Collection)

Caracciola really made his name – and earned the title 'rain master' – it was also the day on which Neubauer (a) realised that he would never be a top driver, and (b) began thinking in terms of what practical support could be offered to a competing driver from the pits during the course of a race. His future in organisation, management and planning was beginning to unfold. In his own mind, at least.

Now came a distinct change of emphasis at Mercedes. Late in 1924 the motoring press had been shown a brand new, 3.9-litre supercharged Mercedes touring car. Developed by Professor Porsche, it was a short-lived model soon to be superseded by 6.2-litre supercharged version which retained the same individual cylinder dimensions of the 28/95 model which Sailer had driven to second place in the 1921 Targa Florio. 'The DMG board ordered a prestige touring car, and Ferdinand Porsche gave them a racer,' is how Karl Ludvigsen summed it up.

In 1927 the 24/100/140K – as this sporting model was designated – was the subject of a major revamp to make it more suitable for front-line motor racing. The revised car was substantially lower than its immediate forbear,

although it retained the same wheelbase and track as the 'K', and the new model was duly designated the 'S'.

This season saw the opening of the dramatic 14-mile Nürburgring circuit deep in the Eifel mountains. Caracciola won the first race on 19 June 1927 in a Mercedes S, ahead of team-mate Adolf Rosenberger. The German Grand Prix, held there the following month, was another home victory, won by Otto Merz from Christian Werner and Willi Walb. The Nürburgring was a venue which would play a dramatic role in the unfolding history of Mercedes-Benz and its racing involvement over the decades to follow.

In 1928, further developments produced the legendary SS and SSK designations for these huge, elegant sports cars. The naturally aspirated version was offered with two different compression ratios that gave outputs of 140 and 160bhp respectively at 2,800rpm. The supercharged version was officially quoted as developing 200bhp at 3,000rpm.

Originally the 'Model SS' designation was applied from the start of the 1928 season when the car's 6.9-litre engine was further expanded to 7.1 litres, by which time this huge

More than half a million people lined the famous Ards road circuit, near Belfast, for the 1929 Ulster Tourist Trophy, won by Caracciola in a Mercedes SS. (David Hodges Collection)

six-cylinder unit with its long crankshaft had of necessity been fitted with a damper ring in order to reduce the effect of unsettling torsional vibrations at around 1,500rpm. These were pivotally important cars for Mercedes, and the prodigiously powerful six-cylinder engines were installed in a variety of chassis, being used in high speed touring cars and hill climbers as well as out-and-out racers.

That year Caracciola won the German Grand Prix at the Nürburgring; Werner shared the driving. In 1929 he won the Tourist Trophy on the famous Ards road circuit, near Belfast, and also took an SSK to the inaugural Monaco Grand Prix street race in 1929, losing an almost certain victory to the Bugatti of William Grover-Williams only when he made a late race refuelling stop.

It seemed that Caracciola was riding the crest of a wave, honing his reputation as the finest German driver of his era. But there was trouble brewing. Racing achievement has to be buttressed by commercial success. For every car maker, there is a financial bottom line below which it dare not sink. In 1930 came the bad news.

A letter from Daimler-Benz Managing Director Wilhelm Kissel very nearly stopped Caracciola in his tracks, both figuratively and literally. The economic ripple effect of the Wall Street Crash was wide-ranging and relentless. The Mercedes driver learned that his contract could not be renewed. Neubauer swung into action to set up an independent team for Caracciola in 1931 which included himself, riding mechanic Wilhelm Sebastian and mechanic Willy Zimmer. The team acquired a specially prepared and lightened SSK in addition to a contribution towards operating expenses from Daimler-Benz AG.

By this time Ferdinand Porsche was no longer involved in the project. In October 1928 he had resigned his position at D-B during a stormy board meeting. His successor as Technical Director was Benz man Hans Niebel who would encourage the career of younger colleagues such as Max Wagner and Fritz Nallinger, the latter having a major hand in the development of the W196 Grand Prix cars some 25 years later.

Caracciola's development car was designated the 'SSKL' –

for lightweight – and he achieved considerable success with it. In 1931 he won the Mille Miglia and a memorable victory in a soaking German Grand Prix at the Nürburgring. After an impromptu celebration dinner at the Adenauer Hof Hotel in the village close to the circuit, Caracciola received some depressing news. He recalled it thus:

'Toward morning Neubauer and I stepped outside a moment to cool our wine-heavy heads. In the east it was already light, but the sun was not up yet. Between the black humps of the mountains lay wisps of an early-morning fog. "We must win many more such victories," I said. "This year and next year."

'Neubauer looked at me. He was silent. Finally he spoke. "Next year, my boy, Mercedes won't run any races. We're short of money. We'll have to go easy."'

D-B had made it clear that it could not continue its level of support for Caracciola into 1932, with the result that he switched to the Alfa Romeo team. Caracciola was clearly torn between loyalty to the Mercedes marque and his need, as a self-styled professional driver, to go racing. His final decision to sign for Alfa seems to have been taken on New Year's Eve, 1931, at the home he shared in Arosa with his wife Charlotte. Both the dejected Neubauer and Alfa Romeo racing manager Aldo Giovannini were seated at the dinner table and, reading Caracciola's memoirs *A Racing Car Driver's World*, one might be forgiven for thinking that Rudi was trying to play each off against the other – even though Mercedes was quite clearly not participating in this particular game.

Eventually Caracciola agreed the contract with Alfa Romeo. Yet Neubauer almost begged him 'not to go over to the other side'. Rudi replied that he had to drive, adding 'Don't you see?' Caracciola later wrote: 'He didn't reply, but he still held onto me. It was a strange moment, the two of us standing in the dimly lit hall and in both of us the vivid memory of eight battle-filled years together. At that

Rudolf Caracciola heads for victory on handicap in the 1930 Irish Grand Prix at the wheel of his Mercedes-Benz SSK. (DaimlerChrysler Classic Archive)

moment Neubauer was closer to me than a brother.

'He took a deep breath and said: "Promise me one thing, Rudi – if Mercedes ever races again, you'll come back to us?"

'"Yes," I said and shook his hands.' Caracciola would be as good as his word.

For the 1932 season, the SSKL 'independent' racing campaign was taken over by the experienced and enthusiastic Hans Stuck. A tall genial man whose son, Hans-Joachim, would become an accomplished Grand Prix and sports car driver in the 1970s and 1980s, Stuck was born in Warsaw on 17 December 1900 although he was not Polish. His parents happened to be on a business trip when they were blessed with the somewhat premature arrival of their new son!

Stuck started racing in the early 1920s and his successes brought him to the attention of Austro-Daimler who loaned him a car in which to take part in hill climb events. Even though he broke his leg in the 1926 Freiburg event the A-D directors retained their faith in his promise and the following year he became one of their factory drivers. A dramatic monetary setback in 1928 left Stuck in a state of acute penury, but Austro-Daimler again stood by him and in 1929 he won them the German, Swiss, Austrian, Italian, Hungarian and French Mountain (hill climb) Championships.

In 1931 Austro-Daimler pulled out of racing so Stuck picked up the threads of his competition career in the SSKL – a deal reputedly made all the easier thanks to his friendship with Crown Prince Wilhelm (a son of the exiled

A hero's welcome for Caracciola, sensational winner of the 1931 Mille Miglia in an SSK. He achieved a new speed record of 1635km in 16 hours 10 minutes, making an average speed of 101kph. (David Hodges Collection)

Kaiser) who helped negotiate a genuinely favourable price with the Daimler-Benz management.

Stuck opened his 1932 season with races in Argentina and Brazil, where he set a new national speed record, then finished second in the Czechoslovakian Grand Prix at Brno and clinched the European Mountain Championship yet again. That year also saw Manfred von Brauchitsch make his début in a customer SSKL, the purchase of which had been funded by a cousin. He commissioned engineer Reinhard Koenig-Fachsenfeld to build it an aerodynamically streamlined body for the prestigious Avus race on 22 May.

Despite potential overheating and tyre problems the race eventually settled down to a battle between von Brauchitsch and former Mercedes ace Caracciola in an Alfa Romeo. In the end, von Brauchitsch emerged victorious – returning a top speed of 143mph which was some 13mph higher than Caracciola's standard bodied SSKL had managed the previous year.

These aerodynamic lessons were certainly not lost on Daimler-Benz which developed its own streamlined bodywork for the SSK in preparation for the same race the following year. The 1933 car was entrusted to Otto Merz. It was readied late, and the bear-like Merz had driven the car from Stuttgart to Berlin by the light of a full moon in order to be present at Avus in time for practice.

Perhaps caught off-guard by a combination of over-exuberance and aerodynamic instability, Merz crashed heavily. Far away, at a hospital in Bologna, Caracciola was recuperating from a serious accident he had been involved with at the wheel of his Alfa Romeo during practice for the Monaco Grand Prix a month earlier. Listening to reports of the Avus meeting on the radio, Rudi forgot his own suffering when the shattering news came through that Merz was dead.

'Another great one, another of the grand old guard,' Caracciola wrote in his memoirs. 'What a man he had been! What a man, with the heart of a child. He was so strong he could lift a racing car himself while they put on fresh tyres. He always laughed when they talked about the dangers of road racing and said he felt sorry for the milestone his head would crack one day. And now he had been carried out of the curve into the great darkness.'

During his recuperation, Caracciola and his wife Charlotte went to stay at a friend's house overlooking Lake Lugano. In November 1933 Neubauer telephoned him there with the news that Mercedes-Benz would be building new cars for the 750kg Grand Prix formula which was scheduled to start the following year. Neubauer was keen to get a deal together with his old colleague.

In fact the Daimler-Benz board had been considering a major racing programme under the new 1934 regulations

as long ago as 1932 when the AIACR announced the proposed new formula which, interestingly, was intended to endure to the end of 1936.

There was definitely an air of rivalry between Mercedes and the other great German team Auto Union, which was a group based in Saxony and composed of the Horch, Audi, Wanderer and DKW marques. Some people considered Auto Union to be the more technically innovative of the two, favouring rear-engined configuration for their new generation of racers, but Mercedes was supremely confident when it unveiled its first prototype W25. This would win its first race.

Tough guy Otto Merz who was killed at Avus in May 1933. He was a great inspiration to Rudolf Caracciola during the formative years of the future European Champion who held him in great awe and respect. Caracciola was devastated at the news of his death. (DaimlerChrysler Classic Archive)

THE GOLDEN AGE, 1934–1939

ON THE FACE OF IT, one might have been forgiven for thinking that the new Mercedes-Benz W25 was rather orthodox, even unimaginative. Powered by a 3.36-litre, straight-eight cylinder, twin overhead camshaft engine, it hardly represented a great break from tradition. Yet the company's engineers spared no effort or expense when it came to methods and materials used in its manufacturing process. The engine developed 314bhp at 5,500rpm which easily eclipsed the 255bhp at 5,400rpm developed by the 2.9-litre Alfa Romeo P3.

The Mercedes W25 transmitted its power by means of a central prop shaft through to a four-speed gearbox in unit with the rear axle. Independent suspension was fitted all round with swing axles at the rear working in conjunction with short, transverse quarter elliptic springs. At the front there was a wishbone arrangement working in conjunction with bell cranks which operated horizontal coil springs. The whole package was clad in an elegant aluminium body with neatly cowled radiator and distinctive head fairings behind the driver.

Manfred von Brauchitsch and Luigi Fagioli were signed from the outset as the team drivers, but it was clear that Caracciola was hoping for a recall. Still handicapped by the lingering after-effects of that Monaco accident, he was nevertheless game for a bold new challenge. In January 1934 Caracciola, still limping badly, visited the Daimler-Benz

The Mercedes W25s, nicknamed the Silver Arrows, made their race début at the 1934 Eifelrennen at the Nürburgring. Luigi Fagioli was faster than Manfred von Brauchitsch, but Mercedes wanted a German not an Italian driver to give them this prestigious victory and – thanks to interventions by Neubauer which resulted in a furious Fagioli, after a row with the Mercedes team manager, refusing to continue racing – that is what they finally achieved. Fagioli finished second at the German Grand Prix held at the Nürburgring the following month. (David Hodges Collection)

management in Stuttgart and agreed a contract. He and Charley then returned to their chalet in Arosa, but tragedy struck again. Frau Caracciola died of a heart attack on 2 February whilst out on a skiing trip on the slopes close to nearby Lenzerheide.

Caracciola had borne his Monaco injuries with scarcely any complaint, but this was a devastating blow. For weeks afterwards he hid away, depressed and withdrawn, refusing to see any friends. It took his old pal Louis Chiron to draw him out of his lethargy and invite him to Monaco where he drove round in the course car. Soon afterwards, he tried one of the new Mercedes W25s at Avus and convinced himself that he was sufficiently recovered to face up to the challenge of racing. He finally returned to the revived Mercedes-Benz in the French Grand Prix at Montlhéry but did not win a major event until Monza where he shared the winning car with Luigi Fagioli, handing over the reins to the Italian after the strain of braking for the succession of new chicanes put too much strain on his injured hip. Fagioli won again in Spain, with Caracciola second.

In 1935 Caracciola really came alive again to win six of the 11 races he entered, clinching the European Championship title. His personal life was also looking up. He was becoming very close to Alice Hoffman-Trobeck, former wife of Alfred Hoffman, heir to the Swiss Hoffman-La Roche pharmaceuticals empire, who had been living

with Chiron for some years. 'Baby,' as she was known, would later become the second Mrs Caracciola. They were married in 1937 at Lugano, and lived there for the remaining 22 years of Rudi's life. For the second time, Caracciola was to experience the matchless benefits of a

Rudolf Caracciola (no.8) and Luigi Fagioli (no.30) at the 1934 French Grand Prix at Montlhéry. (David Hodges Collection)

Retirements at Montlhéry, 1934. Luigi Fagioli's Mercedes is flanked by the Auto Union of August Momberger (no.10) and René Dreyfus's Bugatti.
(David Hodges Collection)

deeply devoted and supportive wife who enhanced his racing career no end.

Meanwhile, the use of international motor racing as a way of aggrandising a nation's prestige abroad was not lost on Benito Mussolini and Adolf Hitler. Thanks largely to the splendid achievements of Alfa Romeo engineer Vittorio Jano throughout the 1920s, Mussolini decided that Italy's

sporting prowess could be demonstrated to great advantage with the onset of the new 750kg Grand Prix regulations introduced in 1934.

Unfortunately the prospects for the P3 Alfa Romeo and the corresponding 2.9-litre Maserati took a dive when Auto Union and Mercedes-Benz – lavishly backed by the Nazi regime – joined in the fray. It had originally been Hitler's

Caracciola's 'racing saloon' styled W25, used in 1934 for record-breaking attempts.
(David Hodges Collection)

34 / MERCEDES IN MOTORSPORT

Glum faces in the pits during the 1934 Swiss Grand Prix which proved a rare failure for the Mercedes squad. Rudolf Caracciola (second left), Manfred von Brauchitsch and Hanns Geier (hands on hips) confer with Alfred Neubauer. (DaimlerChrysler Classic Archive)

Luigi Fagioli pits for fuel with the winning Mercedes W25 he has taken over from Rudolf Caracciola during the 1934 Italian Grand Prix at Monza. The temperamental Italian driver had a hair-trigger temper and once hurled a tyre hammer at Caracciola in a fit of pique! (DaimlerChrysler Classic Archive)

intention to pay the substantial state subsidy of around £60,000 exclusively to the long-established Mercedes-Benz company, but Professor Ferdinand Porsche, now Auto Union Chief Designer, persuaded the German government to split the contribution equally.

The technical regulations in force at the time of their début did not place any restriction on engine capacity, but required a weight limit of between 546 and 750kg. While being scrutineered prior to their first race at the Nürburgring, the eight-cylinder, 78 x 88mm, 3,360cc supercharged Mercedes W25s tipped the scales fractionally over the maximum weight limit. This deeply alarmed Neubauer, but someone cleverly suggested that it might be a good idea to strip off the car's white paint overnight prior to the race.

Neubauer later claimed credit for this inspired piece of improvisation which left the W25s just inside the maximum weight limit, but now sporting bare silver aluminium bodywork. Hence their new nickname which was also applied to the Auto Unions for the remaining years in the run-up to the Second World War. And, indeed, well beyond.

With Caracciola still recovering from the effects of his previous year's accident at Monaco, there were just two Mercedes W25s at the Eifelrennen on 3 June 1934, driven by Manfred von Brauchitsch and Luigi Fagioli. Despite a

RUDOLF CARACCIOLA
A convivial fellow

Birth of a legend. At the 1922 Krähberg hill climb, 22-year-old newcomer Rudolf Caracciola makes his début for the Daimler company at the wheel of a 1.5-litre supercharged Mercedes. (DaimlerChrysler Classic Archive)

A hero of the pre-war European racing scene, Rudolf Caracciola was the most successful member of the factory Mercedes-Benz team from 1934 to 1939, winning the European Championship crown – effectively the forerunner of the World Championship – in 1935, 1937 and 1938.

Caracciola had contested minor league races in the mid-1920s which led to a job, initially only as a salesman, with Mercedes. He later raced their formidable SSK sports cars, dominating the 1931 Mille Miglia, becoming the first non-Italian to win this famous road race.

In 1932 Caracciola drove for Alfa Romeo, then established his own private team for 1933 with Frenchman Louis Chiron, running ex-works Alfas. Unfortunately Caracciola crashed badly during practice at Monaco and did not race for more than a year, battling to recover from a shattered hip which would leave one of his legs shorter than the other for the rest of his life. He returned to Mercedes-Benz in 1934 and by the time the Second World War rang down the curtain on this epic motorsport era, had won 16 races out of 52 starts, a 30.8 per cent success rate which was only exceeded during that period by the legendary Bernd Rosemeyer who won ten races from 33 starts.

When war broke out, Daimler-Benz director Dr Kissel

arranged for Caracciola's pension to be remitted to Switzerland in an acknowledgement of Rudi's contribution to the Mercedes racing legend. Amazingly, Caracciola still harboured thoughts of racing through to 1941 – the height of hostilities – when he actually made a trip to Stuttgart to discuss the possibility of taking over one of the 1.5-litre supercharged 'Tripoli' Mercedes and returning with it to Switzerland. Kissel told Caracciola that, although it might seem a good idea, export restrictions forbade such a transfer. Worse was to come. The National Socialist Automobile Corps stepped in to block Caracciola's pension payments in 1942 which left Rudi and Baby having to live on their savings. In July that year Dr Kissel died and Caracciola received a phone call suggesting that he did not attend the funeral. 'I was told the cool weather might be bad for my health and it would be better if I stayed at home.'

At the end of the war, Caracciola tried again to obtain the release of the 'Tripoli' Mercedes. He was aided in part by the intervention of the 1925 Indy 500 winner Peter de Paolo who was serving as a colonel in the US Army Air Force, stationed in Geneva to take care of those Flying Fortress bombers which might be forced to land in 'neutral' Switzerland after bombing raids on Germany.

In reality, Caracciola was well past his best by the time racing resumed. Although aged only 45, he had taken more punishment than most drivers and when he tried to race again, he suffered a very serious smash in 1946 at Indianapolis. Thereafter he was a shadow of his previous self – shaky and unsteady on his feet, walking with a stick. Yet still he would not give up. He was determined to race again and Neubauer, touchingly, gave him the chance. When Mercedes decided to take their pre-war W163s to Argentina in 1951, Caracciola shrewdly declined, judging that the cars were too old. But when the opportunity came to contest the 1952 Mille Miglia in one of the new 300SL coupés, he jumped at the chance.

He finished fourth in this epic race which he had won with the SSKL Mercedes some 21 years before. Even so, he complained: 'Later I was told that Lang and Kling had been given two faster, more recent models and that I'd been assigned a slower and – they figured – more reliable car. I was annoyed. They should have given me the choice. I felt in such good form that I'd have insisted on driving the more advanced model with Lang.'

Thus emboldened, Caracciola was planning to race at Le Mans, but a few weeks before the 24-hour marathon he entered a sports car race at Berne with the 300SL. Perhaps caught out by a grabbing brake, he slammed into a tree, breaking a leg and knee. It was the end of an illustrious career. Rudolf Caracciola died in 1959 at the tragically early age of 58.

Forty years later, Manfred von Brauchitsch reflected to the author: 'Caracciola was the best driver I competed against. He was very good and fair, a convivial fellow. We had a good relationship for many years, both on and off the circuit. We were slightly older than most of the others and forged a deep personal bond.'

Rudolf Caracciola at Monaco, 1937. (David Hodges Collection)

Geier finished fifth while Fagioli wound up second behind Hans Stuck's winning Auto Union.

Problems preparing the W25s in the time available resulted in Mercedes missing the Coppa Ciano at Livorno and the Belgian Grand Prix, so there was gap of a month before Fagioli won the next race, the Coppa Acerbo on the daunting Italian Pescara road circuit close to the Adriatic coast. This race was marred by a fatal accident. The brilliant Alfa Romeo driver Guy Moll's car was reportedly blown off the road by a gust of wind just as he was coming up to lap slowcoach Ernst Henne's Mercedes.

The Swiss Grand Prix at Berne's Bremgarten circuit then produced more disappointment for Mercedes with Fagioli being the best-placed W25 in sixth place. But the gritty Italian shared the winning car at Monza with Caracciola and then scored Mercedes' fourth win of the season in the Spanish Grand Prix at San Sebastian where Caracciola was placed second. The final race of the season, on 30 September 1934, was the Masarykuv Okruh Grand Prix on Czechoslovakia's bumpy, rutted Brno circuit. It was won by Stuck's Auto Union with Fagioli's Mercedes in second place.

The Mercedes team now returned to Untertürkheim for the winter break which lasted through until 22 April when the 1935 season would kick off at Monaco. During this interval more power was squeezed from the up-rated W25B engine which would go into the fray producing 370bhp at 5,800rpm. Transmission and brakes were also up-rated for 1935 as Mercedes wanted to be well prepared from the start and not have a repeat of the unreliability problems which bugged their progress during the early races the previous year.

As far as the driver line-up was concerned, Mercedes remained committed to Caracciola, von Brauchitsch and Fagioli. Ernst Henne's contract was allowed to lapse and in his place, Hermann Lang – now chief mechanic on Fagioli's car – was adopted for training with the intention of developing his motor racing talents. If Fagioli in any way felt threatened by Lang's presence in the background, he didn't show it. Fagioli won at Monaco ahead of René Dreyfus in an Alfa Romeo, but although von Brauchitsch and Caracciola failed to finish, the team was pleased that Rudi seemed to be right back in the groove once again.

It would have been difficult to find a venue that offered a greater contrast to Monaco than the next stopping point on the international racing schedule. The 8.14-mile Mellaha track in Libya, scene of the Tripoli Grand Prix, was easily the fastest road circuit in the world. This was very much a Formule Libre race, but Mercedes stuck to fielding a trio of W25Bs and Caracciola scored something of a lucky victory

Rudolf Caracciola swings the Mercedes W25 through one of the makeshift chicanes installed at Monza in 1934 to give a chance to the less competitive Italian cars. He later handed over to Fagioli, but they beat the opposition including the Alfa Romeo of Achille Varzi and Tazio Nuvolari's Maserati which are seen chasing him here.
(Ludvigsen Library)

display of indiscipline on the Italian's part when he harried his partner against team orders – Mercedes liked its home victories to come from German, not Italian, drivers – eventually von Brauchitsch won when Fagioli withdrew after a pit lane row with Neubauer!

Neither Mercedes driver finished the French Grand Prix at Montlhéry and then the team suffered quite a significant setback during practice for the German Grand Prix at Nürburgring. Trying too hard, too soon during practice, von Brauchitsch crashed heavily, overturning his car and breaking his arm. This put him out of the racing equation for a few weeks and Neubauer nominated competition department sub-manager Hanns Geier to stand in for him.

HERMANN LANG
Working-class champion

Hermann Lang started out as a mechanic working for Daimler-Benz in 1932. Seven years later he was European Champion, having dominated the 1939 season at the wheel of a factory Mercedes W163 with five wins out of eight starts.

Although a natural driver, Lang had a diffident manner. Beneath the surface he was resilient and tough, however. He needed to be as his working-class origins were regarded with a certain disdain by his team-mates, most notably the aristocratic Manfred von Brauchitsch. He was a loyal team player and a devoted Mercedes man – so much so that he turned down a lucrative offer to join the Auto Union team in the mid-1930s. He returned to racing after the war, sharing the winning Mercedes 300SL at Le Mans with Fritz Riess in 1952.

Lang's last F1 outing came in the 1954 German Grand Prix, by which time this pleasant man was not quite up to front line international racing. Had it not been for the war cutting short the prime of his career, he might have achieved even greater things.

Hermann Lang's Mercedes W154 at Donington Park, 1938. Only a smashed windscreen ruined the German driver's chances of victory in the face of a 170mph breeze. (LAT)

after Achille Varzi's Auto Union suffered a tyre failure while leading with five of the 40-lap race still to run.

Fagioli followed this up by winning the triple-heat Avusrennen before the teams convened again at the Nürburgring for the Eifelrennen. This was to prove another dramatically unlucky day for Manfred von Brauchitsch who, having qualified on pole position and led Caracciola by almost a minute after three laps of the 14-mile track, then over-revved his engine and had to retire.

Meanwhile, Caracciola had come under pressure from the dramatically talented former motorcycle racer Bernd Rosemeyer who was now driving for Auto Union. The tenacious youngster eventually forced his way through into the lead going into the final lap, but Caracciola just regained the upper hand by the time they reached the chequered flag. Nevertheless, a new star had been born.

The French Grand Prix at Montlhéry saw the 3.7-litre Maserati of Goffredo Zehender finish in third place, upsetting the symmetry of a Mercedes grand slam in which Caracciola finished first ahead of von Brauchitsch, with Fagioli coming home fourth. Before this, at the Penya Rhin Grand Prix at Barcelona Fagioli had decided to freelance again, ignoring Neubauer's orders and overtaking Caracciola for the lead despite a 'hold position' signal being brandished on the instructions of the frustrated team manager. Perhaps wisely, Caracciola was satisfied with second place, mindful that the volatile Fagioli had been known to throw tyre hammers at people who crossed him in motor racing matters!

Fagioli was something of a handful by this stage in the

MANFRED VON BRAUCHITSCH
Grand but unlucky

Manfred von Brauchitsch was the nearest thing Mercedes-Benz had to royalty. He was the sole surviving member of the legendary *Silberpfeile* team from the 1930s, an elite throw-back to the days when he, Rudolf Caracciola, Dick Seaman and Hermann Lang went out to do battle against the rival Auto Unions in the heyday of the 'Silver Arrows'.

Born in Hamburg into a Prussian dynasty of army officers, von Brauchitsch enlisted in the forces immediately after finishing school. He rose to the rank of sergeant by 1928 when he was invalided out of the army. His uncle, General Walther von Brauchitsch, would become commander-in-chief of Hitler's armies.

Manfred retained the composure of a man who had known status and respect. He was also one of the unluckiest drivers of that era, winning just three major international races in six seasons. His first triumph came in the 1934 Eifel races at the Nürburgring. It was the weekend on which the *Silberpfeile* were informally christened with a tag which would endure throughout their racing life.

Disappointingly, it is for his ill-fortune behind the wheel and his stylish manner away from the circuits that Manfred von Brauchitsch will be best remembered. His only other wins were at Monaco in 1937, where he ignored Neubauer's orders and stayed ahead of team-mate Rudi Caracciola, and the 1938 French Grand Prix.

Unquestionably, he looked down on some of his colleagues, most notably the somewhat scruffy Luigi Fagioli and even (although Karl Kling rejects this suggestion) perhaps his own compatriot Hermann Lang who had risen from the ranks to eclipse Manfred in terms of talent and achievement. Reflecting that mood is an anecdote recounted by BRM founder Raymond Mays shortly before his death in 1980. Sitting down with his two team-mates in Berlin's swanky Roxy Bar in the 1930s, von Brauchitsch summoned a waiter.

'A bottle of champagne for Caracciola and myself,' he said commandingly. 'And a beer for Lang.'

Manfred von Brauchitsch, fresh from his victory in the 1934 Eifelrennen in the Mercedes-Benz W25, proffers the Nazi salute to Korpsführer Hühnlein, one of Hitler's cronies who was responsible for overseeing the efforts of the German racing teams during the 1930s. (DaimlerChrysler Classic Archive)

Mercedes began the 1935 season as they meant to go on. Race winner Luigi Fagioli's Mercedes stole the show at Monaco, on and off the track, and Mercedes would win eight more races during the next five months. (David Hodges Collection)

season and matters did not improve when it came to the Belgian Grand Prix at Spa-Francorchamps. Caracciola led from the start with von Brauchitsch initially second, but after Manfred retired, Fagioli picked up the pace and began to challenge the leader. This latest display of Italian independent-mindedness was rewarded with another flurry of pit signals from the agitated Neubauer in response to which Fagioli stopped at the pits and became embroiled in an argument with the team manager. Neubauer ordered Fagioli to hand over his car to von Brauchitsch who then continued, to finish second.

For the 1935 German Grand Prix more than 300,000 race fans flocked into the Nürburgring, confident in the knowledge that either Mercedes-Benz or Auto Union would deliver them a glorious home victory. With Caracciola, von Brauchitsch and Fagioli armed with the Mercedes W25s, and the 4.9-litre Auto Unions handled by Achille Varzi, Hans Stuck and the emerging star Rosemeyer, there was surely little hope for the opposition.

Yet Tazio Nuvolari – who despite driving inferior cars was a constant challenge to the mighty German teams – had

other plans. The dogged little Italian was in a three-year-old Alfa Romeo P3 fielded by the Scuderia Ferrari and went to the start with a private score to settle. He was convinced that a conspiracy between Stuck and Varzi had kept him out of the Auto Union team the previous year. Now he wanted to settle that account.

Mercedes-Benz were feeling good: their cars had won no fewer than seven major races so far in 1935, compared to a single victory for Auto Union. Moreover, it looked as though this trend was to continue as Caracciola, the crowd's great favourite, wheel-spun his way into an immediate lead from the start, brilliantly controlling his 440bhp, thin-tyre monster on a treacherously damp track.

Two months of fine summer weather had given way to dank, showery conditions on race morning, but Caracciola seemed master of the situation. He came storming through in the lead after 22 laps. But Nuvolari had made an absolutely brilliant getaway from his position further down the grid and was next up, only 12 seconds behind after 14 miles of racing. Second time round it was the brilliant Rosemeyer, wrestling his Auto Union with breathtaking

flair, who pushed up into second place. Von Brauchitsch was third, then Fagioli, Louis Chiron's Alfa Romeo and Nuvolari who had temporarily dropped back.

For the next few laps it was not Nuvolari but Rosemeyer who captured the imagination of the crowds. On lap three, the Auto Union star sliced a full five seconds off Caracciola – and then another second on lap four. But the leading Mercedes driver seemed suddenly awake to the challenge and promptly steadied his advantage.

Rosemeyer was already in trouble. Early in the race he had glanced an earth bank, damaging a rear wheel. He stopped for attention at the end of lap seven and resumed after some delay in fifth place. Now all eyes began to focus on Nuvolari's Alfa Romeo. By lap seven the little Italian was up to third place, trading lap records with Rosemeyer and, on lap ten, he stormed past Caracciola to take the lead. It was amazing, impossible. The crowds fell silent. Then came the routine pit stops for fuel at the end of lap 12.

Mercedes serviced von Brauchitsch in 47 seconds, which was quick for those days. At the other end of the scale,

Rudolf Caracciola on his way to winning the 1935 French Grand Prix. That season, finally coming back to life again after a period of injury and personal tragedy, he won six of the 11 races he entered, and took the European Championship crown.
(David Hodges Collection)

problems with Nuvolari's refuelling system meant that his stop took well over two minutes. The Italian had to stand and watch his hard-fought lead evaporate in front of his eyes. Then, resuming sixth, he took everybody's breath away by forcing the old Alfa past Stuck, Caracciola, Rosemeyer and Fagioli on the following lap. Now only von Brauchitsch's Mercedes lay between him and the victory he craved.

In the Mercedes pit, you could cut the tension with a knife. Von Brauchitsch was doing everything he could, but the red Alfa, angular and outmoded, was steadily hunting down his sleek silver machine. Down, down came the gap. From 1 minute 26 seconds on lap 14, Nuvolari chiselled it down to just under 30 seconds as the two cars set out on their final lap. It was going to be close, but surely Manfred had done enough?

Sadly for the fans, they had reckoned without tyre problems. In his determination to keep ahead, von Brauchitsch had been mercilessly caning his tyres. Mid-way round that final lap, the Mercedes's left rear tyre flew apart and the German driver was a sitting duck. Nuvolari dodged through to post one of the most brilliant wins

of his remarkable career. Stuck finished second, ahead of Caracciola. Crossing the line on three wheels and a shredded tyre, the crestfallen von Brauchitsch limped in fifth.

'Two laps before the finish, the tyres were starting to show their marker strips which indicated they were getting down to the carcass,' recalled von Brauchitsch to the author 64 years later. 'I could see from the reaction of the spectators, particularly on the descent to Adenau bridge, that they understood I was in trouble. After the race Neubauer blamed me because I did not stop, but I didn't want to come in and perhaps find myself in the same sort of situation which faced Eddie Irvine at the Nürburgring in 1999. Not enough tyres!'

Mercedes opted to miss the Coppa Acerbo at Pescara, resuming their programme at the Swiss Grand Prix at Berne where trainee driver Hanns Geier suffered a fearful accident during practice. Hurled from his wrecked car, Geier was found with multiple injuries, jammed beneath a parked car at the trackside. Had it not been for immediate attention from Dr Peter Glaser, the retained doctor for both the German teams, he would almost certainly have died on the

At the 1935 German Grand Prix, the race famously won by Nuvolari for Alfa Romeo, the best Mercedes could give to the more than 300,000 race fans who had flocked to the Nürburgring was a third place finish for Caracciola. (David Hodges Collection)

A rain-soaked Monaco Grand Prix opened the 1936 season with the harbour-front chicane claiming three of the four Mercedes entries. Louis Chiron (no. 10), here leading Rudolf Caracciola, will soon depart from the fray, leaving his team-mate alone to surf to victory ahead of the Auto Unions of Achille Varzi and Hans Stuck. (David Hodges Collection)

joining the line-up for the Italian Grand Prix at Monza. This proved to be a disastrous race for Mercedes with all its four entries retiring, leaving Stuck to win for Auto Union. Thankfully the team finished 1–2–3 in the final race of the European season, the Spanish Grand Prix at Lasarte. This would be Rudi's sixth win of the year, clinching him the European Championship title, and setting the seal on his complete recovery from the Monaco smash more than two years earlier.

Meanwhile, Hermann Lang had gradually been making his presence felt within the Mercedes team. In the early 1930s he had been so short of work that he even took a job as the engine driver on a light railway at a gravel pit near his home. He recalled cycling to work each day past the Daimler-Benz factory and thinking 'if only I could get a job there!' In due course, he did of course. Many years later he would be shown an internal Daimler-Benz memo which read: 'Since we have taken on Mr (Hanns) Geier and we are not short of racing drivers, I do not consider Mr Lang as the right man'. Racing drivers were clearly considered to be employees, nothing more. Rather like mechanics.

Lang impressed the Mercedes team with his culinary skills however, and would sometimes be persuaded to do a bit of cuisine for the team at the circuits. He later recorded:

The straight-eight cylinder 5.6-litre engine which powered the 1937 W125 developed almost 650bhp, endowing the cars with a top speed of as near 200mph as made no difference. (DaimlerChrysler Classic Archive)

spot. As it was, he eventually recovered and outlived most of his racing colleagues, surviving well into the 1980s.

Caracciola won the Swiss race ahead of Fagioli, with Hermann Lang taking sixth place, the former mechanic also

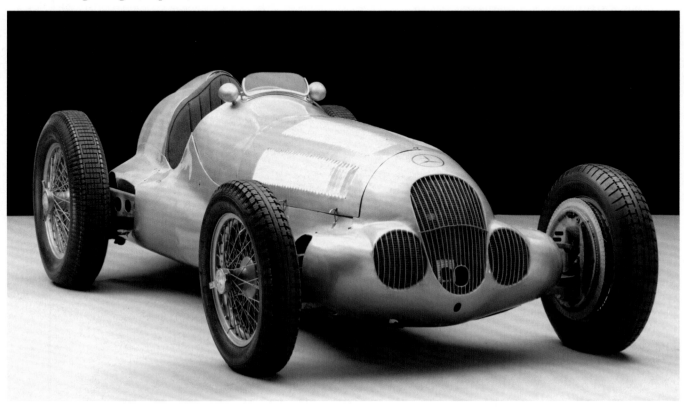

A studio shot of the mighty Mercedes-Benz W125 which in 1937 won at Tripoli and Avus, and the Grands Prix of Germany, Monaco, Switzerland, Italy and Czechoslovakia. (DaimlerChrysler Classic Archive)

'We cooked on an electric stove in the workshop lorry, or at a stove in the open, fired with old cotton waste and oil drainings!'

In 1934 Lang became a test driver in the production car department and was included in a group of hopefuls invited to test one of the Grand Prix cars at Monza. He and his colleagues were told by Neubauer: 'If one of you runs out of road, he might as well buy a train ticket home'. After Geier's Berne smash, Lang was promoted to reserve driver for the 1936 season. In fact, he became the only reserve driver left in the team.

The driver from Bad Cannstatt would emerge as an extremely promising contender during 1936, although he might never have got the opportunity to establish his name after a close shave during pre-season testing at Monza. Hurtling through the first Lesmo right-hander, Lang suddenly felt a painful impact on his arm. When he stopped the car he found a stone 'as big as a fist' in the cockpit. Neubauer chased off round the circuit with security men and found a group of guilty boys who had been competing in a 'bullseye' competition. As Lang later reflected: 'If I had been involved in a fatal accident, probably nobody would have discovered the reason'.

The 1936 season also saw Lang promoted to foreman of the racing department. A contemporary analogy would have been if Olivier Panis, third driver in the 2000 McLaren-Mercedes line-up, was also working as McLaren's factory manager. Times change, and so do ambitions. Lang's essentially modest character could be seen from the fact that his immediate off-track ambition at this point was to build a small house on a patch of land he had acquired near Stuttgart. Talking of his racing activities, he added charmingly: 'My mother and my fiancée shared my pleasure and the sun seemed to shine upon us'.

Meanwhile, Mercedes was hard at work completing the development of the revised W25C for the 1936 season, an even more powerful 4.7-litre version of the straight-eight cylinder engine now developing between 430 and 450bhp at 5,800rpm, dependent on supercharger pressure. Perhaps surprisingly, Mercedes did not take this opportunity to dispense with the services of the temperamental Fagioli, but it did, with Hitler's approval, sign up Caracciola's old pal Louis Chiron.

A rain-soaked Monaco Grand Prix opened the season with the harbour front chicane claiming three of the four Mercedes, leaving Caracciola alone to speedboat away to victory ahead of the Auto Unions of Achille Varzi and Hans Stuck. Then it was off to the bright sunshine of North Africa for races at Tripoli and Tunis. Fagioli and Caracciola could not better third and fourth places at Mellaha, but

a week later Rudi recovered the team's equilibrium to win the Tunis Grand Prix ahead of Carlo Pintacuda's Alfa Romeo.

Yet the elegant, short wheelbase Mercedes W25Cs were not without their performance problems. After the Tunis

Hermann Lang tries an experimental aerodynamic body fitted to a 1936 Grand Prix Mercedes at Avus in 1937. (David Hodges Collection)

A fast tyre change for Hermann Lang at the 1937 German Grand Prix. (David Hodges Collection)

Turning on the power. Manfred von Brauchitsch leads Rudolf Caracciola to victory at the 1937 Monaco Grand Prix. Christian Kautz would make it a 1–2–3 finish for Mercedes. (David Hodges Collection)

race, everything seemed to unravel for the Three-Pointed Star. Nuvolari's Alfa Romeo won in Barcelona, Rosemeyer's Auto Union triumphed in the Eifelrennen, Nuvolari won again in the Hungarian Grand Prix at Budapest, and Jean-Pierre Wimille/Raymond Sommer won the French Grand Prix for Bugatti.

Neubauer was extremely anxious that the Mercedes team should reverse this depressing trend. A huge push was made for the German Grand Prix on 26 July, when more than 300,000 madly enthusiastic spectators swarmed all over the Nürburgring to catch a glimpse of their heroes. The line-up consisted of Caracciola, von Brauchitsch, Chiron, Fagioli and Lang, with the competent Zehender hired as reserve driver. Yet although von Brauchitsch led again from the start, it was not long before things began to go wrong. Manfred glanced an earth bank, stopped briefly out on the circuit to check his steering and then resumed.

Caracciola had fuel feed problems and retired, taking over Lang's car when the new boy broke the little finger on his right hand during a gearchange. Then von Brauchitsch came in and Lang, his finger heavily bandaged, took over for the run to the finish. To add to the chaos, Fagioli pulled into the pits from fifth place and shouted at Neubauer that the car was useless. Caracciola now took over his third car of the day to finish a distant fifth, with Lang bringing his machine home seventh although 'every time I changed gear, the wooden splint on my finger touched the bodywork and I almost howled with pain'.

Mercedes clearly needed a major re-think about its Grand Prix programme. The team returned to Untertürkheim where an ambitious and very promising 30-year-old engineer would be transferred from the production car side to work under Fritz Nallinger, chief of the technical department. His name was Rudolf Uhlenhaut and over the next 20 years he would probably contribute more to the Mercedes motor racing legend than just about any other single individual.

After an abortive outing in the Swiss Grand Prix at Bremgarten, Mercedes withdrew for the balance of the season. Over the winter a heavily revised car was duly produced with a 12-in longer wheelbase and an enlarged 5.6-litre engine, developing a minimum of 550bhp at 5,800rpm.

The Mercedes-Benz W125 was built round a totally new, much stiffer oval-tube chassis with coil sprung independent front suspension and a modified de Dion rear end with longitudinal torsion bars as the springing medium and single radius arms. This new suspension was softer and provided more vertical movement, thereby making the car more driver-friendly and progressive to handle. The W125 also featured gearbox improvements and benefited from the use of uprated Lockheed brakes.

During the development phase of the new car, Rudolf Uhlenhaut carried out much of the test mileage at Nürburgring where he had previously done M-B road car testing. This was supplemented by tests carried out in the Mercedes racing department using a 'chassis dynamometer' which was effectively a predecessor of the seven-post static rigs on which F1 cars were being assessed and developed at the start of the new millennium.

The W125 was perhaps a more forgiving car – at least by the he-man standards of the day – than the corresponding Auto Union which needed a genius like Tazio Nuvolari or Bernd Rosemeyer to extract its ultimate potential.

Of course, the driver selection process operated by a top team such as Mercedes-Benz in those days was stark in the extreme, if fairly organised – in principle not unlike the driver training programmes initiated by the company in the 1990s. Imagine, if you can, Ron Dennis inviting 30 youngsters to turn up to Silverstone for a preliminary test in a DTM 2000 Mercedes CLK, then whittling them down to a handful of hopefuls who would be allowed behind the wheel of an F1 McLaren Mercedes.

This was precisely the method Neubauer employed at the Nürburgring late in 1936. A huge collection of hopefuls

Brilliant partnership – Caracciola and Neubauer, 1937. (David Hodges Collection)

After the disappointment of the Coppa Acerbo, Rudolf Caracciola showed his mettle with a fine victory in the 1937 Swiss Grand Prix at Bremgarten, heading home Lang and von Brauchitsch in a Mercedes 1–2–3. (David Hodges Collection)

ran riot round the 14-mile circuit in a fleet of 2.3-litre Mercedes sports cars. British writer George Monkhouse recalled the episode in his excellent volume *Motor Racing with Mercedes-Benz*: 'The majority of these drivers did badly, and some unpleasant accidents resulted, including one fatality caused by a car going clean over the top of the Karussel bend.

'During these trials the cars suffered badly. The worst incident was when one of the "cadet" drivers had the misfortune to run his car off the road. The car immediately caught alight and by the time the Mercedes lorry in charge of Neubauer had arrived, was blazing furiously. Neubauer with his usual thoroughness decided that it was a little too dangerous to go too near the car in case the petrol tank exploded, and immediately shouted for a revolver, which was duly produced. Neubauer then took careful aim, firing two shots through the petrol tank, which amazingly enough proved to be empty.'

Dick Seaman – one of Britain's most promising young drivers, who had come to prominence with some strong performances in his own ERA – was invited to Monza to test the 1936 Grand Prix cars, together with Swiss driver Christian Kautz and Germans Hans-Hugo Hartmann, Walter Baumer and Heinz Brendel. The two best talents to emerge from this process were Seaman and Kautz. However, while recruiting Seaman represented a huge political coup for Mercedes, it was just another complex factor for Neubauer to take into account in his dealings with Caracciola.

Eventually the final driver line-up for 1937 was decided. Fagioli was dropped, switching instead to Auto Union, while Chiron decided to have a break from Grand Prix racing after escaping unscathed from a horrifying accident at the Nürburgring the previous summer. Thus the Mercedes squad consisted of Caracciola, von Brauchitsch, Lang and Seaman, with Kautz being retained as reserve. Rudolf Uhlenhaut continued his share of development testing and was almost as quick as the regular drivers, so there was precious little prospect of anyone pulling the wool over the eyes of this perceptive engineer.

The opening race of the 1937 Grand Prix season was at Tripoli where Mercedes arrived with five W125s. As always

Start of the inaugural 1937 Donington Grand Prix with Hermann Lang taking an immediate lead ahead of Mercedes team-mates (from left) Dick Seaman, Rudolf Caracciola and Manfred von Brauchitsch. The British 1,500s are already being left behind, to form a secondary race of their own. (LAT)

on the challenging and abrasive Mellaha circuit, conserving tyres would be the key to success and Lang duly emerged the winner from the Auto Unions of Rosemeyer and Ernst von Delius. He led from flag to flag at an average speed of 134.42mph.

This was Lang's big day, a breakthrough which guaranteed his status as a world class driver. Yet he was still quite a shy man and, together with his wife Lydia, had to be coaxed from his hotel room on the evening after the race by an insistent Neubauer who demanded they attend the lavish prizegiving ceremony. Lang's memoirs are full of remarks which reflect a sense of wide-eyed surprise and innocent excitement over the manner in which his life was unfolding. 'How pleasant to leave our home and to arrive at our destination with hotels booked and everything prepared by the provident Neubauer,' he noted modestly.

Lang would win his second consecutive race at Avus that year. The North Curve loop had been replaced, apparently on Hitler's instructions, by a formidable 43-degree banked curve which made lap speeds of 180mph possible. The race took place over three heats and the Mercedes driver,

Donington was one of the few races Mercedes-Benz did not win that year from midsummer onwards. Here Rudolf Caracciola rounds the Melbourne hairpin during the race which saw Bernd Rosemeyer triumph for Auto Union. (LAT)

Manfred von Brauchitsch pressing on at Donington Park, 1937, in his energetic pursuit of Rosemeyer. (DaimlerChrysler Classic Archive)

using a streamlined version of the W125, won at an average of over 162mph. Lang's hopes for a hat trick were thwarted at the Eifelrennen where all the Mercedes cars had fuel pump problems and the best Caracciola could manage was a tyre-troubled second place behind the Auto Union of Rosemeyer.

Next came a divided programme between the Vanderbilt Cup race meeting at Long Island, New York, and the Belgian Grand Prix a week later at Spa-Francorchamps. Caracciola and Seaman were despatched to the USA on the liner *Bremen*, while von Brauchitsch, Lang and Kautz went to Belgium. Rosemeyer's Auto Union won the US race after Seaman's Mercedes spluttered low on fuel at half distance while leading (he went on to finish second), and Caracciola's retired. Meanwhile, at Spa, Lang battled transmission problems and high tyre wear, ending up third behind the Auto Unions of Rudolf Hasse and Hans Stuck. Kautz was fourth, and von Brauchitsch retired from the fray.

The 1937 season also saw preliminary plans laid for participation at Indianapolis the following year. Untertürkheim, mindful of the team's Vanderbilt Cup experience, duly prepared cars for von Brauchitsch, Caracciola and Lang. These entries were cancelled late in April, however, due to Neubauer's perhaps mistaken belief that the Mercedes' oil consumption was high enough to make things extremely marginal in this race where there were strict limitations on how often oil levels could be topped up.

Caracciola sets out on a wet track at the start of the 1937 Freiburg hill climb. The mountain championships were always well supported by Mercedes-Benz and Auto Union throughout the 1930s. (Ludvigsen Library)

Start of the 1938 Tripoli Grand Prix with eventual winner Hermann Lang blasting off the grid ahead of Mercedes team-mates Manfred von Brauchitsch and Rudolf Caracciola. (Ludvigsen Library)

The team was back together in one cohesive unit for the German Grand Prix at Nürburgring. Caracciola won superbly after an early wheel-to-wheel battle with Rosemeyer's Auto Union. Von Brauchitsch finished second, but disaster struck when von Delius in the Auto Union tangled with Seaman's Mercedes coming up the long straight towards the start/finish line.

The two cars were running side-by-side as they leaped the second hump on this section. Then von Delius landed slightly askew, spinning round right in front of the Englishman before crashing end-over-end through the perimeter hedge and landing in a field on the other side of the main highway to Cologne. Seaman braked as hard as possible to avoid the out-of-control Auto Union but the Mercedes careered along the edge of the circuit before slamming into a metal post, pitching into a crazy pirouette.

Seaman was flung out onto the track. He struggled to his feet with a broken nose, thumb and severe facial cuts, but was still able to help marshals push his damaged car out of the way before going off to hospital in Adenau.

It was clear that von Delius was extremely badly hurt. *Autocar* journalist John Dugdale summed up the poignant scene amidst the hustle and bustle of post-race traffic in Adenau village. He wrote: 'Up one short street, into a lane and I was in the cool silence of the small hospital. It looked like a private house, but outside was a large Horch decorated with celluloid-protected Nazi flags and belonging either to race officials or to the Auto Union team inquiring after Delius. [We] went through to see Seaman who put a brave face on it all. But nothing could alter the fact that Delius was far too badly injured to have a chance of surviving the night.' So it proved.

Former mechanic Hermann Lang, here on his way to third place in the 1938 French Grand Prix, would go on to dominate the following season at the wheel of a factory Mercedes W163. (David Hodges Collection)

Manfred von Brauchitsch won the 1938 French Grand Prix. With Caracciola in second place and Lang in third, it was a good day for Mercedes. (David Hodges Collection)

Start of the 1938 German Grand Prix at Nürburgring with Dick Seaman (16) closest to the camera amongst a trio of Mercedes-Benz W154s. Hermann Lang (14) just gets the jump on Manfred von Brauchitsch (12). (John Dugdale/ Ludvigsen Library)

The next Grand Prix on the 1937 schedule came at Monaco which Lang had to miss owing to a particularly virulent bout of influenza which kept him confined to bed. Frustrated, Lang admitted that he swore at the radio commentary in frustration. His wife Lydia silenced him by remarking: 'Now you know what I feel when I listen to the radio or when I sit in the pits waiting while you race.' Lang did not reply, fearing his wife might throw the radio set out of the window if he responded with a clever rejoinder.

Meanwhile, tensions were building elsewhere in the Mercedes-Benz team. Von Brauchitsch seemed to be not terribly keen on Neubauer. But if so, then the legendary, rotund team manager could rightly have claimed another view after his driver won at Monaco in 1937, against team orders, ahead of fellow Mercedes driver Rudolf Caracciola.

There was clearly no rancour between the two rivals, who continued to get on splendidly. 'We ate a lot and drank a lot together,' said von Brauchitsch with a sly grin, remembering the good times more than 60 years ago. 'We had the same interests. But after Monaco, Neubauer didn't speak to me anymore and I began to suffer small, inexplicable problems with my cars. For example, in 1939 I had mysteriously high fuel consumption all weekend at Pau, causing me to stop for a top-up while I was leading which gave Lang the win. Accidents? Coincidences? Who knows?'

Many dispassionate observers see the outcome of the 1937 Monaco Grand Prix as one of the most clear manifestations of von Brauchitsch's superiority in his own mind. Having won that race against team orders, he pulled into the pits and fixed Neubauer with a penetrating glare. It was a defiant gesture, effectively daring the team manager to offer a single word of censure. It seems that Neubauer was sufficiently shrewd not to press the point, but von Brauchitsch could well be correct in his judgement that the Mercedes team manager never felt about him the same way again.

Neubauer got his own back, however. In his memoirs he details von Brauchitsch's defection to East Germany in an unsympathetic fashion, pulling no punches and referring to the suicide of his former driver's first wife Gisela after she had apparently been abandoned by her husband with massive tax debts. This contention is repeated as a fact by Chris Nixon in his highly detailed volume *Racing the Silver Arrows* and is also widely accepted in Germany as being an accurate portrayal of these troubled events.

Lang was still sidelined by illness for the Coppa Acerbo at Pescara, so Seaman was pressed into service only for him to crash heavily in practice. Although Dick was unhurt, his car was extremely badly damaged with the result that there were only two Mercedes entries versus four Auto Unions

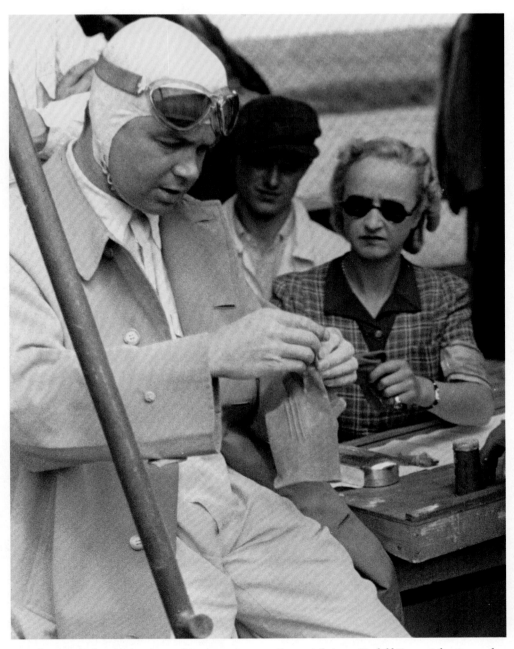

on the grid for the start. Once again, a Caracciola/Rosemeyer battle between the two German teams held the spectators' attention in the early stages of the race, but after Rudi built up almost a one minute lead his W125 lapsed onto seven cylinders. That left Rosemeyer an easy winner from von Brauchitsch, with Seaman taking over Caracciola's stricken car and nursing it home fifth.

Caracciola made up for that disappointment with a fine victory in the Swiss Grand Prix at Bremgarten, heading

Rudolf Caracciola sits on the pit wall at Nürburgring during the 1938 German GP meeting watched by his wife. Caracciola lent his name to a brand of trench coat still being sold as late as 1982. (John Dugdale/ Ludvigsen Library)

Despite some pit lane petulance Dick Seaman won the 1938 German Grand Prix and found himself having to make the Nazi salute. He wasn't happy about this, but then second-placed Hermann Lang and Neubauer don't look fired with nationalistic fervour either. (David Hodges Collection)

home Lang and von Brauchitsch in a Mercedes 1–2–3. The Italian Grand Prix at Livorno produced a Mercedes 1–2 with Caracciola and Lang only feet apart at the chequered flag, but come the Czechoslovakian Grand Prix at Brno it was Lang's turn to experience spectacular misfortune. On the fifth lap of the race he crashed heavily. His Mercedes overturned, killing two spectators sitting in a prohibited area on the edge of the circuit, and it took almost five years before the courts absolved Lang of responsibility for the accident.

Caracciola won the Czech race from von Brauchitsch, after which the team hurried off to Donington Park for what

was the first major international race in Britain. The Langs flew direct from Czechoslovakia in a Junkers 52 airliner via Munich, Frankfurt and Brussels, meeting up with the rest of the team in the palatial splendour of the Grosvenor House Hotel on London's Park Lane.

After three seasons running riot across the Continent, the Silver Arrows were making the first of their two pre-war visits here. The venue was the Donington Park circuit near Derby, a spectacular parkland track which exists, albeit in heavily modified form, to this day. It was a sight for which the British fans could hardly have prepared themselves. During the 1930s, British motor racing was something of an anachronism, bearing little similarity to what was going on in Europe. The sport was largely the preserve of well-heeled amateurs who amused themselves amidst the slightly haughty world of Brooklands – 'the right crowd, and no crowding' – and later at Donington. Although some had sallied forth to do battle with the Europeans on their home ground, the domestic scene remained an insular backwater. Until 2 October 1937.

One of the great factors to trigger the public imagination in the Mercedes-versus-Auto Union confrontation was the fact that the dashing, popular Seaman had been recruited to drive for the Three-Pointed Star. Not only was Seaman one of the most talented new performers in the business, but his inclusion in the German line-up was seen in some quarters as an expression of the Hitler regime's regard for the British. Two years later, perhaps, that might not have seemed to be too obvious, but at Donington Park that autumn day in 1937, politics were not at the top of the agenda.

With British participation confined to a handful of out-classed ERAs driven by the likes of Earl Howe, Raymond Mays and Arthur Dobson, there was clearly nothing to stand in the way of an all-German battle for supremacy. Mercedes's 5.6-litre W125s dominated the front row of the grid with von Brauchitsch and Lang lining up first and second. Seaman was fourth, on the outside of row one, but the Mercedes symmetry was broken up by Bernd Rosemeyer's Auto Union in third place. After a superb 1936 season, Auto Union had again taken a back seat to Mercedes-Benz throughout much of the following year, but the team's hopes were inevitably pinned on Rosemeyer to reverse that trend.

When the Union Jack fell, Seaman made a terrific start in front of his home crowd, but Lang just beat him to the first corner as Caracciola's Mercedes came rocketing through from the second row to nip in front of Rosemeyer. In the opening phase of the race it looked as though Mercedes-Benz was going to round off the season with another victory, but things began to go wrong after an early collision between Seaman and Hermann P. Müller's Auto Union resulted in the British driver's premature retirement.

The spectacle proved awesome. Lang, von Brauchitsch, Rosemeyer and Caracciola battled closely for the lead, their howling silver monsters topping a staggering 170mph on Donington's longest straights and even leaping into the air as they crested the rise before the pits. Rosemeyer's car control was spellbinding. The Mercedes drivers seemed to be having an easier time with their W125s, but Bernd was simply not letting them get away with it. After ten laps the race average had rocketed to 83mph and Rosemeyer's irresistible challenge was driving von Brauchitsch ever closer to Lang in the lead.

On lap 14, von Brauchitsch finally squeezed through to take over at the head of the pack, thereafter edging slightly away from Lang. But Rosemeyer was still in close touch and, when the Mercedes drivers made their first routine fuel stops at the 20-lap mark, the Auto Union tore past into the lead. With 25 laps completed, Rosemeyer had half a minute in hand over Caracciola. Disappointingly, Lang's early efforts had proved fruitless, his Mercedes retiring with

Rudolf Caracciola (no.10) recalled the anguish Manfred von Brauchitsch (no.12) suffered when, after a pit stop fire, he returned to the 1938 German Grand Prix only to have the steering wheel come off in his hands. What followed next is the stuff of fairy tales. (David Hodges Collection)

Still the master, Rudolf Caracciola gets on with the job of winning the 1938 Coppa Acerbo. (David Hodges Collection)

Dick Seaman in practice for the 1938 Donington Grand Prix. (David Hodges Collection)

Mercedes's front tyres as he locked up under frantic braking for the Melbourne hairpin. But Rosemeyer was inspired. Straining every rivet and body panel of the Auto Union, he edged ever closer to his front-engine rival.

Eventually von Brauchitsch had to capitulate and Rosemeyer confidently grabbed the lead. Yet the drama was by no means over as the Mercedes ace then suffered a major front tyre failure at high speed on the straight, somehow wrestling the car back under control and coaxing it round to the pits for fresh rubber.

With just 20 of the 80 laps left, Rosemeyer had the race in the bag with a half-minute lead over the recovering von Brauchitsch. Despite this, the Auto Union team – amazingly – called Rosemeyer into the pits with only five laps left, for a precautionary tyre change. The mood in the pits was electrifying. Rosemeyer, goggles lifted, frowning over his shoulder back down the track, strained to see if either of the pursuing Mercedes was coming.

It could hardly have been judged any closer. That final Auto Union stop had been orchestrated as precisely as anything the McLaren-Mercedes team could do today. Rosemeyer fishtailed back into the race barely one second ahead of the Mercedes and had opened out a 37-second advantage over von Brauchitsch by the chequered flag. Caracciola finished third.

Owing to an organisational mix-up, there was no champagne waiting on the rostrum, so the delighted Rosemeyer toasted weary von Brauchitsch in lemonade. It was to be his final win. On 28 January 1938, the star which had streaked so brilliantly across the Grand Prix skies was abruptly extinguished – Rosemeyer died in a record attempt on the Frankfurt-Darmstadt autobahn.

Caracciola and von Brauchitsch were particularly stunned by the death of a man they regarded not only as a rival, but respected as a close friend and colleague. The entire Mercedes-Benz team attended his funeral in Berlin. He was laid to rest in the same cemetery as that other Auto Union star, Ernst von Delius, who had died in the German Grand Prix the previous year, battling with Seaman's Mercedes.

The 750kg formula had finally run its course by the end of 1937. It was replaced with new rules for 4.5-litre naturally aspirated or 3-litre supercharged engines, both running to an 850kg minimum weight limit. This change represented an effort on the part of the rule makers to somehow rein in Grand Prix car performance, a strategy which has failed time and again over the years.

As author George Monkhouse rightly pointed out in his detailed chronicles of Mercedes pre-war racing efforts, by 1939 the 3-litre supercharged cars were easily eclipsing the

deranged steering. Rosemeyer stayed out until lap 30 before making his stop, and at the same time Caracciola also came in for a quick stop, emerging in second place behind von Brauchitsch and with Rosemeyer now briefly back to third.

Yet the Auto Union star could not be shaken off, fighting back into contention again with a relentless determination. Rosemeyer soon re-passed Caracciola and then closed in on von Brauchitsch. Manfred fought like a tiger against his challenger. Great plumes of smoke poured from the

lap times set by the huge 5.6-litre cars of two years earlier. In 1937, Rosemeyer's Auto Union had set a record lap of 9m 46s for the Nürburgring *Nordschliefe* in a 6-litre car, but this was reduced to 9m 43s by Lang two years later in a 3-litre Mercedes. A lower centre of gravity and ever-improving braking performance were the two key reasons behind this.

The driver line-up at Untertürkheim remained pretty well unchanged for 1938. However, it is worth mentioning that at the end of the previous season the convivial Bernd Rosemeyer had approached Lang with the suggestion that he might consider switching to the Auto Union team. Rosemeyer explained that he was trying to race almost single-handedly against the three regular Mercedes drivers, so perhaps Lang might like to join the opposition to even things up a bit? Lang replied: 'I've grown up with Mercedes-Benz and there I'll remain'. Rosemeyer admitted that he understood perfectly and the matter was never mentioned again.

For the new season, Mercedes came up with a 3-litre supercharged engine for the W154 challenger which

developed around 430bhp at 7,800rpm. The new 60-degree V12 engine had a one-piece crankshaft which ran in ten roller bearings, each bank of cylinders had twin overhead camshafts and the engine/transmission line was angled to the left of the cockpit which meant that the driver could sit lower. As before, the gearbox was in unit with the de Dion rear axle, but it now had five speeds, and the W154 also benefited from further improved braking. The car was slightly heavier than the W125, but this did not result in any performance handicap.

The season opened with an unexpected upset when the Delahaye of René Dreyfus put it across the Mercedes team to win the street race at Pau, in South Western France. The French car won by dint of needing fewer refuelling stops and Dreyfus believed that Caracciola was simply in a bad mood – and didn't want to be seen to be beaten – when he handed over to Lang for the closing stages.

'Finally Rudi came in for fuel and got out of the car,' recalled Dreyfus. 'His hip hurt, he said, (and) he wanted Hermann Lang to take over. Rudi had suffered a bad

Mercedes reserve driver Walter Baumer leads Rudolf Hasse's Auto Union, Donington Park, 1938. Both these drivers would survive racing in the 1930s only to die during the Second World War. (Ludvigsen Library)

RECORD-BREAKING
Speed and self-aggrandisement

The Nazi drive to glorify the homeland was a major factor behind the proliferation of land speed record attempts made by both Mercedes-Benz and Auto Union during the 1930s. In 1936 Daimler-Benz produced a 5.5-litre V12 engine and a special car, clad in an all-enveloping aerodynamic body, to bid for the Class B records from 10km to one hour.

On 26 October 1936, Rudolf Caracciola launched the assault on a specially closed section of the Frankfurt-Darmstadt autobahn next to Frankfurt airport. He posted a new Class B record of 226.4mph for the kilometre and 228mph for the mile. On 11 November Mercedes returned to try for records over the longer distances, but poor weather and mechanical problems prevented this.

Up to that stage Auto Union had held a decisive edge when it came to record breaking, the driving force behind their motivation coming from the determined and extremely brave Hans Stuck. However Mercedes – perhaps wanting to give its workforce, and especially the racing department – a boost during a disappointing Grand Prix season, stepped up its efforts.

Over the winter of 1936/37 Dr Ferdinand Porsche, who had by now left Auto Union to establish his own independent design studio, developed the T80, mid-engined, six-wheeler car which was intended for an all-out assault on Sir Malcolm Campbell's outright land speed record of 301mph.

Porsche told Mercedes that its 33.9-litre aero engine would need over 2,200bhp to achieve the huge leap to 340mph which he intended. For almost three years development of the T80 continued behind the scenes, its existence variously hinted at and then denied by senior Mercedes personnel. In the meantime, in August 1938 George Eyston raised the record three times culminating in a speed of 357mph, and within another 12 months John Cobb raised it to 369.74mph within a few weeks of the outbreak of war.

This might have proved too much for even the proposed enlarged 44.5-litre version of the V12 engine in the T80 which Porsche requested in the hope that 3,000bhp might eventually be unlocked. In fact the Second World War made the T80 a museum piece overnight, later to be analysed in fascinating detail by Cameron C. Earl in his UK Government-backed investigation into the technology involved in the German Grand Prix cars which had so dominated the immediate pre-war era.

Ferdinand Porsche (left) with Mercedes racing boss Max Sailer in 1938.
(Ludvigsen Library)

accident five years before at Monaco, which had left him with a tender hip, but that wasn't the real reason he didn't want to finish Pau.

'We both knew, without ever saying it, that he just didn't want to be beaten by me. Lang wasn't even in his overalls – he had his regular trousers on – but he hopped in. And he did his very best, getting the lap record in the process. But I had whistled by during the pit stop and it was useless. I won easily, by one minute and fifty seconds.'

Next on the schedule was Tripoli, where Lang won at the head of a Mercedes 1–2–3 ahead of von Brauchitsch and Caracciola in a race sadly marred by the death of Lazlo Hartmann after a collision with Giuseppe Farina's Alfa Romeo.

Von Brauchitsch won the French Grand Prix at Reims quite easily, but only after Caracciola and Lang were delayed was he able to stroke it home unchallenged ahead of his team-mates. Rudi finished second after the W154 lapsed onto 11 cylinders. Lang was third – his car had proved reluctant to restart after a pit stop.

This was a rare moment of glory for the unfortunate von Brauchitsch. However the satisfaction he derived would be dramatically diluted by one of the greatest disappointments of his career which came at the next race on the calendar, the German Grand Prix. He and Dick Seaman dominated the race but, as their team-mate Rudi Caracciola later recalled, Manfred was extremely irritated by the way in which the Englishman shadowed his every move.

'Neubauer, that Seaman is driving me insane,' shouted von Brauchitsch in abject frustration at his second refuelling stop. 'He drives up so close behind me that each time I brake, I think now we'll crash. We'll both end up in the ditch if this keeps on.'

While this exchange was taking place Seaman, who was about 10 seconds behind von Brauchitsch, also pulled in for fuel. Neubauer ran across to the second Mercedes and told Dick to take it easy, not to hassle his team-mate. At that point the Mercedes team manager glanced over his shoulder to see von Brauchitsch's car suddenly enveloped in flame after fuel had spilled out over its exhaust pipes. Neubauer fell on the blazing car, clawed von Brauchitsch from the cockpit and helped beat out his burning overalls. Seaman, petulantly conforming to the letter of Neubauer's instructions not to challenge von Brauchitsch, simply sat in the pits and watched the fun.

'God, is the man out of his mind?' roared Neubauer. 'Go on, Seaman, take off. What are you doing?' Seaman replied, deadpan: 'You said not to chase Brauchitsch'. Then, according to Caracciola, he flagged Seaman away into the lead after promising him that it would not be challenged

either if he was ahead at the forthcoming Donington Grand Prix in England.

Meanwhile, von Brauchitsch's car was cleaned up and he accelerated back into the race. Unfortunately his Mercedes' removable steering wheel had not been properly re-attached and it came off in his hands mid-way round the next lap. With great presence of mind he claimed – ridicu-

Rudolf Caracciola and the Mercedes streamliner set off on a record-breaking attempt on the new Reich autobahn near Dessau, February 1939. (David Hodges Collection)

One of the remarkable little 90-degree 1.5-litre Mercedes W165 V8s is warmed up prior to the 1939 Tripoli Grand Prix, its only race outing. (Cyril Posthumus)

walk home by the side of the circuit, carrying the offending steering wheel and consoled by vociferous cries of support from the grandstands. He reported that the wheel had come off on its own, but engineer Rudolf Uhlenhaut shrugged aside that explanation. In his view the wheel had not been properly re-secured by the driver after that chaotic refuelling stop.

This retirement was a huge blow for von Brauchitsch and, while at the track he concealed his true feelings beneath a suave and debonair exterior, the truth was that the German driver was close to tears. Lang finished second, taking over from an unwell Caracciola in the closing stages after his own car had started misfiring early on, and Hermann had relinquished it to Walter Baumer.

Caracciola, his senior by four years, regarded von Brauchitsch with affection and respect. Sadly Caracciola died at the early age of 58 and we only have his memoirs to draw on. But they certainly make interesting reading on the subject of his colleague. During the evening of the 1938 German Grand Prix, back at their hotel in the nearby village of Adenau, Caracciola suddenly noticed that von Brauchitsch was missing. He went to his room where he found 'the Big Fellow stretched out on the bed, sobbing with anger and disappointment.

'Baby [Rudi's wife Alice] sat on the edge of his bed and ran her hand over his tousled head and I sat on a chair. We let him give vent to his feelings and then I ordered an enormous jug of cold orange juice. After a warm bath there remained only the victory celebration to be gotten over with a smile. In the morning the fellow with the proverbial bad luck would be over the worst of his grief.'

Von Brauchitsch simply could not shake aside his ill-fortune. After taking the chequered flag to apparently win the Coppa Ciano at Livorno on 7 August, he was duly presented to Countess Ciano on the rostrum only to be disqualified from the results. He had slid off the road into some straw bales while jousting with Lang and received outside assistance – strictly prohibited – to get going again. As a result of this unfortunate controversy, Lang was handed the victory for Mercedes ahead of the Alfa Romeos of Farina and Jean-Pierre Wimille/Clemente Biondetti. Caracciola had stopped much earlier on with a split fuel tank.

The Coppa Ciano also marked the début of the 1.5-litre supercharged Alfa Romeo 'voiturette', the significance of which was certainly not lost on Neubauer or Uhlenhaut. This machine would, of course, be developed into the Alfa Romeo 158 which so comprehensively dominated the immediate post-war Grand Prix racing scene.

Lang's own fortunes took a horrifying lurch on the

lously in many people's view – to have grabbed the steering wheel spindle and gently steered the car into a shallow ditch. It was a contention questioned by von Brauchitsch's mechanic for the rest of his life – he believed the Patrician driver just made a mistake.

Seaman won the race and 'Unlucky Manfred' was left to

fourth lap of the Coppa Acerbo at Pescara when his Mercedes W154 suffered a major engine failure. Debris from this severed a fuel line and the car erupted in flame. Lang baled out with his overalls flaming, but survived virtually intact. The car was burned to a cinder by the trackside. Von Brauchitsch had retired even earlier with a broken connecting rod, so it was left to Caracciola to get on with the business of beating the remaining makeweight opposition.

Caracciola again demonstrated his unique feel and sensitivity in the wet by dominating the Swiss Grand Prix at Bremgarten after displacing Seaman from an early lead. Rudi was driving a lightened and revised Mercedes W154 which had repositioned fuel tanks intended to minimise changes to the weight distribution as they emptied. Seaman drove superbly to finish second ahead of von Brauchitsch in a 'standard' W154 while Lang was fortunate to escape without serious injury after his goggles were shattered by a stone. He had to stop for medical attention, reserve driver Baumer taking over the car and finishing in tenth place.

There was to be little in the way of good cheer remaining for Mercedes over the last two races of the 1938 season. At Monza in the Italian Grand Prix, Tazio Nuvolari proved truly formidable at the wheel of the Auto Union and won commandingly. Seaman, Lang and von Brauchitsch all succumbed to engine failures and Caracciola was so affected by a leaking exhaust that he handed over to his pal Manfred for several laps, the pair of them eventually finishing third behind Farina's Alfa Romeo.

For the second successive year the international racing season in Europe ended with the Donington Grand Prix. The British fixture had originally been scheduled for 1 October, but due to the growing threat of war the Mercedes and Auto Union teams – who arrived in Britain during the Munich crisis when Neville Chamberlain was negotiating with Hitler and Mussolini – both packed up and headed for Germany. Lang's memoirs record that the Mercedes mechanics were under instructions to spike their trucks' fuel tanks and set fire to the rigs if they were apprehended by the British authorities.

The German driver also recalled Dick Seaman at a banquet in London making light of the tensions in Europe. 'If it [the war] starts,' he said, 'and you're still here, you won't have such a bad time. We are sportsmen.' All very well, thought Lang to himself, but home is home!

In the event – following Chamberlain's 'peace in our time' – the race eventually took place on 22 October. Lang surged into the lead after a slow start, only for a stone thrown up by another car to shatter the windscreen on his Mercedes. He almost suffocated in the 190mph slipstream

Caracciola passes the packed stands on his way to second place at Tripoli, 1939. (Cyril Posthumus)

Hermann Lang, Alfred Neubauer (centre) and engineer Rudolf Uhlenhaut at Tripoli, 1939. (Cyril Posthumus)

Quick pit stop for Hermann Lang, who went on to win the 1939 Tripoli Grand Prix. Safety rules were rather different then – note the cigarette-smoking mechanic. (David Hodges Collection)

and had no choice but to ease off and allow Nuvolari's Auto Union to go through to victory. Seaman finished third, with von Brauchitsch fifth.

Extraordinarily, a full programme of racing was planned for the 1939 season despite the hostilities. Mercedes further uprated the W154 with more elegantly aerodynamic bodywork and a more powerful 480bhp M163 engine. This led to the car being widely referred to as the W163.

Lang opened the season by winning at Pau ahead of von Brauchitsch, but then emerged the secret development in the form of the 90-degree 1.5-litre V8 voiturette which Mercedes had developed exclusively for the prestigious Tripoli Grand Prix which was being run that year for the 1.5-litre regulations.

Work on the car had started at Untertürkheim in the

middle of November 1938 and on 7 May 1939, from a starting grid of 28 Italian cars and two Mercedes, Lang headed Caracciola home to score his third straight win at the Mellaha circuit. Emilio Villoresi finished third in the sole surviving Alfa Romeo 158. For the Italian opposition, the arrival of the little Mercedes W165s – as the 1.5-litre cars were dubbed – was unwelcome in the extreme. They were never raced again.

Lang was by now the fastest driver within the Mercedes team. The technically astute former racing mechanic had an instinctive feel for preserving his machinery and scored his third win of the season at the Eifelrennen. Von Brauchitsch and Caracciola were both complaining earnestly to Neubauer about the treatment they were receiving, perhaps unable to believe that they were being beaten by a former mechanic. Interestingly, Dick Seaman wrote to his friend George Monkhouse that summer to the effect that Lang was a good guy, 'not a sulky child like the others'.

But Lang's fourth straight win of the season came in bitterly tragic circumstances at Spa-Francorchamps. He only inherited the lead when Seaman's Mercedes crashed on the fast left-hand bend prior to the La Source hairpin. Dick was trapped in the car after it caught fire and later that evening died in hospital from his burns.

Lang was aghast. 'I will never forget this appalling sight as long as I live,' he wrote after the war. 'The car had almost completely wrapped itself around the tree, no doubt through the considerable force of impact, the fuel tank had burst and, wedged in the seat like a stone statue, sat Seaman surrounded by a sea of flames. At the pits Neubauer saw from my shocked expression that the worst had happened.'

Lang can have taken no pleasure from his victory and the following week he, along with his colleagues and rivals from the two German national Grand Prix teams, flew to London for the funeral of the man who Lang would always remember as 'kind hearted, cool and fair as a sportsman, just as I had always pictured Englishmen to be'.

Dick Seaman at the 1939 Belgian Grand Prix where he died after his car crashed and caught fire. (David Hodges Collection)

Manfred von Brauchitsch in the 1939 French Grand Prix where retirement deprived him of any chance of scoring a repeat victory. (David Hodges Collection)

Rudolf Caracciola acknowledges the roar of the crowd as he brings glory to the homeland, winning the 1939 German Grand Prix. (David Hodges Collection)

Caracciola's Mercedes W154 slams through a fast right-hander on Bremgarten's treacherous pavé surface on his way to third place in the 1939 Swiss Grand Prix. (Ludvigsen Library)

Other recollections of those times come from Karl Kling, who worked in the sports department before the war. 'Dick Seaman was a gentleman,' he said. 'I never like to talk about who was the best. Caracciola was dominant, until Rosemeyer and Lang came along. At first, Lang was not allowed to drive as fast as he could – you could write a novel about what went on in those times. Some would be flattered by it, some would not. But I'm not writing this novel.

'It wasn't true that von Brauchitsch hated Lang. They had a much better relationship than Lang and Caracciola, for sure. Or Fagioli or 'Caratsch'. The personal relationship between the drivers at that time, well, some were very good, but others were very poor. Seaman was a great driver, but also a great man, friendly with everybody.'

After Seaman's funeral, the Mercedes drivers flew directly from London to Reims for the French Grand Prix where none of the W154s managed to finish, leaving former motorcycle racers Hermann Müller and Georg Meier to score a 1–2 for the Auto Union team.

By now it was clear to most people that war was only a matter of weeks away. With the airship *Graf Zeppelin* looming large over the Nürburgring, the German Grand Prix took place on 23 July in conditions of nervous euphoria. Lang was determined to round off his European Championship bid with another victory here and shot off into an immediate lead. At the Karussell, a teenager by the name of Günther Molter – later to become a respected journalist and the Mercedes PR chief almost 40 years later – watched, spellbound.

'It was absolutely fascinating,' he told the author. 'Lang just stormed away from the opposition, completing the opening lap 27 seconds ahead of von Brauchitsch.' Unfortunately carburettor failure sidelined a bitterly disappointed Hermann after just three laps on the damp circuit. Then von Brauchitsch was eliminated with a split fuel tank, leaving Caracciola to demonstrate that his unique talent was still lurking close to the surface, posting his sixth German Grand Prix victory. Nobody was to suspect it at the time, but this was also the final victory of his distinguished career.

The penultimate race of the season took place at Berne's Bremgarten circuit. There Lang wound up by giving the veteran Caracciola a driving lesson, the Mercedes duo finishing in 1–2 formation with von Brauchitsch third. It was a victory which clinched Lang's European Championship crown in addition to the European Mountain title which he earned thanks to excellent hill climb victories at Vienna and the Grossglockner.

Finally, the epic story of the Mercedes-versus-Auto

DICK SEAMAN
Contract ratified by Hitler

Dick Seaman's wealthy parents encouraged him to pursue a career in the diplomatic service. Instead, he channelled his financial resources into funding his progress up the rungs of the motor racing ladder to the point where he was recognised as Britain's most accomplished international driver of the pre-war era.

He left Cambridge in 1934 at the age of 21 absolutely determined that he was going to become a professional driver and bought the MG K3 Magnette which fellow student Whitney Straight – later to become Chairman of BOAC – was all too willing to sell. Fighting against a robust seam of parental disapproval Seaman secured sufficient finance to clinch a deal to drive a factory-prepared ERA in 1935. Unfortunately this coincided with a downturn in the standards of preparation at Bourne, and Dick decided to cancel the agreement, preferring to have his car prepared by the highly respected Giulio Ramponi, who he hired as his personal mechanic.

In 1936, frustrated by the ERA performance, he was coaxed into acquiring a nine-year-old Grand Prix Delage, driven in its heyday by Earl Howe. The car was extensively re-worked and lovingly fettled by Ramponi, and Seaman drove it to four prestigious wins that year, gaining the reputation as the most impressive 1500cc driver in Europe.

Joining Mercedes was the Englishman's chance to make the big time. His contract was personally rubber-stamped by Adolf Hitler, a measure of just how seriously the Nazi government regarded its investment in Grand Prix racing during the 1930s. Hitler had always been a fan of the English and would clearly have had no reservations in approving the appointment.

Little success came Seaman's way during his maiden season with Mercedes. Indeed, his first test after signing resulted in an accident at Monza from which he was fortunate to escape with relatively minor injuries. Despite this Neubauer and the Mercedes racing management remained relaxed and philosophical. Dick was also involved in a very serious accident at the German Grand Prix, involving Ernst von Delius (see text).

Later that year Seaman was disappointed not to have posted a good result in the first Donington Grand Prix, being pushed off by an Auto Union early in the race. Amazingly, he did not race again until the following year's German Grand Prix. When he won he was faced with the embarrassing situation of having to give an admittedly somewhat tentative Nazi salute on the rostrum.

In December 1938, Dick Seaman married Erica, the 18-year-old daughter of BMW founder Franz-Joseph Popp. They were to have less than a year together before Seaman's death at the 1939 Belgian Grand Prix.

Dick Seaman won the 1938 German Grand Prix. (David Hodges Collection)

Union era came to an end when Nuvolari beat von Brauchitsch into second place at the Yugoslav Grand Prix in Belgrade on 3 September 1939, the day on which the Second World War began.

This already dramatic event was marred by a potential team controversy. Von Brauchitsch left for Belgrade airport after breakfast on race morning, telling Lang to inform Neubauer that he was going home. Apparently Neubauer stormed after him to the airport and pulled him off the plane, only later realising that the flight von Brauchitsch had boarded was going to Switzerland. Not Germany.

If you read between the lines of Caracciola's autobiography you can easily draw the conclusion that von Brauchitsch was planning to join his team-mate in Switzerland, where Rudi had lived since the early 1930s. Caracciola recalls that Manfred 'gave us his luggage for safe keeping'. As von Brauchitsch departed for Belgrade, he said to his compatriot: 'Goodbye, dear old Bear'. Caracciola replied: 'Goodbye – or rather, come back soon'.

After the war, which he spent working as a private secretary to a General in Berlin, von Brauchitsch briefly moved to Argentina before returning to his homeland where in 1948 he became Sports President of the Automobilklub von Deutschland. However, he remained a free spirit and has since admitted that he 'could not stand the system' in reference to Dr Konrad Adenauer's immediate post-war conservative government. This is somewhat at odds with suggestions that he 'fled' to East Germany simply to escape massive tax debts.

Mercedes insiders think that the Eastern bloc appreciated the prestige involved in luring away one of West Germany's most famous sportsmen. In 1955 von Brauchitsch made the move and was quickly appointed President of the German General Motorsport Association. Günther Molter later reflected: 'Rudolf Uhlenhaut told me that von Brauchitsch was very much to the left politically. I have a photograph of the Mercedes drivers meeting Hitler in the 1930s and it is clear that he [von Brauchitsch] was not enjoying it. Manfred was one of the very fastest, but he certainly needed a strong car.'

For the moment, however, the party was over. Six years of war lay ahead before there could be any thoughts of resuming motor racing. And for many of the leading players in this story so far, the golden days were over for good.

RESTORATION

I N THE FIVE AND A HALF YEARS which separated Tazio Nuvolari's victory in the Auto Union over Manfred von Brauchitsch's Mercedes at Belgrade in September 1939 and the surrender of German forces to General Montgomery at Luneburg Heath in May 1945, the world had changed for ever.

Large parts of Britain and Germany had been razed to the ground and, while England's industrial heartland had been seriously damaged, Allied bombing had virtually laid waste to many of Germany's large cities. The Daimler-Benz

plants had been almost totally wrecked. The destruction wrought in Untertürkheim amounted to about 70 per cent, in Sindelfingen 85 per cent, in Mannheim 20 per cent and in Gaggenau 80 per cent, while what remained of the plant at Marienfelde was so badly damaged that there was no choice but to demolish its remains.

According to a brief statement issued by the Board of Directors: 'Daimler-Benz had ceased to exist in 1945'. A subsequent business report on the years immediately following offers an insight into the post-war economic

Disinterred. A convoluted sequence of events resulted in one of the 1939 Mercedes W154s crossing the Atlantic in 1947 where owner Don Lee entered it in the Indianapolis 500. Here Lee's chief mechanic Mal Ord is at the wheel of the car attempting to coax the supercharged V12 engine back into life.
(Ludvigsen Library)

situation facing German manufacturing industry in general and the Three-Pointed Star in particular:

'Germany's surrender resulted in the disruption of all connections between the various plants and branches. Only after an agreement had been reached concerning the various zones of occupation did it become possible to re-establish contact with the Untertürkheim, Sindelfingen and Mannheim plants situated in the American zone.

'The Gaggenau plant in the French zone, however, remained excluded from the Daimler-Benz community for a long time and we only had a very limited influence on its management. Similar problems also arose in Berlin, but in this situation, which was anything but hopeful, it is deeply gratifying to note that the basically sound structure of the company enabled it to overcome these difficulties.

'A new start was made; the staff were recalled, and they made short work of the debris, thus enabling the company to embark upon a provisional programme chiefly consisting of vehicle repair work. During the initial period of rehabilitation, the position was not made easier by requisitions and pilferage and, although hopes ran high that it would be possible to restore the old order, it soon became evident that this task was going to require an immense amount of tedious work.'

The German motor racing fraternity had also been scattered. Walter Baumer, a pre-war Mercedes reserve driver who shared the winning BMW 328 with Huschke von Hanstein in the truncated 1940 Mille Miglia, had died on active service, a fate shared by Auto Union racer Rudolf Hasse.

Hermann Lang was briefly and mistakenly imprisoned after the war for supposed pro-Nazi feelings. Caracciola had opted for self-imposed exile in Switzerland. Hermann Müller, von Brauchitsch and Stuck all survived, the latter duo becoming involved in small-time racing as soon as sufficient cars and resources could be scraped together.

Even Neubauer was in a spot of bother when he was dismissed from Daimler-Benz without notice on 15 November 1946. His 'crime' was supposed criticism of German prisoners-of-war in American camps as well as suggestions that the D-B management had appointed Nazis to its board. Thankfully, it did not take long for Neubauer to marshal a strong defence against these allegations and he was soon rehabilitated.

Daimler-Benz, of course, had its hands full rebuilding the factories. Many of its Grand Prix cars had been dispersed for safety's sake into what ended up as the Russian

The Mercedes factory took a trip down memory lane early in 1951 when a trio of 14-year-old W154s were despatched to Argentina for a couple of races. Here (from left) the front row of the grid for the Presidente Peron Cup race is made up by Karl Kling, Hermann Lang and Juan Manuel Fangio. They were all beaten by Froilan González in a 2-litre Ferrari. (DaimlerChrysler Classic Archive)

occupied zone, and retrieving them would prove an almost insuperable problem.

In 1946 Caracciola went to Indianapolis where he crashed heavily during a practice run in the 4.5-litre Thorne Special after failing to gain the release of one of the two 1.5-litre Tripoli Mercedes which he'd originally hoped to use in this race.

The following year, thanks to a convoluted sequence of events, one of the 1939 W154s turned up in Czechoslovakia. It then found its way to Britain and was soon packed in the hold of the liner *Queen Mary* on its way to America where one Don Lee of Los Angeles had purchased it for a reputed $25,000.

In reality, trying to get to grips with the intricacies of the Mercedes two-stage supercharger and multi-jet carburation was the 1947 equivalent of do-it-yourself maintenance on a Boeing 747. Far away from those who built and developed it, the fact that the car was made to function at all was quite a credit to mechanic Mal Ord. In fact, driven by Duke Nalon, the old Mercedes worked its way up to fourth place before a piston failed.

In 1948 the Mercedes was back again at the Brickyard, this time with 45-year-old Chet Miller at the controls.

Blighted by persistent overheating, the W154 lasted 390 of the 500 miles before being retired after having made several unscheduled pit stops.

Then came utter humiliation for the gallant old stager. In 1949 the car was sold to another amateur racer, Joel Thorne, who replaced its 12-cylinder engine with a 4.5-litre, six-cylinder Sparkes-Thorne engine. Needless to say, this was not a success.

Meanwhile, back in Germany, by the middle of 1950 Daimler-Benz was thinking in terms of a possible return to racing. Neubauer had managed to track down and recover three of the 1939 cars and they were given a preliminary airing on the overgrown and dilapidated Nürburgring later that summer.

The initial plan was to take the cars to Argentina for two races in Buenos Aires at the start of 1951, after which they would contest that year's Indy 500. Neubauer approached Caracciola who reportedly replied: 'Count me out. You won't win any prizes with those old soapboxes'.

In the event the three drivers signed for the Argentine races were Karl Kling, Hermann Lang and rising star Juan Manuel Fangio. However, the tortuous Costanera road circuit seemed to have been laid out with many tight

Karl Kling wrestles with the Mercedes W154 at Buenos Aires, 1951. This significant outing for the 41-year-old from Giessen confirmed him as a potential front-line driver. (DaimlerChrysler Classic Archive)

Caracciola's last race. The great Mercedes ace, far right, now 52 years old, starts the sports car race supporting the 1952 Swiss Grand Prix from the front row in his 300SL. Within a few laps he had smashed head-on into a tree, sustaining injuries that brought his epic career to an end. (DaimlerChrysler Classic Archive)

The Mercedes 300SL coupés of Hermann Lang/Fritz Riess and Theo Helfrich/Helmut Niedermayr achieving that memorable 1–2 success at Le Mans in 1952. (DaimlerChrysler Classic Archive)

corners, perhaps deliberately to handicap the big German cars. The trio of Mercedes faced relatively makeweight opposition, but Froilan González put his own name up in lights by beating the silver cars in both the Presidente Peron Grand Prix and the Eva Peron Grand Prix.

Lang and Fangio were second and third in the first race, Kling and Lang second and third in the second. But the old Mercedes were caught out again by their 'traditional' carburation problems in South America's sweltering heat and the whole project was dubbed a failure. Caracciola had been correct in his prediction and Neubauer faced some embarrassing adverse press reports on his return to Germany. The planned Indianapolis foray was immediately scrapped.

However, while the Mercedes team was away in Buenos Aires, events in Europe were to shape the company's future competition plans. Perhaps inspired by Jaguar's success at Le Mans in 1951 with the C-type, Mercedes decided to develop its new 300SL sports car.

The D-B management committee meeting on 15 June 1951 gave the green light to a limited programme of racing with the new GT coupé which had been developed under the guidance of Fritz Nallinger and Rudolf Uhlenhaut. The end result was a straight six-cylinder 85 x 88mm, 2,996cc engine developing 171bhp at 5,200rpm. This may have seemed a relatively modest output, but it was combined with absolute reliability and therefore an ideal basis for a long distance racing sports car. The 300SL was fitted with distinctive 'gullwing' doors which were hinged in the centre of the roof, and the whole package clad in an aerodynamic bodyshell. It ran on 15in wheels and was fitted with highly developed drum brakes.

The new 300SL coupé made its début in the 1952 Mille Miglia. Three such machines were on hand for the veterans Rudi Caracciola and Hermann Lang, plus the new boy Karl Kling. Much was made of the fact that this was the first time a German factory team had contested the classic Italian road race, excepting, of course, the victory of Huschke von Hanstein and Walter Baumer in the BMW coupé on the truncated 1940 route.

Caracciola's victory in 1931 had been the only previous occasion on which a non-Italian had won the Mille Miglia and, in most people's eyes, it was unlikely that the German driver was about to repeat that feat at the age of 51. Similarly, Lang was suspected of being a little too keen to demonstrate that he'd lost none of his 1939 European Championship winning form. So most folk reckoned that 41-year-old Kling represented the best bet on this occasion for the new Mercedes-Benz coupés.

British participation was, perhaps as usual for that era, too little too late. There was a single works Jaguar C-type

MERCEDES-BENZ

Double victory

after the most strenuous stress in the 24-Hour-Race at Le Mans

1st Lang - Riess
2nd Helfrich - Niedermayr

in Mercedes-Benz type 300 SL

New absolute distance record – 2320.428 miles run within 24 hours

for Stirling Moss, plus a trio of Aston Martin DB2 coupés aiming to clean up the GT class in the hands of George Abecassis, Reg Parnell and Tommy Wisdom.

Interestingly, at pre-race scrutineering the Mercedes team

ALFRED NEUBAUER
The Big Man in the pits

Shortly after the end of the Second World War, Enzo Ferrari wrote in his diaries about receiving a visit from Alfred Neubauer, the former Mercedes-Benz racing manager. Ferrari was struck by how gaunt and haunted Neubauer looked, a shadow of his former self.

A few years later, Ferrari observed that his German colleague and rival had regained much of his lost girth. This led the Commendatore to speculate that if his country was recovering its stature at the same rate as Neubauer was regaining his weight, then perhaps Germany was preparing for the Third World War!

Alfred Neubauer was the man who virtually invented the role of the motor racing team manager. That fact did not mean that he fulfilled a subordinate role to the drivers under his command, of course. Far from it. He was a shrewd organiser and a man with a well-honed sense of the theatrical.

Clad in a double-breasted suit, an ever-present Homburg perched atop a head which seemed too small for his gargantuan frame, Neubauer stamped his identity on Mercedes-Benz motor racing history across a period of four decades. Yet if his outward countenance looked stern and unbending, it was definitely a penetrable facade. On duty, he could well chase unwanted photographers and journalists out of the Mercedes pit. But off duty, with a twinkle in his eye and a glass in his hand, he was an enchanting social companion with a splendid sense of fun.

Alfred Neubauer was born in 1891 in the region of Czechoslovakia then known as Northern Bohemia. Having served in the Austro-Hungarian armed forces during the First World War, he was offered a job in the road test department of the Austro-Daimler company – ironically by Professor Ferdinand Porsche who would go on to design the Auto Unions against which Neubauer's Mercedes cars would later race.

Initially, Neubauer wanted to be a driver. He achieved this aim for Austro-Daimler and Mercedes-Benz, although in subsequent years he was quick to admit that he was not in the first rank. At the time, his fiancée, seeking to speed him up, remarked that he drove 'like a night watchman'. Neubauer took the hint.

Following the 1924 Italian Grand Prix, where Louis Zborowski crashed fatally, Neubauer swapped the steering wheel for the stop watch and effectively conceived the job of team manager simply to keep himself involved in the racing business which he loved so fervently.

He assumed the role of team manager at the 1924 Solitude Grand Prix, at the same time carving himself a distinctive niche within Mercedes-Benz and also becoming a lifelong friend of the legendary Rudi Caracciola who began racing Mercedes cars in the mid-1920s.

At the end of the 1930 season, the depressed economic climate in Europe saw Mercedes withdraw from motor racing. That concerned Neubauer greatly. Not only could he see his own position in jeopardy, but he was also worried that if Caracciola was allowed to slip through their fingers, then should Mercedes ever return to racing they might well have lost one of their biggest assets for good.

Neubauer thus approached the Mercedes management with a proposition: the company should loan Caracciola an SSKL sports car to race on an independent basis throughout 1931. Naturally, Neubauer proposed himself for the role of team manager, and while the arrangement proved very successful, Mercedes felt it could not continue the programme into 1932.

This was a heart-rending situation for the devoted Neubauer, whose loyalty to Mercedes was matched only by his enthusiasm for racing. Shortly afterwards, Auto Union offered him a job, only for Daimler-Benz Managing Director Dr Wilhelm Kissel to intervene with the strong hint that Mercedes did in fact have a racing future and would eventually return to the motorsport scene, probably in 1934.

This was great news for Neubauer, but to his considerable dismay, Caracciola crashed heavily during practice for the 1934 Monaco Grand Prix. It was not until the middle of 1935 that his close friend and protégé returned to the scene, his recovery further set back by the shattering loss of his wife Charly in a skiing accident earlier that same year.

Happily for Neubauer, Caracciola regained his previous form and stormed away to win the 1935 European Championship. Despite this, the Mercedes team manager found himself obliged to assume the role of diplomat as he attempted to balance the wider interests of the team's success with his private regard for Caracciola. It seems certain that the great German driver was something of a handful to deal with, often suspecting that his team-mates were attempting to undermine his number one position in the pecking order.

During the period of Caracciola's convalescence after his Monaco accident, Neubauer found himself forced to look outside Germany for suitable driving talent. With apparent reservations about hiring either Achille Varzi or Tazio Nuvolari, Neubauer instead opted for Luigi Fagioli. Fagioli stayed only until the end of 1936 and did not attract Caracciola's approval.

There was more trouble with Rudi over the next few years as he seemed to take umbrage with the manner in which former mechanic Hermann Lang began emerging as a front-line ace in 1937. By then, Neubauer's shrewd judgement had also resulted in the arrival of an Englishman in the Mercedes ranks – Dick Seaman.

Eventually, Caracciola's truculent attitude towards Lang erupted during the 1939 season. At Tripoli there was a dispute over who was to race the new 1.5-litre 'voiturette' and later at the Eifelrennen voices were raised over how much fuel was necessary to top up the cars' tanks at a routine pit stop. At this point, Caracciola decided that Neubauer had turned against him and the whole dispute got so serious that it was placed before the Mercedes directors for due consideration. Rightly, the directors told everybody involved not to be so stupid and to sort out the issue on their own. But from then on, Caracciola was always rather cool towards Neubauer, the man who had championed his cause for so many years.

After the war, Neubauer reappeared in the pit lane to mastermind the Mercedes-Benz return, first with the 300SL sports cars which won Le Mans in 1952 and later with the dominant W196 Grand Prix machines in 1954/55.

Just as he had been responsible for signing up Dick Seaman,

so he now proved instrumental in getting Stirling Moss into the team. As reward for his faith in the young Englishman, Neubauer watched with pride from the pits as Stirling won the 1955 British Grand Prix at Aintree, 17 years after Seaman had won at the Nürburgring.

Alfred Neubauer died in 1980 at the grand old age of 89, a Mercedes man to the last, but his ghost surely stalks the pit lanes to this day as the descendants of his beloved *Silberpfeile* write yet another chapter in motor racing history.

My boys! The elegantly attired Alfred Neubauer puts an approving arm round Stirling Moss and Denis Jenkinson after their historic 1955 Mille Miglia win. (DaimlerChrysler Classic Archive)

Prepared in roadster form, the Mercedes 300SLs produced a grand slam 1–2–3–4 finish in what amounted to little more than a promotional race at the Nürburgring in 1952. (DaimlerChrysler Classic Archive)

got into a heated debate over the legality of the distinctive 'gullwing' doors fitted to the cars. It took more than four hours of coaxing and cajoling for Neubauer to convince the organizers that these were within the regulations, and although the Mille Miglia officials eventually accepted this there were plenty of pointed remarks to the effect that they certainly did not comply with the *spirit* of the rules. It seemed a particularly harsh and uncompromising stance to adopt.

Ferrari's works armoury was slightly blunted for this classic race. Ascari had an abiding distaste for the Mille Miglia, and Villoresi was recovering from injuries sustained in the Swiss Grand Prix. Maranello thus put its shoulder behind Piero Taruffi's efforts, providing him with what looked like a 225 Vignale spider, but powered by a 4.1-litre V12 developing around 260bhp. In addition, there was an experimental 230bhp 250S-engine berlinetta coupé for hill climb ace Giovanni Bracco.

Even by the standards of the Mille Miglia, this promised to be an epic. Bracco led at Ravenna on the southbound leg with an advantage of around five minutes over Kling's Mercedes, but as the field reached Rome the German driver was ahead. On the northward sprint home, Taruffi had nosed ahead of Kling by the time they reached Sienna, only to fall victim to transmission seizure as he began tackling the Futa and Raticosa passes.

What followed from Bracco was, in Enzo Ferrari's words, probably 'the most spectacular success of all my racers'. Bracco was a man who liked his drink and would eventually die prematurely, partly it was said due to this inclination. He was two minutes down on Kling arriving at Florence,

but he looked at his co-driver and promised they would be leading by the time they reached Bologna.

Fortified by a bottle of Chianti – and reputedly an endless supply of brandy fed to him by the co-driver – the chain-smoking Bracco simply hurled the Ferrari 250S berlinetta across the Futa and Raticosa passes to arrive in Bologna over a minute ahead of Kling. On the final sprint back to Brescia, Bracco added another three minutes to that advantage. Many years later, a German journalist would write that Kling never quite recovered from this Mille Miglia defeat.

Two weeks after the Mille Miglia, four 300SLs ran in the 131km sports car race supporting the Swiss Grand Prix at Berne's Bremgarten track. Kling had experienced locking rear brakes on the Mille Miglia and now Caracciola was caught out by the same problem, the veteran Mercedes ace crashing heavily in an incident which marked the end of his career. The race was won by Kling ahead of Lang and Fritz Riess.

Le Mans was next on the agenda where one of the 300SLs was tried with a rear-mounted air brake as a possible option for this gruelling race. In the event this was not used, but it laid valuable groundwork for the forthcoming 300SLR sports racer which would have such a system at the French endurance classic three years later.

The Mercedes line-up for Le Mans was Lang and Riess in the lead car backed up by Theo Helfrich and Helmut Niedermayr. Yet the key to this race – and, indeed, a man who would go on to play a tragic role in Mercedes-Benz racing history – was not driving for the Three-Pointed Star on this occasion. His name was Pierre Levegh.

Levegh started his career as a menial apprentice, pushing a broom in a small French provincial garage. While nurturing great ambitions to be a racing driver, he displayed no particular talent. He toiled away at his craft and was eventually nominated as reserve driver at Le Mans in 1938 with the Talbot team.

In the event, Levegh failed to prove himself behind the wheel and would have to wait another 13 years to make his Le Mans début in 1951, by which time he was 46. He finished a respectable fourth, sharing a 4.5-litre Talbot with Rene Marchand, and returned the following year with the same co-driver.

Most people judged that the main battle would be fought out between the Mercedes 300SLs and the Jaguar C-types, one of which had won the previous year. Unfortunately for the British team, modifications to the bodywork of the Jaguars, intended to enhance their aerodynamics, caused all three cars – driven by Stirling Moss/Peter Walker, Peter Whitehead/Ian Stewart and Tony Rolt/Duncan Hamilton – to retire early on with overheating.

With the two Mercedes running at a rigorously preplanned, disciplined pace, it was Levegh who moved the Talbot up into contention as the shadows lengthened and darkness fell over this most famous of all endurance events. The French crowd looked on in rapturous appreciation.

Midnight came and went with the Jean Behra/Robert Manzon Gordini still leading the pack, but in the Talbot pit an air of concern could be detected. Levegh was running well, no question about it, but he just would not give up the wheel. Each time he stopped for tyres and fuel, Marchand counselled him – with ever increasing concern – to take at least a brief rest. But each time, the Frenchman declined the offer, preferring to race on single-handed. On the face of it, Levegh was being a hero. In reality, he was asking for trouble.

The first bitter blow for the French fans came in the small hours of Sunday morning. After grappling with fading brakes, the leading Gordini finally retired just after 3am. Into the lead went Levegh's rumbling Talbot, its driver hampered by an inoperative rev counter.

As a misty dawn broke, the Frenchman forced his way onwards, damp and aching in his open cockpit. Snug in the comfort of their closed coupés, Helfrich/Niedermayr and Lang/Riess lay second and third. By mid-morning on Sunday, Levegh was four laps ahead of the nearest Mercedes, but courting disaster like few men in the history of the sport. Dazed, almost hypnotised with fatigue, Levegh was driving like a robot. Logic and reason had long since gone out of the window. At each successive pit stop, he sat resolutely in the cockpit, recognising nobody.

Marchand continued to plead with him. But Levegh wanted all the glory for himself. In the early afternoon, Lang and Riess moved into second place but Levegh still seemed out of reach. Then came catastrophe. Into the final hour, Levegh's dream came to an end. Too numb to know what he was doing, he accidently shifted into first gear instead of third and the Talbot's crankshaft snapped.

Levegh had let down his fans. The 300SLs droned on through that final hour to take strong first and second places. In the pits, Levegh quietly sipped some water as tears rolled down his wife's cheeks.

Some observers felt that there was still much residual anti-German feeling at Le Mans in 1952. Only seven years

Running repairs. Hans Klenk pushes out the remains of the smashed screen while Karl Kling prepares to don his helmet during a maintenance stop with the winning 300SL during the 1952 Carrera Panamericana. The distinctive 'gullwing' doors were a controversial feature of this Mercedes coupé. (DaimlerChrysler Classic Archive)

American John Fitch shared this Mercedes 300SL roadster with mechanic Eugen Geiger during the 1952 Carrera Panamericana, but they were excluded for a rule infringement. (DaimlerChrysler Classic Archive)

Karl Kling (right) and Hans Klenk pause for breath with the winning Mercedes 300SL during the 1952 Carrera Panamericana. (DaimlerChrysler Classic Archive)

had passed since the end of the war; the wounds remained painful. Motor racing insiders can still recall the lukewarm reception which greeted the 300SLs as they took the chequered flag.

Günther Molter, a former Luftwaffe pilot who was mercifully returned injured to Austria shortly before the Battle of Stalingrad, needed no lessons on the anguish of war. Here as a freelance journalist, covering Mercedes events, he discerned no hostile anti-German feelings, however.

'There were certainly people who suffered under the occupation of the Germans,' he reflected to the author. 'But there was no adverse reaction from the great mass of spectators. In fact, it was almost the contrary. When the [Mercedes] team returned at Reims for the 1954 French Grand Prix there were some French people inquiring about Manfred von Brauchitsch, who they'd seen racing there before the war. So perhaps there was something very special about Mercedes.

'When I travelled the world a lot helping Neubauer as assistant team manager – and later as the company's longest serving press chief – I always felt at home. China, Hong Kong, anywhere. They used to say Mercedes was in more countries than the United Nations!'

With that Le Mans victory under their belt, Mercedes put the 300SLs through some dramatic surgery, emerging as open roadsters for a race at the Nürburgring on 2 August. Kling was entered in this race at the wheel of a special supercharged model which for some reason was no quicker during tests on the 14-mile circuit. As a result, all four cars competed in 'standard' unsupercharged trim. Come the race, Kling led initially until an oil leak into the cockpit made life somewhat precarious. It also caused him to slow up, allowing Lang through to beat him. Third and fourth were Riess and Helfrich.

The next event on the calendar was the daunting Carrera Panamericana, an escapade which made the legendary Mille Miglia look like a small-time club race. The Carrera, which was run only from 1950 to 1954, is still recalled by those associated with it as one of the single most remarkable automotive adventures ever to have been staged.

The event ran initially from Ciudad Juarez on the Mexican/US border to El Ocatel on the Guatemalan border, a distance of 2,135 miles. Only in 1950 was the event run in the north-south direction. For subsequent events the 'inverted' route ran from Tuxtla Guittérrez (north of El Ocatel) which reduced the distance to 1,984 miles and

then in 1953 to 1,912. It was also run in eight rather than nine legs from 1951 onwards.

'That was the longest road race of the time and Mercedes decided to take part with the newly developed 300SL,' recalled Kling. 'Seven prototypes were built, and shipped to Mexico. We then drove the race cars to the start in Guatemala. We had a top speed of about 240kph (150mph), which came not from the power of the engines, but from the excellent aerodynamics.'

Kling shared his car with former wartime fighter pilot Hans Klenk, and another 300SL coupé was shared by Lang/Erwin Grupp, with American John Fitch sharing a roadster with mechanic Eugen Geiger. The whole project was managed as usual by Neubauer. Günther Molter was working as his unofficial assistant, and also filing reports back to Stuttgart on a daily basis – not the easiest of tasks in this era before e-mail had been invented.

There was another 300SL on hand which Molter drove from Tuxtla Guittérrez to Mexico City. This was also kept as a test and back-up car, while Neubauer went ahead of the field in a 200S so that he could be waiting when his racers arrived.

Kling and Klenk won the event in splendid fashion,

Karl Kling and Hans Klenk gave the 300SL its most commercially significant victory in the 1952 Carrera Panamericana. It was a victory which gave the Mercedes image a substantial boost on the crucial US market. The 'bracing bars' across the windscreen are the legacy of a vulture smashing the windscreen at high speed. (DaimlerChrysler Classic Archive)

III. Carrera Panamericana Mexico

Triumphant Double Victory

1st **Karl Kling**   2nd **Hermann Lang**

After 5 days of hardest contest supreme victory with a new distance record of "Type 300 SL", developed out of the custom-built passenger cars of

MERCEDES - BENZ

despite a horrifying moment when the windscreen of their 300SL was smashed by a vulture.

'All of a sudden, my windscreen went bang, and my co-driver was hurt,' said Kling. 'He almost lost consciousness, but told me to go on until the next depot. There was a really nasty stench, and I thought he'd shit in his trousers, but it wasn't the case. The vulture was in the back of the car, and that was what stank so much.

'At the next depot we put in some small steel rods – they had to be bent a little, so I got a barrel, and bent them round that. These we then fitted, to prevent birds from hitting us again. It almost happened again – not with a vulture, but another big bird. Anyway, we won all the stages after that, and won the race overall.'

This was a fantastic performance. 'It was a great moment for us all, a victory that all Germany needed,' said Günther Molter. 'The success in Mexico was a sign that German industry had recovered from the damage of the war. I believe that the victory in that Carrera Panamericana was more important to Mercedes-Benz in the years after the war than all the victories in F1 and sports cars during 1954 and 1955. The world's press wrote all about it, especially the Americans, who represented a very important market for Daimler-Benz.'

Karl Kling endorsed that view. 'It was a great result for the whole of German industry. A perfect visiting card. At the time the German economy was coming round after the disaster of the war. What we may call the national importance of the Mercedes victory in the Carrera Panamericana was underlined by the then-president of Germany, Theodor Heuss.'

Lang finished second in this event with the unfortunate Fitch excluded for a rule infringement. The lanky American was driving on the recommendation of US Mercedes importer Max Hoffman, who reckoned that the inclusion of an American in the team would be commercially beneficial.

The event was also a good deal for the successful Mercedes drivers. Prior to leaving for Mexico, Neubauer asked whether they wanted to go for the final prize money or be paid a flat fee for this race. Kling opted for the prize money and the conservative Lang would later thank him for persuading him also to change his mind. The prize money was easily the better bet.

According to official records, Kling won $17,422 and, after deductions, the driver recalled taking home 42,000 marks – a tidy sum at a time when the average monthly wage in Germany was between 400 and 500 marks. 'I invested everything in my house,' said Kling with obvious satisfaction.

The Carrera Panamericana was certainly a unique and unrepeatable event which was described by respected photojournalist Bernard Cahier as 'a mixed grill of the Mille Miglia, the Coupes des Alpes, the Rallye do Portugal, Targa Florio and Coppa Dolomiti'.

W196 REVIVES
FORMULA 1 GLORY

A S FAR AS POTENTIAL GRAND PRIX involvement was concerned, Mercedes had toyed with the idea of competing with an uprated pre-war car in the 1.5-litre supercharged/4.5-litre naturally aspirated category in 1952, but shelved the idea for a variety of reasons, not least because it was clear that this category would be very thinly supported.

Instead, it was decided to clear the decks for a totally fresh challenge when the new 2.5-litre F1 regulations began in 1954. Germany's economic resurgence in the early 1950s continued at a remarkable rate and nothing symbolized that recovery more graphically than the sight of three sleek 'Silver Arrows' lined up in front of the pits for the 1954 French Grand Prix at Reims.

Ranged against the Ferrari 625s and Maserati 250Fs, the Mercedes W196 was an extremely sophisticated and technically advanced machine. It was perhaps matched only by the Lancia D50 but this was at the time still undergoing a

Dominant début. Juan Manuel Fangio and Karl Kling, both in streamlined Mercedes W196s, on the front row for the start of the 1954 French Grand Prix at Reims. Alberto Ascari is in a factory Maserati.
(Günther Molter)

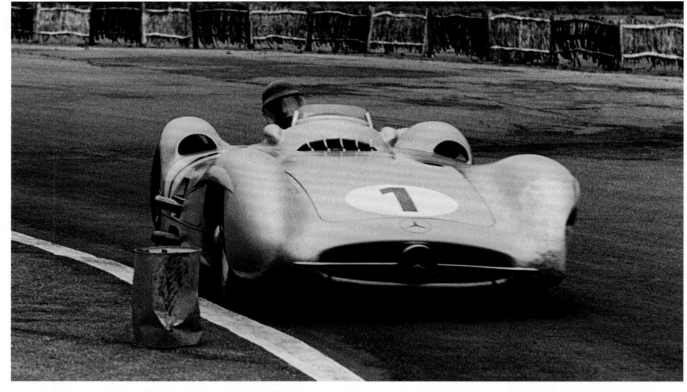

Barrelling round. Juan Manuel Fangio at Silverstone, 1954. (David Hodges Collection)

Fangio's Mercedes W196 open wheeler leads Stirling Moss's Maserati 250F, Hermann Lang's Mercedes open wheeler and Hans Herrmann's streamliner W196 behind the Nürburgring pits on the opening lap of the 1954 German Grand Prix. (DaimlerChrysler Classic Archive)

protracted development phase and would not race for the first time until the end of the season.

The Mercedes was built round an advanced tubular spaceframe which carried an in-line eight-cylinder engine, canted over at a 70-degree angle to keep the car's profile as low as possible.

Designed by a team under the direction of Professor Fritz Nallinger, Dr Manfred Lorscheidt and brilliant engineer Rudolf Uhlenhaut, the car featured inboard drum brakes and Bosch direct fuel injection and, with a capacity of 2,496cc, developed 260bhp at 8,500rpm. This was the starting point on what was originally anticipated to be a five-year development programme which would see the W196 developing more than 300bhp by the end of 1958.

The M196 eight-cylinder engine was also designed with desmodromic valvegear: the valves were forced open and shut by a system of two cams for each valve, thereby enhancing cylinder charging at high revs to produce the requisite high power outputs.

Juan Manuel Fangio was the only world-class driver in the Mercedes line-up, which also included Karl Kling and Hans Herrmann. Moreover, time has tended to throw many people's memories into soft focus: the W196s were not quite the all-conquering titans they were expected to be, at least not as far as the 1954 season was concerned.

Fangio and Kling finished 1–2 at Reims using cars fitted with streamlined all-enveloping bodywork. But this configuration was certainly not the ideal choice for Silverstone which, in those days, was regarded as a medium-speed circuit at best. (In retrospect, this seems amazing as it was the fastest track of all by 1985 when Keke Rosberg put his Williams-Honda on pole position for the British Grand Prix at an average speed of 160mph!) The Mercedes W196 bodies had been developed in the one-fifth scale wind

The Mercedes streamliners lead during the non-title Avusrennen in 1954 where Karl Kling was permitted a deserved home win over Fangio and Hans Herrmann. Here Jean Behra's Gordini hangs on in the slipstream of the Silver Arrows, a performance which encouraged team manager Alfred Neubauer to consider signing the Frenchman for 1955 only to find that Maserati had beaten him to the draw. (DaimlerChrysler Classic Archive)

Juan Manuel Fangio, eventual winner of the 1954 Italian Grand Prix at Monza, outsmarts Ferrari driver Froilan González. (David Hodges Collection)

Chief engineer Rudolf Uhlenhaut (with folded arms) stands with Prof Fritz Nallinger and Dr Hans Scherenberg in the pit lane at Monza, 1954. (DaimlerChrysler Classic Archive)

tunnel at Stuttgart's technical college and represented the first serious post-war attempt at delving into the intricacies of F1 aerodynamics.

Thus while these streamliners were just the job at Reims, they were nowhere near as effective when it came to the British Grand Prix. Whereas Fangio had taken the lead at the start of the French race, at Silverstone it was his old compatriot and sparring partner Froilan González who set the pace with the Ferrari 625.

Contemporary reports suggested that González's confident style was making Fangio's driving appear scrappy by contrast and that his progress was punctuated by several excursions across the grass. Eventually, González emerged a convincing winner from his Ferrari team-mate Mike Hawthorn with Onofre Marimon's Maserati 250F third ahead of Fangio, both a lap down on the victorious red cars from Maranello.

Fangio's car crossed the line with its silver bodywork carrying several ungainly dents, acquired when he clipped the oil drums laid out to delineate the insides of several corners on this bleak former airfield track.

There was another problem too. The race had been run in changeable weather conditions and it was quite evident that the Mercedes tyre supplier, Continental, had quite a bit of work to do to match up with the performance of the rival Pirellis. In fact, at Monza later in the season the team tested on Pirelli rubber which initially proved quicker.

However, the Continental technical staff – strengthened by the recruitment of Hans Klenk who had quit active driving after being badly injured while testing a Mercedes 300SL at Nürburgring in 1953 – reduced the tyre pressures and the 'Contis' proved even quicker. It was an early lesson in an element of F1 technology which today is taken absolutely for granted, namely that pressures need to be tailored from circuit to circuit in order to optimise the performance of the rubber.

For Mercedes's home race at Nürburgring, Fangio was allotted a W196 prepared to conventional open-wheeled specification. He won this race in commanding style but with a heavy heart. During practice his young friend and compatriot Onofre Marimon had crashed his Maserati 250F at *Wehrseifen* and suffered fatal injuries. González was so distraught that Mike Hawthorn had to take over his Ferrari to finish the race second behind Fangio.

'Nobody gave a thought to safety in those days,' reflected Kling. 'Even in the development of the cars that was true. Safety simply wasn't in the concept of the car. I welcome the fact that it has changed – in terms of both cars and circuits. I think it's a big step forward in motor racing. In my time, nobody mentioned it.

'I had a very bad accident at the Nürburgring, in the Alfa Romeo Disco Volante, in 1953. Mercedes at that time were preparing for the F1 return in 1954, and were not racing, so I asked them if I could drive for Alfa Romeo that year. They were interested in what the other teams were doing, so they said yes!

'As for the accident ... I don't want to say what happened, as a courtesy to the team, who were very nice to me, but something happened which shouldn't have happened. It wasn't my fault, I can say that. Onofre Marimon crashed at almost the same place when something broke on his car. Every company has problems of that kind – we did with Mercedes-Benz, too. It's normal, if you go to the limit everywhere. It's part of the game.'

In this particular race at Nürburgring, Kling had perhaps demonstrated rather less restraint than the Mercedes team had hoped for when it came to battling Fangio.

The 2.5-litre Mercedes W196 was built round an advanced tubular spaceframe which carried an in-line eight-cylinder engine, canted over at a 70-degree angle to keep the car's profile as low as possible. (David Hodges Collection)

Ready for action, a W196 setting forth on the distinctive Mercedes transporter built at Rudolf Uhlenhaut's behest. (David Hodges Collection)

Stirling Moss in the Mercedes W196 on the starting grid prior to the Buenos Aires City Grand Prix in 1955. This was a Formule Libre race, so the W196 was fitted with one of the 3-litre engines destined for the 300SLR sports racer. Stirling finished second to Fangio in this event. (Roebuck Collection)

Understandably, he wanted to do very well in front of his home crowd, but some people seemed to think he extended himself a little too far.

Kling freely acknowledged that team orders were in Fangio's favour during 1954, a fact which was unsurprising. Alfred Neubauer and his Buenos Aires-based intermediary, Mercedes director Baron Arnt von Korff, had expended a great deal of effort to secure the great Argentine driver's services and did not wish to squander their asset.

'Yes, there were [team orders], but what was important was that Mercedes should win,' said Kling. 'In 1954, the team orders were in Fangio's favour, but that was correct, because he had the best chance to win the World Championship – he had already scored a lot of points that season with Maserati, before Mercedes returned.'

Kling lost a wheel on his first lap of practice, damaging his W196 and sustaining a black eye. As a result, he started at the back of the grid and just went flat-out. He drove superbly to climb from tenth to third in just three laps and was behind Fangio and pre-war veteran Hermann Lang with seven of the 22 laps completed. Lang's retirement left Kling storming along in second place, but he was more than a minute behind Fangio and – according to the team's standing rules at the time – should therefore have refrained from challenging his team-mate. Yet Kling was determined to have a crack at winning the German Grand Prix. It would have been the absolute pinnacle of his achievement had he managed to score Mercedes' first win on home soil since 1939, but the pit crew was becoming increasingly restive.

Firstly, drivers Lang and Hans Herrmann stood out in front of the pits jointly holding a signalling board with a large 'L' – for *Langsam* or slow – only for Kling to ignore it. Then Neubauer tried. Kling ignored him. Finally, Dr Fritz Nallinger – technical director of the racing department – brandished the signal, shaking his fist at Kling for good measure. But the German driver pressed on at high speed, overtaking Fangio for the lead. By his own admission, Fangio was 'wondering what it was all about' and simply sat on Kling's tail, then went ahead to win after Kling came into the pits.

'I had to stop for fuel,' recalled Kling, 'so I really had to step on it. The Nürburgring was my home track and the pits made frantic signals at me for attacking Fangio. But I was only attacking him because I needed to make an extra stop for refuelling.'

When Kling finally came into the pits for repairs to a damaged rear suspension arm – probably caused by sliding into a grass bank somewhere round the epic 14-mile *Nordschleife* – Neubauer really gave him a roasting. More seriously, Dr Nallinger wanted him fired. 'Kling must not drive for us again,' he fumed. 'A man who's incapable of team discipline and who drives his car to death is no use to us.' Thankfully, Nallinger changed his mind when Neubauer relayed the driver's explanation for why he had pressed on so hard!

'Of course, technical development was nothing like as radical as it is today,' reflected Kling in 1997. 'We tested a lot at home – in Stuttgart – on moving dynos, rolling road, as the team do today. [But] between the races, development did not progress. In those days, we didn't talk in terms of hundredths and thousandths of a second, but of whole seconds. Engines were run for two or three races – not for one practice session! Of course, the engines were far less sensitive than they are now. We were only allowed to rev them to 8,500–9,000 at the most.'

So did Kling run flat-out through most Grands Prix in those days, or did he take a more tactical approach?

'It depended on your position,' he said. 'You wanted to go as fast as possible, but this depended on how the race was going. In the 1954 German Grand Prix I was flat-out all the way. In Saturday practice, I did only one lap, because then I lost a front wheel. I had to start from the back, and I ran my car to the limit – more was not possible. I was at 9,000 revs for a lot of the way that day, and I didn't care about it.

'In the fifties, the contact between the drivers was more friendly than today, I think. Everything was less commercialized, more … gentlemanly … than now. Even before the war, Mercedes and Auto Union would very often eat together in the evening. I can only go by what I hear and read these days, of course, but I don't get the impression it's like that now.'

Impressive victory on the Rio de la Plata
Grand Prix of Argentina 1955

1. World champion J. M. Fangio
4. Herrmann / Kling / Moss

MERCEDES-BENZ

(engl.)

Stirling Moss (no.6) and Juan Manuel Fangio (no.2) head the pack at the 1955 Monaco Grand Prix. (David Hodges Collection)

Alberto Ascari follows Fangio at the 1955 Monaco Grand Prix. It was the Italian maestro's last race. (LAT)

The Nürburgring race also marked the last Grand Prix outing for Hermann Lang, who ran off the road at Flugplatz while running third. Later it transpired that the engine had seized, but not before stories circulated to the effect that the 45-year-old former Champion had simply dropped it. People said he had lost his touch. Rumours abounded that he was also drinking too much. He was not in the team for the Swiss Grand Prix at Bremgarten where Fangio won again ahead of González's Ferrari and young Hans Herrmann who had been drafted into the Mercedes team. Kling retired with engine failure.

At Monza, Fangio again scraped home the winner in the W196 streamliner, but not before two key rivals fell by the wayside. The Ferrari team was determined to do well on its home turf and negotiated for Alberto Ascari to be released from his Lancia contract for this specific event. The Italian driver had been sitting around for much of the year vainly waiting for the new high-tech Lancia D50 to be readied and now jumped at the chance of displaying his legendary skills.

Driving brilliantly in a Ferrari 625 powered by the later type 553 'Super Squalo' engine, Ascari shook himself free of Fangio and pulled out a nine second lead before a valve broke. That let Stirling Moss through into the lead in his Maserati but this suffered a fractured oil pipe, allowing the Mercedes through to win ahead of Mike Hawthorn's Ferrari.

Lang made another appearance in practice at Monza where Neubauer required him to prove himself against Herrmann. The young man won the confrontation and Lang was obliged to stand aside.

This race was followed by a patriotic interlude at Berlin's Avus track where a non-championship F1 race took place, the Mercedes team squaring up to only makeweight opposition. The streamlined W196s played to the crowd with Kling being allowed a diplomatic win ahead of Fangio and Herrmann. Even so, much attention was grabbed by the Frenchman Jean Behra who gamely kept his underpowered Gordini running hard in the Mercedes' slipstream until its over-taxed engine finally broke.

Behra made quite an impression on Neubauer that day and the Frenchman was considered as a possible team-mate for Fangio in 1955. Unfortunately, by the time the Mercedes team manager was ready to make a bid, Behra had committed himself to Maserati. Avus also saw Lang again try to make the field, but again Neubauer opted for

Fangio, the master. Monaco, 1955. (David Hodges Collection)

Herrmann. It was the end of the road for Lang's career.

Mike Hawthorn then gave the Ferrari a win in the Spanish GP at Barcelona's Pedralbes circuit, followed home by Luigi Musso's Maserati and Fangio in the Mercedes. It was sufficient to clinch Fangio's second World Championship crown with 42 points (net) ahead of González (25) and Hawthorn (24.5). Five scores out of nine counted.

Hawthorn would remember that race with particular satisfaction. After seeing off an early challenge from privateer Harry Schell's Maserati, he recalled: 'The Squalo was going beautifully, while the Mercedes was giving trouble and Fangio was struggling on, covered in oil and black dust. The pit signalled each lap to tell me what the gap was between Fangio and I, but towards the end the Mercedes began to trail a smoke screen and was beaten into second place by Musso's Maserati.'

For the 1955 season Moss duly gained his promotion to the Mercedes works team, but that season the German equipe was scheduled to face possibly its most formidable opposition – Lancia's new D50 in the hands of Ascari. It didn't show in the race results, but on the car's début in the 1954 Spanish GP, Ascari was pulling away at two seconds a lap before retiring with what was officially described as clutch trouble.

Weighing in at 1,367lb (620kg), the D50 was one of the lightest Grand Prix cars of its era. The Mercedes W196 tipped the scales at 1,587lb (720kg) in aerodynamic trim and 1,521lb (690kg) in open-wheeled form, while the Ferrari 625 weighed 1,433lb (650kg), the 553 'Squalo' just over 1,300lb (590kg) and the Maserati 250F 1,389lb (630kg).

The history of Mercedes' domination might have been very different had Ascari been able to début the Lancia at Reims on the same day as the W196. But it was not until Ascari lapped Monza during testing a full three seconds faster than Fangio's best in the Mercedes streamliner that Gianni Lancia gave the green light for the D50's racing début.

Fangio scored a decisive victory in the 1955 Argentine GP season-opener at Buenos Aires, with González a solid second sharing his Ferrari 625 with Trintignant and Farina. A week later Fangio and Moss finished 1–2 in the Gran Premio de Buenos Aires Formule Libre race in which the W196s were fitted with the 3-litre engines from the 300SLR sports racers.

This was followed by the long haul back home from South America. The European F1 season started in Monaco, which proved a total disaster for Mercedes. Hans Herrmann crashed in practice, breaking a hip, and his place was taken in the team by the relatively slow French driver André Simon.

Although the Mercedes team produced several permuta-

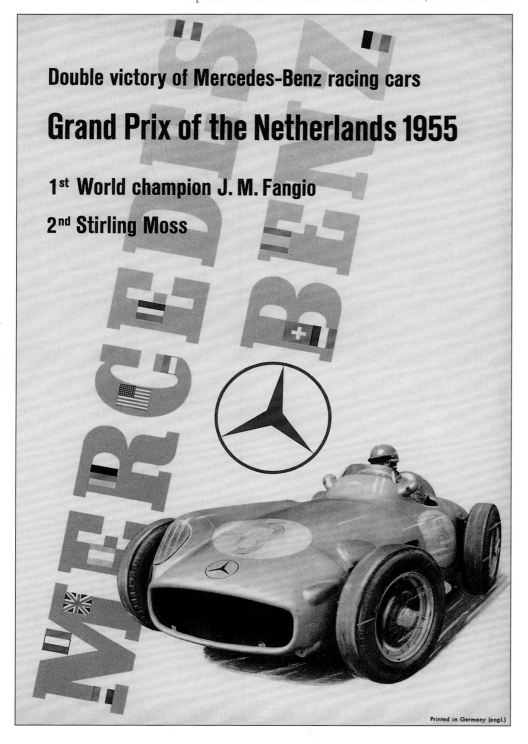

Double victory of Mercedes-Benz racing cars

Grand Prix of the Netherlands 1955

1st World champion J. M. Fangio

2nd Stirling Moss

Printed in Germany (engl.)

tions of chassis, with various wheelbases and the choice of either inboard or outboard brake set-ups, neither Fangio nor Moss could win. Victory fell to Maurice Trintignant's reliable Ferrari 625, while Ascari crashed his Lancia into the harbour when poised to take the lead. Four days later Ascari was killed testing a Ferrari sports car at Monza.

Thereafter, the Mercedes W196s finished first and second in the four remaining races on the World

Championship calendar. Fangio led Moss across the line at Spa-Francorchamps and Zandvoort, but in front of Stirling's home crowd in the British Grand Prix the positions were reversed. Britain's 'Golden Boy' – who had insisted on carrying the Union flag on the tail of his silver Mercedes – won by a nose from the canny Argentine ace.

Forty-five years later, Stirling Moss admitted that he was still not totally certain whether or not Fangio allowed him

Start of the 1955 British Grand Prix at Aintree with the four Mercedes W196s accelerating into an immediate lead in the order Fangio (10), Moss (12), Kling (14) and Taruffi (50). (DaimlerChrysler Classic Archive)

At this stage Fangio still leads Moss at Aintree. (David Hodges Collection)

to win that sunny afternoon at Aintree. 'I know I was driving well that day but, boy, the Old Man seemed to be able to haul up alongside me whenever he liked!'

When questioned on the matter in the years prior to his death in 1995, Fangio would simply grin and adopt a self-effacingly dignified response. 'No, no, Stirling beat me,' he would say. 'He had a lower final drive ratio fitted to his car before the race, and there was no way my car could catch his under acceleration.'

There had been few days like it in the history of Formula 1. Mercedes came, saw and conquered at Aintree in a quite remarkable tour-de-force which had Karl Kling and Piero Taruffi finishing third and fourth in a unique grand slam.

Some people have suggested that Moss's victory was nothing more than a PR exercise, but this under-sells both drivers. They had a tremendous respect and affection for each other which spanned the 20-year gap between their ages. Stirling, at 25, was motor racing's great new hope. Fangio, at the peak of his success, was only three years

STIRLING MOSS
Golden boy

Stirling Moss's versatility and consistency were the key qualities which made him such a great driver. He drove with the unflustered artistry of a natural star, never had an off-day, seldom made a mistake and, had it not been for his patriotism, would have been World Champion several times over.

Having made his name in the cut-and-thrust of the immediate post-war 500cc Formula 3 scene, this son of a wealthy dentist graduated to international racing with the HWM team in 1951. Yet it was not until 1954 that Moss stepped up into the F1 front line when, thanks to financial support from BP, he was able to acquire his own Maserati 250F.

Prior to this, Moss's manager Ken Gregory had approached Neubauer, saying that he'd heard Mercedes was after Fangio's services, but it would be much better to sign up Stirling as the young Englishman was a better bet. Neubauer remembered that when Moss's name was first mentioned 'it meant no more to me than Herbert Smith or Alfred Jones'. He told Gregory to get 'his friend' to buy an old Maserati and prove that he was better than Fangio. If he did so, then Neubauer promised they would talk again 12 months later.

Although this was not a factory-entered car, it was a state-of-the-art F1 machine and enabled the youngster to blow away Juan Manuel Fangio's Mercedes in the 1954 Italian Grand Prix at Monza before the Maserati's oil pressure wilted. It was a performance which earned Moss a drive in a works Mercedes in 1955, a season which would see him win the British Grand Prix at Aintree by inches from Fangio.

However, when Stirling accepted the Mercedes drive for 1955 there was some indignation at Maserati who felt that he

had committed to drive for their works team. But no contract had been signed, so Moss was free.

The hard-boiled brigade in post-war Britain also 'tut-tutted' furiously at the notion of Stirling going over to drive for the Germans, but Moss defused that controversy by saying he would be very willing to drive for a British F1 team if they had a competitive car. At that stage, none of them did.

Yet it was perhaps the 1955 Mille Miglia, in which his Mercedes 300SLR was navigated by journalist Denis Jenkinson, which was the most remarkable victory of Moss's entire career (for the full story see Chapter 6). The whole adventure was a tour-de-force of organisational genius, detailed preparation and iron nerve.

It was also an example of Moss's extraordinary energy. After they had finished the 1,000-mile route in fractionally over ten hours, Moss showered, attended the prize-giving and drove off over the Alps in his Mercedes 220A 'company car' to Stuttgart where he lunched the following day with the Daimler-Benz directors. He then drove on to London, arriving at the end of the following day.

Moss – thrifty as well as hyper-active – recalls that the Mercedes racing drivers were given a one dollar a day allowance to have their cars cleaned, the feeling being that a dirty car projected the wrong image. He admits that he pocketed the dollars and cleaned the car himself, 'not every day, you understand, but certainly when Neubauer was around!'

In 1956 he drove for the works Maserati team, then for millionaire bearing magnate Tony Vandervell's Vanwall team for the following two years. Thereafter he preferred to race mainly for British private owner Rob Walker through to the accident which ended his career at the age of 32 at the Easter Monday Goodwood international meeting in 1962.

Ready for the great adventure. Stirling Moss and Denis Jenkinson in the cockpit of their Mercedes 300SLR prior to the start of the 1955 Mille Miglia. (DaimlerChrysler Classic Archive)

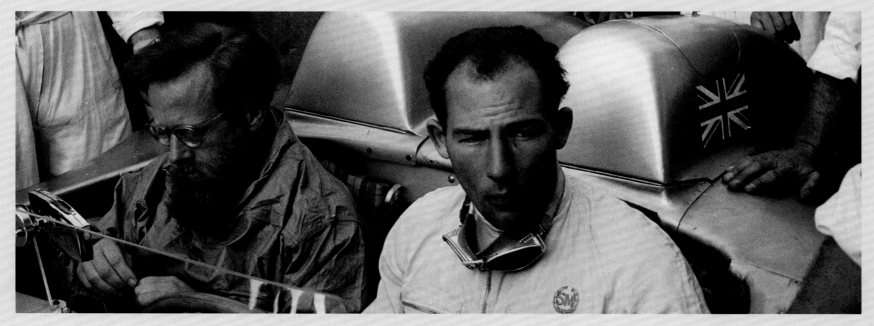

JUAN MANUEL FANGIO
Inspirational to the end

One of the great masters of the 1950s, the Argentine driver achieved his dazzling success quite late in life and was already past his 40th birthday when he clinched his first World Championship for Alfa Romeo in 1951.

Fangio combined great self-belief with a diffident outward manner which some rivals misread at their peril. He was a master tactician with unswerving judgement and a physical resilience bred from racing rugged Chevrolet-engined specials in dusty road races across South America.

In 1949 he came to Europe to drive an F1 Maserati sponsored by the Argentine government. His exploits with that car earned him a seat in a factory Alfa Romeo for the 1950

The characteristically relaxed Fangio dominated the 1955 Monaco Grand Prix until his Mercedes W196 suffered valvegear failure. (David Hodges Collection)

season, which saw the start of the official Drivers' World Championship. After winning the first of his five titles the following year, he switched to the Maserati team for the next two seasons during which the championship was contested by F2 machines owing to a shortage of proper F1 cars.

In 1954 Mercedes-Benz returned to Grand Prix racing and Fangio was the obvious choice as team leader. The following year he was partnered by Stirling Moss, then he moved to Ferrari in 1956, then back to Maserati to win his fifth title, four of them in a row.

Fangio was competitive right to the end of his career, a fact underlined by his stunning defeat of the Ferrari team in the 1957 German Grand Prix. On the 14-mile Nürburgring the Argentine driver broke his own lap record no fewer than six times. He was truly inspirational.

away from retirement. They were both professionals, with a shrewd and accurate perception of each other's worth. If Aintree 1955 was a demonstration run, then the 'Old Man' certainly made Stirling work for his money.

In fact, Fangio sprinted into the lead at the start, only to let Moss ahead without any fuss after just three of the race's 90 laps. From then onwards the two W196s simply streaked away from their opposition, Jean Behra's dogged challenge from third place coming to a premature end after just ten laps when the engine on his Maserati blew apart.

On lap 17, Fangio asserted his authority once more and retook the lead, but it was only another nine laps before Stirling, encouraged by the crowd's vociferous support, went ahead again. It was a tantalising chase. But how would it be resolved? On the face of it, all Stirling had to do was to keep out of trouble, but the pressure on him was enormous. Unflustered, he pressed on, picking his way through the backmarkers with expert precision.

With ten laps left to run, Moss seemed to have his home Grand Prix in the bag. He'd opened a four-second margin over his team-mate, yet Fangio came back relentlessly at him in the closing stages. Stirling just held on to finish his historic task. This was an unashamedly emotional moment. As they celebrated their joint success Stirling generously placed his winner's laurels around Fangio's neck, which conveyed his true feelings more dramatically than any words could ever have done.

The race encapsulated the role of well-matched team-mates in the Mercedes-Benz motor racing story, a legend which has repeated itself in differing circumstances over the decades. All these pairings have been spawned – directly or indirectly – by the commitment of Mercedes and its partners to employ the best drivers available at all times. There had been no obvious team orders at Aintree. Neubauer merely relied on the well-ordered good sense of his drivers to race competitively while keeping in mind the overall interests of the company.

Transmission problems caused Moss to retire at Monza, but Fangio led Taruffi home to the final 1–2 of the season, winning his third World Championship with 40 points to Moss's 23 counting five scores from seven races. Yet it was all coming to an end for Mercedes-Benz and Formula 1.

After the 300SLR of Stirling Moss and Peter Collins had scored the Targa Florio victory which clinched Mercedes the Sports Car World Championship, Neubauer returned to the villa the team was renting to find an envelope addressed to him marked 'Personal and Confidential'.

This was from Professor Fritz Nallinger. It read: 'The Board of Directors has decided, after the most careful consideration, to withdraw from motor racing for several years'.

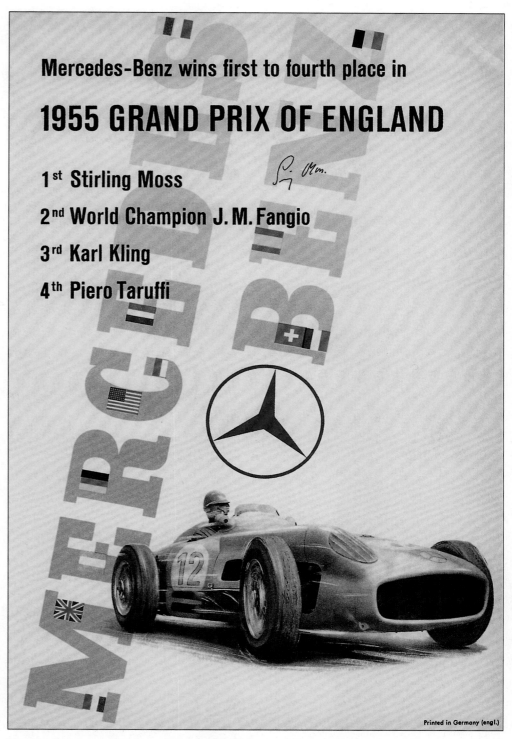

Mercedes-Benz wins first to fourth place in

1955 GRAND PRIX OF ENGLAND

1st Stirling Moss

2nd World Champion J. M. Fangio

3rd Karl Kling

4th Piero Taruffi

Printed in Germany (engl.)

For Neubauer, to whom motor racing had been almost as important as food and drink, it was the moment he had been dreading.

THE 300SLR WEAVES
ITS MILLE MIGLIA LEGEND

With Alfred Neubauer watching from behind the starting ramp (right, wearing hat), Moss and Jenkinson prepare for the Mille Miglia start. (DaimlerChrysler Classic Archive)

IT IS GIVEN TO A MERE HANDFUL of cars to win a major international motor race on their first appearance, but the remarkable success of the elegant Mercedes-Benz 300SLR on its début outing in the 1955 Mille Miglia certainly continued a great Stuttgart tradition.

Like the W25 in 1934 and the W196 twenty years later, the 300SLR was not simply designed and developed for a specific purpose. It was also tested, rigorously and methodically, by a company with all the necessary resources to hand, before it rolled out on the circuit in competitive anger for the first time. This meticulous attention to engineering detail would add more lustre to the already enviable Mercedes legend.

Alongside F1, throughout 1955 Mercedes was cam-

paigning a full programme of sports car races with the elegant 300SLR. Powered by a 78 x 78mm, 2,992cc version of the Grand Prix engine, it also used a basic chassis which was very closely related to the W196 with slight modifications incorporated to provide for an enlarged fuel tank and two-seater cockpit. The end result was clothed in an aerodynamic body which took more than a few design cues from the central-seat W196 streamliner.

The 300SLR would go down in history as one of the most famous of all the Mercedes-Benz competition cars. Tragically, a 300SLR was also involved in the most dreadful accident in motor racing history when Pierre Levegh's car vaulted into the crowd at Le Mans a month after the Mille Miglia triumph, killing more than 80 onlookers.

In the immediate post-war years Denis Jenkinson spent all his money on a racing Norton to embrace a gypsy-like existence in Europe, earning a bob or two racing in predominantly minor league events. By 1949, he paired up with Eric Oliver to ride 'in the chair' and helped win the sidecar World Championship. In 1954, he partnered John Heath in an HWM-Jaguar on the Mille Miglia.

Jenks recalled that Mercedes' preparation for the 1955 event took a full three months, and could remember the very moment at which the germ of the idea took hold in his mind. It was Monday 6 September 1954, the day on which he watched at Monza as the prototype of what would become the Mercedes-Benz 300SLR was put through its preliminary trials. American driver John Fitch was also watching this test and hoping that he might be included in the Mercedes factory sports car team on the strength of his competitive performance with the 300SL in the 1953 Carrera Panamericana.

Jenks fell into discussion with Fitch about the possibility of making pace notes for the 1955 Italian road race and agreed to partner him. In the end, all Mercedes could promise Fitch was a position as the team's reserve driver, plus the loan of a 300SL 'gullwing' coupé for an attempt at winning the GT category of the Mille Miglia. Moss also heard of the idea and, with Fitch's agreement, Jenkinson switched to drive with Britain's F1 rising star in a works 300SLR.

The generous-minded Fitch later wrote: 'I was especially interested in the prospects for Stirling Moss who, besides being a good friend on the same team, though in a different class, carried with him the red-bearded journalist Denis Jenkinson, one of the Mille Miglia's greatest enthusiasts.

'Jenks is utterly captivated by the event for its physical length and variety, its place in the history of motor racing and perhaps as a kind of throwback to the spectacles of the Middle Ages. His passion for it made him extraordinarily

They're off. The 300SLR accelerates away down Brescia's Via Rebuffone into the rising sun. (DaimlerChrysler Classic Archive)

good in his navigating job; he could remember whole sections of the long single lap without reference to notes. Previously, we had planned to form a team, before Stirling had joined the Mercedes factory, so I was anxious to see him succeed in the contest which had so captured his imagination.'

Preparations for the race were characteristically thorough and detailed, as one would have expected from the Mercedes-Benz squad. Moss and Jenks ran many laps at Hockenheim, deciding on which windscreen configuration would give them the most comfortable ride and even experimenting with intercom systems to help with the navigation process. Stirling eventually opted for Jenks's special repertoire of hand signals as the best way of tackling the challenge, explaining that the idea of somebody talking to him through a headset would be unnecessarily distracting.

Of course, practice for this epic event took place on crowded public roads, with all the drama and chaos that involved. The preparation was pretty evenly split for Moss and Jenks between Stirling's Mercedes 220A road car, a 300SL 'gullwing' coupé and the full blown 300SLR racer.

Jenks explained that the prototype 300SLR was provided to give them an early run round the route. It was a particularly important assessment to see just how well this bespoke racing car's engine, transmission and running gear coped with the thumping, banging and general abuse involved in pounding round the public roads of Italy.

'We were given instructions not to exceed 170mph in fifth gear, always fill the fuel tank with Agip Supercortemaggiore petrol, not to hurry, and to take two days to complete the first lap, and not to drive in the dark,' he recounted.

The initial overall feeling was very upbeat. The car performed well and they were both amazed by its staggering mid-range acceleration, 'the feeling that its acceleration between 50 and 150mph was absolutely constant'. Moreover, on that first run Moss and Jenks arrived in Pescara easily in time for lunch, having averaged 80mph in traffic from their start in Brescia.

The first practice lap was completed without any problems. On the third day they embarked on their second lap once the 300SLR had been examined from top to bottom. Tyre wear was monitored in precise detail, front brakes checked for wear and stripped down, the engine checked for oil leaks, and the transmission and clutch dismantled.

On this second lap Stirling managed to average 95mph

The Moss/Jenkinson equipe on its way to victory in the Mille Miglia, 1955...
(David Hodges Collection)

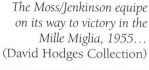

for the first hour and a half, then everything began to go wrong. First it started to rain, then a stone punctured the radiator and, after a spare radiator had been rushed out and fitted to the stranded SLR, it began to snow. 'We struggled another 200 miles in conditions which ranged from hail to three inches of slush on the road, and ice forming on the windscreen and our goggles faster than we could rub it off,' said Jenks.

Happily, by the time they reached Rome the conditions cleared and everything looked fine. Then they hit a hump, spun and a rear wheel struck a low concrete bollard as the Mercedes lurched into a ditch. That was that. Soon afterwards, Kling and Herrmann arrived in their 220, picking up Moss and Jenks who continued the second lap in the rear seats. The next morning they woke to find snow covering the whole of central Italy. All of which put paid to any further practice for the moment.

Jenks would also recall how one day he and Moss set out for a practice run in a 300SL 'gullwing' coupé and Fangio, driving one of the pukka 300SLRs, caught them as they went into the section through the Abruzzi mountains.

'Speed and power were not important on that section,' mused Jenks. 'Rising to the challenge, as any good racing driver would, Stirling tucked in behind and drove on the limit to stay with the Old Boy. That was exciting, but the open car gradually pulled away from us.

'On another practice run, Fangio was in his pale blue Mercedes cabriolet touring car and we were in Stirling's 220 saloon. We were going down the Adriatic coast road, in and out of the normal daily traffic, and were astounded by the way Fangio was carving his way through gaps with this big, dignified cabriolet.

'After about ten minutes of this, Stirling backed off and said, "if I try and keep this pace, we'll collect a donkey cart or a truck". Then he grinned and added, "or collect the Old Boy when he bounces back off a rock". But inwardly we knew that Fangio would not be doing that.

'One night at Modena, as darkness was falling and we had finished for the day, there was a roaring noise outside the hotel so we went out to take a look. There was Fangio in the 300SLR "practice car" with only one headlamp working, saying that he was pressing on back to Brescia,

"only three more hours…" He had started out that morning and was completing a whole practice lap of the 1,000-mile route without a break, something we never managed.'

Another memorable incident took place on 1 April 1955, exactly one month to the day prior to the Mille Miglia itself. Moss and Jenks set off from Brescia at 6.30am in a competition 'gullwing' coupé. They had just left Forli, on the outward leg to Pescara, and were accelerating back up to a decent speed when an army lorry turned across their path.

Stirling did everything he could to avoid a collision, but the right front corner of the 300SL ploughed into the truck and was very definitely not going anywhere else that day. They didn't quite know what to do, but it was clear that they needed to get in touch with Neubauer as quickly as possible.

Jenks took up the tale: 'Arrangements were made to get the wrecked Mercedes to the Fiat garage in Forli. A middle-aged dark and swarthy man offered to take us in his Fiat Topolino, so Stirling got in the front and I got in the back.

'The man explained that he owned the Fiat garage and

… and exultation and exhaustion as they take the chequered flag. (David Hodges Collection)

his breakdown truck would deal with the Merc. Then he said, "you are practising for the Mille Miglia? I won the Mille Miglia in 1937 with [Carlo] Pintacuda". When I replied, "you are Paride Mambelli?" he smiled and said "yes" and drove us quietly back to his garage.'

Neubauer was totally sympathetic when he heard about the accident, relieved only that Moss and Jenkinson had emerged without injury. He told them to wait in Forli while mechanics were dispatched with Stirling's own 'company' 220A saloon car to bring them back to Brescia.

Meanwhile, Moss and Jenks were preparing for an interview with the local Chief of Police. They approached this with some trepidation feeling, perhaps naturally, that one of the locals might be less than sympathetic to the antics of a famous racing driver such as Moss.

'Our interpreter took us to the fortress-like building that was the police headquarters,' said Jenks, 'and after being escorted down endless corridors into the very depths of the huge building, we were ushered into a vast office, and behind a large desk sat a very imposing gentleman in an immaculate pale blue uniform, with gold epaulets.

'We were beginning to tremble a bit because we thought we were in for trouble, driving too fast, a racing car on the road, driving without due care and attention, and everything else in the book.

'The Chief of Police indicated us to take a seat and we sat down there like two schoolboys in front of the headmaster. Putting his elbows on the desk, he placed his fingertips together in a most elegant fashion and said in perfect English, "the Mille Miglia is a wonderful race, I drove it myself three years ago in a small 750cc Stanguellini. Unfortunately it broke down, so I did not finish. But I am proud to say I drove in the Mille Miglia. It is a wonderful race."'

Moss and Jenks breathed a silent sigh of relief. The only thing the Chief of Police was slightly disappointed about was the fact that Mercedes had agreed to pay for the repairs on the 300SL if the army repaired its own truck.

'A pity,' he said. 'We have been waiting for something like this for a long time.' It transpired that the army trucks were always causing traffic accidents but, being the military, they were untouchable. But now they had been involved in an accident with 'foreign tourists' the Police Chief saw this as a golden opportunity to take them to the cleaners. Unfortunately not on this occasion.

Jenks committed the entire 1,000-mile route to a 17-ft long sheet of paper which was encased in a little metal box and scrolled past a perspex window. He kept Moss guided by a series of pre-agreed hand signals for the ten-hour marathon – and they won commandingly.

Anybody wishing to read Jenkinson's epic account of what it was like sitting alongside one of the most talented

Twentieth anniversary. Denis Jenkinson and the author together with a road test Mercedes 450SE retracing the Mille Miglia route over the Raticosa Pass, April 1975. (LAT)

racing drivers of all time during a 1,000-mile dash round Italy should beg, borrow or steal a copy of the June 1955 edition of *Motor Sport* magazine. It is a riveting piece of journalism.

Jenkinson, a profoundly logical and pragmatic fellow, manages to build the tension superbly while at the same time reflecting his inner confidence that all the pre-race preparation, allied to the superb standards of engineering which had gone into the 300SLR, would be vindicated. He was right.

At 7.22am on the morning of 1 May 1955, the Mercedes mechanics pushed the gleaming 300SLR up onto the starting platform in Brescia's Via Rebuffone in order to save undue wear on its clutch. Moss and Jenks settled in their seats and, once the starting signal was given, accelerated hard away into the fierce rising sun which would be shining brightly into their faces from the eastern sky for the first couple of hours of the event.

By the time the Mercedes duo reached Padua, Moss could see a red speck in his mirror. This proved to be the 4.4-litre Ferrari of Italian hero Eugenio Castellotti which dodged ahead of the silver 300SLR when Stirling slid wide and bumped its nose on a trackside hay bale shortly afterwards.

It did not take long for Moss to pull back onto Castellotti's tail, but the Italian was really thrashing his Ferrari to keep in front, great plumes of smoke pouring from the tyres. At the Ravenna control the Mercedes re-passed while Castellotti was having his tyres replaced. From then on it was flat-out down the Adriatic coast to Pescara with not a moment to enjoy the view of the shimmering Adriatic waters on their left-hand side.

At Pescara the 300SLR was refuelled. Jenks remembered that there was just enough time for somebody to hand him a slice of orange, a peeled banana, and a sheet of paper telling him they were second behind Taruffi and ahead of Herrmann, Kling and Fangio, before Moss dropped the clutch and they were accelerating back into the fray.

Exiting Pescara the Mercedes had another bump with straw bales but survived intact. Over the mountains to Rome Moss picked up more time, driving with an assurance and cool which was underpinned by his absolute faith in Jenkinson's navigating notes.

Despite bottoming out at speed over a level crossing going into Rome, the Mercedes pressed on towards the control which effectively marked the half distance spot. Moss jumped out for a brief pee, the windscreen was quickly cleaned, new rear tyres fitted and the car fuelled up again.

By this stage they were running first by more than a

minute from Taruffi and were determined to disprove the old Mille Miglia legend which predicted 'he who leads in Rome is never the winner'.

Accelerating hard out of the city, Moss and Jenkinson were depressed to see Kling's 300SLR badly damaged well off the road in amongst the trees. Mercifully, their team-mate had not been badly hurt and the leaders pressed on, putting the thoughts of his unfortunate excursion quickly out of their minds.

Up over the Radicofani pass they stormed towards Florence with the 300SLR never missing a beat, then up across the Futa pass before coming down onto the flat lowlands of the Emilia Romagna where the next port of call was the Bologna control.

Moss continued to pile on the pressure, knowing that if they could get back to Brescia within ten hours they would have averaged 100mph for the entire event. They nearly made it. Having dodged almost every hazard, and with the Mercedes eight-cylinder engine still singing along happy at 7,500rpm any time it was required to do so, the winning partnership roared home into Brescia to become only the second non-Italian to win the prestigious event.

Their total time for the 1,000 miles was 10hr 7m 48s, an average of nearly 98mph, a remarkable achievement.

As Jenks summed it up in *Motor Sport*: 'It was with a justified feeling of elation that I lay in a hot bath, for I had

Denis Jenkinson, Stirling Moss and Karl Kling together with one of the Mercedes 300SLRs at the factory test track, Untertürkheim, in April 1975. (LAT)

had the unique experience of being with Stirling Moss throughout his epic drive, sitting beside him while he worked as I have never seen anyone work before in my life, and harder and longer than I ever thought it possible for a human being to do.

'It was indeed a unique experience, the greatest experience in the whole of the 22 years during which I have been interested in motor racing, an experience that was beyond my wildest imagination, with a result that even now I find extremely hard to believe.

'After previous Mille Miglias I have said, "he who wins the Mille Miglia is some driver, and the car he uses is some sports car". I now say it again with the certain knowledge that I know what I'm talking about and writing about this time.'

Jenks felt it was an enormous privilege to have become what can best be described as an 'associate member' of the Mercedes-Benz family. He was highly impressed with Alfred Neubauer's organisational capabilities, even though some other members of the team regarded the rotund team manager as a little too much of a self-publicist.

'He brooked no interference with his decisions and was the absolute commander-in-chief. Strict as he was, he had a great sense of comedy at the right time, and to see him impersonating the walk of Marilyn Monroe or to listen to some of his stories in an after-dinner session was wonderful.

'He could drink anyone else under the table, especially on Strega, and just when you thought he was losing control and his eyes were closing into an alcoholic sleep, he would spring up, clap his hands and say "Moss, Jenkinson, in der bed, start six hours in the morning, come" and you just had to go to bed at 10pm and be ready to start practice at dawn next morning.

'The incredible thing was that as you staggered down at 6am, having been woken by Neubauer's booming voice on the phone, there he was in his slippers and pyjamas to see that everything was in order and that you had all you wanted before starting out on a 1,000-mile practice lap.

'Many times the hotel manager told me that he had left Neubauer at 2.30am, still knocking back the Strega, yet he never missed seeing you off.

'One thing that will always endear that grand old gentleman to me was when we crashed the factory training 300SL, and went into his office to tell him about it, feeling like two naughty schoolboys.

'His first words were, "are you both unhurt? The car is nothing, we can repair that, but to repair you is more difficult". I am sure that anyone who came under his strict, but exceedingly warm influence, had the greatest respect for him, not only as a team manager but as a man.'

Jenkinson's affectionate views were perhaps not totally shared by Hans Herrmann who, being the 'baby' of the team in the early 1950s, has rather more irreverent memories.

'Uhlenhaut was in technical charge, while Neubauer knew other important things like where the best restaurants were, the best wine,' he told the author in 1999.

'No, I joke. He busied himself in the pits kicking out journalists who were standing in the way. He also controlled which trousers we wore and when we went to bed. I shared a room with him during the period before the start of the 1955 Mille Miglia and he snored so hard I could hardly sleep.

'I remember one evening I was late out and he told the man on the reception desk to wake him when I returned. I didn't get back until one o'clock in the morning and he simply exploded at me, telling me that I "had endangered the expedition".

'I replied, perhaps flippantly, "why – we're not in Greenland, are we?" and Neubauer immediately fired me from the team. It took Uhlenhaut to calm him down the next morning and get me reinstated. On my last lap of training I sent a postcard from Rome to Neubauer to prove I'd been there. But we'd been off out for the day with some girls and I got a mechanic to post the card for me!'

For his part, Günther Molter sides with Jenkinson's

A hydraulically operated air brake was fitted to the 300SLRs at Le Mans, 1955. It was controlled by the driver, but interlocked with second gear for automatic retraction as the car accelerated away from the corners. The additional 'window' aperture was fitted during practice. Poignantly, this is the very car in which Pierre Levegh had his catastrophic accident. (Ludvigsen Library)

memories. 'You could not compare Uhlenhaut with Neubauer,' he said. 'Uhlenhaut was a soft-speaking man who, even after he retired, would visit the factory twice a month just to keep in touch.

'Neubauer was Falstaff! An actor, a PR man and an excellent organiser. I remember when we prepared for Mexico in 1952 he had everything to hand: books, script, medicine for Montezuma's Revenge. To have dinner with Neubauer was a joy. I loved the man!'

By the spring of 1975 the author was working on the editorial staff of *Motoring News*, the sister journal to *Motor Sport*, and had struck up a close friendship with Jenkinson. Together we hatched a plan to celebrate the 20th anniversary of the 300SLR victory with a drive round the route of the famous road race in order to produce a lengthy feature.

Mercedes-Benz helped enormously, providing us with a magnificent 450SE saloon for the journey. Thus one morning in late March, we arrived at Heathrow Airport together with Stirling Moss, Mercedes UK press officer Erik

Johnson and *Motor Sport* managing editor Michael Tee to fly to Stuttgart where we would pick up the car.

During our visit there Moss and Jenks posed at the test track with Karl Kling and one of the 300SLRs – not their winning race chassis, I hasten to add – after which Stirling and Erik flew back to London leaving Jenks, Michael and myself to head off towards Brescia in the big Mercedes limo.

It was one of the most memorable trips of my entire journalistic career. Starting out from Brescia's Via Rebuffone – whence the 300SLR, its side exhausts belching smoke, had hurtled off on its journey into the motor racing history books 20 summers before – we managed to trace pretty well the full route. Sections were missing, by-passed or straightened out, but generally it was pretty well discernible.

Jenks was still fêted as a hero amongst the Italian motor racing community and even in 1975 people on the street would still spin round with a bemused gesture of half

Prelude to disaster. A ferocious battle for the lead raged throughout the early stages of the 1955 Le Mans 24-hour classic with Mike Hawthorn's Jaguar D-type struggling to keep ahead of Juan Manuel Fangio's Mercedes 300SLR, here with its air brake deployed as it chases the British car into the Esses. (David Hodges Collection)

recognition. The little bearded man – who some observers had identified as a padre when he sat alongside Moss in the 300SLR! – was still absolutely in his element and had an anecdote relating to pretty well every twist, turn, hump, level crossing and village on the entire 1,000-mile route.

We detoured into the centre of Forli at one point and actually located the garage which had recovered the 300SL coupé which Stirling and Jenks had bounced off an army lorry full of munitions during one of their Mille Miglia reconnaissance runs. Grins and exclamations of pleasure greeted Jenks's arrival at the garage, the one that had been owned by Paride Mambelli who had partnered Carlo Pintacuda to win the Mille Miglia in 1937.

Unfortunately Mambelli had died some years earlier and we continued on our nostalgic way down the coast to Pescara, the big 450SE rumbling away unobtrusively as we reeled off the miles in considerably more comfort than Moss and Jenks had enjoyed in the 300SLR.

On the return leg from Rome we detoured from another bypass to follow the original route through the centre of a small village, the main street so narrow that there was only room for a single car at a time. We stopped and chatted to the locals and Jenks struck up a conversation with an elderly lady, asking 'do you remember the great race which used to come through the village?'

Barely pausing for a second, she replied with a mixture of indulgent bewilderment and confusion, 'yes, of course, it came up the main street here' as if to say 'where else did you think it could have gone?' Scarcely halting her monologue sufficiently to draw breath, she added, 'now, did I tell you about the time the Pope came to our village?'

Then came the blast over the famous Futa pass from Florence to Bologna and Michael Tee wrestled himself into a state of some exhaustion trying to imitate Moss's efforts in the 300SLR. By the time we reached the top of the Futa we were all ready for a break, stumbling out of the 450SE which stood there ticking quietly, the needles on its water temperature and oil pressure gauges having never wavered throughout all this Boy Racer stuff.

Much too soon we were back in Stuttgart, our brief

Kling brakes for Tertre Rouge corner, with Fangio behind. Shortly after this, Mercedes would withdraw from the 1955 Le Mans race following Levegh's tragic accident in which more than 80 onlookers were killed. (David Hodges Collection)

odyssey into Mille Miglia history itself just a happy memory. Then came the most curious tailpiece imaginable. While waiting in the departure lounge at Stuttgart airport, Jenks was showing me a little album of photographs from the 1955 Mille Miglia. One was of the refuelling stop at Pescara where a young mechanic had briefly slid off the tail of the 300SLR while slamming the filler cap as Stirling suddenly dropped the clutch and accelerated away from the service point.

As we were flicking through the album, a well-dressed, middle-aged gentleman approached us, introduced himself formally and shook Jenks's hand. 'Perhaps you don't remember me, Mr Jenkinson?' he said politely. Jenks frowned, obviously searching his memory. Our new acquaintance gestured to the picture of the Pescara refuelling stop. 'I was that mechanic,' he smiled, pointing to the lad at the rear of the silver Mercedes racer.

After their 1955 win, Jenkinson had written: 'I think that Stirling Moss is the greatest driver, and a genius.' The two men remained lifelong friends.

In June 1995, they celebrated the 40th anniversary of their Mille Miglia victory by being reunited with the winning Mercedes at the Goodwood Festival of Speed. As Jenkinson remarked, it was an overwhelmingly emotional moment. 'I haven't sat in this car since I hopped out of it in Brescia on 1 May 1955,' he recalled. It was a sweltering weekend and Jenks was clearly beginning to wilt, but his joy was unmistakable. Both men were fêted like heroes. And rightly so.

On the Monday morning after the Goodwood extravaganza, many British national newspapers carried photographs of Moss and Jenks climbing the hill in the 300SLR. It was as if the years had fallen away and they were storming the Raticosa and Radicofani passes deep in the heart of Italy four decades earlier.

Jenks had a tear in his eye. And he was certainly not alone. It was a momentous reunion. Full of symbolism, full of pathos.

For his part, Moss had fulsome praise for Jenkinson's contribution to their historic victory. 'No amount of

Battered but unbowed, the 300SLR in which Stirling Moss (pictured) and John Fitch won the 1955 Tourist Trophy at Dundrod. (David Hodges Collection)

money, nothing, would persuade me to sit for ten hours in a car that somebody else was driving at 170mph over blind brows,' he later said in tribute after his old friend died in November 1996 at the age of 75.

The Mille Miglia was followed by the Eifelrennen event where Fangio won ahead of Moss, with Kling fourth, around the Nürburgring, before the team prepared itself for the challenge of Le Mans.

In order to help match the braking performance and stability of the very aerodynamic rival Jaguar D-types, Mercedes arrived at Le Mans with a full-width air brake fitted across the rear bodywork of the 300SLRs. This device was designed to ease the strain on the drum brakes, particularly at the end of the long Mulsanne straight where sustained, consistent retardation from 170mph would be required throughout the gruelling event.

Hans Herrmann had been injured when he crashed at Monaco, so Frenchman André Simon, something of a journeyman, was invited into the team to drive with Karl Kling. Fangio and Moss naturally were paired together as the team's prestige entry, while the most controversial selection of all was the signing of 49-year-old Pierre Levegh to drive with John Fitch, the American being an experienced Le Mans performer in the early 1950s at the wheel of a Cunningham.

Chaps in slacks. From left, John Fitch, Stirling Moss, Hans Herrmann and Peter Collins with the Mercedes 220A in which they thrashed round the Targa Florio course in 1955, learning the circuit. (DaimlerChrysler Classic Archive)

From the start of the race Mike Hawthorn's Jaguar D-type and Fangio's Mercedes 300SLR were locked in combat at the head of the field with records tumbling lap after lap. Such was their pace that just after 6pm the leaders were coming up to lap Kling and Levegh whose 300SLRs had been running in fifth and sixth places.

At precisely 6.20pm, as they came up to complete the 35th lap, an interlocking sequence of events conspired to produce a disaster.

Hawthorn, aiming to stop in the pits this time round, pulled across in front of Lance Macklin's Austin-Healey and braked hard. Macklin pulled out to the left just as Levegh came up at high speed, Kling having already pulled off.

Author Douglas Rutherford, who was taking photographs on the bank opposite the pits, was able to chart the whole catastrophe in minute detail.

'It [Levegh's Mercedes] was still on the road when it hit the bank about ten feet to my right,' he recalled. 'Instead of becoming embedded in the safety wall, the left front wheel rode up it and the car leapt.

'The next instant was curiously drawn out, like a film suddenly in slow motion. I could see the under part of the Mercedes as it passed over my head, still in one piece and identifiable as a car with a driver aboard. It seemed to fly on as leisurely as the horse going over Becher's Brook in the newsreel.

'Though I did not realise it at the time, it snapped a wire at a point 18 inches above my head and sprinkled the hair of the lady on my right with tiny morsels of silver coachwork.

'Even while the silver car was still hurtling to earth again there was time to feel emotion. First came the anguish for the driver, imprisoned in that airborne car, utterly committed to the crash. Then came the sensation of violation, of tremendous forces suddenly out of control. Last and most terrible was the realisation that the machine was falling amongst a mass of humans and must surely crush them.'

The Mercedes disintegrated in the first impact and its front suspension, engine and brakes scythed through the crowd. Poor Levegh died instantly, mercifully never knowing that his wayward Mercedes killed 82 people during its doomed flight into the packed enclosures.

Macklin marched straight to the Jaguar pit, effectively to ask Hawthorn what the hell he thought he'd been doing. Mike over-shot the Jaguar pit as the disaster unfolded around him and team manager Lofty England immediately dispatched him on one more lap before he stopped and handed over the D-type to Ivor Bueb.

Hollow-faced and trembling, he was helped away,

blaming himself for the whole awful affair. Mercedes press chief Artur Keser went to Neubauer and asked what should happen next. Should the German team retire from the race?

It was a difficult decision. Neubauer suggested that if Jaguar withdrew, so would Mercedes. Artur Keser approached Lofty England on the matter only to receive a firm rebuff. As far as the Jaguar manager was concerned, the episode had nothing to do with the British company. Which it most demonstrably did, of course.

Eventually the 300SLRs were withdrawn on the instruction of the Daimler-Benz management in Stuttgart early on Sunday morning, but not before a considerable amount of lobbying on the part of Levegh's co-driver John Fitch who was outraged that the race was being permitted to continue. By this time Fangio and Moss were running in the lead several laps ahead of the rest of the field.

That left Hawthorn and Bueb to cruise home to a dishonoured victory. Mercedes-Benz faced being put under the magnifying glass with allegations that the ferocity of the inferno which enveloped Levegh's wrecked 300SLR was caused by the use of nitrate of methane as a performance-enhancing fuel additive.

Neubauer recalled: 'In fact, the car did burst into flames. When the fire brigade tried to put the fire out, there was a fresh cloud of thick white smoke and flame. We held a press conference in Stuttgart and proved that when water is poured on burning electro-plated metal, precisely this effect is produced.'

Inevitably, the question of who was to blame preoccupied the headlines for weeks, particularly as the French Grand Prix that year was immediately cancelled and circuit racing in Switzerland banned from that day forth. Mercedes-Benz faced some very uncomfortable questions, particularly from the German media. Chairman of the Board Dr Fritz Konecke suggested to Professor Fritz Nallinger, technical director of the racing department, that it might be wise not to take part in the next event on the calendar, the Dutch Grand Prix. Quite boldly, however, Nallinger told his senior colleague that he did not agree. He felt such a move could be interpreted as a tacit admission of responsibility for the disaster.

On the face of the available evidence – which has been debated endlessly over the past four decades – Hawthorn was the prime culprit who triggered the accident. Yet Mercedes was surely taking too much of a gamble allowing the veteran Levegh into such a powerful car in such emotional personal circumstances. The Frenchman was in over his head.

Respected French journalist Jabby Crombac told the author during the preparation of this book: 'Levegh was a

very second-rate driver who had never won anything of importance. A very pleasant fellow indeed, but certainly not a top ranker. No, in my view, Mike Hawthorn pulled the trigger of the loaded gun set up by the circumstances of the narrow track in front of the pits.'

The season continued. In the Tourist Trophy at Dundrod, Moss partnered Fitch in the winning 300SLR, although Stirling drove the lion's share of the race. They were challenged throughout by the dramatically driven works Jaguar D-type shared by Mike Hawthorn and Desmond Titterington, a keen 27-year-old Ulsterman whose family produced linen in Belfast. Only a missed gearchange in the closing stages of the race caused Hawthorn's retirement from second place.

The 1955 sports car season was rounded off by the Targa Florio. This would see Moss and Peter Collins winning from Fangio and Kling in a success which gave Daimler-Benz the championship title by a whisker ahead of Ferrari.

On the strength of his performance at Dundrod, Desmond Titterington was invited, probably via Stirling Moss's manager Ken Gregory on the recommendation of Stirling himself, to crew the third 300SLR with Fitch. Some 45 years later, Titterington shared his recollections with the author:

Desmond Titterington shared the fourth place 300SLR with John Fitch on the 1955 Targa Florio. (DaimlerChrysler Classic Archive)

Hard driving and a frantic pit stop (opposite) to patch up the winning Stirling Moss/Peter Collins Mercedes 300SLR on the 1955 Targa Florio … (David Hodges Collection)

'I suppose I was very lucky to get noticed but I think Stirling gave me some support. He knew I had been brought up in racing in the Irish road circuits rather than the airfield tracks.

'I had been racing sports cars with Ecurie Ecosse, of course, and I was completely obsessed with racing at the time, although I was always an amateur. I received this telegram from Mercedes-Benz inviting me to go down to Sicily so I accepted, met up with Peter Collins in London and we flew down together via Rome.

'It was a truly wonderful two weeks. We did what you might call our pre-practice sharing Mercedes 220 saloons with each other and I think we all learned a lot from that.

'On one occasion I went round with Stirling who told me that there were about five places on the circuit which were really dangerous. "If you make a mistake there, it's curtains," he told me. On the next day, I went round with Fangio and he pointed to the very same five corners while at the same time as pulling a hand across his throat. He couldn't speak English, of course, but he was giving me the same message as Stirling had done!'

Titterington recalls spending about one week driving these saloons before trying his hand in the 300SLR test car which was available. 'The race cars didn't arrive from Stuttgart until a day or so before practice started, and we were only allowed one lap of official practice in them prior to the race.

'The 300SLR impressed me as a pretty strongly made job. You always had the feeling that the Jaguar D-type was more brittle. If they won, then fine; if they didn't last, then too bad.

'The Mercedes was very robustly engineered and reliable, and the team's attitude was superbly professional. Stirling just told me, "it's up to you, the car won't let you down". By contrast you had to treat the Jag with kid gloves.'

In the race Titterington drove for ten laps of the race, Fitch for three, and together they finished the race fourth. As events at Dundrod had proved, the American driver was struggling to keep up on circuits which really demanded high levels of skill and precision. During his three-lap stint on the Targa Florio, he managed to side-swipe the 300SLR into a bridge parapet, closing up its side exhaust exits.

'That obviously reduced the power,' recalls Titterington. 'During practice we were pulling 160mph on the long straight bordering the Mediterranean, but now we were down to 140mph which meant we were losing a lot of time. It was too much of a deficit to pull back on the mountain sections where some of the smaller cars were quite capable of cornering as hard as our Mercedes.'

Titterington has fond memories of the whole exercise. 'Neubauer was a great chap, but a little aloof, perhaps, which was accentuated by the fact that he could not speak English. He was a typical practical German and everything had to be done by the book. What he said went. I formed the impression that Uhlenhaut was rather upper class, whereas Neubauer had progressed up through the ranks and remained rather conscious of that.

'I also got to know Denis Jenkinson much better on that trip. I thought he was a delightful journalist, a clever and able fellow.'

Titterington recalls that the entire driving team seemed stunned when Neubauer announced at the prize-giving immediately after the Targa Florio that Mercedes was withdrawing from racing.

'The retirement may have been anticipated by the older generation of drivers, like Fangio and Kling, but the news conveyed to us after the race took us completely by surprise. Stirling, Peter, John and myself were anticipating our future spots or careers with Mercedes for the following season, so we were dismayed at the news. On reflection now, I suppose it was inevitable that, having won everything that year, this was the best time to call a halt.'

Titterington was offered a works Ferrari sports car drive for 1956 but turned it down in favour of staying with Jaguar and also racing for Connaught in some F1 events. 'In those days one tended to move through into F1 from sports cars, so who knows what might have happened if I'd accepted that offer?'

In the event, Desmond Titterington retired from racing for good at the end of the 1956 season, instead turning his hand to golf as a recreation. He now lives in Scotland and retains a distant interest in the sport which gave him so much pleasure during his twenties.

… their victory clinched the Sports Car World Championship for the Three-Pointed Star. (DaimlerChrysler Classic Archive)

INTERMISSION

AT THE END OF 1955 IT WAS TIME to stop racing. Commercial pressures meant that Mercedes needed to forge ahead with expansion of its road car production as the European economic climate finally shrugged aside the aftermath of war and started to boom. Mercedes had enjoyed a tremendous run of success in motorsport and, even though there had been plans to continue racing the 300SLRs into 1956 after the F1 programme had been finished, the decision was taken to call it a day.

Neubauer retired soon afterwards. He was 64 when, at the end of the 1955 season, his position as competitions chief was taken over by Karl Kling. Kling's own active

Although Mercedes-Benz was officially out of racing from 1955, the 300SL 'gullwing' coupé continued to have a competitive life in the hands of privateers. Here Belgian Willy Mairesse (right) waits by his car during a brief break on the way to victory in the gruelling 1956 Liège-Rome-Liège rally.
(DaimlerChrysler Classic Archive)

circuit racing career had effectively finished with the retirement of the Silver Arrows – although his last competitive success came four years later when he and Rainer Gunzler won the Algiers to the Cape rally in a Mercedes 190D saloon.

Rallying and production car racing would sustain a Mercedes-Benz presence in motorsport into the early 1960s when the image of the Three-Pointed Star would become synonymous with the name of Eugen Böhringer.

Böhringer, whose family ran an inn and a vineyard on the slopes above the Untertürkheim factory, served in the German Army on the Russian front and suffered a protracted spell as a prisoner-of-war before being repatriated. He started rallying in the late 1950s and reached the peak of his achievement in the early 1960s.

In 1960 Mercedes decided to concentrate on international rallying with production cars and, to this end, entered three 'fintail' fuel-injected 220SEs on the Monte Carlo Rally. They were driven by Walter Schock/Rolf Moll, Eugen Böhringer/Hermann Socher and Eberhard Mahle/Roland Ott.

The prevailing rules at the time permitted only stripped down production cars which could be lightly modified with

The Walter Schock/Rolf Moll Mercedes 220SE on its way to victory in the 1960 Monte Carlo Rally. (DaimlerChrysler Classic Archive)

such accessories as sump guards plus additional foglights and main-beam headlights.

The 3,600km route saw the Mercedes team electing to start from Warsaw and the whole route had to be managed at an average of 60kph. It was quite a challenge.

'When ice, snow and fog made life difficult for us, sometimes we had no choice but to travel at the specified average speed of 60kph without being able to see,' recalled Rolf Moll. 'When we finally reached the Alpes Maritime, we went off the road – as did Böhringer – after quite a lot of "snow chains on, snow chains off" switching around. Fortunately we got the cars back on the road again.'

Yet it was the 350km circuit of the Alpes Maritime which proved to be the key to winning the rally and, after being tipped off by colleagues out on the route, Schock and Moll opted for 'summer tyres' which just happened to have been 'organised' from the car of the then Daimler-Benz press officer Artur Keser.

Rolf Moll continued: 'On the very winding roads, Walter always beat my time by one or two seconds. He took the corners very tightly, even more so than the road sometimes allowed! His specialities were snow and ice where he was almost as quick as on dry roads. And he had an infallible sense of timing. On the second lap of the "circuit" we were a bit behind schedule. So we built up speeds, the snow chains came off sooner than they had on the previous lap and we travelled for a few kilometres at the top of the pass

between banks of snow more like a bobsled than a car. But ever so fast!'

It was enough to give Schock and Moll victory with Böhringer/Socher second and Mahle/Ott in third place.

In 1961 Böhringer was third in the European Rally Championship behind Hans-Joachim Walter (Porsche) and Gunnar Andersson (Volvo). That season he took another class win on the Monte, and was fourth on the Tulip, Acropolis and Liège-Sofia-Liège events. He also won the Polish Rally, partnered by young Finn Rauno Aaltonen who was immediately snapped up by BMC competitions chief Stuart Turner for the British manufacturer's increasingly formidable mid-1960s international rally challenge.

Still driving the tank-like 220SE Böhringer excelled himself in 1962 with victories on the Acropolis and Liège-Sofia-Liège which helped him towards clinching the European Championship ahead of Saab's Erik Carlsson, Peter Lang (Böhringer's own co-driver) and Pat Moss.

Summing up the year in his *Autosport* Seasonal Review, John Gott wrote: 'In my view Böhringer was just the best. It was a wonderful performance for the middle-aged man to outdrive the youngsters, and his win on the Liège was in many ways not unlike Fangio's epic drive on the Nürburgring…'

In 1963 Böhringer won the Acropolis again in a bigger-engined saloon, the 300SE, as well as triumphing on the Liège-Sofia-Liège in one of the smaller 230SL roadsters

Team celebration after the
Mercedes 1–2–3 victory in
the 1960 Monte Carlo Rally.
From left, second-place
finishers Eugen Böhringer
and Hermann Socher,
winners Walter Schock and
Rolf Moll (separated by team
manager Karl Kling), and
third-place finishers
Eberhard Mahle and Roland
Ott. (DaimlerChrysler
Classic Archive)

Eugen Böhringer's winning
Mercedes 220SE on the
1961 Polish Rally on which
his co-driver was a young
Finn named Rauno
Aaltonen. BMC
Competitions Manager
Stuart Turner snapped him
up for the following season
and he developed into one of
the great rally aces of the
1960s. (DaimlerChrysler
Classic Archive)

Even in the early 1960s, Mercedes-Benz was pretty shrewd when it came to promoting its image. The all-woman team of Sweden's Ewy Rosqvist (driving) and Germany's Ursula Wirth attract plenty of male attention at the start of the 1962 Gran Premio Argentina. They were a very competitive duo, more than a match for their team-mates on this gruelling, no-holds-barred, high-speed South American road race. (DaimlerChrysler Classic Archive)

Ewy Rosqvist and Ursula Wirth on the harbour front at Monaco after the 1963 Monte Carlo Rally in which they convincingly won the Coupes des Dames award in their Mercedes 220SE. (DaimlerChrysler Classic Archive)

which had recently been introduced. That earned him second in the European Championship and he came back to take another third place on the Liège-Sofia-Liège, again in the 230SL.

On that occasion he was beaten – ironically – by Stuart Turner's BMC best in the form of Rauno Aaltonen, sharing the Austin-Healey 3000 with Tony Ambrose, and the Saab of Erik Carlsson/Gunnar Palm.

'The 230SL was a splendid car for undulating roads,' recalled Böhringer in 1999. 'The 300SE was fast, of course, but not so good on tracks with a lot of curves.'

It had been a golden era for Mercedes and their rallying programme, but once BMC got their act together with the Mini-Coopers and Healey 3000s, the big saloons from Stuttgart were simply no longer fast enough. Wisely, Karl Kling decided to withdraw from any further international rallying programme.

It was almost the end for Böhringer as well. At the start of 1965 he had a one-off outing in the Monte Carlo Rally in a Porsche 904 and finished second. Then he finally retired for good.

Seventeen years later, Mercedes-Benz tempted Böhringer out of retirement to tackle Britain's first 'historic' rally – the Golden 50 of 1982, when they refurbished one of the old works cars they had kept in store, and he put up a remark-able performance, winning his class once again!

Yet this European rallying programme was just one dimension to the Mercedes-Benz competition effort in the early 1960s. In 1961 Kling and the management decided to despatch four 220SEs to compete in the 2,756-mile Argentine road race which started and finished in Buenos Aires.

For four years Mercedes would dominate this gruelling event. Walter Schock won ahead of Hans Herrmann on their first attempt, while in 1962 the glamorous female line-up of Ewy Rosqvist and Ursula Wirth led all six stages and won at the record speed of 78.78mph.

In 1963 and 1964 the thinly disguised road race was dominated by Eugen Böhringer and his regular co-driver Klaus Kaiser, although it initially turned into a no-holds-barred contest between all the competing Mercedes drivers. In 1964 Ewy Rosqvist – by now Ewy von Korff, having married Baron Arnt von Korff who would succeed Kling as manager of the motorsport programme – won two of the five stages, but she still had to settle for third at the finish.

'Ewy Rosqvist was as good as Pat Moss – and on rough roads, she was even better,' Böhringer told the author as he reflected on the South American adventures. 'Perhaps it was her Swedish background. Those Argentine road races were *very* fast. On one day we touched 204kph at night on

Circuit racing had not been completely abandoned by Mercedes-Benz during the early 1960s. Here Eugen Böhringer hurls his works 300SE round the Nürburgring during the Six Hour touring car race in July 1963. (DaimlerChrysler Classic Archive)

Eugen Böhringer and Klaus Kaiser at speed in their Mercedes 300SE on their way to victory in the 1964 Gran Premio Argentina, leading a Mercedes 1–2–3 finish at an amazing average speed of 85.72mph over open roads. (DaimlerChrysler Classic Archive)

Eugen Böhringer and Klaus Kaiser used the compact 230SL coupé to finish third on the 1964 Liège-Sofia-Liège rally. (DaimlerChrysler Classic Archive)

a dirt road section. We didn't do much in the way of training, though. Just no drinking or smoking.' At which point, Ewy Rosqvist von Korff, listening intently to our conversation from the opposite side of the table, burst into laughter.

Touring car racing in the European Championship was also on the Mercedes menu in the early 1960s. In 1964 Böhringer won his class at the wheel of a 300SE in the Brands Hatch Six-Hour race and also led in the Spa 24-hour race, sharing with Dieter Glemser, only to be disqualified for replacing a damaged front hub assembly with pieces from the retired Herbert Linge/Peter Lang car. The race was won by Robert Crevits and Gustave Gosselin, the latter going on to share the second-place Ferrari 275LM in the following year's Le Mans 24-hour race.

Experimentation with production car racing continued into the 1970s. Development engineer Erich Waxenberger

managed to get together support for a team of the formidable 6.3-litre V8-engined 300SEL saloons to contest the prestigious 1969 Spa 24-hour race. Unfortunately tyre 'chunking' problems during pre-event testing led to the decision to withdraw the cars from the race. The project was kept on the back burner for a year or so, punctuated from time to time by various testing forays, but it gradually ran out of steam. It did, however, give a few worthwhile cues to the fledgeling AMG organisation which later played such an important role in Mercedes competition history.

As the years rolled on, D-B continued to look indulgently upon various rallying projects. In 1977 four Mercedes 280E saloons entered the London to Sydney marathon and finished first, second, third and fifth. In 1979–80 Daimler-Benz concentrated its efforts on the 450SLC coupés powered by 5-litre V8 engines which were formally homologated on 1 April 1979 after Andrew Cowan drove one to victory on the marathon-length South American rally the previous September.

The energetic Erich Waxenberger oversaw these efforts which were rewarded later that year by Hannu Mikkola heading a Mercedes 1–2–3–4 on the Bandama Rally. The following year Bjorn Waldegaard was back in the same gruelling event in the Ivory Coast to repeat Mikkola's victory at the wheel of a 450SLC.

Just days after that success Mercedes-Benz announced that it was retiring from rallying. The 450SLC had been an ambitious project, but it was disproportionately costly when weighed against the benefits achieved and the big coupé from Stuttgart was far from the ideal all-round rally machine. Yet there were other tantalising prospects for Daimler-Benz and motorsport a few years down the road.

Rallying revived. Hannu Mikkola and Arne Hertz with the Mercedes 500SLC back on the marque's traditional stamping ground in Argentina, on the way to second place in the 1980 Codasur Rally.
(Ludvigsen Library)

CONSOLIDATION

Mike Thackwell, John Nielsen and Henri Pescarolo drove this Sauber-Mercedes C8 to eighth place in the 1986 Kouros 1000 race at Silverstone. (Sutton)

THE DEVELOPMENT OF THE MERCEDES 190E 2.3/16 into a potential competition car represented a crucial element in revamping the company's youthful and sporting image during the 1980s. However, it was the arrival of the Three-Pointed Star on the Group C sports car racing scene during that same decade which marked the start of a process which would carry Mercedes back to the high profile, international racing front line.

The conduit for the eventual return of the Silver Arrows was provided by the Swiss racing entrepreneur Peter Sauber who had been manufacturing his own racing sports cars since 1970. Initially Sauber had been involved primarily in

the 2-litre category, but his engineering ingenuity was demonstrated to very positive effect in 1981 when he decided to design and build a special version of the 3.5-litre BMW M1 coupé using a lightweight carbon fibre composite monocoque manufactured by neighbouring Swiss company Seger and Hoffman.

In this car Hans-Joachim Stuck and Nelson Piquet won that year's Nürburgring 1,000km race, benefiting enormously from the fact that their car was some 70kg lighter than the equivalent standard model.

Suitably encouraged by this performance, Sauber moved into the Group C category in 1982 with a car powered by a 3.9-litre Cosworth DFL engine. Unfortunately, like other users of this engine, the Sauber suffered badly from vibration problems and the team's record of achievement over the next few years was patchy. Not until 1985 came the crucial turning point when Sauber arrived at Le Mans with its all-new C8 challenger powered by a 5-litre twin-turbo Mercedes-Benz V8.

Under the direction of Dr Hermann Hiereth, technical director of the Mercedes racing programme, development of the engine was monitored with increasing seriousness. Although it was to be another three years before Mercedes became officially involved in this Group C programme, Dr Hiereth and his staff kept a paternal eye on the Sauber programme.

In fact, the first serious study of what Group C might have to offer the German car maker had come in 1984 when Peter Sauber approached Daimler-Benz with a request to use their wind tunnel to assess the aerodynamic performance of the Sauber C76, a car equipped with a 3.5-litre engine at the time.

Prior to Peter Sauber's decision to use the Mercedes V8, Dr Hiereth's team had decided to assess the performance of MB's 16-valve type M117 engine – the 5-litre V8 which powered its top-of-the-range limousines and coupés – when boosted by a twin turbocharger set-up.

The Mercedes team quickly became absorbed in the challenge. It was quite clear that delivering a stable power output while at the same time satisfying Group C's fuel consumption requirements would not be the work of a moment. And there were obvious practical limitations as to the amount of data that could be accumulated from dynamometer testing.

It was therefore decided to agree to Peter Sauber's requests that MB should release development engines for his own Group C project. Even so, it was made clear from the outset that this would be very much an arm's length involvement.

The chassis design and development work on the Sauber C8 was entrusted to Leo Ress, technical director of the Swiss operation. The maiden outing at Le Mans was far from a

John Nielsen and Henri Pescarolo on their way to ninth place for Sauber-Mercedes in the 1986 Monza 1000km race. (Sutton)

The Sauber-built Mercedes C11s dominated the 1990 international sports car racing scene. Here the two C11s are seen heading the sprint to the first corners at Nürburgring and Monza in this final year of fuel-restricted Group C racing. (DaimlerChrysler/Wilhelm)

success. Danish driver John Nielsen was at the wheel when the C8's undertray worked loose, causing the car to become airborne over the hump at the end of the Mulsanne straight. The Sauber performed a mid-air loop before crashing back onto its wheels, the driver thankfully unhurt but its chassis badly damaged. In 1986 Sauber duly expanded its operation to run a second car, but the C8 chassis had inadequate ground-effect qualities to enable it to compete on equal terms with the opposition from Porsche and Jaguar, even though it generally proved extremely reliable.

In August 1986, Mike Thackwell and Henri Pescarolo notched up what would be the first of a multitude of victories for the Sauber-Mercedes alliance, in streaming wet conditions at the new Nürburgring. It was a promising trailer for the 1987 season, which was marked by the advent of the new Sauber-Mercedes C9, built round a much stiffer bonded aluminium monocoque and demonstrating dramatically enhanced ground-effect properties.

Disappointingly, Sauber failed to win a single race that season, but at least the team managed to come away from

Le Mans with a new outright circuit record to its credit. However, there were potentially serious commercial problems ahead. At the end of the year Peter Sauber and his colleagues were dismayed to hear that the team would be losing its sponsorship from Kouros, the men's toiletries brand owned by Yves St Laurent, but this was replaced by backing for 1988 from AEG, one of Daimler-Benz's associate companies.

This subtle change in attitude – and signal of tacit blessing from within D-B – had been prompted by the arrival of Mercedes-Benz CEO Dr Werner Niefer as Deputy Chairman. Moreover, supplementing the substantial commercial support from AEG, the technical back-up was also enhanced with the team's engines now being developed using the highly efficient Bosch Motronic 1.7 engine management system.

To this end, four factory technicians were now assigned to

the Sauber team, attending each race to look after the engines. Mercedes also offered valuable assistance in developing the Hewland VGC transmission which used gears designed by Mercedes with the UK-based Staffs Silent Gears.

On 12 January 1988, the Daimler-Benz directors formally ratified the company's support for the Sauber Group C programme, a move which meant that Jaguar would have some very determined opposition indeed.

The programme was based round an updated version of the 1987 Leo Ress-designed Sauber C9 powered by the 700bhp Mercedes V8. The season began with Jean-Louis Schlesser, Jochen Mass and Mauro Baldi winning the opening race at Jerez before the TWR Jaguar steamroller really hit its stride and notched up wins in the next four events, including Le Mans.

Schlesser and Mass then won at Brno and Nürburgring

The old and new order. Suzuka, 1990, saw the race début of the naturally aspirated flat-12-engined Mercedes C291 (right) seen here alongside the V8 turbo C11. Jean-Louis Schlesser and Jochen Mass are by the C11 with the new machine entrusted to Mercedes 'babies' Michael Schumacher and Karl Wendlinger. (DaimlerChrysler/Wilhelm)

before Baldi and Stefan Johansson posted Sauber's fourth win of the year at Spa-Francorchamps. At the end of the day the Swiss team finished second in the Teams' Championship, a long way behind Jaguar even though it was generally accepted they had turned the corner.

The following year, 1989, saw the return of the Silver Arrows to sports car racing. Granted, the Saubers were still called Saubers, but they now were painted silver and had large three-pointed stars on their nose sections. The Sauber C9 remained the backbone of the team's challenge, but much additional development work was carried out on the M119 V8 engine which now produced around 720bhp at 7,600rpm.

This was good enough to give the team a World Championship winning edge. Schlesser and Mass started with a win at Suzuka. Thereafter, Sauber seldom looked back, winning at Jarama, Brands Hatch, Nürburgring, Donington Park, Spa-Francorchamps and Mexico City. Jaguar did not get a look in and Schlesser eventually took the drivers' crown by just eight points from his Sauber team-mate Jochen Mass.

The prestigious Le Mans 24-hour event remained outside the championship after a major dispute with the FIA over the assignment of television contracts and other commercial rights to the governing body. Only three weeks before the race took place did it become clear that the impasse was insoluble.

Learning the ropes. Michael Schumacher in the cockpit of the Mercedes C291. He and Karl Wendlinger won the final race of 1991 in this car at the Japanese Autopolis circuit. (DaimlerChrysler/Wilhelm)

The Sauber-Mercedes squad still took part and was rewarded with a victory thanks to the efforts of Jochen Mass, Manuel Reuter and Stanley Dickens who won in front of team-mates Mauro Baldi, Kenny Acheson and Gianfranco Brancatelli. It was only the second Le Mans win for Mercedes ever, the first being the Lang/Riess 300SL victory in 1952.

For the 1990 season, Leo Ress had produced what was effectively an evolutionary version of the C9, but this was now officially dubbed the Mercedes-Benz C11. The Silver Arrows were now out in the open for all the world to see. Leo Ress commented: 'With this car we had the opportunity to build a new machine for the final year of the Group C regulations as they were then. Nobody else in the pit lane had this advantage; it was a good package.

'Our first C11 prototype chassis was made in Switzerland, but we never raced it. It was too heavy and it wasn't right.' Instead the team came to Britain, to Dave Price's DP Composites in Surrey, where all future sports car chassis for the Swiss constructor would be made.

'We were racing for Mercedes-Benz, so we could not take risks and had to do our very best,' reflected Ress. 'The chassis of the C11 had double the stiffness of the C9 [aluminium monocoque] which meant that we had to be more careful with the selection of the springs and shock absorbers. We had to be more precise in the way we set up the car, but a stiffer chassis definitely offered us more in the way of advantage.'

Jochen Neerpasch, then the Mercedes motorsport chief, admitted that he regarded the 1990 season as very much a learning year and underpinned that philosophy by introducing what amounted to a junior driver training scheme. From the ranks of the German Formula 3 championship he selected three likely lads in the form of Michael Schumacher, Karl Wendlinger and Heinz-Harald Frentzen who all took turns to partner the veteran Jochen Mass in the number two Mercedes C11.

Mass was fully in support of this idea. Always keen and unselfish when it came to tutoring young talent, Jochen was perhaps in the minority when it came to taking this view. Fierce rivals in 1989, World Champion Jean-Louis Schlesser and Mauro Baldi now found themselves partnered together in the number one Mercedes and nobody was very happy that the popular Ulsterman Kenny Acheson had been dropped by the team to make way for the new boys.

As it turned out, Schlesser and Baldi romped to the Championship, although Mass might have run them very close had it not been for some typical misfortune, but the former F1 driver nevertheless put in his share of truly spectacular performances.

Schlesser and Baldi won six of the nine races, but Mass and Schumacher were consistently quicker throughout the weekend of the season's finale in Mexico City. The Franco-Italian pairing eventually came through to win after Mass made a tactical error in delaying a change to wet rubber during a late rainstorm. However, after the race the win reverted to Mass and Schumacher when it was found that the Schlesser/Baldi C11 had taken on 0.1-litre more fuel than permitted at its final refuelling stop.

Yet, from an historical perspective, the most important contribution from the Mercedes-Benz Group C1 team was the introduction of that talented trio of youngsters who would eventually make an indelible mark on the Grand Prix scene later in the 1990s. Sadly, Wendlinger's F1 career would lose its momentum for good in the wake of a life-threatening practice accident at Monaco with the Sauber-Mercedes in 1994, but Michael and Heinz-Harald remain firmly in the F1 spotlight to this day.

Reflecting on the performance of the 'Mercedes babies' during 1990, Adam Cooper wrote in *Autocourse*: 'Wendlinger, Schumacher and Frentzen [who appeared only at Donington] did an outstanding job all year, benefiting from the thousands of miles of testing they were allowed over the winter.

'Each combined pace with economy, and was not afraid to fight it out with either the crew of the number 1 car or old hands like [Jaguar drivers] Brundle and Lammers. And, against expectations, mistakes were few; Schumacher had a big practice off in the rain at the 'Ring, Frentzen spun in the race at Donington, and Wendlinger picked up a puncture when he hit a slower car at Montreal, but otherwise they all drove impeccably.'

The Swiss-German alliance finished the year well advanced in the preparation of the new 3.5-litre Mercedes C291 which displayed radical thinking, being powered by a totally new 180-degree flat-12 cylinder engine. As things transpired, this would come to be regarded as something of a technical error of judgement which never quite managed to deliver the goods.

The Daimler-Benz board had given the green light to develop a 3.5-litre challenger for the new regulations as far back as 1988 and Dr Hiereth recalled that a total of 14 concepts were considered:

'The required power output of the engine involved us setting a target of 650bhp, combined in a package which would weigh in at the minimum 750kg while enabling us to produce an ideal aerodynamic package.

'We considered using 10 and 12 cylinders, and finally

reached the conclusion that the flat 12-cylinder engine would offer us a low centre of gravity without any penalty concerning aerodynamic efficiency.'

The initial development engine for this programme started out as a conventional V12, but eventually Leo Ress concluded that a single, full-width under-car venturi would be aerodynamically preferable to two 'tunnels' on either side of the car. Consequently the flat-12 engine configuration got the final vote.

'It was hard work to get the package balanced, because although the flat engine allowed a low centre of gravity, the gearbox drive taken from the centre of the crankshaft made it a little higher. We moved the gearbox a bit during the initial tests in the wind tunnel, but when we looked at the result we redesigned the gearbox. In the end, however, we reached a good compromise.'

In terms of chassis packaging, the Mercedes C291 was yet another evolutionary version of what had gone before. Like most of its rivals in this category, it was structurally an extremely strong car, producing excellent wind tunnel results. The engine – questionable configuration or not – incorporated the very advanced TAG Electronics management system, future versions of which would be seen on the F1 McLaren-Ford MP4/8 from the start of the 1993 Grand Prix season.

Despite this, the C291 was not destined to go down in history as one of the world's most successful sports racing cars. At the end of the day, the Mercedes flat-12 engine

Developments behind the scenes. The first Sauber F1 prototype is towed back for attention after a 1992 test run at the Lurcy-Levis aerodrome circuit in central France. (DaimlerChrysler/Wilhelm)

proved heavy, lacked power and was over-complex to install in the chassis. Despite Ress's professed ambition that it should be possible to change in three hours, the reality was that it was too cumbersome to replace between practice sessions at the races.

The new rules allowed the old Group C turbo cars to continue racing, but at a 1,000kg limit – 100kg more than the latest naturally aspirated racers. Nevertheless, that provision worked in the Mercedes team's favour at the start of the 1991 season as their front-line driver partnership of Schlesser and Mass was slotted into the heavier C11 for the first few races in the hope of at least picking up a few championship points from the Jaguar and Peugeot opposition.

The troublesome C291 was therefore entrusted to Michael Schumacher and Karl Wendlinger who proved that, despite its problems, the new car was really quite quick. More likely, it proved what everybody in F1 would soon learn, namely that this Austro-German alliance was outstandingly talented. Wendlinger ran competitively at Suzuka, Michael starred at Monza, and at Silverstone the two youngsters achieved an

impressive second place overall. Then came Le Mans, a race which Mercedes had missed in 1990.

The C11s should have easily got the job done, but outside observers noted just a hint of complacency about the Mercedes effort this time round at the Sarthe. The cars were crushingly quick, but an obscure alternator failure sidelined two of the C11s whilst in the lead two hours from the finish, and would have probably accounted for the third car had it not retired with other technical problems. The 'junior' salvaged fifth place, but Mercedes was shell-shocked with disappointment.

However, the strong showing of the C291 at Silverstone meant that Mass and Schumacher took one of these machines for the sprint race at Nürburgring. The Mercedes was on the competitive pace, but this event marked the beginning of a technically disastrous sequence of races.

A flawed batch of flat-12 cylinder blocks had got into the system and their dangerously thin walls prompted a whole sequence of abrupt and extremely embarrassing engine failures. This unreliability also badly affected performance

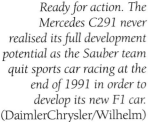

Ready for action. The Mercedes C291 never realised its full development potential as the Sauber team quit sports car racing at the end of 1991 in order to develop its new F1 car. (DaimlerChrysler/Wilhelm)

during practice and qualifying to the point that there were times when it seemed as though there might be insufficient flat-12s available overall to sustain the team's racing programme.

Schumacher, of course, made his F1 début with the Jordan team in the 1991 Belgian Grand Prix before switching to Benetton. Whenever he returned to drive the Mercedes C291 his confidence seemed to be soaring ever higher and a super win in the final race at Japan's Autopolis circuit was the high spot of the team's year.

In the end Jaguar won the Teams' Championship with 108 points, but Mercedes ran Peugeot close for second place, the German marque's total of 70 points ending up just nine behind their key French rivals. At the end of the year Jochen Mass bowed out into a well-earned retirement, having contributed a great deal towards embellishing the long-established Mercedes sports car racing legend.

In 1992, Sauber effectively took a year out preparing its own F1 operation. Having carried the Mercedes-Benz standard in sports car racing for seven years, the infrastructure was certainly in place to start a full-scale Grand Prix operation,

even if the personnel had little experience of such a project.

Peter Sauber decided to embark on his own F1 project after Mercedes-Benz initially declined to do so. When such a high profile project was being envisaged, F1 engineers Harvey Postlethwaite and Steve Nichols had both spent time at the team's base near Zurich, working on the project. They left when it was clear that Mercedes would not be fronting up the programme, so it was down to Leo Ress to get things moving.

By developing the new C12 challenger during the course of 1992, the Sauber team was well prepared when the time came for Karl Wendlinger and J.J. Lehto to début the car at Kyalami in 1993. The steely black machines still had a link with Mercedes through the 'concept by Mercedes-Benz' imagery which at least kept open the prospect of a continuing project with their longtime partners.

The team did well enough, scoring a total of 12 points in the Constructors' Championship to clinch joint sixth place with Lotus. Good, but not outstanding. Remember, they had a year's run-up in which to prepare for the programme, a luxury not afforded to those rivals who were established in the F1 business.

Karl Wendlinger at speed with the first Sauber F1 prototype. Note the 'concept by Mercedes-Benz' branding. From little acorns…
(DaimlerChrysler/Wilhelm)

NORBERT HAUG
A modern Neubauer

As Mercedes-Benz motorsport director, Norbert Haug has had an influence on modern Mercedes motorsport involvement every bit as profound as the legendary Alfred Neubauer's contribution in the 1930s and 1950s. And that's not where the similarity ends.

Haug is a committed, intense professional during working hours. Yet, like Neubauer – and indeed most of the Mercedes management down the ages – when off-duty he is a gregarious party animal with huge reserves of stamina and enthusiasm. Like Neubauer's legendary imitations of Marilyn Monroe half a century before, Haug ad-libbing a favourite pop song from the 1960s is a feature of Mercedes racing parties today.

Back in the 1930s, Dick Seaman's wife Erica expressed her amazement at the way in which the Daimler-Benz directors could party into the small hours – and still be back at their desks, fresh and ready for a full day's work the following morning. Haug was cast in that mould.

Norbert Haug originally joined Mercedes on 1 October 1990 with a brief from Jurgen Hubbert to develop an F1 racing plan. Unfortunately this was rejected by D-B Chairman Edzard Reuter and the company concentrated on touring car racing until the low-key partnership with Sauber began initially in 1994.

Yet even at this early stage, Haug was absolutely convinced that motorsport would benefit the Mercedes image. It was Haug who correctly identified the limitations of the marque's link with Sauber. In particular, he realised there could be no

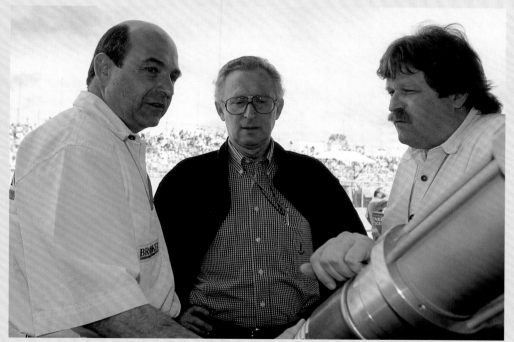

Norbert Haug (right) with Peter Sauber (left) and Jurgen Hubbert at the 1994 Brazilian Grand Prix. (DaimlerChrysler/Wilhelm)

serious future with them when Mercedes was obliged to step in and effectively finance the team after some much-publicised sponsorship from the non-existent *Broker* magazine came to nothing.

The initial seasons with McLaren were not always easy for Haug. The McLaren-Mercedes package had not yet reached the competitive level that many had hoped for, underlining the complexity of the chassis/engine relationship in contemporary F1. Haug had to explain this to the Mercedes senior management. There was speculation that it put him under a lot of pressure, that it was difficult to persuade the grey suits, concerned primarily with profit and loss, that the five-year collaboration would eventually reap the appropriate benefits.

Haug was always positive and optimistic, however. 'It's just a matter of time, and of discipline, to continue the process of improvement,' he observed mid-way through the first year of the McLaren-Mercedes alliance in 1995. 'It is altogether a very young team and our new engine is only effectively four months old as it ran for the first time at the beginning of February on the dynamometer. That put the pressure on us to catch up quickly, but if you try to catch up in such a short time, under a lot of pressure, you cannot guarantee you have 100 per cent reliability at the same time.'

Soon it became clear that Mercedes could be in F1 for the longer term, which seemed to be confirmed at the start of 2000 when DaimlerChrysler took a 40 per cent stake in the TAG McLaren Group.

Regarding extending the initial five-year collaboration, Haug said: 'This is what you might call a planning rhythm. But anything further than that will obviously be down to the Mercedes board of management to decide, and that decision will obviously become easier if we are going forward, making progress and becoming successful.

'But you have to be open and as self-critical as possible in such situations, otherwise there is no way in which you can move forward.'

So did he feel it was necessary for him to educate some of the board members as to the precise subtleties of F1? Or were they sufficiently sophisticated to understand it all for themselves?

'No, you do not need to educate them,' said Haug. 'They really know what it is about and it is my duty to report back to them absolutely objectively, and that is what I have been doing for the past five years. Otherwise, they would not believe in the system. I have always tried to describe things very precisely, and I think there is a firm belief from the responsible board members that our small group can make a competitive impact on the F1 business.'

Moreover, as a former journalist – editor of *SportAuto* and later deputy editor at *Auto Motor und Sport* – Haug knows how frustrating it can be attempting to get information from within reluctant teams. 'To be honest, I never enjoyed being an F1 journalist. I hated waiting hours for the big stars, and that's why we try to be very open and help the media.

'We need the communication. We don't hide.'

PROGRESSION

9

INTO THE 1990s MERCEDES-BENZ extended its involvement in motorsport and forged some important new alliances to support these activities. We will come to the impact of the Three-Pointed Star on the US Champcar arena in due course, but one company which contributed to the Mercedes legend in the touring car and GT racing categories – not to mention the production of bespoke

modifications to enhance the marque's road car range – was AMG.

In 1967, Hans-Werner Aufrecht and Erhard Melcher, both former employees at Mercedes-Benz, started their engineering company AMG in the village of Grossaspach near Stuttgart, for the manufacture and development of racing and sports cars. In 1978, AMG moved from its initial

A sense of history runs through the Mercedes racing involvement like a silver thread. Here Mika Hakkinen prepares to demonstrate the Mercedes W196 during the 1996 ITC race meeting held at Helsinki. (DaimlerChrysler/Wilhelm)

Bernd Schneider keeps his AMG Mercedes C-class ahead of the opposition round the twists and turns of Helsinki, 1996. (DaimlerChrysler/Wilhelm)

premises, the Old Mill in Burgstall, to a larger plant near Affalterbach.

From the very beginning a degree of good fortune accompanied the steady growth of this small tuning specialist into a car constructor in its own right. Whether it was technical or aesthetic refinements for production road cars or the development, construction and operation of high performance production racing cars, its Mercedes-Benz branding remained unchanged.

AMG signed a co-operation agreement with Mercedes to regulate not only the motorsport activities but also to sanction the production of small numbers of sports cars for use on the road. These included such mouthwatering machines as the C36 AMG, then the C43 AMG as well as the E50 AMG and its follow-up model E55 AMG.

'I need racing,' Hans-Werner Aufrecht once said, perhaps explaining the philosophy that has sustained the company's business over more than 30 years.

As early as 1971, AMG entered a Mercedes 300SEL powered by a 400bhp, 6.9-litre eight-cylinder engine in the Spa 24-hour touring car race. This was driven to an impressive second overall place by Hans Heyer and Clemens Schickentanz. Later Schickentanz and Jorg Denzel also drove a Mercedes 450SLC to victory in the 1980 Nürburgring Touring Car GP.

In 1988, AMG became the official partner team for Mercedes-Benz in the German Touring Car Championship (DTM). It was responsible not only for entering the cars, but also for the complete development and construction of the racing technology, as well as supplying parts for and supporting private teams.

With four drivers and five team titles, AMG Mercedes rose to be the most successful competitor in the German Touring Car Championship, both with the 190 and C-class saloons and later in the International Touring Car Championship (ITC) with the C-class.

With 91 victories to its credit between 1988 and 2000 and 15 titles spread across the DTM, the ITC and the FIA GT Series, AMG Mercedes certainly demonstrated their capability and versatility.

The racing division of AMG is now called HWA GmbH, but while the name is changed, the spirit and performers are both well established. The owner and boss of HWA is Hans-Werner Aufrecht. On 1 January 1999, 51 per cent of the AMG shares passed into DaimlerChrysler hands and by 2009 the takeover of this compact, but extremely special, company will be complete. The new DaimlerChrysler subsidiary will be known as Mercedes AMG. Aufrecht may be leaving AMG, but he will retain the racing division as a newly independent company.

Aufrecht's credo has always been that his workforce should not waste any time looking for reasons why something doesn't work: 'We have to concentrate on the question of how it can be made to work.'

One of the first examples of this was the Mercedes CLK-GTR. After the 1996 season, the situation in touring car racing became extremely difficult and lacking in credibility. Alfa Romeo and Opel both withdrew from the International Touring Car Championship at short notice, a controversial decision which left the AMG Mercedes squad lacking a backdrop against which to continue their challenge.

However, for the 1997 season the new FIA GT Championship offered a viable alternative and, in a remarkable effort which took only 128 days, the new AMG-built Mercedes CLK-GTR was produced to contest this series.

For the opposition, the message was writ large on the wall when the series opened in the second week of April. Bernd Schneider's CLK-GTR may only have been finished at 7am on the Friday, yet it was able to claim pole position, almost a second faster than the next quickest rival which – with a supreme irony – was the BMW-engined McLaren F1 GTR of former Benetton driver J.J. Lehto.

What followed was six victories in 11 races and two title crowns, one for Bernd Schneider in the Drivers' Championship and one for AMG Mercedes in the Teams' Championship. In fact, at only the second race in the series the car was a contender for victory: the combination of Schneider and Alexander Wurz was ahead at the Silverstone event when it was red-flagged due to a multiple accident on the flooded circuit. In these circumstances the results are back-dated by a single lap, which handed victory to the Roberto Ravaglia/Peter Kox McLaren GTR.

The CLK notched up its first win at the Nürburgring in late June. By this time Lehto and his team-mate Steve Soper had built up a 12-point lead at the head of the table after scoring two wins in the first three races. Lehto and Soper won again in the mixed weather conditions at Spa-Francorchamps after which Mercedes bounced back with a

1–2 at the A1-Ring thanks to the efforts of Klaus Ludwig/Bernd Maylander/ Bernd Schneider and Alessandro Nannini/Marcel Tiemann. Then came a freak accident at Mugello which deprived Schneider of an almost certain victory after Mercedes had added another two wins to their tally at Suzuka and Donington Park.

Schneider and Ludwig rounded off the series with US victories at both Sebring and Laguna Seca, Schneider taking the Drivers' Championship by 72 points to the 59 total shared by Lehto and Soper.

In November 1997, after winning the FIA GT Championship, Mercedes-Benz made the decision to field a

Bernd Schneider in the AMG Mercedes CLK-GTR at the opening round of the 1998 FIA GT Championship at Oscherslaben, Germany. (LAT)

CLR
Disappointment after freak accidents

In 1999 Mercedes redoubled its efforts to score yet another victory at Le Mans. The new CLR contender was powered by a restricted 5.7-litre engine that developed 600bhp at 7,000rpm. It was a direct descendant of the twin turbo V8 which triumphed at the Sarthe ten years earlier when it powered the Sauber C9 to a 1–2 success.

By the time the trio of sleek CLRs arrived at the French circuit it had undergone more than 35,000km of testing, much of which took place at the super-fast Fontana speedway in California. The team was extremely optimistic about its prospects and motorsport manager Norbert Haug understandably passed up the opportunity to attend the Canadian Grand Prix in order to preside over the Silver Arrows in the French endurance event.

Former GT and saloon ace Klaus Ludwig had retired from racing at the end of the 1998 season, but there was still a formidable line-up in the Mercedes squad. Heading them was the hugely experienced 35-year-old Bernd Schneider, partnered by a group of drivers who had all competed for the AMG Mercedes squad in the previous year's FIA GT championship.

These included Schneider's compatriot, 25-year-old Marcel Tiemann, Australia's Mark Webber (22), plus Frenchmen Jan-Marc Gounon (36) and Christophe Bouchut (32). They were joined by four new additions – German F3000 star and McLaren-Mercedes F1 test driver Nick Heidfeld, former Lotus F1 team member Pedro Lamy, Frenchman Franck Lagorce and the very promising young Scot, Peter Dumbreck.

By any standards here was a strong equipe, including as it did no fewer than seven former national F3 champions, two Monaco F3 winners and one F3 race winner. Haug commented with some satisfaction at the time: 'This shows how good the training and competitive base of our Le Mans driver line-up really is. Someone who has managed to win a title in one of the most important F3 championships is a consistent potential winner. They should not only have speed, but also discipline, a crucial combination required at Le Mans.'

Yet what was billed by many pundits as having all the promise of a real classic event proved a disaster. On a weekend when BMW emerged the winners, the AMG Mercedes team found their CLRs pitched into a horrifying sequence of aerial accidents.

In fact, the troubles had started even in May during pre-qualifying when Webber's CLR crashed on the Mulsanne straight after a suspension wishbone pulled out. Moreover, the cars did not prove as quick as expected during qualifying and there seemed to be some doubt as to whether they would be able to match the ultra-fast Toyotas

Webber suffered his second major accident at the wheel of a CLR in Thursday practice and had another somersault during the race day warm-up on Saturday. Much debate and consideration was then expended over whether the cars should be raced. Having made some aerodynamic adjustments, the decision was taken to start. In retrospect, this was a mistake. Nearly a tragic one.

Peter Dumbreck's accident occurred at 200mph on the Indianapolis section of the 13.8km circuit. Following closely behind one of the rival Toyotas, the silver car hit a kerb and suddenly became airborne. It rocketed high above the circuit, somersaulting before crashing over the safety barrier and landing in an area of scrub and small saplings which had only recently been cleared of larger trees.

Mercedes personnel were stricken as the spectre of the most spectacular accident in motor racing history was paraded before their eyes, not least by the media. Only when it was confirmed that the 25-year-old driver was unhurt and that there were no other casualties could they catch their breath and begin to banish memories of the 1955 Le Mans disaster. The remaining CLR was immediately withdrawn from the race. 'With the data we had on Saturday morning, we were convinced of having made the right decision to start,' said Haug.

The Mercedes CLR problem was believed to have been multifaceted, something which had previously affected other sports cars with an underside plan area which creates disastrous aerodynamic consequences if excessively exposed to a 200mph airflow. In addition, the Mercedes seemed to have been particularly pitch sensitive, possibly due to running with very soft rear springs in an effort to pick up straight line speed. This apparently promoted an instability which eventually proved untenable as the aerodynamic 'centre of pressure' was disrupted.

Needless to say, Mercedes received much media criticism for not having withdrawn the cars prior to the start of the race. They had certainly made the wrong call and this potentially catastrophic sequence of events brought down the curtain on the Mercedes Le Mans programme.

Norbert Haug and his Mercedes team colleagues had a deeply frustrating time grappling with the potentially disastrous CLR programme at Le Mans in 1999. (Daimler/Chrysler)

possible entry for the 24-hour race at Le Mans. Immediately, back in Affalterbach the AMG workforce began a race against time.

A mere 120 days after the first stroke of the pen on the drawing board, the CLK-LM rolled onto the tarmac. At Le Mans it celebrated a remarkable début with the best practice time – Schneider qualified for pole at an average speed of 141.194mph. Disappointingly, however, the first AMG Mercedes effort to rekindle the Sauber team's winning ways in the French classic was to prove disappointing in the extreme. The CLK-LM crewed by Schneider, Ludwig and Australian rising star Mark Webber

was out after only 19 laps with engine failure, and the sister car of Jean-Marc Gounon, Christophe Bouchut and Ricardo Zonta lasted just another 12 laps before succumbing to a similar fate. It was not a race to remember.

However, the FIA GT series was another matter altogether. The AMG Mercedes team won all the races, starting the season with two wins for the uprated CLK-GTR before the V8-engined LM version joined the party after its abortive experience at Le Mans. There were five wins apiece for Schneider/Webber and Ludwig/Zonta, but the latter pairing finally made it to the championship title crown thanks to better placings in the races that they failed to win.

The AMG Mercedes CLK-GTRs of Bernd Schneider and Mark Webber run nose to tail at the A1-Ring, 1998. (DaimlerChrysler/Wilhelm)

Heinz-Harald Frentzen in the Sauber-Mercedes C13 at Interlagos during the 1994 Brazilian Grand Prix. (DaimlerChrysler/Wilhelm)

Back on the Grand Prix scene, it was at the 1993 Australian Grand Prix, the race where Ayrton Senna scored his final victory for McLaren, that Mercedes-Benz finally confirmed its long-expected involvement in F1 with the news that it had acquired a 25 per cent stake in Ilmor Engineering.

This not only ensured that Mercedes-Benz would become involved in the US Champcars in 1995, but that the 'Concept by Mercedes-Benz' image by which it had rather loosely been associated with the Sauber team would be reinforced in the future.

By the end of the 1993 season there was a huge sense of anticipation within the F1 community that one of the most famous names in the sport's history would soon be back in Formula 1 again.

This decision effectively realised the initial plan whereby Mercedes-Benz helped the Swiss team to get its F1 programme up and running while keeping almost out of sight behind the scenes. The idea was to go international motor racing in the most cost-effective manner.

Jurgen Hubbert, the Mercedes-Benz board member who was head of passenger vehicles and in charge of motorsport, would later expand on the company's philosophy: 'In 1991 we had stated that our company was interested in F1, but that finances would not permit us to race the *Silberpfeile* in Grand Prix contests. In retrospect, and when we see how the automobile industry has since developed, our decision was clearly the right one at the time.

'At the end of 1993 we were able to reverse our decision, because a brand-new, less expensive motorsports programme was submitted. This concept links us with teams that are in charge of development and use of vehicles in the respective racing series. We see motorsports as one of the pillars of our marketing offensive. By being active in the German Touring Car Championship, in F1 and, from 1995 on, the American Indycar series, we want to show people just how strong our competitive edge is.'

Achievements over the next few seasons would demonstrate that philosophy to spectacular effect.

In 1994 the Sauber team carried 'Powered by Mercedes-

The Sauber-Mercedes C13 with drivers Andrea de Cesaris (left) and Heinz-Harald Frentzen. Sadly Wendlinger's F1 career had already ended after a serious accident in 1994 during practice at Monaco, although the popular Austrian driver made a good recovery. (DaimlerChrysler/Wilhelm)

Benz' identification on their bodywork, and in 1995 the works supported Penske Champcars were scheduled to carry 'Powered by Mercedes-Benz'. The third element was scheduled to be the DTM assault by AMG C-class saloons carrying the 'Made by Mercedes-Benz' legend.

Less than a year later Mercedes-Benz would decide that it needed a much stronger partner than Sauber with which to fashion its future F1 success. By the summer of 1994 it was becoming clear that Mercedes was on course to forge a partnership with McLaren. Norbert Haug and Ron Dennis, McLaren's Managing Director, instinctively recognised the synergy between the two companies. McLaren would benefit from association with the up-market Mercedes image while Mercedes could see that here was a technical partner with whom they could finally start out on the long road to the F1 big-time.

Much time was wasted at the start of the 1995 season grappling with an ill-judged and short-term partnership with Nigel Mansell. The former World Champion – winner of back-to-back F1 and Indycar titles – had become reacquainted with Grand Prix racing in the second half of 1994 when he drove four guest races for Williams in the wake of Ayrton Senna's death.

Yet the new McLaren MP4/10 just wasn't up to scratch. Mansell wasn't prepared to struggle with an uncompetitive car at this stage in his career and the partnership was quickly dissolved. But not before McLaren had wasted many man hours designing an enlarged monocoque to accommodate the British driver. In terms of squandered resources, it was a bruising, not to say rather embarrassing, experience.

The alliance between McLaren and Mercedes-Benz also illustrated just how long it can take F1 car and engine suppliers to blend into an effective partnership. For example Mercedes's engine maker Ilmor expended massive effort on improving the driveability of its V10 concept. Brand new engines were also introduced for both 1996 and 1997, offering enhanced scope for better installation in the chassis. The work never let up.

'I believe that at all times you should have the best – or at least try to have the best,' says McLaren boss Ron Dennis. 'This is not simply about money, it is mainly about commitment. We try to inspire it into the very fibre of everyone's approach to their work for the team.'

It goes not only for the racing team, but also the £150 million technology centre – Paragon – designed by Sir Norman Foster and being built in former green belt land near McLaren's Woking base.

'Winning is not just about winning on the circuit, it is also about winning off the circuit,' says the man for whom

Frustrated man. Nigel Mansell won the final race of the 1994 season in a Williams-Renault and had been hoping to sustain that momentum when he switched to the McLaren-Mercedes team. But things simply didn't work out. (DaimlerChrysler/Wilhelm)

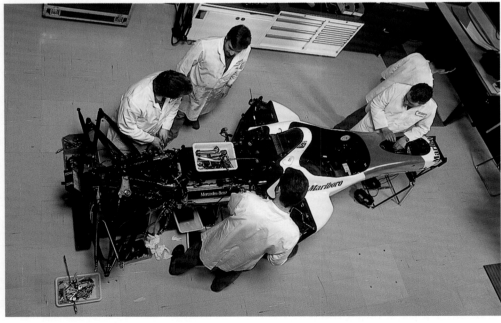

Building the enlarged McLaren MP4/10B chassis required to accommodate Nigel Mansell comfortably at the start of the 1995 season. (Sporting Pictures UK)

MARIO ILLIEN
Pushing the boundaries of F1 engineering

Mario Illien is one of F1's most celebrated back room boys. When Mercedes-Benz set out to dominate Grand Prix racing in the 1990s, they turned to British technology to propel them to the top of the victory rostrum.

Instead of building their own engines, M-B bought a stake in Ilmor Engineering, the Northampton specialist race engine builder established by former Cosworth engineers Illien and his partner Paul Morgan back in 1983. This is a very different route from that adopted by BMW which made much of the fact that its new F1 engine, used by Williams from the start of 2000, was built totally in-house.

Illien is a formal Swiss whose usual reserve evaporates when he talks about racing: 'I always wanted to be involved with engines since I was a kid. It is, if you like, a childlike passion which has never left me. But the nature of this business, with all its pressures, is such that you simply have to be passionate about it. Otherwise you quite simply can't put in the hours it requires.'

Mercedes shrewdly tapped into that zeal and expertise. They were quick to appreciate that building a winning F1

engine had precious little to do with making refined road engines for autobahn cruising. It's about quick response and unyielding commitment, about chipping away at a technical advantage in tiny percentages. The key to last season's F1 Mercedes V10 engines came down to a combination of excellent power, low weight and compact overall dimensions.

'If you compare Ilmor's original F1 engine of 1990 to that of today, it has changed dramatically,' said Illien. 'Yet there is a certain philosophy which shows all the way through. For its time, that engine was very small and light and that is something we always strive for.'

On the face of it, saving weight might not seem a very high priority. With the F1 regulations requiring an all-up weight of car and driver of not less than 600kg, teams are quite capable of building comfortably below that requirement. The balance is made up by deploying ballast around the car. But the more weight that can be saved, the more ballast can be positioned in areas of the car which have a positive effect on its handling.

The Ilmor partnership knew its stuff right from the start. In 1979 Illien had joined Cosworth, makers of Ford's F1 engines, where he met Paul Morgan. In 1983 they decided to go it alone in an audacious move to beat their former employers at their own game. 'When we left Cosworth, we considered carefully which racing category to tackle and concluded that taking on Cosworth's monopoly in US Indycar racing would make most sense,' said Illien.

With backing from US Champcar team owner Roger Penske, General Motors and, more recently, Mercedes-Benz, Ilmor became firmly established. When GM decided to withdraw its backing at the end of 1993, Mercedes took over their 25 per cent stake, Penske having earlier sold half his shares to the US motor giant. Since establishing its partnership with McLaren in 1995, Mercedes is estimated to have poured over £30 million annually into Ilmor, enabling its British subsidiary to expand both in terms of workforce and technical equipment. Mercedes also makes test and development facilities available at Stuttgart.

Today Ilmor has a workforce of more than 400, a far cry from the first three months of the company's existence when Illien and Morgan were the sole employees. Illien grins when he says he is the Technical Director, and Morgan is the Managing Director: 'I still try to be more of an engineer than a businessman'. Not surprisingly perhaps, despite working at the very heart of this high tech world he believes that an engineer's feel is the most important element in the equation. 'A computer doesn't give you ideas. Feel is very important, because even with all of today's computing power, there is not enough time to calculate everything that could be calculated. That is what differentiates a good designer from an average one.'

Illien feels it is important to take risks, to push the frontiers of F1 engineering knowledge to its absolute limit: 'We decided we had to take risks to progress. That brings pressure, of course, but it speeds up your learning tremendously, first in the new knowledge it brings and second through the pressure itself!'

Ilmor co-founder Mario Illien by one of his company's dynamometers at its Brixworth, Northamptonshire, headquarters. (DaimlerChrysler/Wilhelm)

perfection is only just good enough. 'Consequently, when people pass less-than-favourable remarks about the things we do, most of the time those remarks broadly reflect the fact that they recognise we have higher standards than they have achieved.'

One of the keynotes of the McLaren-Mercedes alliance is that from the outset it has been a partnership in the truest sense of the word. Both Ron Dennis and Norbert Haug have worked hard to ensure that, should problems arise, there has never been any apportioning of blame between chassis and engine maker. 'We suffered together when things went wrong, and we celebrated together when every-thing went right,' said the McLaren chief. 'There was nothing to be gained by picking holes in each other's con-tribution, so when we achieved success we did so as a unified operation. Which is the only way it could be.'

Yet the 1995 season was a bruising period for that mutually supportive alliance. There were some compro-mises in the design of the MP4/10; Mansell's retirement from the team had a knock-on effect in terms of time wasted; and Mika Hakkinen was not yet in a position to offer the seasoned and mature performances he would later provide with such spectacular effect.

Behind the scenes, Dennis and Haug were always

pushing their respective teams to the absolute limit in an effort to catch up lost ground. The Mercedes V10 was not the easiest engine to drive from the viewpoint of power delivery, but the team displayed a strength in adversity which indicated the potential of things to come.

For example, after a spate of engine failures at the 1995 Hungarian Grand Prix, Ilmor engineers stripped the V10s, assessed the problem, manufactured and installed fresh components, bench tested the revised engines and had them back at Silverstone for a pre-Belgian GP test.

In parallel, McLaren produced a revised gearbox casing to accommodate a new rear suspension geometry at Spa where Hakkinen blotted his copybook with a spin on the second lap.

Determined to sustain the tempo of progress, McLaren pushed ahead with the development of a further revised C-spec engine before the end of the year, but design problems with yet another new suspension geometry left them flagging. In the European GP at Nürburgring, a race attended by many senior Daimler-Benz directors, the McLaren-Mercedes MP4/10s of Hakkinen and Mark Blundell performed dismally, but at Suzuka the Finn qualified third and finished a competitive second.

The 1995 season bumped along towards its conclusion,

Nigel Mansell in the McLaren-Mercedes MP4/10B in the 1995 San Marino Grand Prix. The car was not as competitive as the 1992 World Champion had expected. (DaimlerChrysler/Wilhelm)

Mark Blundell surfs across one of the Monza gravel traps with his McLaren-Mercedes MP4/10B during the 1995 Italian Grand Prix. (DaimlerChrysler/Wilhelm)

ending on another potentially catastrophic note when Hakkinen crashed heavily in practice for the Australian GP at Adelaide. He suffered serious head injuries from which, thankfully, he was to make a total recovery.

The team ended the year a distant fourth in the Constructors' Championship on 30 points, 107 behind the title-winning Benetton-Renault marque. Hakkinen wound up seventh in the Drivers' Championship, Blundell tenth. Clearly there was a lot more work ahead if the alliance's ambitions were to bear fruit.

The steady improvement continued for 1996 when the popular Scottish driver David Coulthard joined McLaren-Mercedes as Hakkinen's team-mate. The all-new MP4/11 was powered by a totally new Phase 3 version of the Mercedes F0110 75-degree V10 engine which ran on the

dyno for the first time on 3 February, barely a week before the new car had its maiden airing at the Estoril test. Power was transmitted through a totally new McLaren six-speed longitudinal gearbox with a semi-auto gearchange by TAG Electronics. The car also featured a new TAG 2000 integrated engine and chassis control data acquisition system.

To supplement the services of Hakkinen, Coulthard, and test driver Jan Magnussen, the team could also call upon engineering input from Alain Prost, who had won three of his four World Championships in a McLaren and – pending the purchase of his own team – rejoined on a consultancy basis. Prost carried out some extremely valuable test and development work, especially in terms of cross-referencing the input as regards the MP4/11's sustained handling problems.

DOMINATION

'**M**OTORSPORT IS NOT ABOUT the short term, it is about the long term,' says Ron Dennis. 'As we have taken the blows that have been administered to us by our fellow competitors and the media I have said, "well, they don't understand". We have been in a position of dominance in the past and we will regain that position in the future.

'The problem is that many observers fail to understand the complexity of Formula 1 motor racing. The top 20 tennis players at Wimbledon could borrow each other's rackets and probably play within a very small percentage of how they played with their own.

'The more you look at many sports, you realise that the role the equipment plays in the overall equation is very small. By contrast, a Grand Prix car is one of the most complex pieces of equipment you could ever place in the hands of a sportsman. That is what sets motor racing apart, and why it is so enormously difficult to win a Grand Prix.'

It is this bullish approach which sustained Dennis and the McLaren team through those dark, uncertain days of 1993–94 and strengthened their resolve to bounce back as major players in partnership with Mercedes-Benz.

At the end of 1996 Dennis freely acknowledged how much the team had benefited from the presence of Alain Prost: 'He helped the drivers' understanding when it came to the art of setting up the car. He helped the engineers with things only a driver could explain and, although it is very difficult to quantify precisely how much his collaboration produced, I believe we have had value for money and that he positively contributed to the way in which the MP4/11 was developed.'

Dennis also regularly paid tribute to the amount of effort Mercedes poured into the programme as part of the support for Ilmor Engineering, the MB F1 engine manufacturers. Not only are any new specifications run for at least 550km in the race car – if possible – but they are also put

through a rigorous series of test runs on the computer-controlled transient dynamometers at Stuttgart which are capable of simulating a race distance over any predetermined circuit on the championship programme.

'When Mercedes and McLaren formed its current partnership, it was always intended that we take a very well considered and strategic approach,' says Dennis. 'We have very much a desire to win as many races as possible. The simple fact is that you win Grands Prix and World Championships not by considering the next race, or even the race after that, but you do it by means of what you plan for the future.

Step in the right direction. David Coulthard's McLaren-Mercedes MP4/11 leads the opening stages of the 1996 San Marino Grand Prix at Imola ahead of Michael Schumacher's Ferrari and Jean Alesi's Benetton. (DaimlerChrysler/Wilhelm)

Mika Hakkinen's McLaren-Mercedes MP4/11 clips the tyres at the first chicane, Monza, 1996. After repairs, Mika's comeback drive to third place was one of the highlights of the race. (DaimlerChrysler/Wilhelm)

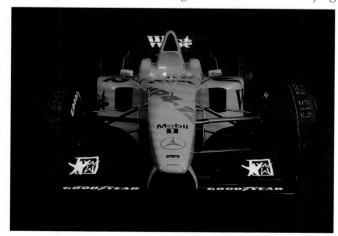

The 1997 MP4/12 was originally unveiled to the media in McLaren's traditional orange racing livery, which dated back to the 1960s. The team was keeping its new silver livery under wraps until the official launch at Alexandra Palace. (LAT)

'Our approach with Mercedes is many years into the future, to try and give our respective engineering groups the very best facilities for them to contribute to us winning races. To make it possible, you have to have everybody around you with the same long-term vision. We are trying to develop a long-term strategy to win consistently, for McLaren and Mercedes, both of whom have a distinguished heritage.'

It began slowly. In 1996 Coulthard scored his best result with a second place at Monaco behind the Ligier of Olivier Panis, McLaren just losing out to its French rival during a spate of mid-race refuelling stops on a drying track.

This was also the scene of Hakkinen's biggest mistake of the year when he wrote off a brand new MP4/11 during a 15-minute extra pre-race acclimatisation session in the pouring rain. What made this accident so embarrassing was that he was running two seconds faster than anybody else on the circuit and merely attempting to beat his own best time. It was the Finn's lowest point of the year, after which he gradually regained his form and confidence, adding strong third places to his record in the British, Belgian, Italian and Japanese Grands Prix.

The times they were a-changing. A major about-turn for McLaren came when it announced that its 23-year partner-

The distinctive silver livery of the West McLaren-Mercedes MP4/12, Alexandra Palace, 1997. (Formula One Pictures)

ship with the Philip Morris cigarette conglomerate would end after the Japanese Grand Prix. Rather than accept reduced funding from Marlboro, Ron Dennis determined to negotiate the team's title sponsorship on his own terms and, to that end, concluded a long-term deal with the German tobacco company Reemtsma. This would bring the West cigarette brand into the F1 front line as the team's prime sponsor.

Then, no matter how it was explained, or what was intended, when the wraps came off the new silver liveried McLaren-Mercedes MP4/12s at Alexandra Palace in February 1997 the British F1 team took a decisive step closer to the German car maker. From the moment these latest Silver Arrows were unveiled, it was inevitable that Ron Dennis would be deluged with questions as to whether this meant that Mercedes would eventually take over his company.

The fact that the status quo remained unchanged is not the point. It was the perception of the new livery which counted, and it was no coincidence that a pre-war

Mercedes W25 was wheeled out for this momentous occasion. The redoubtable Manfred von Brauchitsch, winner of the first 'Silver Arrows' race at the Nürburgring in 1934, had survived to take a bow at Alexandra Palace. He was 91 years old. His presence made one wonder what the

Mika Hakkinen and David Coulthard mingle with the Spice Girls at the high-profile launch. (Sutton Photographic)

1997, offering enhanced scope for better installation in the chassis. The work never let up.

There must have been times when life felt distinctly uncomfortable for both Dennis and Haug. Pressure for results was subtly but clearly mounting. Finishing 1997 without a single victory could well have had terminally damaging implications for the partnership.

Happily, the initial signs looked good. The MP4/12 was a totally new machine with several imaginative design innovations. It also incorporated features such as a rear impact zone, collapsible steering column, reduced winglet area and suspension designed within the limited aspect ratios designated by the new 1997 F1 technical regulations.

Power came from a further revised Mercedes-Benz F0110E 75-degree V10 engine. 'This is another major evolution from the specification which we used in the final race of last season,' explained Ilmor boss Mario Illien. 'It involved a new block design which we decided on both for performance and installation reasons. The inlet system has been completely redesigned and was marginally lighter. We have enhanced the power output, but how much better it is in terms of driveability will only be established once the car starts testing, although indications from the dynamometer suggests that we have certainly made improvements.'

From the outset, Ron Dennis appeared cautiously optimistic about the new car, hinting that some significant aerodynamic improvements had been found as a result of the intensive wind tunnel testing completed over the winter: 'We knew that we had made quantifiable gains in the wind tunnel, but I would be surprised if all the other

David Coulthard signs autographs for the fans after giving the McLaren-Mercedes squad its maiden victory at the 1997 Australian Grand Prix. (DaimlerChrysler/Wilhelm)

Mercedes team would have made of the Spice Girls – the songsters recruited to jazz up this particular evening – had they appeared at Nürburgring 63 years before.

Getting the McLaren-Mercedes to work had been a long job, and not just for the chassis maker. Ilmor expended massive effort improving the driveability of its V10 concept. Brand new engines were also introduced for both 1996 and

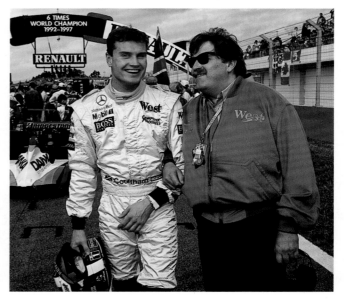

David Coulthard with his girlfriend Heidi Wichlinski, Monaco, 1997. (Formula One Pictures)

David Coulthard and Norbert Haug prior to the start of the 1997 European Grand Prix at Jerez. (DaimlerChrysler/Wilhelm)

teams haven't made corresponding improvements. The only thing we don't know is where they are starting from. That said, I think attempting to evaluate the qualities of the opposition is pretty much a waste of time. We just have to concentrate on developing the best car we can.' That they certainly did.

Coulthard gave the McLaren-Mercedes squad its maiden victory at the 1997 season opener in Australia, then another at Monza. Hakkinen, meanwhile, was left to fume in frustration. Finally, in the European Grand Prix at Jerez – the controversial finale which saw Villeneuve survive the attentions of a ram-raiding Schumacher to win the title – Coulthard acceded to team orders and allowed Hakkinen ahead in the closing stages so that he could at least finish the season with his first ever F1 victory.

It was a process of psychological purging which Ron Dennis felt was extremely important. Mika had been deprived of several victories through misfortunes not of his own making. Now the McLaren boss decided to rectify that situation and, in effect, put Hakkinen's mind at ease by steering the pleasant Finn through a crucial mental barrier. He would never look back.

The summer of 1997 had also seen the McLaren-Mercedes squad make an approach to Damon Hill. The 1996 World Champion, ditched by the Williams team after clinching the title, was now languishing with the embar-

rassingly uncompetitive Arrows team. And the partnership – still struggling to produce consistently competitive form as the season unfolded – felt it was only reasonable to cast

Coulthard, Jerez, 1997.
(DaimlerChrysler/Wilhelm)

Jacques Villeneuve's Williams leads at Jerez from the McLaren-Mercedes of Mika Hakkinen and David Coulthard which are, in turn, sandwiching Eddie Irvine's Ferrari. This would be Hakkinen's maiden victory, gifted by Coulthard on team orders – the Finn would never look back.
(DaimlerChrysler/Wilhelm)

The pit crew tend Mika Hakkinen's McLaren-Mercedes MP4/13 in the team's garage at Interlagos during the 1998 Brazilian Grand Prix. Mika won the race in commanding style ahead of Coulthard. (Formula One Pictures)

David Coulthard with McLaren technical director Adrian Newey at Buenos Aires, 1998. The British driver finished sixth after a controversial collision with Michael Schumacher's Ferrari while challenging for the lead. (Formula One Pictures)

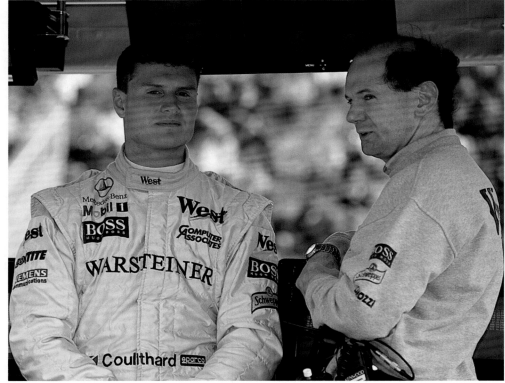

its net as widely as possible when considering the driver line-up for 1998.

Ron Dennis, Norbert Haug, McLaren International Managing Director Martin Whitmarsh, and new Technical Director Adrian Newey – who, as Chief Designer at Williams, had worked with Hill already – were all involved in a systematic programme to evaluate which drivers were available and what they had to offer. Leaving aside Coulthard and Hakkinen whose qualities were well known, a short list was produced.

Rumours began to filter out of Stuttgart that the Mercedes-Benz board of management liked the idea of recruiting a driver of Hill's public profile. McLaren denied that there was ever any pressure brought to bear, one way or another. Hill was definitely worth consideration, however. He had a proven working relationship with Adrian Newey who reckoned his technical input might be positive for future car development. Dennis and Haug clearly tried to shelve their own personal doubts about Hill. Sufficient remarks had been made over the years to give those close to the team the feeling that neither man was wildly enthusiastic. But Hill could not be discounted.

Privately, Dennis was haunted by the Mansell fiasco. Paying top dollar to a man whose best days might have passed was not on his agenda. Hill, approaching his 37th birthday, could be a risk. It was all very well for Damon and his advisors to talk in terms of 'few drivers having the ability to string together a World Championship', but this was to cut no ice.

In the run-up to the Belgian Grand Prix, Dennis did provide Hill with a route to the McLaren-Mercedes enclave. He offered him a one-year contract with a $2 million retainer, supplemented by a bonus structure of $1 million per win scored up to a maximum of 12 wins. With Newey now in firm control of the McLaren technical armoury, the prospects for 1998 – under the heavily revised F1 regulations – looked good.

Hill was holidaying in the South of France when Dennis telephoned him for a preliminary talk, advising Damon from the outset that he was on a three-way line with Whitmarsh and Newey. Dennis was determined to flush out the former World Champion with a proposal which, in his view, would establish his seriousness. When the figures were mentioned, Hill didn't quite put the phone down on the spot. But he came pretty close. 'That is a derisory offer,' he replied. And that was the end of the McLaren/Hill dialogue.

The 1998 season promised to be the best yet for the partnership. The new MP4/13 was the last of the new breed of narrow F1 cars, running on grooved tyres, to be unveiled to the waiting fans. The team had taken the bold decision to switch from Goodyear to Bridgestone rubber in what was seen by some as a gamble to secure a short-term performance advantage prior to Goodyear's withdrawal from F1 at the end of the season. McLaren's contract with Goodyear extended beyond this date so, as the terms of the deal could not now be met, it clearly made sense to change camps as quickly as possible. This proved to be a shrewd move. It was supported with considerable enthusiasm by Mercedes whose CLKs had won the 1997 FIA GT Championship using the Japanese rubber.

The new car was powered by the latest Mercedes-Benz F0110G V10 cylinder engine. This weighed in at around five per cent lighter than its immediate predecessor, as well as being more compact and better packaged with a lower centre of gravity. Its 770bhp power output was enhanced and the driveability significantly improved.

Technical rule changes tend to come thick and fast in Formula 1, but in 1998 they were particularly wide ranging. There is of course an ongoing battle between the rule makers, always seeking ways of slowing the cars down for safety reasons, and the designers, who push their ingenuity to the limits in an effort to make up such lost ground. But now this had taken a more serious turn. With grooved tyres

and narrower front and rear track, the best estimates were that the new cars would start the season between three and five seconds per lap slower than their 1997 predecessors.

By making the track narrower, the crucial airflow over the cars was reduced, theoretically taking the edge off their lap

Majestic victory. Hakkinen scored a runaway victory in the 1998 Monaco Grand Prix. (Formula One Pictures)

speed by reducing their grip. The grooved tyres also generated less grip, putting a premium on a driver's sensitive use of the throttle pedal rather than simply hurling a car into a high speed corner and allowing a combination of huge aerodynamic downforce and awesome adhesion from slick tyres to do the rest.

Mika began the 1998 season as he meant to go on. By winning. He started with the Australian Grand Prix and, by the time he took the chequered flag at Suzuka seven months later, he had won exactly half the season's 16 races, becoming only the second Finnish World Champion after Keke Rosberg.

Hakkinen appreciated that his first win had been far too long in coming: 'I would fly to all the races last season thinking to myself "we're gonna win this one". But, yes, there were times that I didn't think it would happen. And when I finally did win, I was surprised that perhaps I didn't feel quite so elated as I might have expected. Then I realised this was because, inwardly, I felt that I should have been winning as a matter of course for a long time. So it did not perhaps have quite the impact. It should have been normal.'

Those who watched Hakkinen and Coulthard apparently toying with the opposition to score 1–2 grand slams in

Hakkinen on his way to a strong third place in the 1998 French Grand Prix. (Formula One Pictures)

Hakkinen looks cool as he prepares for the 1998 British Grand Prix at Silverstone. He led, but lost out to Schumacher's Ferrari after an off-course excursion on a near-flooded circuit. (Formula One Pictures)

Australia and Brazil could have been forgiven for thinking that they were destined to enjoy a 1998 season no more challenging than a brisk walk in the park. Yet nobody was underestimating the opposition.

After a slow start, Michael Schumacher and the Ferrari team mounted a spectacular counter-attack. To begin with the Bridgestone-shod McLaren was overwhelmingly the best package in the business, but when Goodyear's development programme slipped into top gear it was clear that the McLaren drivers had a fight on their hands.

Those two wins at the start of the season gave Hakkinen a valuable mathematical cushion which would work in his

Seldom has a single World Championship point been so hard-earned. Hakkinen struggled with dire handling problems to salvage sixth place from the 1998 Hungarian Grand Prix. (Formula One Pictures)

For McLaren, the 1998 World Championship marked their final step in the long process of restoration. (LAT)

Erja Hakkinen wishes her husband good luck…
(DaimlerChrysler/Wilhelm)

… after a light breakfast.
(DaimlerChrysler/Wilhelm)

had somehow found its way into the McLaren supply chain. This was a rare fault indeed and exhaustive steps were taken to ensure that there was no repetition of the episode.

The Spanish and Monaco Grands Prix then yielded outstanding wins for the Finn. Characterised by unerring high speed precision, Hakkinen started both races from pole and vanquished the opposition to come away from the Mediterranean principality with a healthy-looking 22 point lead over Michael Schumacher. It was all beginning to look distinctly promising for the man who, 12 months before, had still to post his first F1 success.

Yet Hakkinen also showed his mettle when events were running against him. Both McLarens retired from the Canadian Grand Prix, Mika with gearbox problems at the start, and David with troublesome throttle linkage when he had looked on course to beat Schumacher's Ferrari in a straight fight.

Montreal raised the curtain on a run of three Schumacher victories. Mika had to settle for third in France behind a Ferrari 1–2, but at Silverstone he drove with great skill in a torrential downpour to lead the Ferrari ace – only to slide off the road when the conditions became absolutely appalling. He was lucky to find his way back onto the track after this excursion and, although the McLaren's nose wings were damaged, it seemed that his 30-second lead over Schumacher would be sufficient to sustain his advantage. Unfortunately the safety car was deployed to slow the field as the rain intensified and that entire advantage disappeared. When the re-start was given, those damaged nose wings meant that Mika was unable to keep Schumacher back in second place.

This was a highly controversial race. Schumacher actually took the chequered flag while entering the pit lane to take a 10-second stop-go penalty, imposed after he overtook a slower car under a yellow flag earlier in the race. Unfortunately this penalty had not been correctly posted and the stewards adjudicating at Silverstone later had their licences suspended for what the FIA regarded as a serious maladministration.

As a result of this debacle, after Silverstone Schumacher had closed to within two points of Mika at the head of the championship table, but the Finn then redressed the balance with two straight victories in the Austrian and German Grands Prix.

With 16 points in hand, Hakkinen headed into the Hungarian race in confident mood. He led from the start only to be slowed when a front anti-roll bar worked loose on his car which forced him to slow his pace dramatically. From an easy win, he struggled home sixth after a brilliant

favour. In the third race at Buenos Aires he was happy to take second to Michael Schumacher on a circuit the Finn did not particularly like.

Then came the San Marino GP where David Coulthard scored his sole win of 1998, a race in which Hakkinen stopped with gearbox failure. A rogue, counterfeit bearing

performance of car conservation. But he could now seriously feel the pressure with Michael closing to seven points behind.

The Belgian Grand Prix at Spa-Francorchamps effectively put the title chase on hold for one race. Neither Mika nor Michael made it to the finish, but most of the pack scarcely managed to get beyond the start. To begin with anyway.

Coming out of the La Source hairpin for the first time in torrential rain, Eddie Irvine's Ferrari and Coulthard's McLaren touched and the Scot spun broadside, triggering one of the most spectacular multiple collisions ever seen – 12 cars were wrecked and the race was immediately red-flagged to a halt.

Prior to the restart – where spare cars were very much in evidence – McLaren switched Hakkinen's car from full Bridgestone wets to intermediate tyres, effectively duplicat-ing Michael Schumacher's decision to make a similar change on his Goodyear-shod Ferrari. Unfortunately Bridgestone intermediates were not yet in the same class as Goodyear's with the result that Hakkinen slid wide at La Source on the restart, spun after making light contact with Michael and was then rammed by Johnny Herbert's Sauber.

For his part Schumacher, apparently unsighted in the tor-rential rain which marred the entire race, later became involved in a controversial collision with Coulthard. The impact ripped off the Ferrari's right front wheel. Back in the pits an ugly scene threatened as Schumacher squared up to Coulthard, but it was defused largely thanks to the Scot's calm dignified attitude.

The Italian Grand Prix saw an emotional Ferrari 1–2, although McLaren-Mercedes certainly had the faster cars on this occasion. Disappointingly, Coulthard's engine failed

Mechanics and engineers tend David Coulthard's MP4/14 in the pit lane at Monaco, 1999. (Formula One Pictures)

In what Ron Dennis later described as 'the most heroic seven laps of the season', Mika recovered to nurse his car home fourth, with only the rear brakes working. This was a great display of damage limitation, but it meant that Mika and Michael left Monza sharing the title lead with 80 points apiece. It could go either way.

Hakkinen now proved publicly that he had come of age. At the Luxembourg Grand Prix at Nürburgring he spent the first 14 laps of the race boxed into third place behind Irvine's Ferrari as Schumacher raced away into the distance. However, once second, Mika drove a stupendous race to emerge from his first refuelling stop ahead of Michael.

It was the defining moment of the season as Hakkinen went on to win in front of the Mercedes senior management. He had proved that Schumacher could be beaten, against the odds, in a straight fight. Michael's face was a picture of disbelief as they shared the winners' rostrum. He just could not accept that he had been outrun.

That gave Hakkinen the psychological edge. Five nail-biting weeks remained before the final race at Suzuka in Japan. Michael qualified on pole position, then stalled at the start, a transgression which required him to go to the

while he was leading, and a rare brake problem pitched Hakkinen into a 175mph spin as he was closing on Schumacher in the second half of the race.

back of the grid for the re-start. Mika had finally broken his challenge. Both men had withstood huge pressure, but at the end of the day it was Schumacher who wobbled first.

For McLaren, this first World Championship since 1992 marked the final step in their long process of restoration. For Mercedes-Benz, it was the realisation of a dream.

This view was strongly endorsed by Mercedes-Benz board director Jurgen Hubbert: 'I think this success is very important for the Mercedes tradition. Motorsport is something quite special and belongs firmly to our heritage.

'When we resumed F1 racing again in the 1990s the image of the Silver Arrows was still there, even for those people who had never seen them in the 1930s and 1950s. It shows how competitive and innovative the company is which is very important in these difficult and commercially competitive times. We are all delighted that Mika has achieved this World Championship.'

Yet Mika had not finished. More than anything, he wanted to retain the title in the manner that his arch-rival Michael Schumacher had managed back in 1995.

From the technical standpoint, McLaren certainly did not waver when it came to applying development resources to ensure that the new MP4/14 was a significant improvement over its predecessor.

'We changed the packaging quite a bit,' explained Adrian Newey at the start of the 1999 season, 'which was actually something I'd wanted to do with the previous year's car but I arrived with the team too late to make those changes. We re-packaged the oil tank and the hydraulic system which I think ought to be an improvement.

'The gearbox is also all new, slightly shorter, but still a six-speed longitudinal configuration. We've also fitted torsion bar rear suspension, which is another thing we didn't have time to do for 1998, but the front suspension was very similar to what had gone before.'

In truth, from the moment Schumacher's Ferrari F399 speared into the tyre barrier on the opening lap of the British Grand Prix at Silverstone, it should have been a stroll for the McLaren-Mercedes squad. Yet it didn't quite work out as planned.

At the end of the day, although Mika Hakkinen deservedly became only the seventh driver in the 50-year history of the official World Championship to win back-to-back titles, McLaren lost out by two points to Ferrari in the

The opening lap of the 1999 Belgian Grand Prix with David Coulthard already sprinting away from team-mate Mika Hakkinen … (DaimlerChrysler/Wilhelm)

battle for the constructors' crown. Ferrari's first world title of any sort since 1983 was achieved largely due to the consistency of Irvine in his role as Schumacher's understudy.

The Ulsterman opened the year with a lucky win at Melbourne and went on to add another three victories to his personal tally by the end of the year. Irvine knew that his Ferrari F399 didn't quite have the legs on the latest McLaren MP4/14, but it did have technical, if not operational, reliability on its side. Maranello's temporary number one driver was also good at mind games, most notably winding David Coulthard off the clock during a brief mid-season spell of psychological joshing.

A win in Malaysia kept Irvine in play right up to the final race of the year and it was only on Saturday morning at Suzuka that his composure finally began to crack and the mental advantage passed back to the resurgent Hakkinen. It was effectively all over for Eddie when he slammed off the road and could only qualify fifth.

Hakkinen blitzed the final race and retained the crown.

It had been a close call for Hakkinen, not least because his team had made a huge leap forward with the new MP4/14, paying for their technical audacity with a raft of early season unreliability.

Powered by a lighter and lower 72-degree Mercedes

F0110H V10 engine developing around 785bhp at 16,700rpm, the new car represented Adrian Newey's formula to claw back some of the grip lost by the fourth groove now required in the front tyres by the revised 1999 technical rules. With extra weight trimmed off the entire chassis/engine package, the new car had even more scope for strategic placement of ballast around the chassis. It was also more complex than its predecessor in terms of the positioning of many of the ancillary components within the monocoque walls.

The MP4/14 was not quite as user-friendly as the 1998 car, failing initially to instill its drivers with the same sense of confidence and 'chuckability'. On the limit, however, it represented an appreciable step forward even though the more powerful V10 had rather less in the way of progressive power delivery than the previous engine.

One of the main issues which particularly affected McLaren – and most other cars, come to that – was the reduction in the front tyre contact patch caused by the introduction of a fourth circumferential groove. Complicating that issue, what came as something of a surprise was the reduction in rear grip produced by the latest generation of Bridgestone rubber.

This only became apparent during the early development

ADRIAN NEWEY
The crucial ingredient

In August 1997 former Williams Chief Designer Adrian Newey joined McLaren as its new Technical Director in a reputed £2 million deal which at a stroke destabilised his former employers while providing McLaren with a crucial technical boost that has underpinned their winning efforts ever since.

A quiet, self-effacing man, Newey is regarded as one of the very best designers of his generation. He has a particular penchant for aerodynamic ingenuity at a time when the wind tunnel is probably the most important single asset in the process of developing a Grand Prix car. Yet for all that, Newey primarily regards himself as a team player, knowing that the complexities of today's F1 car design far out-strip the capabilities of a single individual: 'I try to be good at delegation. I do believe it is important that people are given a reasonably free rein so that they can express themselves in engineering terms, within the overall team structure, of course.'

Newey had a long-term contract with Williams until 1999, but left the company at the end of 1996 after a dispute about whether or not he should have been consulted over the decision by Frank Williams and his Technical Director Patrick Head to drop Damon Hill from the team. 'I think, ultimately, Patrick and I got on well, but when it came to it, he was my boss. The title Technical Director as such doesn't interest me. But I wanted more freedom, if you like, more influence and, basically, a fresh challenge. I had been there for seven years.

'At Williams I had a very great degree of engineering autonomy, but no influence in other areas. I have more responsibility here at McLaren, and not just on the technical side. That's obviously the side I'm good at, but it is nice to be involved in other things like drivers, the new factory and so-on.'

For nine months after leaving Williams, Newey was on 'gardening leave', sitting at home waiting for the legal loose ends to be resolved before he could join McLaren. As rival team owner Eddie Jordan observed wryly, this worked out particularly well for McLaren: 'He spent the best part of a year sitting in his garden shed, if you like, pondering over the best way to interpret the new 1998 technical regulations. And I think that helped McLaren a lot in 1998 with the MP4/13 challenger.'

Newey wasn't always a star player. He admits that he struggled academically and was lucky to get a place at Southampton University where he graduated with a degree in astronautics and aeronautics. His subsequent position with the March company at Bicester provided the launch pad for his career. In particular, he would gain a reputation for innovation in terms of aerodynamic development.

'I took that particular degree course because I felt that racing cars were closer to aircraft than they were to road cars. Add to that the fact that the March, McLaren and Brabham teams all came along to use the Southampton wind tunnel and my interest in this area was sharpened.'

March co-founder Robin Herd was something of a mentor to Newey and the diversity of the company's business in the mid-1980s meant that the fledgeling engineer learned a great deal in a relatively short time. Specifically, it was on the high speed ovals of the US CART Championship that Adrian really honed his skills. This led to the post of Chief Designer with the March team when it returned to Formula 1 in 1988, a role he retained until the move to Williams.

From left, DaimlerChrysler chairman Jurgen Schrempp, board director Jurgen Hubbert, McLaren technical director Adrian Newey and TAG McLaren Managing Director Ron Dennis at the 1997 European Grand Prix. (DaimlerChrysler/Wilhelm)

Coulthard and Hakkinen draw up alongside each other after their 1–2 victory in the 1999 Belgian Grand Prix. The race had started with the cars making light contact at the first corner. (LAT)

Mr and Mrs Hakkinen in a relaxed mood. (DaimlerChrysler/Wilhelm)

of the MP4/14 after various fixed parameters of its design were established. It resulted in the need to alter the deployment of ballast around the car, but eventually everything was satisfactorily resolved in time for the opening race of the year. Even so, assimilating all the lessons from the 1998 car and incorporating them into a ground-up re-design resulted in too many risks. It needed honing in the interests of reliability, and that process ate into too much of the season.

Unquestionably, Ferrari posted some of the best victories of the 1999 season. The most contentious as well. Virtuoso performances by Schumacher at Imola and Monaco seemed to be launching the German ace towards his third World Championship until events at Silverstone cut short his challenge, while Irvine's defeat of David Coulthard in Austria was probably his best single drive of the year.

Yet the aftermath of the inaugural Malaysian Grand Prix at Sepang cast an unfortunate shadow over the way Ferrari sometimes operated. Schumacher's return to the cockpit after recovering from a broken leg, was soured not only by the debate in the scrutineering bay over the legality of the Italian cars' aerodynamic 'bargeboards' but also by the manner in which he deliberately blocked Hakkinen's McLaren as they raced for second place.

It was simply not good enough to retreat behind the rule book and say 'this is not prohibited', as did many of

Michael's star-struck supporters. Varying one's lap times by more than a couple of seconds and backing off in high speed corners may not actually contravene any written regulation, but was plainly unsporting and ruthlessly unethical.

After Sepang, for Michael then to have the brass neck to accuse Coulthard of balking him at Suzuka – and for Bernie Ecclestone to pile in with suggestions that DC should have been black-flagged – was simply laughable. The Scot's McLaren delayed the Ferrari team leader for three corners and three seconds. Nothing more.

McLaren understandably expressed indignation at the manner in which officialdom seemed intent on spoon-feeding Ferrari its World Championship, no matter how blatant the favours appeared. Yet the fact remains that Ron Dennis and his crew should never have been remotely vulnerable to a Ferrari challenge in the second half of the year. When Hakkinen scored his flag-to-flag victory in Hungary, it ought to have been the win which clinched the title. As it was, this proved no more than a happy interlude in a summer blighted by mistakes and technical problems.

Certainly, McLaren made more unforced errors in 1999 than during any season in recent memory. Mika threw away

20 points by crashing out of the lead at both Imola and Monza. A loose wheel at Silverstone, tyre failure at Hockenheim and David Coulthard pitching him into a spin on the second corner in Austria – surely the silliest moment of the year – all added to the sense of impending crisis.

There was another area which threatened to undermine McLaren's title challenge. The team's unyielding commitment to give Coulthard and Hakkinen an equal crack at the championship, while exemplary behaviour in an increasingly political sport, meant that they were sometimes tripping each other up. For example Mika was hard pressed to see the fairness of the situation when Dennis refused to call team orders at Spa, allowing Coulthard an unchallenged – and admittedly brilliant – victory barely a month after that stupid tangle in Austria. And all this in the face of a Ferrari team which, by contrast, accorded unchallenged number one status first to Schumacher and then, in his absence, to Irvine.

But taken as a whole, Hakkinen did a markedly better job than Coulthard who continued his patchy race form and could count himself lucky not to lose his McLaren seat to Eddie Irvine for the 2000 season. Despite this, paddock pundits had the strong impression that both McLaren and

The slip that could have cost him the title. Hakkinen spins out of the lead of the 1999 Italian Grand Prix. (LAT)

That winning smile. Mika Hakkinen and the McLaren-Mercedes team after the Finn successfully retained his World Championship crown by winning the 1999 Japanese Grand Prix. (DaimlerChrysler/Wilhelm)

Sweeping through the right-hander at Monte Carlo's harbour front swimming pool, Coulthard heads for an outstanding victory in the most prestigious race on the 2000 F1 calendar. (Formula One Pictures)

Mercedes were more than willing for Coulthard to smooth out the peaks and troughs in his performance in order to justify keeping him on.

Yet for all the problems and minor setbacks in 1999, the McLaren team's record was looking pretty impressive by the end of the year. McLaren International had won 99

Grands Prix since 1981, a cumulative total of 123 races since 1968. This included eight drivers' and constructors' World Championships. In that time, closest rivals Williams won 99 GPs, including an all-time record nine constructors' and seven drivers' crowns. By contrast Ferrari had won 52 GPs (two constructors' and one drivers' championship),

RON DENNIS
The practical visionary

McLaren have always had a self-built, practical image which was started by Bruce McLaren himself and sustained by Ron Dennis who took over control in the early 1980s when the team became McLaren International.

Dennis is a visionary. He was never what one would describe as a dyed-in-the-wool car enthusiast, but had a fascination for technical matters, and preferably technical excellence. He started as a mechanic with the works Cooper F1 team in the summer of 1966. In those days it was quite a tough life. Paddocks were often scarcely more than gravel-strewn fields. At best there was some protection from temporary awnings erected alongside the transporters but generally, work on the cars was conducted in the open.

Ron concedes that he's always been something of an 'old woman' when it comes to cleanliness and order. He never saw any merit in grubby equipment or personnel. Within half an hour of getting home from the factory after a day's work, Ron would wash, change into fresh clothes and appear as clean as a new pin. It is a philosophy he has sustained to this day.

After learning the motor racing ropes with Cooper, Ron Dennis switched to the Brabham team for 1968 and by the end of 1970 had been promoted to Chief Mechanic. In fact, for the last two races of that season he was effectively operating as team manager. He was now sufficiently confident to strike out on his own.

That single-minded focus has carried Dennis to his current position as Chairman and CEO of the TAG McLaren group. Within his company he is surrounded by a group of employees who have followed a similarly focused path.

One of the most loyal members of the factory-based group is Neil Trundle, Ron's original partner in the Rondel Racing F2 team back in 1971. Now in charge of the specialist gearbox department at McLaren, he has stuck with the company through good times and bad: 'Things are always changing, but the team spirit stays. Ron was always trying to keep morale up when we went through a bad patch.'

McLaren team co-ordinator Jo Ramirez is a relative newcomer with 14 years of service under his belt. But his racing experience extends way back to the early 1960s when he did odd jobs for his friend Ricardo Rodriguez who he got to know in Mexico City. Jo paid $60 to cross the Atlantic, steerage, in the old *Queen Elizabeth* and became a 'gopher' for Ferrari. Later he would work for Lamborghini, Ford, Eagle, Tyrrell, Copersucar and, eventually, McLaren.

Dave Ryan, now the McLaren team manager, was another who began from absolute base camp. A New Zealander trained as a mechanic, he found himself stranded in San Francisco without enough money and spent his final few dollars on what started as a 14-day trip to Britain. He went to the 1974 British Grand Prix at Brands Hatch, liked what he saw, and soon afterwards wandered into the McLaren factory where he was told to pick up a broom and start sweeping. Another classic example of how commitment pays off.

Staying in control. Ron Dennis on the pit wall at Monaco, 1999. (Formula One Pictures)

HAKKINEN AND COULTHARD
'They're getting better all the time'

German ace Michael Schumacher got the thumbs-down as a possible McLaren-Mercedes driver in 1999 when Jurgen Schrempp, the Chief Executive Officer of DaimlerChrysler, announced that he preferred sticking with Mika Hakkinen and David Coulthard. Dismissing the prospect of Schumacher joining McLaren as 'absolute nonsense', Schrempp made it clear that the team was happy with its current line-up: 'We have two very successful drivers, they are getting better all the time and they are two very likeable people.'

Schrempp went on to praise the Mercedes-Benz motorsport division. 'What it has achieved is exemplary for the whole company,' he added to a standing ovation from 14,000 DaimlerChrysler shareholders gathered in Stuttgart.

This was quite an endorsement. Going into the 2000 season, Hakkinen and Coulthard were starting their fifth year together as Mercedes team-mates, a record previously only exceeded by Rudolf Caracciola and Manfred von Brauchitsch who were

Coulthard, Hakkinen and Schumacher at the pole winner's press conference prior to the 1999 Australian Grand Prix. None of them finished in the points, as it turned out. (DaimlerChrysler/Wilhelm)

paired in the Mercedes-Benz factory team from 1934 to 1939.

Mika and David have very different personalities and, while it might be difficult to imagine them sharing a bottle of champagne with back-slapping familiarity in the manner of the pre-war duo, they both have a deep commitment to their chosen profession. They are cordial towards each other rather than convivial. Both are quite controlled, pragmatic personalities which means that they fit well into the McLaren-Mercedes environment.

Each graduated to stardom via karting and then the British F3 Championship, which Mika won in 1990; David finished second to Rubens Barrichello the following year. Hakkinen then went straight into F1 with Lotus before switching to the role of McLaren test driver in 1993 and being promoted to the race team to replace Michael Andretti towards the end of the season. David spent three years in F3000 before landing the job of test driver in the Williams-Renault squad. The tragic death of Ayrton Senna saw him promoted to the race team and he duly scored his first victory in the 1995 Portuguese Grand Prix before joining Hakkinen at McLaren the following season.

1999 QANTAS AUSTRALIAN GRAND PRIX

Benetton 27 GPs (one constructors' and two drivers' championships) and the now-defunct Brabham team 15 GPs and one drivers' title. The remaining wins had been shared out between Renault (15), Lotus (8), Ligier (4), Jordan (3) Tyrrell (2) and Stewart (1), making a grand total of 127 Grands Prix between them. McLaren headed the all-time leader boards and, together with Mercedes-Benz, were determined to continue that enviable state of affairs.

From the touchlines it always seemed clear that Mercedes-Benz and McLaren would move closer as the years rolled by. It was not always obvious precisely how this would manifest itself, until decisive plans were announced at the 1999 British Grand Prix to the effect that DaimlerChrysler would purchase a 40 per cent stake in the TAG McLaren Group under the terms of a share option. Both parties were bound by on-disclosure agreements in

A man with a lot on his mind. Mika Hakkinen in the cockpit of his McLaren-Mercedes MP4/15.
(Formula One Pictures)

David Coulthard takes the chequered flag to win the 2000 French Grand Prix at Magny-Cours, a splendid triumph by the popular Scot. (Formula One Pictures)

Worth all the effort! Hakkinen celebrates after taking pole position at Spa-Francorchamps. (Formula One Pictures)

respect of the terms and conditions of the deal, but motor industry insiders put the value of the alliance at not much short of £700 million.

It was the second major coup for the Anglo-German partnership, coming just 24 hours after confirmation that McLaren Cars would build the forthcoming 540bhp AMG V8-engined Mercedes SLR supercar at the new TAG McLaren headquarters, Paragon, which was currently under construction near Woking.

'This element of our long-term strategy is designed to further enhance our products and to differentiate the Mercedes-Benz brand in an increasingly competitive market,' said Schrempp. 'This option is consistent with our acquisition of the majority of AMG and the Mercedes-Benz Maybach project.'

The link would strengthen immeasurably the McLaren-Mercedes F1 programme which, Ron Dennis was quick to emphasise, remained the McLaren core business: 'It is absolutely essential to our strategy to keep a dominant position in F1', confirming that under the new arrangement he and TAG boss Mansour Ojjeh would each retain 30 per cent stakes in TAG McLaren. 'The new project will have no impact at all on the F1 budget. We are well structured and disciplined in the handling of our F1 budget. It is certainly not necessary for DaimlerChrysler to provide additional funding.'

DaimlerChrysler board member Dr Jurgen Hubbert said there were no plans to take more than a minority share in TAG McLaren: 'It is a relationship which is more than just business.' Dennis confirmed that 'one of the pre-requisites from Mr Schrempp was that there should be nothing in place to detract from the [McLaren] entrepreneurial spirit. That value cannot be stripped out of the company.'

The new SLR was to be dubbed a Mercedes-Benz

David Coulthard's McLaren-Mercedes photographed in the race morning warm-up for the 2000 Belgian Grand Prix by the eagle-eyed John Townsend. In a rare slip, the McLaren pit crew have left on the protective nose wing covers – which will fly off, much to Coulthard's surprise, a few seconds later! (Formula One Pictures)

High level discussion. From left: Coulthard's manager Martin Brundle, McLaren Chairman Ron Dennis and DC himself. (Formula One Pictures)

McLaren. 'McLaren is a strong brand,' said Dennis, 'and we believe it will bring added value to this particular car.'

The deal was finally confirmed in March 2000 to make the McLaren-Mercedes alliance unquestionably the closest between an F1 team and its engine partner to be seen on the contemporary F1 stage. However, Martin Whitmarsh added a note of caution to the long-term future: 'We still have a contractual relationship with Mercedes which has resulted in an extension of the engine supply agreement with McLaren at least until the end of 2004. Clearly, because of their equity participation there would be an expectation that they will be in for longer. But a commitment for five years is a long time in F1 terms.

'When you look at what is also happening with Honda, BMW and Toyota, the commitment of the major automotive manufacturers now is much higher than it has ever been. Inevitably, when you look back at the history of the major car makers' commitment to F1, it has been cyclical. But now, of course, uncoupling and reshuffling will be much more difficult. So you could argue there were inherent risks for McLaren becoming more closely linked and embroiled with a major manufacturer like Mercedes. This is inevitably an issue. Yet with the changing ways of F1, you need to have large scale commitment from an automotive manufacturer in order to be competitive. They

naturally want to have a higher level of participation and what we're seeing is a natural consequence of this.

'In five years time, can Honda, BMW, Toyota, Jaguar and Mercedes-Benz *all* be winning in F1? The answer of course is no. So can those brands, which by definition are premier brands, be seen to be participating in a very public and committed manner and not succeeding? I think that is a stage we have yet to face. Inevitably, some of them will drop out. How the F1 teams manage that process could be quite a challenge.'

In preparation for the 2000 season, testing became even more of a priority for the McLaren-Mercedes squad. To that end former Prost team driver, and 1996 Monaco Grand Prix winner, Olivier Panis was signed up to support Mika and David who were starting their fifth straight season together as the team's regular drivers.

Unquestionably, Panis's contribution to the sustained development of the evolutionary McLaren MP4/15 was one of the key factors behind the car's competitiveness. The Frenchman not only proved to be a methodical and very intelligent test and development driver, but he was also seriously quick. From a career standpoint, Panis was taking one hell of a risk stepping down from the F1 mainstream to tackle this new challenge. But it would pay off. By the end of the season, reputation sparkling, he was offered a full-

With the giant Indianapolis grandstands as the momentous backdrop, Coulthard leads the field away from the line at the start of the inaugural 2000 US Grand Prix.
(Formula One Pictures)

Coulthard energetically squeezes Michael Schumacher as the German driver's Ferrari takes the lead at Indianapolis. David jumped the start slightly and was later given a 10sec stop-go penalty. Hakkinen watches the fun from third place. (Formula One Pictures)

Compact jewel. The tiny Mercedes F0110G 72-degree V10 which powered the McLaren MP4/15s, seen in a rare unclothed moment on the starting grid at Suzuka. (Formula One Pictures)

Dramatic moment. Mika Hakkinen leads Michael Schumacher as they sprint for the first corner of the 2000 Japanese GP at Suzuka, the race at which the Ferrari team leader claimed his third World Championship crown and the Finn lost his chance of winning a legendary three titles in a row. (Formula One Pictures)

time seat with British American Racing for 2001.

As it happens, the MP4/15 underwent its preliminary trials in the hands of Hakkinen while Coulthard initially continued his pre-season test work with the interim MP4/14 development chassis, both machines fitted with the latest Mercedes FO110J V10 engines.

Hakkinen and Coulthard went into the first race of the season confident they had a car quick enough to do the job. The speed was demonstrated pretty convincingly, but initial reliability was a sore point. Running first and second in Australia they both succumbed to pneumatic valve filter problems on their engines.

It was a bitter blow as these failures handed Ferrari an easy 1–2 victory. Ilmor Engineering worked hard to ensure there was no repetition of this, but in Brazil Hakkinen's car wilted with an engine problem while the Finn seemed right

on course for a strategically astute win on a one-stop strategy. As it was, Schumacher won again and then took a third straight win at Imola where Hakkinen at last got his Championship points score off the deck with second place.

Interlagos also produced a bitter blow for Coulthard who had battled with gearbox problems to cross the finishing line second. After the race, following a lengthy period of scrutineering during which his car was examined and re-examined exhaustively by officials, the FIA technical delegate Jo Bauer concluded that the front wing was 7mm too low according to the regulations. McLaren appealed against the disqualification, but the FIA Court of Appeal supported the stewards' original exclusion.

There was already no doubt, however, that MP4/15 was a better car than its predecessor. 'It was better in responding to [set up] changes and more comfortable to drive on the

162 / MERCEDES IN MOTORSPORT

limit,' explained Whitmarsh. 'Development was structured and routine, although there were no hugely radical technical developments during the course of the year. Routine development of the aerodynamic package, including a variety of diffusers, was part of the programme and eventually we returned to using a power steering system, not least because the drivers were saying "well, everyone else has them" even though this involved slight issues of complexity and additional weight.'

Coulthard finally gave McLaren-Mercedes its first win of the season in the British Grand Prix at Silverstone, round four of the title chase. Hakkinen then took the initiative, posting a strong second to Schumacher's Ferrari at the Nürburgring and then winning the Spanish GP ahead of Coulthard only four days after DC survived the crash landing of a chartered Learjet at Lyons Satolas airport in which both the pilots died.

Coulthard's determined run to second place in Spain heralded a golden month of achievement for the Scot who, from the touchlines, seemed to have gone up a gear in terms of confidence and all-round accomplishment. He kept out of trouble to score a well-judged and precise win through the streets of Monaco, and while Canada saw him picking up an unfortunate 10 second stop-go penalty after his mechanics stayed on the dummy grid too long prior to the formation lap when he stalled his engine, his victory in the French GP at Magny-Cours was an absolutely top drawer performance.

Having removed the tailplane from his rear aerofoil on the starting grid to ease a touch of last-minute understeer, Coulthard found his McLaren-Mercedes perfectly balanced through the fast Estoril right-hander beyond the pits and was able to press home a successful onslaught on Schumacher's Ferrari. He boldly overtook the German ace and was pulling away when the Ferrari's engine failed.

Throughout this period Hakkinen was feeling rather stressed-out, the cumulative result of the two years' endeavour involved in winning and defending his 1998 World Championship. Ron Dennis would blame himself for not having recognised the problem earlier, and he duly despatched Hakkinen on a well-deserved mid-season holiday.

On his return in Austria, Mika won commandingly. He then went on to finish second at Hockenheim where – ironically – a disgruntled former Mercedes employee wandered onto the circuit, triggering the emergence of the safety car, which badly disadvantaged the McLaren drivers, who were leading by more than 30 seconds, in terms of their overall race strategies.

Hakkinen continued to dominate the Hungarian Grand Prix and wrested the lead of the Belgian race at Spa-

The line-up for 2001 – Hakkinen, Coulthard, and new test driver Alexander Wurz. (Formula One Pictures)

Francorchamps in a daring display of overtaking, squeezing ahead of Michael Schumacher with three laps to go as they both lapped Ricardo Zonta's BAR-Honda. Thereafter, Ferrari took the initiative at Monza and Indianapolis, where Hakkinen was closing on Schumacher when his engine failed, and he led the lion's share of the crucial Japanese Grand Prix until a rain shower tipped the outcome of the title battle in the German's favour.

In total McLaren won seven races. Coulthard squandered the opportunity to make it four each after running off the road while leading in Malaysia, the resultant debris picked up in his radiator ducts overheating his engine to the point where the team had to make damaging amendments to his race strategy.

The McLarens fell under the scrutiny of FIA officials again during the course of the season with Hakkinen's Austrian victory jeopardised after an official paper seal was found missing from his car's electronic control box. It did not matter that it was probably the FIA who'd omitted to fit this in the first place for it was McLaren's responsibility to ensure it was present. The net result was a $50,000 fine and loss of the ten Constructors' Championship points which went with the win, but Hakkinen was permitted to retain his own points in the Drivers' Championship.

THE TWO-SEATER MP4-98T
It's quite quick, eh?

It was the ferocious way in which the mere act of gearchanging sent seismic tremors through McLaren's ultimate promotional tool which really caught the author's attention.

The McLaren MP4-98T seemed to shake from stem to stern each time Olivier Panis flicked the electro-hydraulic gearchange and the drive from the 750bhp Mercedes V10 was disconnected for a split second as we went up through the ratios. Yet while the initial acceleration was enough to slam my helmet back into the headrest, it was sustained in third, fourth and fifth gears, the McLaren seeming to surge off with the relentless force of Concorde until, just as one was waiting for it to take off, the huge carbon-fibre brakes grabbed it to a halt into the braking area like a huge hidden hand.

On the Thursday prior to the 2000 Australian Grand Prix, I followed Panis out onto the circuit at Melbourne less than 24 hours before the start of the first F1 practice session of the new millennium.

I sat just 18 inches behind the 1996 Monaco Grand Prix winner, snug in the tailored seat of the McLaren two-seater for the treat of a lifetime. Ahead of me beckoned three hot-making laps round the Albert Park circuit. It served as a terrific reminder of just how fit the current F1 drivers must be to perform in this frenetic cauldron of competitive activity.

The whole affair had started ten days earlier when Ron Dennis rang and proffered the invitation: 'You can wimp out now, in which case only you and I will know about it.' He paused. 'Until I get to Melbourne and tell everybody, of course…'

It was at this point that I found myself recalling the classic definition that a hero is somebody who is an abject coward – but does it anyway. I snivelled my thanks down the telephone, privately confident that I would fail the necessary medical. Having passed my 50th birthday, I clearly fell into that category of a potential passenger whose cardio-vascular system might not survive the eight-mile white-knuckle ride. Consequently, they insisted on full cardiac stress ECG, neck X-rays and top-to-toe check. I passed. The barriers separating me from the cockpit of the two-seater were collapsing by the minute.

On arrival at Melbourne, I reported to a makeshift garage outside the F1 paddock proper for a pre-briefing from the crew of the McLaren 'adrenaline programme'. The car is run by a small group of engineers under Dermot Walsh, together with the McLaren F1 GTR coupé which is also part of the programme.

The first task was to have a seat mould taken and made on the spot. Slipping down into the cockpit, I was amazed how much room there seemed to be. Then I remembered that Panis had to go in front! A carbon-fibre crossbeam was dropped in ahead of my chest. It was a deeply claustrophobic experience, but nothing compared with the mounting feeling of anxiety as Panis's seat was then squeezed between my legs. I was now trapped; in somebody else's hands and a hostage to McLaren fortune.

Author Alan Henry is fitted into the 'rear seat' of the McLaren-Mercedes MP4-98T at Melbourne, 2000, prior to his ride with Olivier Panis. The driver's seat is still to go in, between his legs. It was all a very snug fit, not for the claustrophobic. (LAT)

As I sat, my hands crossed over my chest, the top bodywork – complete with that confining headrest – was added. Truth be told, the whole feeling of confinement was extremely unpleasant. However, the soothing and reassuring manner in which the crew took me through an explanation of precisely what was going to happen made life much more bearable. Sweltering in the 30-degree heat inside my full overalls, helmet and balaclava, I slipped into a trance-like state, resigned to my fate.

Twice during my ride we pulled almost 4-G, a chirp from the right front tyre as Panis swung into a tight right-hander after braking from 170mph in 40 metres testifying to the fact that he wasn't exactly hanging about. Yet it was the slingshot effect of the acceleration in the intermediate gears as we slammed round the two long right-handers on the return leg of the circuit, retaining wall looming ominously close to my left ear, which really grabbed my attention. I suppose it was slightly reassuring that Olivier's right elbow dug into my knee as he negotiated the tighter right-handers. Nice to know he was still there…

'This compares very closely with the proper race car,' said Panis afterwards. 'The level of grip is much the same, although it feels pretty heavy with two passengers and, when you exit low speed corners, the rear-end starts to slide and lose grip.' Tell me about it.

'Maybe we lose five or six seconds a lap as compared with the pure single-seater. It's quite quick, eh? Obviously I was braking a little earlier than I would in the race car, because the responsibility while carrying a passenger is very great. But I am sure that, if the passenger did not mind, it would be possible to push a little harder.'

Plans for this amazing one-off machine had originally been revealed just two years before, on the eve of the 1998 Australian Grand Prix. For several years Mansour Ojjeh – Chief Executive Officer of the TAG group which is McLaren's parent company – had been trying to coax Ron Dennis into building a two-seater Grand Prix car so that outsiders might at last experience that intoxicating world which is F1 motoring.

Finally the green light was given. The design brief was to construct a bespoke machine incorporating the highest standards of constructional safety for both driver and passenger. McLaren Cars Technical Director Gordon Murray and Chief Designer Barry Lett, who was to lead the programme, took a long look at the Rocket two-seater sports car which Murray had designed some time earlier. With its tandem driving position, this project had clearly given him some ideas on how to tackle the one-plus-one F1 cockpit layout.

The MP4-98T has been used to chauffeur a wide range of celebrities all over the world. It has done much to raise F1's international profile, also generating many thousands of dollars for charitable causes. Riding in the extraordinary vehicle gave me membership of an exclusive club of barely 30 people, ranging from Murray Walker to violinist Vanessa Mae, from FIA president Max Mosley to Spain's King Juan Carlos.

US SCENE
AND TOURING CARS

Al Unser Jr heads for victory in the 1994 Indianapolis 500 at the wheel of the sensational pushrod Mercedes V8-engined Penske which was developed in secret especially for this one event.
(DaimlerChrysler)

AFTER GENERAL MOTORS WITHDREW its backing from Ilmor at the end of 1993 it was decided to have a gap year before the Mercedes-Benz involvement in the US series would come on stream. Perhaps it was felt somewhat cynical simply to re-badge the GM motors as 'Mercedes' overnight, but certainly both Daimler-Benz and Ilmor's management regarded this as a more credible strategy.

However, as a taster for what was to come, Mercedes, Ilmor and the Penske team got together for the 1994

Indianapolis 500 to run a one-off engine which would put the opposition very firmly in the shade for the Memorial Day classic. Taking advantage of USAC's illogical equivalency rules, the works Penske of Al Unser Jr would dominate the 500 using a specially designed two-valves per cylinder, pushrod Mercedes V8. After detailed discussions with Ilmor partners Mario Illien and Paul Morgan, team chief Roger Penske agreed that the extra 800cc cylinder capacity and additional permitted turbocharger boost for

cam-in-block, two valve engines would be just the way to go for a one-off assault on America's most important motor race.

'The engine went from discussion, to drawings, to casting and onto the dyno in 25 weeks,' remembers Paul Morgan. The hardware they produced was a 72-degree, 3.43-litre V8 weighing 273lb and developing around 750bhp. That was all the outside world would know or, in the opinion of Mercedes and Ilmor, needed to know. The rest would speak for itself.

The green light was given to the project in June 1993 – five months before Daimler-Benz agreed to take a stake in the Ilmor operation – and by Sunday, 20 February 1994 the new engine was installed in a Penske chassis, testing behind closed doors at the Penske-owned Nazareth oval track which had been specially cleared of heavy snow for the occasion.

Al Unser Jr remembers very specifically when he was first told of the plan. 'I was in a dug-out with Roger (Penske) at a charity baseball game in Reading, Pennsylvania. Roger says, very quietly: "Al, we've got an engine that we're gonna take to Indy and it's gonna blow 'em off. Nobody knows about this."

'I mean, he's telling me this in a dug-out! And then he says: "Mum's the word here, Al. Ilmor is building it, specially for us. This is gonna be the one!"

'It showed up for the first time in a '93 car at Reading. We had to plough the race track because it was December and the snow was four feet deep. I had snow walls, not just the outside wall, but the inside wall as well. They took snow blowers and literally cut the race track out of the snow. Boy, it was cold! I remember the crew had to climb the snow banks because otherwise they couldn't see the car on the front straightaway.

'So I was the first driver to actually hear it! It was the neatest sounding engine, real throaty. And when I first drove it, I mean this thing had so much bottom end torque. It was a low revver; 9,000rpm, tops. But from 7,000 on up, this thing just grunted. They said: "What you think? Can we go to Indy with it?" I said: "Hey man, I don't know because I can't use the throttle enough here at Nazareth to tell you. But it runs great, it's got a lot of power but we need to get on a race track so that we can leg this thing."

'Of course, we couldn't take it to Indianapolis because everybody would find out about it. So, we went to Michigan. I drove it there and this thing had so much power. I mean, a big lift in the corners. It was 240mph down the straightaway; big power!

'The development process was so intense that, when it

would blow up, they would take it out of the car right away and disassemble it immediately so that they could phone up Mario and all the staff and say what went wrong. And they would start working on it immediately.

'You would run 300 miles and go away; then run 350 and go away. I remember going there day after day and it being so cold because it was during the winter months. I did most of the development. Paul (Tracy) would drive it every now and then. Then Emerson (Fittipaldi) would get in it. I

Former double World Champion Emerson Fittipaldi won no fewer than 11 CART victories for Penske between 1990 and 1996, his last at Nazareth in April 1995 being scored with Mercedes-Benz power. (DaimlerChrysler/Wilhelm)

remember Emerson driving the day that Senna died. I was doing promotional work up in Canada. I had to cut the visit short. They flew me in and by 2pm that day I was sitting in the car at Michigan and continuing the development.

'Each time I drove it, there was a little bit less hit and a little bit less horsepower to make it live. But it still was running 240 down the straight, always with big lifts in the corners. And at least we could leg it. I remember telling Roger that if we could make it live at Michigan then it would live at Indy, no problem. And he knew that.

'Then the month of May started and everybody knew about it by then. The one big thing I remember was, man, if I went out and ran a quick time, Roger parked me instantly. He'd say: "You're done. Go back to the garage." I'd say: "But Emerson is getting more out of the car, Tracy is getting more out of the car", and he would say: "That's fine, that's fine. But you're parked."'

It was a shrewd move. Penske did not want Indianapolis

Paul Tracy scored three wins for the Penske-Mercedes squad during the 1997 CART season. (LAT)

owner Tony George to fully appreciate the performance advantage the Penske-Merc really had. He knew only too well that George might pass an overnight rule restricting its performance if he was worried about a cakewalk. But he didn't – and Unser duly delivered the longed-for result.

Unser Jr qualified on pole with a four lap average of 228.011mph. In the race, Fittipaldi and Unser ran away from the field although Al stalled when trying to leave the pits which lost him time at his first stop. With less than 50 miles to go to the chequered flag, Fittipaldi lapped Unser, but Al repassed the Brazilian in traffic and then Emerson hit the wall as he was running hard in Unser's slipstream. Al recalls it as a great day: 'That's when I knew for sure this was the strongest team I had ever been with. I was still making mistakes because I messed up that first pit stop again. It was my third race in a row that I couldn't get out of the pits at the first stop, but we still ended up winners.'

In 1999, Unser would reflect: 'I have had great relation-

ships with Mario Illien and Paul Morgan; perhaps more so with Mario. He's somebody I've always looked up to; I've always wanted to drive his engines, right from when the Ilmor and Chevrolet were first introduced. My Dad was part of Penske Racing at that time and I always wanted one. Now I was winning with this incredible engine at Indy.

'I was aware of the need to win, if only for the Ilmor and Penske guys not being able to take losing after all the effort they had put in. But I was just doing my job. I'm there to win and I know the effort it takes for me to get out there and do my job and the sacrifices I've had to make with my family and all that kind of thing. The hours that I see these people put in – I'm not there doing it with them but, believe me, I know what they're doing because I did those things in my sprint car days.

'My Dad would drill me about all this kind of stuff when I was being raised. So, to actually see it all going on was an honour. I've never seen an engine disassembled – bham – just like that before. That's why I was so very proud to be part of such a magnificent team.'

At the start of the 1995 season Ilmor produced a new 2.65-litre V8 engine which would launch the CART involvement for Mercedes-Benz.

The front line of the Mercedes CART challenge was the works Penske PC24s. The season started with Al winning at Long Beach and Emerson Fittipaldi following that up with victory at Nazareth. But – defying belief – neither driver managed to qualify at Indianapolis. This was the equivalent of Mika Hakkinen being unable to make the 107 per cent qualifying cut in a 2000 World Championship race and remains inexplicable to this day. It was also the first time a defending Indy 500 winner had failed to make the field.

Unser and Fittipaldi bounced back into contention after this painful debacle and, between them, steered the Mercedes-engined Penskes to five wins throughout the course of the season. Unser worked undeniably hard for the balance of the year, but was thwarted in his efforts to become the first Mercedes-powered CART champion when Jacques Villeneuve pipped him to the drivers' title by just 11 points with his Team Green Reynard-Honda. In the manufacturers' championship Mercedes at least had the satisfaction of beating Honda into second place with 272 points, taking runner-up spot behind Ford Cosworth who totalled 310 points.

In 1996, Mercedes had a more frustrating time on the CART scene. Jimmy Vasser took the title to start a run of three straight Reynard-Honda championships for the Target Ganassi team, the next two of which would fall to former F1 racer Alex Zanardi. In the Mercedes camp, the Penske flattered to deceive in pre-race testing and failed to win a

single race all season – even though Unser's team-mate Paul Tracy posted three pole positions.

In 1997, although Zanardi would take the drivers' championship, heading a 1–2–3 for Honda ahead of Gil de Ferran and Jimmy Vasser, the CART manufacturers' title would go to Mercedes-Benz after a great season in which four drivers combined to produce nine wins. These

Mark Blundell, leading here in his PacWest team Reynard-Mercedes, won three races for the team during a successful 1997 CART season.
(DaimlerChrysler/Wilhelm)

Dario Franchitti drove for the Hogan CART team with Mercedes support in 1997 before switching to the Team Green Reynard-Honda squad the following year. (DaimlerChrysler/Wilhelm)

Mercedes V8 power in the CART Players Reynard at the first round of the 1999 championship, Homestead, Florida. (DaimlerChrysler/Wilhelm)

included three each for Penske's Paul Tracy and former McLaren F1 driver Mark Blundell at the wheel of Bruce McCaw's PacWest team Reynard, plus two wins for Greg Moore and a single triumph for Blundell's PacWest team-mate Mauricio Gugelmin. And while Blundell and Gugelmin really put the PacWest team on the map, Moore's first win at Milwaukee earned him the historic distinction of becoming the youngest ever Champcar race winner at 22 years, one month and ten days.

After beating Honda in 1997, Mercedes had to take something of a back seat in 1998. Norbert Haug was hard pressed to conceal his disappointment when promising young Scottish driver Dario Franchitti deserted the Mercedes ranks to join the Team Green Reynard-Honda squad. Franchitti, whose professional career had been kept alive thanks largely to the AMG Mercedes team in the International Touring Car Championship, switched to Champcars in 1997 after the saloon series came to an end. With Mercedes support he gained a place in the Hogan Racing squad, but subsequently decided that his career progress would be better served by a change of scene. It was certainly a blow for the Mercedes brigade who regarded Franchitti as an eminently talented performer.

In 1998 Moore won again at Rio for Mercedes and later added to his tally with victory in the US 500 at Michigan. But these were the only wins scored by the Mercedes brigade on the CART scene and the German engine supplier slumped to third in the championship ratings at the end of the year. The season was also a bitter comedown for the once dominant Penske team which did not win a single race – indeed managed just one podium finish – and manifestly failed to get the best out of the compact, almost tiny, Merc 108E engine with its admittedly very promising PC27 challenger.

Penske's commercial interests meant that he would remain committed to Goodyear tyres at a time when all the front runners were using Firestone products and there was a sense that the team had also lost a degree of its bite and purpose. The PacWest squad similarly struggled and failed to win any races that season.

Mercedes and Ilmor were quite understandably concentrating the lion's share of their technical firepower on Formula 1 and this was having a damaging knock-on effect in CART, once a lucrative customer engine market for the British company. The trend continued through the 1999 season with Moore posting the sole Mercedes victory in the opening race at Florida's Homestead oval. Tragically, at the final race of the season, Moore was killed in a horrifying accident when his Reynard-Mercedes spun off the high banking at California's Fontana speedway and slammed

into a barrier. It was a bitter blow for the entire CART community and, in particular, for his close friend Dario Franchitti. It was scant comfort that Franchitti finished the year equal on points with series winner Juan Pablo Montoya, only losing out to the brilliant Colombian driver on number of wins.

The Mercedes CART challenge for 2000 was based round a totally new V8 engine, the IC108F, which was touted as having much enhanced mid-range power. This was scheduled to be supplied to the PacWest and Bettenhausen Motorsports teams plus the all-new Mo Nunn Racing squad which had been established by the

Greg Moore's Reynard-Mercedes stormed to a convincing victory in the 1999 Miami Grand Prix at Florida's Homestead oval. (DaimlerChrysler/Wilhelm)

Greg Moore, a great talent, sadly missed. (DaimlerChrysler/Wilhelm)

famous British engineer Morris Nunn who once competed in F1 with his own Ensign team.

In fact the 2000 season proved extremely disappointing, with the PacWest team fading, and a handful of halfway promising runs by Brazilian rising star Tony Kanaan in the Nunn-entered Reynard-Mercedes usually ending in mechanical failure and non-finishes. Mauricio Gugelmin managed just a single podium finish, a second place at Nazareth in May. By September the mood of optimism had changed dramatically as Mercedes announced its withdrawal from CART against a backdrop of commercial uncertainty over how the US series was going to develop. According to DaimlerChrysler board director Jurgen Hubbert, the return

of a United States Grand Prix to the international racing programme was sufficient to maintain the Mercedes profile in the USA. In addition there had been considerable investment in the emergent DTM 2000 series on the German domestic scene, all of which conspired to drop CART to a low priority in the overall pecking order. It was also made plain that Mercedes intended to focus even more energy and resources on its Formula 1 programme in the future at a time when Grand Prix racing was becoming ever more competitive.

It was a sad note on which to round off a programme which had started with such optimism and promise back in 1994 with that spectacular Indy 500 win.

ROGER PENSKE
Enriching the legend

Roger Penske is the patrician, dynamic founder and chairman of the Penske Corporation, a major diversified transportation services company in the USA whose annual revenues exceed $10 billion. It employs more than 34,000 people in 3,600 facilities across the world.

That is the official profile of the man who has also been one of the most imaginative and successful of American race team owners and an important contributor to the contemporary Mercedes racing legend. His empire is divided into four main business groups: transportation services, Penske Capital Partners, automotive and performance. The corporation's automotive group currently sells more than 39,000 vehicles annually including Toyota, Lexus, Mercedes-Benz, Honda and Jaguar ranges.

Penske began his business life as a salesman for the Alcoa Aluminium company. He was also an accomplished professional racing driver. British fans may recall watching in 1963 when he won the prestigious Guards Trophy sports car race at Brands Hatch at the wheel of the Cooper-Zerex which would – by a historical twist – be sold on to Bruce McLaren and became a forerunner of the McLaren team's first Can-Am sports car.

Prior to that, Penske had enjoyed two F1 outings in the United States Grand Prix at Watkins Glen. In 1961 he finished eighth in a privately entered four-cylinder Cooper T53, four laps behind Innes Ireland's winning Lotus, and the following year he was ninth in a Lotus 24-Climax V8. By 1965 Penske had retired from the cockpit to become general manager of a Chevrolet dealership in Philadelphia. It was the start of his dazzling ascent to multi-millionaire status and the establishment of the most successful Champcar racing team in history.

Despite Penske's decision to switch his team to Honda power for the 2000 season, he remained a joint venture partner in Ilmor Engineering with Mercedes-Benz through Penske Performance Inc. By then his team had scored a total of 99 Champcar race victories, including ten wins in the Indianapolis 500, nine national championships and 119 pole positions. Sadly it was not to be a Mercedes-Benz engine that propelled the team to its 100th Champcar victory.

Emperor of most he surveys: Roger Penske, team owner, millionaire entrepreneur and US circuit owner, with his team in the pit lane.
(DaimlerChrysler/Wilhelm)

MERCEDES AND TOURING CARS
Major shift in image

The arrival on the scene of the 'baby' Mercedes-Benz 190 saloon at the end of 1982 spelled a major shift in marketing policy for the Stuttgart company. Now they had a product with which they could attack the mid-sector executive market which had for so long been the preserve of their arch rival BMW.

For competition purposes, the 190 would transform the Mercedes image. The programme would be based on the high-performance power unit which had been developed specially by Britain's Cosworth Engineering on a sub-contract basis. The result was the Mercedes-Benz 190E-2.3-16 with the potential to develop 270bhp. The car made its high profile public début when a celebrity field of F1 drivers handled a grid of 2.3-16s to mark the opening of the new Nürburgring in May 1984. The race was won by a relative newcomer who soon the whole motorsport world would know, a young Brazilian by the name of Ayrton Senna.

By 1986 Hans-Werner Aufrecht and his team at AMG had started to race prepare the 190Es for the German Touring Car Championship (DTM) and the first Mercedes win in this category was eventually scored at Nürburgring in 1986 by Volker Weidler. Within two years Mercedes had taken a strategy decision to provide direct and substantial support for those teams competing in the DTM. 'There is no better racing series than the DTM,' said DB executive Jurgen Hubbert, 'for a manufacturer to present the sporting qualities and dynamism of cars that are close to the standard specification.'

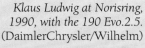

Klaus Ludwig at Norisring, 1990, with the 190 Evo.2.5. (DaimlerChrysler/Wilhelm)

Over the years that followed, Hubbert would continue to be one of the most energetic and unwavering supporters of the Mercedes motor racing ethos. The 190E competition concept would be honed to ever more intense levels of performance. And the DTM would become a crucial marketing tool, every bit as important for its competitors as F1. By 1990 no fewer than 153 million television viewers tuned in to watch at least some of the 63 hours' coverage of the DTM series.

Mercedes redoubled its efforts to win the manufacturers' title, producing two dramatic evolutions of the 190E concept with ever larger wings and more power. BMW were horrified. The 'Evo 2' made its racing début at the Nürburgring in June 1990 in the hands of Klaus Ludwig and his AMG team-mate Kurt Thiim and delivered its first win at Diepholz later in the year, one of five MB victories notched up that season. The Evo 2 racers continued that domination through into the 1991 season and in 1992 DTM history was made when Ellen Lohr – team-mate to former F1 McLaren driver Keke Rosberg – became the first woman to win a round of the championship.

In 1992 the championship was a three-way AMG Mercedes battle between Thiim, Ludwig and Bernd Schneider and that year at last saw Ludwig win the coveted DTM drivers' title for the Three-Pointed Star. For the 1994 season the baton was assumed by the new C-class Mercedes saloon which had taken over from the 190 range as the 'Baby Benz'.

Although the DTM was highly successful, it was certainly out of step with the rest of the world, most of which subscribed to the 2-litre concept as used by the British Touring Car Championship. But nothing could match the wild and woolly

2.5-litre V6 cars in the German series for sheer colour, class and showmanship.

The DTM really flourished in 1994 in a three-way fight between the Mercedes C-class, Alfa Romeo 155 and four-wheel drive Opel Calibras. It was perhaps not surprising that, once its teething troubles had been sorted out, the new C-class proved superior to the four-wheel-driven machines fielded by the opposition. Consequently the evergreen Klaus Ludwig, now 44 years old, did a great job regaining the DTM title which he had first won two years earlier. That said, Bernd Schneider was perhaps the unluckiest Mercedes driver in the category, leading several races but only winning a couple of times. However, in 1995 it was Schneider who shone brilliantly to win both the DTM and the newly instituted International Touring Car Championship for the AMG Mercedes squad. By the end of the season the DTM had vanished, absorbed by the experimental ITC which it had spawned during the very same season.

For the 1996 season it was planned that the 14-round international championship would see six rounds held in Germany and eight more as far afield as Japan and Brazil. Television rights would be owned by F1 commercial czar Bernie Ecclestone. Disappointingly, the ITC never quite realised its potential and, through unfortunate circumstances, would be killed off at the end of 1996 when Alfa Romeo and Opel pulled the plug on their programme. Put simply, the Alfa and Opel management were not prepared to give the new series time to reap the apparent television and promotional benefits which seemed to beckon. In excusing themselves, both marques cited dissatisfaction with the level of television and general media exposure although, in reality, their complicated four-wheel-drive car had become too expensive to run. Mercedes was indignant at being left in the lurch and Ecclestone was thwarted in his efforts to deliver a rounded, professional and televised 'second division' international racing category to those circuits which could not obtain an F1 Grand Prix.

Ironically, it was a great season with plenty of closely-fought events. It enabled Dario Franchitti to establish himself as a convincing supporter under the AMG banner and Schneider eventually wound up second in the overall drivers' championship. It was a bitter disappointment that Opel and Alfa Romeo chose to torpedo the ITC's future and left Mercedes casting around for a replacement second series which it would eventually identify in the form of the FIA GT series.

The failure of the ITC also resulted in the destruction of the DTM, leaving a substantial void facing the German race-going enthusiast. Eventually Norbert Haug and his fellow directors – knowing that as long ago as 1995 there were some 850,000 spectators who supported the last DTM over the entire season – decided on a course of action which would lead to the revival of a DTM series for the new millennium. The new category provided for cars powered by long-life, low maintenance 4-litre V8 engines with a total ban on all active, electronic or hydraulic control systems.

Equally, all brake units must be made of carbon and all gears and differentials must be the same, irrespective of the make of

car. For its part, Mercedes planned to build at least 12 AMG-prepared CLK coupés for this series which would contest the nine meetings planned throughout the season visiting every German circuit in due course. The inaugural championship would duly be won by Mercedes veteran Bernd Schneider.

'Equality is what is demanded these days,' said Norbert Haug in launching the new DTM 2000. 'The DTM is a legend and many people still carry the images of the old days in their minds. On that basis alone, our plans would already seem to be a success.'

Keke Rosberg's AMG Mercedes 190E battles to keep a flock of BMW M3s at bay. (DaimlerChrysler/Wilhelm)

Klaus Ludwig three-wheels his AMG C-class Mercedes to victory at Nürburgring in 1994. (DaimlerChrysler)

BERND SCHNEIDER
Mr Versatility

Driving in the new DTM 2000 series at the wheel of a CLK coupé, Bernd Schneider was contesting his tenth season in an AMG Mercedes branded product. Expert at the wheel of generations of touring cars on the old Nürburgring *Nordschleife*, Schneider had been named after the legendary pre-war Auto Union driver Bernd Rosemeyer who produced so much opposition to the factory Mercedes team on his way to winning the 1936 European Championship and thereby interrupting a run of success for Mercedes ace Rudi Caracciola.

Schneider made his name in karts. He won a German and European title before graduating to single seaters to win the 1987 German F3 Championship. In 1988 and 1989 he was promoted to F1 with the Zakspeed team, but the small German outfit had neither the technical resources nor financial backing to compete at what was even then becoming a formidably competitive level of intensity.

After a two-year dalliance with Porsche in sports car racing, Schneider switched to the German Touring Car Championship (DTM) in 1992, finishing third at the wheel of an AMG Mercedes 190E. Thereafter he became a veritable cornerstone of the Mercedes touring car challenge, finishing third again in the DTM in 1993, tenth in 1994 and then taking both the DTM and International Touring Car Championships with an AMG Mercedes C-class in 1995.

Schneider was runner-up again in the ITC in 1996, but the abandonment of that series saw him switch to the new FIA GT series in 1997 when he won the title with five victories at the wheel of an AMG Mercedes CLK-GTR. The following year he had five victories and shared second place in the title chase with Australian Mark Webber.

Popular and versatile, Schneider continued to enjoy his racing with a passion as he entered his 23rd season of competition at the start of the new millennium. 'Motorsport is a team sport,' he is quick to emphasise. 'We can only achieve our aims if we all pull on the same rope. I like to help everybody because that helps the team.'

Norbert Haug with Bernd Schneider, one of the best Mercedes contemporary racing drivers outside the F1 business, whose run of success culminated in the DTM 2000 title. (DaimlerChrysler/Wilhelm)

Frequently the close-fought nature of the DTM could get a little bit too destructive for the sponsors' bank balances! (DaimlerChrysler/Wilhelm)

BIBLIOGRAPHY

Adventure on Wheels. John Fitch with William F. Nolan. (G.P. Putnam, 1953)

A Racing Car Driver's World. Rudolf Caracciola. English edition translated by Sigrid Rock. (Farrar, Strauss and Cudahay, 1962)

Chequered Flag, The: 100 Years of Motor Racing. Ivan Rendall (Weidenfeld & Nicolson, 1993)

German Racing Cars and Drivers. Günther Molter and Kurt Worner. (Floyd Clymer, 1950)

Grand Prix Data Book. David Hayhoe & David Holland. (Duke, 1996)

Grand Prix Driver. Hermann Lang. English edition translated by Charles Meisl. (G.T. Foulis, 1952)

Grand Prix Who's Who. Steve Small. (Travel Publishing Ltd, 2000)

Great Motor Sport of the Thirties: A personal account. John Dugdale. (Wilton House Gentry, 1977)

Jenks: A passion for motor sport. (Motor Racing Publications, 1997)

Mercedes-Benz Grand Prix Racing 1934–55. George Monkhouse. (White Mouse Editions, 1984)

Mercedes-Benz: Quicksilver Century. Karl Ludvigsen. (Transport Bookman Publications, 1995)

Mercedes-Benz W196: Last of the Silver Arrows. Michael Riedner. (Haynes/Foulis, 1990)

Motor Racing with Mercedes-Benz. George Monkhouse. (G.T. Foulis, 1948)

My Two Lives: Race Driver to Restaurateur. René Dreyfus with Beverly Rare Kimes. (Aztex Corporation, 1983)

Racing the Silver Arrows. Chris Nixon. (Osprey Publishing, 1986)

Speed Was My Life. Alfred Neubauer. English edition edited and translated by Stewart Thomson and Charles Meisl. (Barrie & Rockliff, 1960)

The Carrera Panamericana 'Mexico'. Compiled by R. M. Clarke (Brooklands Books)

Autocourse
Autosport
Motor Sport
Stars & Cars
Racing Line

MAJOR RESULTS

R = retired; D = disqualified; NS = non starter;
W = withdrawn

GRANDS PRIX

1934

Jun 3, Eifelrennen, Nürburgring

M. von Brauchitsch	Mercedes-Benz W25	1
L. Fagioli	Mercedes-Benz W25	R

Jul 1, French GP, Montlhéry

M. von Brauchitsch	Mercedes-Benz W25	R
L. Fagioli	Mercedes-Benz W25	R
R. Caracciola	Mercedes-Benz W25	R

Jul 15, German GP, Nürburgring

L. Fagioli	Mercedes-Benz W25	R
H. Geier	Mercedes-Benz W25	5
R. Caracciola	Mercedes-Benz W25	R

Aug 15, Coppa Acerbo, Pescara

L. Fagioli	Mercedes-Benz W25	1
E. Henne	Mercedes-Benz W25	16
R. Caracciola	Mercedes-Benz W25	R

Aug 26, Swiss GP, Bremgarten

L. Fagioli	Mercedes-Benz W25	6
R. Caracciola/H. Geier	Mercedes-Benz W25	10
M. von Brauchitsch	Mercedes-Benz W25	11

Sep 9, Italian GP, Monza

R. Caracciola/L. Fagioli	Mercedes-Benz W25	1
E. Henne	Mercedes-Benz W25	R
L. Fagioli	Mercedes-Benz W25	R

Sep 23, Spanish GP, San Sebastian

L. Fagioli	Mercedes-Benz W25	1
R. Caracciola	Mercedes-Benz W25	2

Sep 30, Masaryk GP, Brno

L. Fagioli	Mercedes-Benz W25	2
E. Henne	Mercedes-Benz W25	6
R. Caracciola	Mercedes-Benz W25	R

1935

Apr 22, Monaco GP, Monte Carlo

L. Fagioli	Mercedes-Benz W25B	1
R. Caracciola	Mercedes-Benz W25B	R
M. von Brauchitsch	Mercedes-Benz W25B	R

May 12, Tripoli, GP, Mellaha

R. Caracciola	Mercedes-Benz W25B	1
L. Fagioli	Mercedes-Benz W25B	3
M. von Brauchitsch	Mercedes-Benz W25B	R

May 26, Avus GP, Avus

L. Fagioli	Mercedes-Benz W25B	1
M. von Brauchitsch	Mercedes-Benz W25B	5
H. Geier	Mercedes-Benz W25B	R
R. Caracciola	Mercedes-Benz W25B	R

Jun 16, Eifel GP, Nürburgring

R. Caracciola	Mercedes-Benz W25B	1
L. Fagioli	Mercedes-Benz W25B	4
H. Lang	Mercedes-Benz W25B	5
M. von Brauchitsch	Mercedes-Benz W25B	R

Jun 23, French GP, Montlhéry

R. Caracciola	Mercedes-Benz W25B	1
M. von Brauchitsch	Mercedes-Benz W25B	2
L. Fagioli	Mercedes-Benz W25B	4

Jun 30, Penya Rhin GP, Pedralbes

L. Fagioli	Mercedes-Benz W25B	1
R. Caracciola	Mercedes-Benz W25B	2

Jul 14, Belgian GP, Spa-Francorchamps

R. Caracciola	Mercedes-Benz W25B	1
L. Fagioli/	Mercedes-Benz W25B	2
M. von Brauchitsch		

Jul 28, German GP, Nürburgring

R. Caracciola	Mercedes-Benz W25B	3
M. von Brauchitsch	Mercedes-Benz W25B	5
L. Fagioli	Mercedes-Benz W25B	6
H. Geier	Mercedes-Benz W25B	7
H. Lang	Mercedes-Benz W25B	R

Aug 25, Swiss GP, Bremgarten

R. Caracciola	Mercedes-Benz W25B	1
L. Fagioli	Mercedes-Benz W25B	2
M. von Brauchitsch	Mercedes-Benz W25B	R
H. Lang	Mercedes-Benz W25B	6

Sep 8, Italian GP, Monza

L. Fagioli	Mercedes-Benz W25B	R
R. Caracciola	Mercedes-Benz W25B	R
M. von Brauchitsch	Mercedes-Benz W25B	R
H. Lang	Mercedes-Benz W25B	R

Sep 22, Spanish GP, San Sebastian

R. Caracciola	Mercedes-Benz W25B	1
L. Fagioli	Mercedes-Benz W25B	2
M. von Brauchitsch	Mercedes-Benz W25B	3

1936

Apr 13, Monaco GP, Monte Carlo

R. Caracciola	Mercedes-Benz W25C	1
L. Chiron	Mercedes-Benz W25C	R
M. von Brauchitsch	Mercedes-Benz W25C	R
L. Fagioli	Mercedes-Benz W25C	R

May 10, Tripoli GP, Mellaha

R. Caracciola	Mercedes-Benz W25C	4
L. Fagioli	Mercedes-Benz W25C	3
L. Chiron	Mercedes-Benz W25C	9
M. von Brauchitsch	Mercedes-Benz W25C	R

May 17, Tunis GP, Carthage

R. Caracciola	Mercedes-Benz W25C	1
L. Chiron	Mercedes-Benz W25C	R

Jun 7, Penya Rhin GP, Barcelona

R. Caracciola	Mercedes-Benz W25C	2
L. Chiron	Mercedes-Benz W25C	6

Jun 14, Eifel GP, Nürburgring

R. Caracciola	Mercedes-Benz W25C	R
M. von Brauchitsch	Mercedes-Benz W25C	R
H. Lang	Mercedes-Benz W25C	5
L. Chiron	Mercedes-Benz W25C	6

Jun 21, Hungarian GP, Budapest

R. Caracciola	Mercedes-Benz W25C	R
M. von Brauchitsch	Mercedes-Benz W25C	R
L. Chiron	Mercedes-Benz W25C	R

Jul 26, German GP, Nürburgring

L. Fagioli/R. Caracciola	Mercedes-Benz W25C	5
M. von Brauchitsch/	Mercedes-Benz W25C	7
H. Lang		
L. Chiron	Mercedes-Benz W25C	R

Aug 23, Swiss GP, Bremgarten

H. Lang/L. Fagioli	Mercedes-Benz W25C	4
R. Caracciola	Mercedes-Benz W25C	R
M. von Brauchitsch	Mercedes-Benz W25C	R

1937

May 9, Tripoli GP, Mellaha

H. Lang	Mercedes-Benz W125	1
R. Caracciola	Mercedes-Benz W125	6
R. Seaman	Mercedes-Benz W125	7
M. von Brauchitsch	Mercedes-Benz W125	R

May 30, Avus GP, Avus

H. Lang	Mercedes-Benz W125	1
R. Caracciola	Mercedes-Benz W125	R
R. Seaman	Mercedes-Benz W125	5
M. von Brauchitsch	Mercedes-Benz W125	R

Jun 13, Eifel GP, Nürburgring

H. Lang	Mercedes-Benz W125	6
R. Caracciola	Mercedes-Benz W125	2
R. Seaman	Mercedes-Benz W125	R
M. von Brauchitsch	Mercedes-Benz W125	3
C. Kautz	Mercedes-Benz W125	9

Jul 5, Vanderbilt Cup, Long Island

R. Caracciola	Mercedes-Benz W125	R
R. Seaman	Mercedes-Benz W125	2

Jul 11, Belgian GP, Spa-Francorchamps

H. Lang	Mercedes-Benz W125	3
M. von Brauchitsch	Mercedes-Benz W125	R
C. Kautz	Mercedes-Benz W125	4

Jul 25, German GP, Nürburgring

R. Caracciola	Mercedes-Benz W125	1
H. Lang	Mercedes-Benz W125	7
R. Seaman	Mercedes-Benz W125	R
M. von Brauchitsch	Mercedes-Benz W125	2
C. Kautz	Mercedes-Benz W125	6

Aug 8, Monaco GP, Monte Carlo

R. Caracciola	Mercedes-Benz W125	2
M. von Brauchitsch	Mercedes-Benz W125	1
C. Kautz	Mercedes-Benz W125	3

Aug 15, Coppa Acerbo, Pescara

R. Caracciola	Mercedes-Benz W125	5
M. von Brauchitsch	Mercedes-Benz W125	2

Aug 22, Swiss GP, Bremgarten

R. Caracciola	Mercedes-Benz W125	1
H. Lang	Mercedes-Benz W125	2
M. von Brauchitsch	Mercedes-Benz W125	3
C. Kautz	Mercedes-Benz W125	6

Sep 12, Italian GP, Livorno

R. Caracciola	Mercedes-Benz W125	1
H. Lang	Mercedes-Benz W125	2
R. Seaman	Mercedes-Benz W125	4
M. von Brauchitsch	Mercedes-Benz W125	R
C. Kautz	Mercedes-Benz W125	R

Oct 2, Donington GP, Donington Park

R. Caracciola	Mercedes-Benz W125	3
H. Lang	Mercedes-Benz W125	R
R. Seaman	Mercedes-Benz W125	R
M. von Brauchitsch	Mercedes-Benz W125	2

1938

Apr 10, Pau GP, Pau

R. Caracciola/H. Lang	Mercedes-Benz W154	2

May 15, Tripoli GP, Mellaha

R. Caracciola	Mercedes-Benz W154	3
H. Lang	Mercedes-Benz W154	1
R. Caracciola	Mercedes-Benz W154	2

Jul 3, French GP, Reims

R. Caracciola	Mercedes-Benz W154	2
H. Lang	Mercedes-Benz W154	3
M. von Brauchitsch	Mercedes-Benz W154	1

Jul 24, German GP, Nürburgring

R. Caracciola/H. Lang	Mercedes-Benz W154	2
R. Seaman	Mercedes-Benz W154	1
M. von Brauchitsch	Mercedes-Benz W154	R
H. Lang/W. Baumer	Mercedes-Benz W154	R

Aug 7, Coppa Ciano, Livorno

R. Caracciola	Mercedes-Benz W154	R
H. Lang	Mercedes-Benz W154	1
M. von Brauchitsch	Mercedes-Benz W154	R

Aug 14, Coppa Acerbo, Pescara

R. Caracciola	Mercedes-Benz W154	1
M. von Brauchitsch	Mercedes-Benz W154	R

Aug 21, Swiss GP, Bremgarten

R. Caracciola	Mercedes-Benz W154	1
H. Lang/W. Baumer	Mercedes-Benz W154	10
R. Seaman	Mercedes-Benz W154	2
M. von Brauchitsch	Mercedes-Benz W154	3

Sep 11, Italian GP, Monza

R. Caracciola/ M. von Brauchitsch	Mercedes-Benz W154	3
H. Lang	Mercedes-Benz W154	R
R. Seaman	Mercedes-Benz W154	R

Oct 22, Donington GP, Donington Park

H. Lang	Mercedes-Benz W154	2
R. Seaman	Mercedes-Benz W154	3
M. von Brauchitsch	Mercedes-Benz W154	5
W. Baumer	Mercedes-Benz W154	R

1939

Apr 2, Pau GP, Pau

R. Caracciola	Mercedes-Benz W154/63	R
H. Lang	Mercedes-Benz W154/63	1
M. von Brauchitsch	Mercedes-Benz W154/63	2

May 7, Tripoli GP, Mellaha

R. Caracciola	Mercedes-Benz W154/63	2
H. Lang	Mercedes-Benz W154/63	1

May 21, Eifel GP, Nürburgring

R. Caracciola	Mercedes-Benz W154/63	3
H. Lang	Mercedes-Benz W154/63	1
M. von Brauchitsch	Mercedes-Benz W154/63	4
H.H. Hartmann	Mercedes-Benz W154/63	8
R. Seaman	Mercedes-Benz W154/63	R

Jun 25, Belgian GP, Spa-Francorchamps

R. Caracciola	Mercedes-Benz W154/63	R
H. Lang	Mercedes-Benz W154/63	1
M. von Brauchitsch	Mercedes-Benz W154/63	3
R. Seaman	Mercedes-Benz W154/63	R

Jul 9, French GP, Reims

R. Caracciola	Mercedes-Benz W154/63	R
H. Lang	Mercedes-Benz W154/63	R

Jul 23, German GP, Nürburgring

R. Caracciola	Mercedes-Benz W154/63	1
H. Lang	Mercedes-Benz W154/63	R
M. von Brauchitsch	Mercedes-Benz W153/63	R
H. Brendl	Mercedes-Benz W153/63	R

Aug 20, Swiss GP, Bremgarten

R. Caracciola	Mercedes-Benz W154/63	2
H. Lang	Mercedes-Benz W154/63	1
M. von Brauchitsch	Mercedes-Benz W154/63	3
H.H. Hartmann	Mercedes-Benz W154/63	7

Sep 3 Yugoslavian GP, Belgrade

H. Lang/W. Baumer	Mercedes-Benz W154/63	R
M. von Brauchitsch	Mercedes-Benz W154/63	2

1951

Feb 18, Presidente Peron GP, Buenos Aires

H. Lang	Mercedes-Benz W154/63	2
J.M. Fangio	Mercedes-Benz W154/63	3
K. Kling	Mercedes-Benz W154/63	6

Feb 24, Eva Peron GP, Buenos Aires

H. Lang	Mercedes-Benz W154/63	3
J.M. Fangio	Mercedes-Benz W154/63	R
K. Kling	Mercedes-Benz W154/63	2

1954

Jul 4, French GP, Reims

J.M. Fangio	Mercedes-Benz W196	1
K. Kling	Mercedes-Benz W196	2

Jul 17, British GP, Silverstone

J.M. Fangio	Mercedes-Benz W196	4
K. Kling	Mercedes-Benz W196	7

Aug 1, German GP, Nürburgring

J.M. Fangio	Mercedes-Benz W196	1
K. Kling	Mercedes-Benz W196	4
H. Herrmann	Mercedes-Benz W196	R
H. Lang	Mercedes-Benz W196	R

Aug 22, Swiss GP, Bremgarten

J.M. Fangio	Mercedes-Benz W196	1
K. Kling	Mercedes-Benz W196	R
H. Herrmann	Mercedes-Benz W196	3

Sep 5, Italian GP, Monza

J.M. Fangio	Mercedes-Benz W196	1
K. Kling	Mercedes-Benz W196	R
H. Herrmann	Mercedes-Benz W196	4

Sep 19, Berlin GP, Avus

J.M. Fangio	Mercedes-Benz W196	2
K. Kling	Mercedes-Benz W196	1
H. Herrmann	Mercedes-Benz W196	3

Oct 24, Spanish GP, Barcelona

J.M Fangio	Mercedes-Benz W196	3
K. Kling	Mercedes-Benz W196	5
H. Herrmann	Mercedes-Benz W196	R

1955

Jan 16, Argentine GP, Buenos Aires

| J.M. Fangio | Mercedes-Benz W196 | 1 |
| H. Herrmann/K. Kling/
S. Moss | Mercedes-Benz W196 | 4 |

Jan 28, Buenos Aires City GP, Buenos Aires

J.M. Fangio	Mercedes-Benz W196	1
S. Moss	Mercedes-Benz W196	2
K. Kling	Mercedes-Benz W196	4
H. Herrmann	Mercedes-Benz W196	R

May 22, Monaco GP, Monte Carlo

J.M. Fangio	Mercedes-Benz W196	R
S. Moss	Mercedes-Benz W196	9
A. Simon	Mercedes-Benz W196	R

Jun 5, Belgian GP, Spa-Francorchamps

J.M. Fangio	Mercedes-Benz W196	1
S. Moss	Mercedes-Benz W196	2
K. Kling	Mercedes-Benz W196	R

Jun 19, Dutch GP, Zandvoort

J.M. Fangio	Mercedes-Benz W196	1
S. Moss	Mercedes-Benz W196	2
K. Kling	Mercedes-Benz W196	R

Jul 6, British GP, Aintree

J.M. Fangio	Mercedes-Benz W196	2
S. Moss	Mercedes-Benz W196	1
K. Kling	Mercedes-Benz W196	3
P. Taruffi	Mercedes-Benz W196	4

Sep 11, Italian GP, Monza

J.M. Fangio	Mercedes-Benz W196	1
S. Moss	Mercedes-Benz W196	R
K. Kling	Mercedes-Benz W196	R
P. Taruffi	Mercedes-Benz W196	2

1994

Mar 27, Brazilian GP, Interlagos

| K. Wendlinger | Sauber-Mercedes C13 | 6 |
| H.H. Frentzen | Sauber-Mercedes C13 | R |

Apr 17, Pacific GP, Aida

| K. Wendlinger | Sauber-Mercedes C13 | R |
| H.H. Frentzen | Sauber-Mercedes C13 | 5 |

May 1, San Marino GP, Imola

| K. Wendlinger | Sauber-Mercedes C13 | 4 |
| H.H. Frentzen | Sauber-Mercedes C13 | 7 |

May 15, Monaco GP, Monte Carlo

| K. Wendlinger | Sauber-Mercedes C13 | NS |
| H.H. Frentzen | Sauber-Mercedes C13 | NS |

May 29, Spanish GP, Barcelona

| H.H. Frentzen | Sauber-Mercedes C13 | R |

Jun 10, Canadian GP, Montreal

| A. de Cesaris | Sauber-Mercedes C13 | R |
| H.H. Frentzen | Sauber-Mercedes C13 | R |

Jul 3, French GP, Magny-Cours

| A. de Cesaris | Sauber-Mercedes C13 | 6 |
| H.H. Frentzen | Sauber-Mercedes C13 | 4 |

Jul 10, British GP, Silverstone

| A. de Cesaris | Sauber-Mercedes C13 | R |
| H.H. Frentzen | Sauber-Mercedes C13 | 7 |

Jul 31, German GP, Hockenheim

| A. de Cesaris | Sauber-Mercedes C13 | R |
| H.H. Frentzen | Sauber-Mercedes C13 | R |

Aug 14, Hungarian GP, Hungaroring

| A. de Cesaris | Sauber-Mercedes C13 | R |
| H.H. Frentzen | Sauber-Mercedes C13 | R |

Aug 28, Belgian GP, Spa-Francorchamps

| A. de Cesaris | Sauber-Mercedes C13 | R |
| H.H. Frentzen | Sauber-Mercedes C13 | R |

Sep 11, Italian GP, Monza

| A. de Cesaris | Sauber-Mercedes C13 | R |
| H.H. Frentzen | Sauber-Mercedes C13 | R |

Sep 25, Portuguese GP, Estoril

| A. de Cesaris | Sauber-Mercedes C13 | R |
| H.H. Frentzen | Sauber-Mercedes C13 | R |

Oct 16, European GP, Jerez

| A. de Cesaris | Sauber-Mercedes C13 | R |
| H.H. Frentzen | Sauber-Mercedes C13 | 6 |

Nov 6, Japanese GP, Suzuka

| J.J. Lehto | Sauber-Mercedes C13 | R |
| H.H. Frentzen | Sauber-Mercedes C13 | 6 |

Nov 13, Australian GP, Adelaide

| J.J. Lehto | Sauber-Mercedes C13 | 10 |
| H.H. Frentzen | Sauber-Mercedes C13 | 7 |

1995

Mar 26, Brazilian GP, Interlagos

| M. Blundell | McLaren-Mercedes MP4/10 | 6 |
| M. Hakkinen | McLaren-Mercedes MP4/10 | 4 |

Apr 9, Argentine GP, Buenos Aires

| M. Blundell | McLaren-Mercedes MP4/10 | R |
| M. Hakkinen | McLaren-Mercedes MP4/10 | R |

Apr 30, San Marino GP, Imola

| N. Mansell | McLaren-Mercedes MP4/10B | 10 |
| M. Hakkinen | McLaren-Mercedes MP4/10B | 5 |

May 14, Spanish GP, Barcelona

| N. Mansell | McLaren-Mercedes MP4/10B | R |
| M. Hakkinen | McLaren-Mercedes MP4/10B | R |

May 8, Monaco GP, Monte Carlo

| M. Blundell | McLaren-Mercedes MP4/10B | 5 |
| M. Hakkinen | McLaren-Mercedes MP4/10B | R |

Jun 11, Canadian GP, Montreal

| M. Blundell | McLaren-Mercedes MP4/10B | R |
| M. Hakkinen | McLaren-Mercedes MP4/10B | R |

Jul 2, French GP, Magny-Cours

| M. Blundell | McLaren-Mercedes MP4/10B | 11 |
| M. Hakkinen | McLaren-Mercedes MP4/10B | 7 |

Jul 16, British GP, Silverstone

| M. Blundell | McLaren-Mercedes MP4/10B | 5 |
| M. Hakkinen | McLaren-Mercedes MP4/10B | R |

Jul 30, German GP, Hockenheim

| M. Blundell | McLaren-Mercedes MP4/10B | R |
| M. Hakkinen | McLaren-Mercedes MP4/10B | R |

Aug 13, Hungarian GP, Hungaroring

| M. Blundell | McLaren-Mercedes MP4/10B | R |
| M. Hakkinen | McLaren-Mercedes MP4/10B | R |

Aug 27, Belgian GP, Spa-Francorchamps

| M. Blundell | McLaren-Mercedes MP4/10B | 5 |
| M. Hakkinen | McLaren-Mercedes MP4/10B | R |

Sep 10, Italian GP, Monza

| M. Blundell | McLaren-Mercedes MP4/10B | 4 |
| M. Hakkinen | McLaren-Mercedes MP4/10B | 2 |

Sep 24, Portuguese GP, Estoril

| M. Blundell | McLaren-Mercedes MP4/10B | 9 |
| M. Hakkinen | McLaren-Mercedes MP4/10B | R |

Oct 1, European GP, Nürburgring

| M. Blundell | McLaren-Mercedes MP4/10B | R |
| M. Hakkinen | McLaren-Mercedes MP4/10B | 8 |

Oct 22, Pacific GP, Aida

| M. Blundell | McLaren-Mercedes MP4/10B | 9 |
| J. Magnussen | McLaren-Mercedes MP4/10B | 10 |

Oct 29, Japanese GP, Suzuka

| M. Blundell | McLaren-Mercedes MP4/10B | 7 |
| M. Hakkinen | McLaren-Mercedes MP4/10B | 2 |

Nov 12, Australian GP, Adelaide

| M. Blundell | McLaren-Mercedes MP4/10B | 4 |
| M. Hakkinen | McLaren-Mercedes MP4/10B | NS |

1996

Mar 10, Australian GP, Melbourne

| M. Hakkinen | McLaren-Mercedes MP4/11 | 5 |
| D. Coulthard | McLaren-Mercedes MP4/11 | R |

Mar 31, Brazilian GP, Interlagos

| M. Hakkinen | McLaren-Mercedes MP4/11 | 4 |
| D. Coulthard | McLaren-Mercedes MP4/11 | R |

Apr 7, Argentine GP, Buenos Aires

| M. Hakkinen | McLaren-Mercedes MP4/11 | R |
| D. Coulthard | McLaren-Mercedes MP4/11 | 7 |

Apr 28, European GP, Nürburgring

| M. Hakkinen | McLaren-Mercedes MP4/11 | 8 |
| D. Coulthard | McLaren-Mercedes MP4/11 | 3 |

May 5, San Marino GP, Imola

| M. Hakkinen | McLaren-Mercedes MP4/11 | 8 |
| D. Coulthard | McLaren-Mercedes MP4/11 | R |

May 19, Monaco GP, Monte Carlo

M. Hakkinen	McLaren-Mercedes MP4/11	6
D. Coulthard	McLaren-Mercedes MP4/11	2

Jun 2, Spanish GP, Barcelona

M. Hakkinen	McLaren-Mercedes MP4/11	5
D. Coulthard	McLaren-Mercedes MP4/11	R

Jun 16, Canadian GP, Montreal

M. Hakkinen	McLaren-Mercedes MP4/11	5
D. Coulthard	McLaren-Mercedes MP4/11	4

30 Jun, French GP, Magny-Cours

M. Hakkinen	McLaren-Mercedes MP4/11	5
D. Coulthard	McLaren-Mercedes MP4/11	6

Jul 14, British GP, Silverstone

M. Hakkinen	McLaren-Mercedes MP4/11	3
D. Coulthard	McLaren-Mercedes MP4/11	5

Jul 28, German GP, Hockenheim

M. Hakkinen	McLaren-Mercedes MP4/11	R
D. Coulthard	McLaren-Mercedes MP4/11	5

Aug 11, Hungarian GP, Hungaroring

M. Hakkinen	McLaren-Mercedes MP4/11	4
D. Coulthard	McLaren-Mercedes MP4/11	R

Aug 25, Belgian GP, Spa-Francorchamps

M. Hakkinen	McLaren-Mercedes MP4/11	3
D. Coulthard	McLaren-Mercedes MP4/11	R

Sep 8, Italian GP, Monza

M. Hakkinen	McLaren-Mercedes MP4/11	3
D. Coulthard	McLaren-Mercedes MP4/11	R

Sep 22, Portuguese GP, Estoril

M. Hakkinen	McLaren-Mercedes MP4/11	R
D. Coulthard	McLaren-Mercedes MP4/11	13

Oct 13, Japanese GP, Suzuka

M. Hakkinen	McLaren-Mercedes MP4/11	3
D. Coulthard	McLaren-Mercedes MP4/11	8

1997

Mar 9, Australian GP, Melbourne

M. Hakkinen	McLaren-Mercedes MP4/12	3
D. Coulthard	McLaren-Mercedes MP4/12	1

Mar 30, Brazilian GP, Interlagos

M. Hakkinen	McLaren-Mercedes MP4/12	4
D. Coulthard	McLaren-Mercedes MP4/12	10

Apr 13, Argentine GP, Buenos Aires

M. Hakkinen	McLaren-Mercedes MP4/12	5
D. Coulthard	McLaren-Mercedes MP4/12	R

Apr 27, San Marino GP, Imola

M. Hakkinen	McLaren-Mercedes MP4/12	6
D. Coulthard	McLaren-Mercedes MP4/12	R

May 11, Monaco GP, Monte Carlo

M. Hakkinen	McLaren-Mercedes MP4/12	R
D. Coulthard	McLaren-Mercedes MP4/12	R

May 25, Spanish GP, Barcelona

M. Hakkinen	McLaren-Mercedes MP4/12	7
D. Coulthard	McLaren-Mercedes MP4/12	6

Jun 15, Canadian GP, Montreal

M. Hakkinen	McLaren-Mercedes MP4/12	R
D. Coulthard	McLaren-Mercedes MP4/12	7

Jun 29, French GP, Magny-Cours

M. Hakkinen	McLaren-Mercedes MP4/12	R
D. Coulthard	McLaren-Mercedes MP4/12	7

Jul 13, British GP, Silverstone

M. Hakkinen	McLaren-Mercedes MP4/12	R
D. Coulthard	McLaren-Mercedes MP4/12	4

Jul 27, German GP, Hockenheim

M. Hakkinen	McLaren-Mercedes MP4/12	3
D. Coulthard	McLaren-Mercedes MP4/12	R

Aug 10, Hungarian GP, Hungaroring

M. Hakkinen	McLaren-Mercedes MP4/12	R
D. Coulthard	McLaren-Mercedes MP4/12	R

Aug 24, Belgian GP, Spa-Francorchamps

M. Hakkinen	McLaren-Mercedes MP4/12	D
D. Coulthard	McLaren-Mercedes MP4/12	R

Sep 7, Italian GP, Monza

M. Hakkinen	McLaren-Mercedes MP4/12	9
D. Coulthard	McLaren-Mercedes MP4/12	1

Sep 21, Austrian GP, A1-Ring

| M. Hakkinen | McLaren-Mercedes MP4/12 | R |
| D. Coulthard | McLaren-Mercedes MP4/12 | 2 |

Sep 28, Luxembourg GP, Nürburgring

| M. Hakkinen | McLaren-Mercedes MP4/12 | R |
| D. Coulthard | McLaren-Mercedes MP4/12 | R |

Oct 12, Japanese GP, Suzuka

| M. Hakkinen | McLaren-Mercedes MP4/12 | 4 |
| D. Coulthard | McLaren-Mercedes MP4/12 | 10 |

Oct 26, European GP, Jerez

| M. Hakkinen | McLaren-Mercedes MP4/12 | 1 |
| D. Coulthard | McLaren-Mercedes MP4/12 | 2 |

1998

Mar 8, Australian GP, Melbourne

| M. Hakkinen | McLaren-Mercedes MP4/13 | 1 |
| D. Coulthard | McLaren-Mercedes MP4/13 | 2 |

Mar 29, Brazilian GP, Interlagos

| M. Hakkinen | McLaren-Mercedes MP4/13 | 1 |
| D. Coulthard | McLaren-Mercedes MP4/13 | 2 |

Apr 12, Argentine GP, Buenos Aires

| M. Hakkinen | McLaren-Mercedes MP4/13 | 2 |
| D. Coulthard | McLaren-Mercedes MP4/13 | 6 |

Apr 26, San Marino GP, Imola

| M. Hakkinen | McLaren-Mercedes MP4/13 | R |
| D. Coulthard | McLaren-Mercedes MP4/13 | 1 |

May 10, Spanish GP, Barcelona

| M. Hakkinen | McLaren-Mercedes MP4/13 | 1 |
| D. Coulthard | McLaren-Mercedes MP4/13 | 2 |

May 24, Monaco GP, Monte Carlo

| M. Hakkinen | McLaren-Mercedes MP4/13 | 1 |
| D. Coulthard | McLaren-Mercedes MP4/13 | R |

Jun 7, Canadian GP, Montreal

| M. Hakkinen | McLaren-Mercedes MP4/13 | R |
| D. Coulthard | McLaren-Mercedes MP4/13 | R |

Jun 28, French GP, Magny-Cours

| M. Hakkinen | McLaren-Mercedes MP4/13 | 3 |
| D. Coulthard | McLaren-Mercedes MP4/13 | 6 |

Jul 12, British GP, Silverstone

| M. Hakkinen | McLaren-Mercedes MP4/13 | 2 |
| D. Coulthard | McLaren-Mercedes MP4/13 | R |

Jul 26, Austrian GP, A1-Ring

| M. Hakkinen | McLaren-Mercedes MP4/13 | 1 |
| D. Coulthard | McLaren-Mercedes MP4/13 | 2 |

Aug 2, German GP, Hockenheim

| M. Hakkinen | McLaren-Mercedes MP4/13 | 1 |
| D. Coulthard | McLaren-Mercedes MP4/13 | 2 |

Aug 16, Hungarian GP, Hungaroring

| M. Hakkinen | McLaren-Mercedes MP4/13 | 6 |
| D. Coulthard | McLaren-Mercedes MP4/13 | 2 |

Aug 30, Belgian GP, Spa-Francorchamps

| M. Hakkinen | McLaren-Mercedes MP4/13 | R |
| D. Coulthard | McLaren-Mercedes MP4/13 | 7 |

Sep 13, Italian GP, Monza

| M. Hakkinen | McLaren-Mercedes MP4/13 | 4 |
| D. Coulthard | McLaren-Mercedes MP4/13 | R |

Sep 27, Luxembourg GP, Nürburgring

| M. Hakkinen | McLaren-Mercedes MP4/13 | 1 |
| D. Coulthard | McLaren-Mercedes MP4/13 | 3 |

Nov 1, Japanese GP, Suzuka

| M. Hakkinen | McLaren-Mercedes MP4/13 | 1 |
| D. Coulthard | McLaren-Mercedes MP4/13 | 3 |

1999

Mar 7, Australian GP, Melbourne

| M. Hakkinen | McLaren-Mercedes MP4/14 | R |
| D. Coulthard | McLaren-Mercedes MP4/14 | R |

Apr 11, Brazilian GP, Interlagos

| M. Hakkinen | McLaren-Mercedes MP4/14 | 1 |
| D. Coulthard | McLaren-Mercedes MP4/14 | R |

May 2, San Marino GP, Imola

| M. Hakkinen | McLaren-Mercedes MP4/14 | R |
| D. Coulthard | McLaren-Mercedes MP4/14 | 2 |

May 16, Monaco GP, Monte Carlo

| M. Hakkinen | McLaren-Mercedes MP4/14 | 3 |
| D. Coulthard | McLaren-Mercedes MP4/14 | R |

May 30, Spanish GP, Barcelona

M. Hakkinen	McLaren-Mercedes MP4/14	1
D. Coulthard	McLaren-Mercedes MP4/14	2

Jun 13, Canadian GP, Montreal

M. Hakkinen	McLaren-Mercedes MP4/14	1
D. Coulthard	McLaren-Mercedes MP4/14	7

Jun 27, French GP, Magny-Cours

M. Hakkinen	McLaren-Mercedes MP4/14	2
D. Coulthard	McLaren-Mercedes MP4/14	R

Jul 11, British GP, Silverstone

M. Hakkinen	McLaren-Mercedes MP4/14	R
D. Coulthard	McLaren-Mercedes MP4/14	1

Jul 25, Austrian GP, A1-Ring

M. Hakkinen	McLaren-Mercedes MP4/14	3
D. Coulthard	McLaren-Mercedes MP4/14	2

Aug 1, German GP, Hockenheim

M. Hakkinen	McLaren-Mercedes MP4/14	R
D. Coulthard	McLaren-Mercedes MP4/14	5

Aug 15, Hungarian GP, Hungaroring

M. Hakkinen	McLaren-Mercedes MP4/14	1
D. Coulthard	McLaren-Mercedes MP4/14	2

Aug 29, Belgian GP, Spa-Francorchamps

M. Hakkinen	McLaren-Mercedes MP4/14	2
D. Coulthard	McLaren-Mercedes MP4/14	1

Sep 12, Italian GP, Monza

M. Hakkinen	McLaren-Mercedes MP4/14	R
D. Coulthard	McLaren-Mercedes MP4/14	5

Sep 26, European GP, Nürburgring

M. Hakkinen	McLaren-Mercedes MP4/14	5
D. Coulthard	McLaren-Mercedes MP4/14	R

Oct 17, Malaysian GP, Sepang

M. Hakkinen	McLaren-Mercedes MP4/14	3
D. Coulthard	McLaren-Mercedes MP4/14	R

Oct 31, Japanese GP, Suzuka

M. Hakkinen	McLaren-Mercedes MP4/14	1
D. Coulthard	McLaren-Mercedes MP4/14	R

2000

Mar 12, Australian GP, Melbourne

M. Hakkinen	McLaren-Mercedes MP4/15	R
D. Coulthard	McLaren-Mercedes MP4/15	R

Mar 26, Brazilian GP, Interlagos

M. Hakkinen	McLaren-Mercedes MP4/15	R
D. Coulthard	McLaren-Mercedes MP4/15	D

Apr 9, San Marino GP, Imola

M. Hakkinen	McLaren-Mercedes MP4/15	2
D. Coulthard	McLaren-Mercedes MP4/15	3

Apr 23, British GP, Silverstone

M. Hakkinen	McLaren-Mercedes MP4/15	2
D. Coulthard	McLaren-Mercedes MP4/15	1

May 7, Spanish GP, Barcelona

M. Hakkinen	McLaren-Mercedes MP4/15	1
D. Coulthard	McLaren-Mercedes MP4/15	2

May 21, European GP, Nürburgring

M. Hakkinen	McLaren-Mercedes MP4/15	2
D. Coulthard	McLaren-Mercedes MP4/15	3

June 4, Monaco GP, Monte Carlo

M. Hakkinen	McLaren-Mercedes MP4/15	6
D. Coulthard	McLaren-Mercedes MP4/15	1

June 18, Canadian GP, Montreal

M. Hakkinen	McLaren-Mercedes MP4/15	4
D. Coulthard	McLaren-Mercedes MP4/15	7

July 2, French GP, Magny-Cours

M. Hakkinen	McLaren-Mercedes MP4/15	2
D. Coulthard	McLaren-Mercedes MP4/15	1

July 16, Austrian GP, A1-Ring

M. Hakkinen	McLaren-Mercedes MP4/15	1
D. Coulthard	McLaren-Mercedes MP4/15	2

July 30, German GP, Hockenheim

M. Hakkinen	McLaren-Mercedes MP4/15	2
D. Coulthard	McLaren-Mercedes MP4/15	3

Aug 13, Hungarian GP, Hungaroring

M. Hakkinen	McLaren-Mercedes MP4/15	1
D. Coulthard	McLaren-Mercedes MP4/15	3

Aug 27, Belgian GP, Spa-Francorchamps

M. Hakkinen	McLaren-Mercedes MP4/15	1
D. Coulthard	McLaren-Mercedes MP4/15	4

Sept 10, Italian GP, Monza

M. Hakkinen	McLaren-Mercedes MP4/15	2
D. Coulthard	McLaren-Mercedes MP4/15	R

Sept 24, US GP, Indianapolis

M. Hakkinen	McLaren-Mercedes MP4/15	R
D. Coulthard	McLaren-Mercedes MP4/15	5

Oct 8, Japanese GP, Suzuka

M. Hakkinen	McLaren-Mercedes MP4/15	2
D. Coulthard	McLaren-Mercedes MP4/15	3

Oct 22, Malaysian GP, Sepang

M. Hakkinen	McLaren-Mercedes MP4/15	4
D. Coulthard	McLaren-Mercedes MP4/15	2

SPORTS CARS

1952

May 3/4, Mille Miglia

K. Kling	Mercedes-Benz 300SL	2
R. Caracciola	Mercedes-Benz 300SL	4
H. Lang	Mercedes-Benz 300SL	R

May 18, Berne, Switzerland

K. Kling	Mercedes-Benz 300SL	1
H. Lang	Mercedes-Benz 300SL	2
F. Riess	Mercedes-Benz 300SL	3
R. Caracciola	Mercedes-Benz 300SL	R

Jun 14/15, Le Mans 24-hours

H. Lang/F. Riess	Mercedes-Benz 300SL	1
T. Helfrich/ H. Niedermayer	Mercedes-Benz 300SL	2
K. Kling/H. Klenk	Mercedes-Benz 300SL	R

Aug 2, Nürburgring

H. Lang	Mercedes-Benz 300SL	1
K. Kling	Mercedes-Benz 300SL	2
F. Riess	Mercedes-Benz 300SL	3
T. Helfrich	Mercedes-Benz 300SL	4

Nov 19/24, Carrera Panamericana

K. Kling/H. Klenk	Mercedes-Benz 300SL	1
H. Lang/F. Riess	Mercedes-Benz 300SL	2
J. Fitch/E. Geiger	Mercedes-Benz 300SL	D

1955

May 1, Mille Miglia

S. Moss/D. Jenkinson	Mercedes-Benz 300SLR	1
J.M. Fangio	Mercedes-Benz 300SLR	2
K. Kling	Mercedes-Benz 300SLR	R

May 29, Eifelrennen, Nürburgring

J.M. Fangio	Mercedes-Benz 300SLR	1
S. Moss	Mercedes-Benz 300SLR	2
K. Kling	Mercedes-Benz 300SLR	R

Jun 11, Le Mans 24-hours

J.M. Fangio/S. Moss	Mercedes-Benz 300SLR	W
K. Kling/H. Herrmann	Mercedes-Benz 300SLR	W
P. Levegh/J. Fitch	Mercedes-Benz 300SLR	R

Aug 8, Swedish GP, Kristianstad

J.M. Fangio	Mercedes-Benz 300SLR	1
S. Moss	Mercedes-Benz 300SLR	2
W. von Trips	Mercedes-Benz 300SLR	R

Sept 22, Tourist Trophy, Dundrod

S. Moss/J. Fitch	Mercedes-Benz 300SLR	1
J.M. Fangio/K. Kling	Mercedes-Benz 300SLR	2
W. von Trips/A. Simon/ K. Kling	Mercedes-Benz 300SLR	3

Oct 16, Targa Florio, Sicily

S. Moss/P. Collins	Mercedes-Benz 300SLR	1
J.M. Fangio/K. Kling	Mercedes-Benz 300SLR	2
J. Fitch/D. Titterington	Mercedes-Benz 300SLR	4

1988

Mar 6, Jerez, Spain

J.Schlesser/M. Baldi/ J. Mass	Sauber-Mercedes C9/88	1

Mar 13, Jarama, Spain

J. Schlesser/M. Baldi	Sauber-Mercedes C9/88	2

Apr 10, Monza 1000km,

J. Schlesser/M. Baldi	Sauber-Mercedes C9/88	2

May 8, Silverstone 1000km

J. Schlesser/J. Mass	Sauber-Mercedes C9/88	2
J. Weaver/M. Baldi	Sauber-Mercedes C9/88	3

Jul 10, Brno, Czechoslovakia

J. Schlesser/J. Mass	Sauber-Mercedes C9/88	1
J. Weaver/M. Baldi	Sauber-Mercedes C9/88	4

Jul 24, Brand Hatch

J. Schlesser/M. Baldi	Sauber-Mercedes C9/88	3

Sep 3/4, Nürburgring

J. Schlesser/J. Mass	Sauber-Mercedes C9/88	1

Sep 18, Spa-Francorchamps

M. Baldi/S. Johansson	Sauber-Mercedes C9/88	1
J. Mass/J. Schlesser	Sauber-Mercedes C9/88	3

Oct 9, Fuji 1000km, Japan

M. Baldi/S. Johansson	Sauber-Mercedes C9/88	1
J. Mass/J. Schlesser	Sauber-Mercedes C9/88	3

Nov 20, Sandown Park, Australia

J. Schlesser/J. Mass	Sauber-Mercedes C9/88	1
M. Baldi/S. Johansson	Sauber-Mercedes C9/88	2

1989

April 9, Suzuka, Japan

J. Schlesser/M. Baldi	Sauber-Mercedes C9/88	1
K. Acheson/J. Mass	Sauber-Mercedes C9/88	2

May 21, Dijon-Prenois

J. Schlesser/J. Mass	Sauber-Mercedes C9/88	2
M. Baldi/K. Acheson	Sauber-Mercedes C9/88	3

Jun 10/11, Le Mans 24-hours

J. Mass/M. Reuter/ S. Dickens	Sauber-Mercedes C9/88	1
M. Baldi/K. Acheson/ G. Brancatelli	Sauber-Mercedes C9/88	2

Jun 25, Jarama

J. Mass/J. Schlesser	Sauber-Mercedes C9/88	1
M. Baldi/K. Acheson	Sauber-Mercedes C9/88	5

Jul 23, Brands Hatch

M. Baldi/K. Acheson	Sauber-Mercedes C9/88	1
J. Schlesser/J. Mass	Sauber-Mercedes C9/88	3

Aug 20, Nürburgring

J. Schlesser/J. Mass	Sauber-Mercedes C9/88	1
M. Baldi/K. Acheson	Sauber-Mercedes C9/88	1

Sep 3, Donington Park

J. Schlesser/J.Mass	Sauber-Mercedes C9/88	1
K. Acheson/M. Baldi	Sauber-Mercedes C9/88	2

Sep 17, Spa-Francorchamps

M. Baldi/K. Acheson	Sauber-Mercedes C9/88	1

Oct 29, Mexico City

J. Schlesser/J. Mass	Sauber-Mercedes C9/88	1

1990

Apr 8, Suzuka

J. Schlesser/J. Mass	Mercedes-Benz C9/88	1
J. Mass/K. Wendlinger	Mercedes-Benz C9/88	2

Apr 29, Trofeo Caracciola, Monza

M. Baldi/J. Schlesser	Mercedes-Benz C11	1
J. Mass/K. Wendlinger	Mercedes-Benz C11	2

May 20, Silverstone

J. Schlesser/M. Baldi	Mercedes-Benz C11	R

Jun 3, Spa-Francorchamps

J. Mass/K. Wendlinger	Mercedes-Benz C11	1
M. Baldi/J. Schlesser	Mercedes-Benz C11	8

Jul 22, Dijon-Prenois

J. Schlesser/M. Baldi	Mercedes-Benz C11	1
J. Mass/M. Schumacher	Mercedes-Benz C11	2

Aug 19, Nürburgring

J. Schlesser/M.Baldi	Mercedes-Benz C11	1
J. Mass/M. Schumacher	Mercedes-Benz C11	2

Sep 2, Donington Park

M. Baldi/J. Schlesser	Mercedes-Benz C11	1
J. Mass/H.H. Frentzen	Mercedes-Benz C11	2

Sep 23, Montreal

J. Schlesser/M. Baldi	Mercedes-Benz C11	1
J. Mass/K. Wendlinger	Mercedes-Benz C11	2

Oct 7, Mexico City

J. Schlesser/M. Baldi	Mercedes-Benz C11	D
J. Mass/M. Schumacher	Mercedes-Benz C11	1

1991

Apr 14, Suzuka, Japan
J. Schlesser/J. Mass   Mercedes-Benz C11   2

May 5, Trofeo Caracciola, Monza
J. Schlesser/J. Masss   Mercedes-Benz C11   3

May 19, Silverstone
K. Wendlinger/   Mercedes-Benz C291   2
    M. Schumacher
J. Schlesser/J. Mass   Mercedes-Benz C11   4

Jun 22/23, Le Mans 24-hours
K. Wendlinger/   Mercedes-Benz C11   5
    M. Schumacher/
    F. Kreuzpointner
J. Schlesser/J.Mass/   Mercedes-Benz C11   R
    A. Ferte
J. Palmer/S. Dickens/   Mercedes-Benz C11   R
    K. Thim

Oct 7, Mexico City
K. Wendlinger/   Mercedes-Benz C291   R
    M. Schumacher

Oct 27, Autopolis, Japan
K. Wendlinger/   Mercedes-Benz C291   1
    M. Schumacher
J. Schlesser/J.Mass   Mercedes-Benz C11   5

INDY/CART VICTORIES

1994

May 29, Indianapolis 500
Al Unser Jr   Penske PC23-Mercedes

1995

April 9, Long Beach, California
Al Unser Jr   Penske PC24-Mercedes

April 23, Nazareth, Pennsylvania
Emerson Fittipaldi   Penske PC24-Mercedes

May 25, Portland, Oregon
Al Unser Jr   Penske PC 24-Mercedes

August 8, Mid Ohio
Al Unser Jr   Penske PC24-Mercedes

September 9, Vancouver, British Colombia
Al Unser Jr   Penske PC24-Mercedes

September 17, Laguna Seca, California
Gil de Ferran   Reynard 951-Mercedes

1997

April 27, Nazareth, Pennsylvania
Paul Tracy   Penske PC26-Mercedes

May 11, Rio de Janeiro, Brazil
Paul Tracy   Penske PC26-Mercedes

May 24, Gateway International Raceway, Illinois
Paul Tracy   Penske PC26-Mercedes

June 1, Milwaukee, Wisconsin
Greg Moore   Reynard 971-Mercedes

June 8, Detroit, Michigan
Greg Moore   Reynard 971-Mercedes

June 22, Portland, Oregon
Mark Blundell   Reynard 971-Mercedes

July 20, Toronto, Ontario
Mark Blundell   Reynard 971-Mercedes

August 31, Vancouver, British Columbia
Mauricio Gugelmin   Reynard 971-Mercedes

September 18, Fontana, California
Mark Blundell   Reynard 971-Mercedes

1998

May 10, Rio de Janeiro, Brazil
Greg Moore   Reynard 981-Mercedes

July 26, Michigan Speedway
Greg Moore   Reynard 981-Mercedes

1999

March 21, Homestead, Florida
Greg Moore   Reynard 991-Mercedes

INDEX